Palgrave Studies in Prisons and Penology

This is a unique and innovative series, the first of its kind dedicated entirely to prison scholarship. At a historical point in which the prison population has reached an all-time high, the series seeks to analyse the form, nature and consequences of incarceration and related forms of punishment. Palgrave Studies in Prisons and Penology provides an important forum for burgeoning prison research across the world.

Irene Marti

Doing Indefinite Time

An Ethnography of Long-Term Imprisonment in Switzerland

palgrave
macmillan

Irene Marti
Institute for Penal Law and Criminology
University of Bern
Bern, Switzerland

The open access publication of this book has been published with the support of the Swiss National Science Foundation.

ISSN 2753-0604 ISSN 2753-0612 (electronic)
Palgrave Studies in Prisons and Penology
ISBN 978-3-031-12592-8 ISBN 978-3-031-12590-4 (eBook)
https://doi.org/10.1007/978-3-031-12590-4

Cover credit: Photo taken by a prisoner in JVA Lenzburg

This Palgrave Macmillan imprint is published by the registered company Springer Nature Switzerland AG
The registered company address is: Gewerbestrasse 11, 6330 Cham, Switzerland

The original version of this book Frontmatter was revised: The OA funding acknowledgement line has been included in the copyright's holder page of Frontmatter. The correction to the book is available at https://doi.org/10.1007/978-3-031-12590-4_8

Acknowledgements

This book is based on my doctoral thesis, which would never have been possible without the support and guidance of various people. I would like to thank them all.

First, I would like to thank Marcel Ruf (*JVA Lenzburg*), and Andreas Naegeli (*JVA Pöschwies*) for opening the doors to me and generously supporting my plans inside these prisons. Special thanks go to all those who allowed me, for some time, to participate in their daily lives in prison—as inhabitants or as staff members—and who shared their experiences, feelings, and thoughts with me. I would also like to thank the representatives from the penal enforcement authorities who made themselves available for interviews, and am deeply appreciative of the Swiss National Science Foundation (SNSF) for its financial support for the research project underlying this book.

Furthermore, I express my gratitude to those who played an important role in the creation and evaluation of my thesis. First and foremost, I thank Prof Ellen Hertz of the University of Neuchâtel, who has been an inspiration to me since my time as an MA student, for her always nuanced and constructive comments and for keeping me on track. I am particularly grateful to PD Dr Ueli Hostettler of the University of Bern, who introduced me to the world of prison research and has supported my work for many years now by providing me with advice, encouragement, and opportunities to gain the experience that allowed me to develop further in academia. I feel honoured that I had both of you as my co-supervisors. Special thanks also are extended to my committee members for their inspiring and critical remarks and their careful evaluation of my thesis: Prof Manuela Ivone P. da Cunha of the University of Minho, Prof André Kuhn of the University of Neuchâtel, and Prof Dominique Moran of the University of Birmingham, who also provided me with very generous support during my stay as visiting scholar at the University of Birmingham.

Finally, I would like to thank current and former members of the Prison Research Group at the University of Bern, namely Anna Isenhardt, Conor Mangold, Marina Richter, Barbara Ryser, and Christopher Young, for always having a ready ear for me and for our countless stimulating discussions and exchanges. My sincere appreciation also to my parents and my brother, as well as my friends and colleagues, who offered me insight and encouragement during this time. These include Barbara Born, Li Duenner, Ana and Christian Ghasarian, Alain Müller, Rahel Müller, Willi Nafzger, Sarah Sägesser, Isabelle Schläpfer, Isabelle Schmied, and Marion Schulze. In particular, I would like to thank Marc Tadorian for his patient and wide-ranging emotional, intellectual, and practical support and encouragement along the way—I am deeply grateful to share my life with you, Charlot and Clay.

Contents

List of Figures

1
Introduction

That's what simply wears you down and destroys you. On the one hand, [the penal enforcement authorities] give you reason to hope, then you see a light again and think: yes, maybe it could be possible [to get out of prison]. Then you do this and that, and afterwards they come back and say: yes, that's all well and good what you've done, but you still can't get out. They just hit you on the head again with a hammer. You are devastated. So what's the point? It makes me sick, it's tedious. That's why I sometimes say that it would be best for me if they would just stand up and clearly say: you will not get out, ever. Then you would know where you stand and you [...] could adjust to it and say: ok, I'll spend the rest of my life in prison, I'll make my life as best as I can and that's it. But as it stands, it just takes a lot of energy. (Hugo, 25.6.2013)[1]

[1] All quotations from prisoners, prison management and staff as well as representatives of penal enforcement authorities in this book have been translated from German by the author. For the sake of anonymity, all names have been replaced by pseudonyms. For quotations from interviews and fieldnotes, the following rules have been implemented: (1) *square brackets* [ ] are used when leaving out words or sentences from the original text, adding an explanation or replacing a word; (2) *round brackets* ( ) denote sounds (e.g. laughing) and gestures; (3) *two slashes* // // mark overlapping talking; and (4) *ellipses* ... indicate pauses in the conversation.

I. Marti, *Doing Indefinite Time*, Palgrave Studies in Prisons and Penology,
https://doi.org/10.1007/978-3-031-12590-4_1

> Will I ever see a stream again, will I ever experience a big overgrown meadow full of flowers again [...] [will I ever go up] a mountain again, to the sea or to a lake, see people in a cafe in the city or in the village? (Rolf, 11.9.2013)

> Me, as an inmate sentenced to indefinite incarceration, I cannot hope to be released. I cannot wait, though. I take the days as they come. You have to adapt to a certain degree to the setting, to know the rules so that you don't ignore them and get into trouble, and to establish your own routine that makes you feel comfortable. Me, I feel safe and comfortable [...] I don't say time passes too slowly or too fast, I take it as it comes. I flow with the time, day after day. But this has nothing to do with simply living for the moment. It just helps me to protect myself and not to think too much about my situation. (Marco, 4.5.2016)

My interest in the experiences of Hugo, Rolf and Marco began in 2013, during a study I conducted on end of life in prison.[2] Most of the elderly prisoners I encountered in the units reserved for ill and elderly prisoners in two 'secure' or 'closed' prisons in Switzerland were in prison for multiple serious offences. The psychiatrists who had evaluated their cases had put them at a high risk of recidivism, and a judge had therefore decided that the public should be protected from them and imposed a security measure called 'indefinite incarceration' (according to Art. 64 of the Swiss Criminal Code [SCC]) in addition to a regular prison sentence.

In Switzerland, lifelong prison sentences without the possibility of release—that is, without reviews of the sentences by the court—are deemed to violate human rights and are unconstitutional (European Court of Human Rights, 2019).[3] However, in Switzerland and elsewhere, changing demands for security and public pressure in recent decades have led to a shift towards a more punitive and hard-line approach to crime and even towards zero tolerance for certain criminals, in particular violent and sex offenders. This 'punitive turn' (Garland,

---

[2] The project *End-of-life in prison: legal context, institutions and actors* was funded by the Swiss National Science Foundation (SNSF). For more information, see http://p3.snf.ch/Project-139296 and https://eolinprison.ch.

[3] In Switzerland, in the case of persons serving a life sentence (according to Art. 40 SCC), parole is possible after ten years at the earliest (Art. 86 para. 5 SCC).

2001) in criminal policy has resulted in more investment in security, repression and control. As a consequence, since the 1990s the number of people not only serving longer sentences but also preventively held in prison for an undetermined duration and sentenced to indefinite incarceration (Art. 64 SCC) has increased rapidly (Kuhn, 2017; Simmler, 2016). Even though release is legally possible, and despite the courts and enforcement authorities evaluating these prisoners' situations on a regular basis, in Switzerland most of those labelled as 'high-risk' offenders will remain in prison for the rest of their lives (see also Künzli et al., 2016, p. 4) and spend the end of their lives in a carceral setting (see Hostettler et al., 2016).

In the sparse literature on the 'punitive turn' in Switzerland, these developments are explained with reference to the emergence of a general sense of insecurity and threat among citizens and a loss of confidence in the criminal justice system due to economic and political changes that challenge material safety and established norms and values (Garin, 2012; Kunz & Moser, 1997; Kuhn, 2017). They are certainly also reinforced by the popular media, which not only reflects but may also reinforce feelings of insecurity and fear of crime. For example, incidents such as (rare) prison escapes are often reported in an emotionally charged manner and presented as political scandals (Young, 2018). Generally, these changes have been considered to contribute not only to a punitive approach towards crime but to a general 'culture of exclusion' (Staerklé et al., 2007) in relation to individuals who are perceived as a threat to the social order and public security—not only criminals but all 'deviant' or 'different' people, such as the poor, welfare recipients, migrants and homosexuals (Garin, 2012; Staerklé et al., 2007).

This changing attitude towards crime is also reflected in several popular initiatives that have appeared over the past decade. Since 2004, Swiss citizens have accepted several initiatives for a more severe penal regime (Queloz, 2013). In 2004, voters approved an initiative on lifelong incarceration—the enabling legislation entered into force in 2008—in the case of violent and sexual offenders classified as 'extremely dangerous' and 'permanently untreatable' (Art. 64 para. 1bis SCC) with no possibility for release on parole unless new scientific findings demonstrate that treatment would render them inoffensive (Baechtold et al., 2016, pp. 335–338). In 2008, the proposal to abolish the statute of limitations for those guilty of crimes involving pornographic acts committed against children under the age of 12 passed by popular vote. In 2010, a programme to deport foreign criminals was widely favoured. Also in 2010, a private committee temporarily considered launching a popular initiative to reintroduce the death penalty for certain offences (Bundeskanzlei BK, 2019). The most recent initiative, which concerned professional disqualification for convicted paedophiles, was accepted in 2014.

While the number of long-term prisoners is currently on the rise, our understanding of indefinite imprisonment—what it *is* and what it *does*—is quite limited. It is mainly left to legal experts or journalists, who rarely include the perspectives of prisoners or penal staff in their analyses.[4] In the dominant public discourse, these prisoners are extremely violent and disturbed criminals, who are often described as 'evil and subhuman' (Waldram, 2009a, p. 4), essentially cold and shallow individuals lacking in empathy for their victims. In the media, they are often represented as 'monsters' (20 Minuten, 2016) or 'beasts' (Blick, 2018). These criminals are not only physically removed from society but also 'morally exiled' (Waldram, 2009b, p. 225). In the words of Greer and Jewkes (2005, p. 21), violent and sex offenders who commit serious or 'unusual' crimes are portrayed as today's 'absolute others', completely detached from 'the social, moral, and cultural universe of ordinary, decent people'. Public interest in these people appears to be limited to their crimes

[4] There are various explanations for this: (1) the 'punitive turn' (Garland, 2001) in criminal policy in past decades, leading to more investment in security, repression and control, going hand in hand with a growing prison population and doors that are gradually closed for external researchers, especially in the US (Wacquant, 2002); (2) institutional barriers (e.g. physical access, permanent surveillance) that classify prisons as extremely challenging research sites (Waldram, 2009a; Rhodes, 2001); (3) a low level of governmental research funding (Crewe, 2009, p. 2); and (4) the fact that offenders are not 'standard' participants, particularly in anthropological research, which is traditionally 'strongly focused on the innocent and disempowered', and academic audiences might view the intention of 'giving voice' to them with suspicion (Waldram, 2009a, p. 4). There are also scholars who (5) emphasize personal and emotional challenges as constraining elements since the researcher is at the heart of the qualitative, and especially ethnographic, approach (Drake & Harvey, 2013; Jewkes, 2012, 2014; Liebling, 2001; Rowe, 2014). The researcher is not only emotionally exposed to the effects of the prison as a 'bad place' (O'Donnell, 2014, p. 179) that leads inmates to experience a wide range of *pains of imprisonment* but also to their personal stories and criminal backgrounds.

and, once they are imprisoned, to possible future illicit or transgressive behaviour.

Although these people are banished from society, they are still *alive*. During my fieldwork in 2013, I quickly realized the extent to which this almost total exclusion from society and the indefinite nature of imprisonment can affect human beings. Almost all the prisoners I talked with said that they accepted the (sometimes very long or even life) sentences they had received but struggled with the lack of perspective that came with indefinite incarceration. Some described it as 'mental torture', an 'inhumanly long-drawn-out death penalty', or as 'suffering from constant depression'. Many said that they would prefer a 'real' life sentence, or even the death penalty, to indefinite incarceration. From an anthropological perspective, prisoners serving undetermined sentences find themselves, in a certain sense, in a condition of 'chronic crisis' (Vigh, 2008) characterized by a lack of perspective and uncertainty regarding their future. Clearly, this prison population suffers very particular 'pains of imprisonment' (Sykes, 1971 [1958]). Among other things, they must find new ways of dealing with space and time.

Researching Long-Term Imprisonment

Although indefinite incarceration occurs in other countries (e.g. Germany, New Zealand and France [see Künzli et al., 2016, p. 9]), few studies explicitly and exclusively focus on this form of sanction, and those that do are mostly law and policy related (see e.g. Annison, 2018; Drenkhahn, 2013; Jacobson & Hough, 2010; Kinzig, 2008). This is no doubt due to the fact that this particular population (still) represents a minority within prisons. In Europe, the trend of reintroducing indefinite incarceration is recent, as it was abolished by many countries after the Second World War, when it was deemed contrary to the rule of law.[5]

Studies on long-term imprisonment concentrate on prisoners who are either serving (finite) long-term or (whole) life sentences. For the prisoners I studied, however, the time-based indefiniteness of their incarceration was a central concern. In contrast to a regular, temporally finite

[5] For an overview, see https://de.wikipedia.org/wiki/Sicherungsverwahrung#Rechtsprechung_des_EGMR_und_des_BVerfG.

(although long) prison sentence, indefinite incarceration may—and in Switzerland indeed often does—become a permanent condition and not 'simply' a discrete period in someone's life course. Yet, in contrast to 'real life sentences' or 'whole life sentences' without the possibility of parole (typically found in the US or the UK), where the fixed end date is usually death (Leigey & Ryder, 2015), in Switzerland, release from indefinite incarceration is legally possible and has to be examined at regular intervals. The amount of time these people will spend in prison is thus indeterminate, and their future remains uncertain. The expression 'doing time' therefore obtains a completely new meaning.

Based on ethnographic data generated in two closed prisons in Switzerland, this book provides extensive and in-depth insights into the overlooked everyday lives of prisoners held in indefinite incarceration, illuminating its conditions and effects.

Although the indeterminate nature of incarceration is the most crucial aspect of these prisoners' everyday lives, there are other issues they deal with that are also important for prisoners serving life sentences, with or without the possibility of release. Studies on long-term imprisonment emerged in the 1970s in the UK and the US. The abolition of the death penalty in 1965, as well as an increase in violent crime in the UK and a shift in sentencing policy in both the UK (Richards, 1978) and North America (MacKenzie & Goodstein, 1985), led to an increase in the long-term prison population. Parallel to these developments, official concerns emerged about 'what to do' with these prisoners: what treatment and regime was appropriate for this prison population, and how could it work to change their lives for the better (Liebling, 2014b)?

These early studies on long-term imprisonment were driven by the widely shared assumption that long-term imprisonment would automatically lead to a higher degree of 'prisonization' (assimilation to 'prison culture') (Clemmer, 1958 [1940], pp. 298–299) and to emotional and intellectual deterioration. Thus, a great deal of this mainly quantitative sociological and psychological research was conducted to explore the *effects* of long-term imprisonment on prisoners' well-being and personality. Generally cross-sectional and longitudinal, this research was usually based on cognitive tests, such as visual reproduction tests or reaction tests (Banister et al., 1973), or questionnaires including a list of 'problems' such as psychological stress, often combined with structured interviews exploring prisoners' coping strategies (Flanagan, 1980; Richards, 1978). However, none of these studies provided hard evidence that long-term imprisonment necessarily led to cumulative or progressive effects on prisoners' experience of problems (see also Heather, 1977; MacKenzie & Goodstein, 1985; Rasch, 1981; Sapsford, 1983). Certain scholars claimed that later stages of imprisonment are less stressful than early stages and that, over time, prisoners adapt and find strategies to cope with imprisonment (Flanagan, 1980; MacKenzie & Goodstein, 1985; Richards, 1978; Zamble, 1992). Generally, being deprived of relationships with the outside world has been found to be much more painful than the deprivations prisoners face within the institution (Flanagan, 1980; Richards, 1978).

During this same period, another strand of research emerged that was critical of these early studies. Pointing to their 'limited' character, these authors claimed that this kind of research design, which relied on pre-defined, specific (psychological) categories and large-scale (sociological) perspectives, was 'not sophisticated and subtle enough' (Cohen & Taylor, 1972, p. 51) to capture the difficulties faced by long-term prisoners. These critiques emphasized *subjective experience* and prisoners' adaptation processes. At their core was the argument that even if there is no evidence of psychological deterioration, long-term imprisonment has 'profound existential implications' (Crewe et al., 2016, p. 3; see also Crewe et al., 2020). Cohen & Taylor (1972), in particular, explored the experience of long-term imprisonment from a phenomenological perspective by considering it an 'extreme situation' similar to an expedition or migration that has significant effects on everyday activities and feelings. Using methods such as unstructured group interviews (conducted during sociology classes held in prison and attended by approximately 50 men), letter-writing and the production of other written texts by prisoners in the maximum-security wing of a British prison, the authors concluded that long-term prisoners are particularly concerned with the passage of time, the making and breaking of friendships, the fear of deterioration and the loss of self-integrity and identity. Moreover, Cohen and Taylor (1972) claimed that the indeterminacy of a sentence represents a specific source of stress. Similar conclusions emerged from a study conducted by Flanagan (1981). Based on qualitative interviews conducted with 59 long-term prisoners in the US, the latter study found that the main challenges faced by this particular prison population are time structuring and management, maintenance of family ties, and the prison's pernicious assault on prisoners' self-esteem. These results were confirmed by studies conducted in Canada (Zamble & Porporino, 1988) and again in Great Britain (Mitchell, 1990).

However, by the 1980s, interest in qualitatively oriented prison research had decreased significantly for various reasons. With respect to long-term imprisonment, Liebling (2014a, p. 260) points out that a lack of riots as well as some major improvements (at least in the UK) during the 1990s helped remove high-security prisoners from the policy agenda and away from public scrutiny. In the 2000s, however, events such as the rise of terrorist attacks and the diffusion of fundamentalism, along with the introduction of new and longer sentences for violent crimes (such as Imprisonment for Public Protection), placed this subject back on public policy and research agendas (Liebling, 2014a, p. 260).

More recent qualitative as well as mixed-method research on the experience of long-term imprisonment still largely derives from the US and the UK. While these studies draw on early research to highlight the challenges prisoners face, they delve more deeply into the heterogeneity of this population, notably in terms of their *age* (for studies on younger long-term prisoners, see Cope [2003], Crewe et al. [2020], and Tynan [2019]), their *gender* (for studies on the experience of women 'lifers', see Crewe et al. [2017], Jose-Kampfner [1990], and Walker and Worrall [2000]), and also the *regime* under which they are imprisoned (e.g. solitary confinement and super-max prisons, typically found in the US [King, 2005; O'Donnell, 2014; Rhodes, 2004]). Among US studies, there are also some autobiographical books about prison life, known as 'convict criminology', written by 'insiders'—that is, prisoners serving life sentences—often in collaboration with academics (Hassine, 2009; Paluch, 2004). Other surveys explore the experience of long-term imprisonment by focusing on specific themes: prisoners' coping strategies in relation to *time* (Brown, 1998; Cope, 2003; Crewe et al., 2016; Cunha, 1997, 2016; Jewkes, 2005; O'Donnell, 2014), their views on the *legitimacy of their sentences* (Schinkel, 2014), or their difficulties with and strategies for finding *meaning and purpose in life* (Jewkes, 2005; Liebling, 2014b).

All of these studies basically agree that long-term prisoners generally find ways of coping over time, making their sentences meaningful by dealing productively with the time they have. For example, prisoners construct 'new narratives of the self' (Jewkes, 2005), learn to 'swim with the tide' (instead of against it) (Crewe et al., 2016), or develop an 'art of living' (O'Donnell, 2014)—a specific attitude that facilitates acceptance of the situation and at the same time the maintenance of self-integrity. Nonetheless, as several authors (see, e.g. Jewkes, 2002) critically remind us, only the 'survivors' can actually be part of these studies. Those who are suffering from acute mental health problems are generally held in secured psychiatric facilities that are rarely accessible to researchers (Crewe et al. 2016). Moreover, as argued by Hulley et al. (2015, p. 789), adaptation also has a 'deep and profound impact on the person' as the process of coping leads to 'fundamental changes in the self, which go far beyond the attitudinal, and may bring about secondary problems of their own' (see also Crewe et al., 2020).

In sum, in the academic literature on (long-term) imprisonment, the prison is usually assumed to be a very particular place, one that is in essence 'bad' or 'dehumanizing' (O'Donnell, 2014, p. 179), where prisoners face a wide range of 'pains', 'deprivations', 'problems' and 'loss' (Hulley et al., 2015; Jewkes, 2005; Leigey & Ryder, 2015; Sykes, 1971 [1958]), and have to invent strategies in order to 'survive' (Toch, 1996 [1977]) this 'extraordinary' or 'extreme' situation (Cohen & Taylor, 1972). Without wanting to downplay these understandings, the ethnographic research project on which this book is based tried to start without a priori ideas of what the prison is and what it does. Rather, I set out firstly to gain an understanding of the prison 'from the inside' (Eriksen, 2015 [1995], p. 8)—that is, as it appears to prisoners—without previously assigning it a set of qualities.

I tried to maintain this outlook without losing sight of the formal organization imposed by the penal system—that is, the political, institutional and social forces at work in prisoners' lives. This research strategy echoes work by Moran et al. (2018), who call for more studies that 'uncover the *subjectivity* and *relativity* inherent in the experience of carcerality, since in its lived experience, the carceral is *relative* rather than absolute'. As they argue,

> the carceral is in the eye of the beholder – its perception is complex, nuanced, contextual and only partially predictable. What is felt acutely as suffering by one individual may not perturb another. What is not intended to punish may deliver significant harm. (Moran et al. 2018, p. 677)

To analyse long-term prisoners' experiences, I propose in this book to shift the analytic lens away from the familiar framework of power and resistance and towards a phenomenological and pragmatist perspective, using *space*, *time* and *embodiment* as key concepts. As embodied individuals, we are spatially and temporally positioned in any social situation we encounter—whether we live in prison or under other conditions. In this book, I explore prisoners' subjective, situated and embodied perceptions of the prison's various everyday contexts, and the forms of agency they express through their multiple means of dealing with space and time, thereby uncovering prisoners' manifold ways of *inhabiting* the prison.

1.1 Observing, Listening and Engaging in Prisoners' Everyday Lives

My research was geographically and institutionally located in prison, more precisely two Swiss prisons, understood as two different organizations. However, the 'institutional logic' (Thornton et al., 2012) inscribed in what I will call the '*penal system*' through its organizing principles was common to both prisons.

As a state institution, the penal system includes all authorities and organizations in charge of implementing criminal sanctions and measures. The most important authorities and organizations include the cantonal penal enforcement authorities, probation services and the prisons themselves. Their fundamental legal principle and purpose (for both prison sentences and measures) is rehabilitation. Their most important goal is the prevention of recidivism and thus future crimes. Security for society and internal security for the prisoners and staff working there are also important (Baechtold et al., 2016). The institutional logic of the penal system is materialized in prison architecture and infrastructure and internal norms and rules, and it shapes the practices of management and staff (Marti et al., 2017).

To carry out the research on which this book is based, I relied on established institutional connections and previous research experience. As a member of a research group at the University of Bern, Switzerland, which has been conducting research in Swiss prisons since 2006,[6] and within the framework of the research project *End-of-life in prison: legal context, institutions and actors,* mentioned above, I obtained privileged access to two closed Swiss correctional facilities: *JVA Lenzburg* and *JVA Pöschwies*. Through two intensive, uninterrupted fieldwork trips (each lasting one month) in 2013 and several day trips between 2013 and 2014, I was able to establish relations with prisoners (most of them labelled as 'dangerous' and thus sentenced to indefinite incarceration) and staff members that allowed me to gain in-depth insights into daily prison life and develop an understanding of this special institutional context. While the research focus was on *the end of* life, I became more and more interested in *living* life in prison under these particular conditions: being entirely excluded from society, stuck in a context that was the same each day (same place, same people, same routines, same food, etc.), and left to wonder if they would ever be released. I discussed these issues in many exchanges with prisoners and prison staff, and little-by-little, my PhD project emerged.[7]

---

[6] See https://prisonresearch.ch.

[7] My PhD project entitled *Living the prison: An ethnographic study of indefinite incarceration in Switzerland* was funded by the SNSF (http://p3.snf.ch/project-159182).

Justizvollzugsanstalt (JVA) Lenzburg

JVA Lenzburg was built in 1864 and can accommodate 366 inmates. It consists of the *Strafanstalt* and the *Zentralgefängnis* (built in 2011), which are about 300 metres apart. The *Strafanstalt* is intended to house 199 male prisoners (including those sentenced to indefinite incarceration) who must serve their sentence in a secure or closed setting. In the *Zentralgefängnis*, 167 places are available for pre-trial detention, semi-detention and short-term sentences for young people, men and women. The prisoners are monitored, supervised and assisted by around 250 employees (Kanton Aargau. Departement Volkswirtschaft und Inneres, 2020).

The *Zentralgefängnis* also has a special unit for ill and elderly prisoners, namely the 60plus unit, inaugurated in May 2011. It has 12 places and is primarily intended—according to Art. 80 SCC, which allows 'other forms of sentence execution'—to offer an appropriate place for long-term prisoners aged 60 and over (JVA Lenzburg, 2012, p. 59). The unit also accommodates prisoners who have not reached their 60th birthday, but who are, due to physical and mental disabilities, not able to live together with the main prison population. In contrast to the regime[8] in the main prison, the *60plus* unit is characterized by longer cell opening times, a reduced workload and more 'rehabilitative, social and leisure-oriented' activities (JVA Lenzburg, 2014, p. 50, my translation). JVA Lenzburg is guided by the principle that prisoners' autonomy should be maintained and promoted. Thus, they carry out everyday activities such as cooking, washing and cleaning independently. Prison officers in the *60plus* unit are required to support and specifically promote the cognitive and intellectual abilities of the prisoners and offer brain-performance, creative or handicraft activities. To counteract social isolation and loneliness, the employees spend a large part of their time with the prisoners in the common rooms of the unit. In order to provide suitable palliative care, the social workers and nursing staff are assisted by external professionals and institutions (e.g. *Spitex*) (Galli, 2016).

---

[8] Here, 'regime' is an emic term used by prison authorities to refer to internal rules and regulations.

Justizvollzugsanstalt (JVA) Pöschwies

JVA Pöschwies is the largest secure or closed prison for male prisoners in Switzerland. It can accommodate 423 adult male prisoners, all of whom have been sentenced to a prison term of at least one year, to an in-patient therapeutic measure according to Art. 59 SCC, or to indefinite incarceration (Art. 64 SCC). It currently employs about 260 people (Amt für Justizvollzug Kanton Zürich, 2019a).

An *Age and Health* (*Abteilung Alter und Gesundheit, AGE*) unit is located within the *JVA Pöschwies*. It offers space for 30 prisoners. Similar to the 60plus unit at *JVA Lenzburg*, the *AGE* accommodates prisoners of advanced age and those with health issues, such as addiction problems or somatic diseases, as well as prisoners who are in a difficult life situation and in need of 'a safe space, protection and more intensive and care-oriented assistance' (Amt für Justizvollzug Kanton Zürich, 2019b, my translation). In addition to these inmates, who need a temporary break from the 'normal' regime, the *AGE* is also designed for long-term prisoners (Amt für Justizvollzug Kanton Zürich, 2019b). The regime of detention in the *AGE* is 'loosened', with detainees receiving 'a high degree of attention and humanity, without losing sight of organizational and security aspects' (JVA Pöschwies, 2014, p. 18, my translation). The employees work together with the prisoners to establish individual daily routines. In this, they are supported by the prison's medical and social services as well as its psychiatric-psychological service (Amt für Justizvollzug Kanton Zürich, 2019b).

I started my PhD fieldwork in 2016 and, as in the previous project on end-of-life situations, explored prisoners' lived experiences inductively, using ethnographic research methods. As Coyle points out, ethnographic fieldwork is particularly suited to gaining a better understanding of 'what goes on behind [prison's] high walls' (Coyle, 2005, p. xi) because it brings the researcher into direct contact with the social and institutional context. Despite this advantage, in many countries, ethnographic studies are (still) 'overshadowed' by quantitative studies (Jewkes, 2015, p. x) despite a revival of ethnographic prison research (see Drake et al., 2015) after its decline—or 'eclipse' (Wacquant, 2002)—in the late 1980s. My previous research experience led me to support Crewe's argument that we have 'insufficient knowledge about the ordinary world of the prison, at a time when both policies and populations are changing rapidly, and that it is through sustained fieldwork that this knowledge can best be accumulated' (2006, p. 348). With my choice to use an ethnographic approach for my study, I join scholars who wish to renew the tradition of prison ethnography (see Drake et al., 2015). In order to gather information on the living conditions of long-term prisoners and to make their lived experience visible, I used a selection of qualitative research methods to generate data, ranging from participation and observation to different forms of interviews and document analysis.[9]

1.1.1 'Being There'

In order to explore prisoners' subjective (embodied) experience and practice of space and time, I relied on Pink's (2009) 'sensory ethnography'. Through this concept, Pink draws our attention to the sensory experience, perception and categories we use when we talk about our experiences and everyday life. The anthropological research process is thus understood as 'personal engagement and embodied knowing' (Pink, 2009, p. 43). More concretely, the process involves the ethnographer not only engaging with the ideas of others, but learning through her or his own sensorial experience, practice and knowledge. Observing, listening, and writing/reading are therefore 'not enough', and must be complemented by multisensory, embodied participation. The 'being there' is hence not simply about observing and playing 'roles' in certain situations in order to 'do things similar to those that they do' (Pink, 2009, p. 67). Rather, through sensory ethnography the researcher focuses on his or her emplaced engagements in the research participants' 'ordinary' practices (such as eating, drinking, walking or passing time) in order to learn how these sensory experiences are lived. Of course, in the prison

---

[9] In conducting my analysis, I made use of all my data, including interview transcripts, postscripts, fieldnotes, memos and documents. I coded and organized my data using the qualitative data analysis software MAXQDA. For analysis and interpretation, inspired by Mayring (2010), I applied a structuring content analysis with the aim to crystallize certain types (distinctive features) and to search for similarities as well as differences in my data. Following Flick (2014, p. 183), the combination of different qualitative methods, research settings and groups of actors allowed me to *triangulate* different methods and information, which provided me with different perspectives on the experience of indefinite incarceration. Triangulation served not as a means to validate results, but rather as a way to overcome the epistemological limitations of any single method.

the scope for (sensory) experience was limited, as my options regarding mobility and involvement in activities were restricted by the management, above all for security reasons. Nevertheless, during my stay within the prisons, I was allowed to participate and to be present in a wide range of daily activities and situations: I worked, played games or music, walked around, had lunch, had coffee breaks and waited with prisoners. This allowed me to explore prisoners' multisensory experiences and relationships to the prison environment, and their feelings about them. From my perspective, 'sensing with' also involves 'feeling with', which I understand as being empathetic and at the same time reflexive, a position I tried to maintain while in prison as well as when I was back home or at my desk at the university. Drawing on my emotions as 'intellectual resources' (Jewkes, 2012) helped me to grasp my impression of the prison atmosphere and the micro-interactions that defined it, and thereby also to become aware of my ethical and moral engagements in and with the field.

During fieldwork, whenever I found the time and space to write undisturbed (usually in staff offices), I took fieldnotes, which I divided into 'observational notes', 'theoretical notes' and 'methodological notes' (Schatzman & Strauss, 1973). These I later coded using MAXQDA and then analysed along with the rest of my data. All in all, between 2013 and 2017, I spent a total of 155 days in the two prisons, including four one-month periods where I spent five whole working days a week in prison (including some weekends) as well as several day trips. As with any ethnographic research, my fieldwork began with the 'problem' of gaining access—to the research setting as well as to the research participants.

1.1.1.1 Gaining Access to the Prison: The Formal Organization of My Fieldwork

Researchers who decide to carry out ethnographic fieldwork in prison face specific challenges, since prisons are considered 'closed' and 'sensitive' institutions not accessible to the public (Bouillon et al., 2006; Drake et al., 2015). Prisons are characterized by power relations, surveillance and control, mutual mistrust (between staff and prisoners and among prisoners) and a wide range of deprivations. Hence, there are many practical challenges and ethical questions specific to prison research, concerning both access *to* and access *within* the prison.

Gaining access *to* the prison is strongly influenced by political conditions, guidelines and the architectural features of the prison, as well as by management's willingness to open the gates, as granting access to an external person constitutes a security risk and disturbs institutional routines. While the Council of Europe has long recommended that prisons be open for social science research (Council of Europe, 1967), institutionalized and pre-established patterns for civilian access are often lacking, and researchers therefore regularly have to break new ground (Reiter, 2014, p. 418). As the *Prison Research Group* (PRG), of which I am a member, had been active in the carceral field for almost ten years at the time of my research, it was relatively easy to negotiate access within the scope of the two research projects on which this book is based. Nonetheless, there were no pre-established institutional procedures to deal with persons external to the penal system. Hence, we had to start our negotiations from scratch. At the core of these negotiations was my role during each research stay and the rules of conduct I had to follow.

In the prison literature, a wide range of possible roles are discussed (Hostettler, 2012). Among them one can find so-called 'prison tourists', visitors who participate in official prison tours (Piché & Walby, 2010; Wacquant, 2002), as well as researchers who are part of the prison staff, so-called 'insiders', who conduct research in the role of 'staff researchers' (Fleisher, 1989; Jack, 1988), and those who work as 'independent researchers' (Waldram, 2009a) coming from the outside. Working with the management of both prisons, we defined my research stays officially as 'internships' for the position of a prison officer. Nonetheless, in both prisons I wore regular clothes rather than a uniform in order to mark my distance from the prison staff (see Sloan & Wright, 2015, p. 151). The status of intern allowed me to be integrated into the prison officers' day-to-day work and to conduct research at the same time. However, in practice my experiences at the two sites turned out to be quite different from each other, oscillating between being part of the system (a quasi-employee) and an autonomous individual (an independent researcher coming from outside the system) (for details, see Marti et al., 2014; Marti & Hostettler, 2016, 2018).

During my pre-doctoral research at *JVA Lenzbrug*, I spent most of my time in the *Zentralgefängnis* unit for ill and elderly prisoners. Like the prison staff, I was given a telephone equipped with an alarm function (that also allowed me to be located at any time) as well as keys (including one to open the prisoners' cells). I could thus move around freely throughout the whole prison. During my stay, I became increasingly integrated into the prison officers' day-to-day work and was assigned different tasks, such as escorting prisoners to the medical unit, the school or the courtyard, and conducting administrative paperwork such as proofreading reports. I also unlocked prisoners' cell doors in the morning and locked them again in the evening. Due to this close involvement in the everyday work of the prison staff, I was treated both by staff and inmates almost like a staff member ('insider'). I became aware that as a quasi-employee, I started to develop strong feelings of loyalty towards the prison staff and their tasks, rules and behaviour. However, I tried to spend as much time as possible with prisoners during their leisure time, mainly in the unit's common room (often playing games with them), but also on the floor and in the courtyard, walking, waiting or simply hanging out.

For my PhD project, I mainly conducted fieldwork in the *Strafanstalt* of *JVA Lenzburg*. As I was known to prison management and some of the prison staff, I very soon became a 'familiar visitor'—though I was barely involved in prison staff activities. As with the unit for ill and elderly prisoners, I was given a key to open the main doors within the building, allowing me to move around unaccompanied. However, I was not given keys to the prisoners' cells. Moreover, during day trips I had to wear a badge that identified me as a visitor. I spent most of my time at the prisoners' workstations and participated in the evening sports programmes. Over time, I also arranged some 'unregulated' time, which allowed me simply to 'hang out', preferably at a junction for prisoners where I could easily engage them in a chat, after work on their way back to the cell, for instance. For reasons of time, I decided not to attend the evening school lessons. I did not spend much time in the courtyard, mainly because most of the long-term prisoners I met avoided the courtyard. Worried that I would disturb prisoners' rare moments of privacy and intimacy, I also avoided the visitation room.

At *JVA Pöschwies*, during my pre-doctoral research as well as for my PhD project, I conducted fieldwork exclusively in the unit for ill and elderly prisoners. Although labelled an 'intern', the prison management and staff treated me as an 'independent researcher' or 'outsider'. I had to wear a red visitor tag for the entire day, signalling to everybody that I was not allowed to walk around the building unaccompanied. I did not receive a telephone or keys and was therefore totally dependent on prison staff. Most of the time, I accompanied prison officers during their daily activities, and whenever possible they delegated minor tasks to me, such as assisting (actively or by counselling) prisoners in their daily work assignments in the unit (e.g. watering plants, handicraft work). Moreover, I was also allowed to perform some tasks when I was in the office. For instance, I received and handed out the prisoners' own cell door keys (which they were obliged to hand in while at work) and delivered letters and newspapers to the prisoners. Furthermore, I carried out some administrative paperwork (proofreading reports and other texts). Because the upper floor where the prisoners' cells are located is not equipped with surveillance cameras (CCTV) for privacy reasons, it would have been impossible for staff to monitor my movements. I was therefore required to stay in the office, the workstation or the courtyard, all locations where I could be seen by staff.

During my PhD fieldwork, I continued to be viewed as an independent researcher; however, I also had the feeling that I was increasingly treated as a 'familiar visitor'. No doubt because I was familiar with the rules and norms of conduct, I was given more latitude to choose how to spend my time and was less involved in staff work and routine assignments. In contrast to my initial stay, when prison officers would worry that I would feel 'bored' and tried to think up tasks to keep me busy, they knew by now that they could just 'let me alone' and that 'hanging around' was just fine with me. I spent my days partially with prison officers and partially with prisoners, whom I preferred to meet at their workstations or during their leisure time, which they, in contrast to the prisoners in *JVA Lenzburg*, liked to spend in the courtyard, where I played games, such as table tennis, or sat or walked around with them.

In both prisons, staff had been informed about the research project in advance by prison management or the principal investigator. During our first meetings in both prisons, I personally informed the prisoners about the research and regularly provided details of its progress as openly and transparently as possible to all research participants.

1.1.1.2 Gaining Access Within the Prison: Establishing and Maintaining Trust

Gaining access is also an issue *within* the prison and—as with any ethnographic research—boils down to how trust between researchers and research participants is established and maintained. This is essential in the prison context because, by default, hierarchy and mutual distrust characterize this particular research site. Research participants can be prisoners, staff or both at the same time. In the literature, different strategies are described for establishing trust, all related to the question of loyalty and 'taking sides' (Liebling, 1999). For instance, independent researchers may find it necessary to prove their neutrality and independence from the prison by engaging in 'unusual [or] unauthorized behaviour' that inmates can interpret as an act of resistance against the system (Waldram, 2009a), or to signal their distance by not attending staff meetings, not reading prisoners' files and/or not wearing staff symbols such as a uniform or carrying keys (Mathiesen, 1965, p. 234). However, even when 'siding with' prisoners, it is obvious that a researcher 'never become[s] "one of them"' (Mathiesen, 1965, p. 236). As Feldmann (1991) puts it: 'in a culture of surveillance, participant observation is [...] a form of complicity with those outsiders who surveil' (Feldmann, 1991, p. 12). It would seem that it is impossible to obtain a 'total view' that includes both prison staff and inmates' perspectives 'without damaging at least some relationships' (Mathiesen, 1965, p. 241). In sum, taking sides is generally regarded as an 'inevitable part of the research process' (Scott, 2014, p. 30).

Certainly, my institutionally ascribed role as trainee created a formal proximity between staff members and myself and consequently a certain distance vis-à-vis the prisoners. Before we even encountered one another, the prisoners were, of course, wondering about me. The majority indeed thought that I was a new prison officer, social assistant or psychotherapist (who generally do not wear uniforms either). Others thought that I was a journalist. However, these inmates soon learned that, in contrast to prison staff, I had no mission to fulfil for the prison or even the penal system as a whole; I remained an 'outsider' with an interest in the prisoners' lives as individuals, not as offenders who needed to be punished or rehabilitated. As I explore further below, it was therefore possible for me to generate a 'neutral' space within the framework of informal interactions and thus to allow the inmates a short 'time out' from prison procedures. This opened up the opportunity to build trust with them through everyday encounters. However, my immersion in the field was also shaped by my own emotions, images and preconceptions of these men. In contrast to 'epistemological violence', defined as 'a form of violence that is produced in "knowledge"' (Teo, 2010, p. 298) and related to the interpretation of data and the way researchers construct 'the *Other'* as inferior or problematic, I had to deal with research participants who have already been designated by society as 'problematic' or 'absolute' (Greer & Jewkes, 2005) '*Others*'.

Probably unsurprisingly, my very first encounter with prisoners was 'marked by a certain fear and inhibitions' (Fieldnotes, 29.4.2013):

> The inmates evoked very different feelings in me, often depending on how they looked at me or watched me. I interpreted their looks as curious, sceptical, deceitful, but also good-natured, childlike, shy ... […] While taking refuge in the staff's office during the whole morning and afternoon, I tried to get in contact with the inmates in the evening, and therefore went out into the corridor. One of the prisoners, Hans, immediately came up to me and we had a short conversation about the pansies that he had planted in the courtyard. He also showed me some of his private photos, which he stored in his cell. However, I didn't dare to enter his cell and asked him to step outside. This didn't seem to be a problem for him; he immediately came out of the cell. The other inmates didn't show much interest in me. Slowly my fear vanished. (Fieldnotes, 29.4.2013)

I quickly realized that I had to block out the prisoners' offences (and forget about the stereotypical images and what I had read in the newspaper about some of them) and to simply approach them as human beings, whose life experiences certainly included many more aspects than 'just' the crime(s) that brought them into prison. For this reason, I also avoided reading their files (although I was allowed to) during the first weeks of my stay. By reflecting on this (initially rather intuitive) attitude towards approaching the prisoners after I completed my first fieldwork trip in 2013, I became more and more aware of its ethical, analytical and methodological consequences.

The 'Everyday' and the 'Ordinary' as Methodological Entry Points

As I came to realize, approaching the prisoners first of all simply as *people*—people living in this particular place—opened up the possibility of encountering them detached not only from stereotypical images, but also from pre-defined assumptions and concepts of what the prison *is* and what it *does*. In contrast to much of the academic literature, in which the prison is characterized as a 'bad' or 'dehumanizing' place (O'Donnell, 2014, p. 179) per se, I propose in this book to approach the experience of being in prison without assigning it any set of qualities at all. To do this, I used the *everyday* and the *ordinary* as methodological entry points.

In the Oxford Dictionaries (2018a) the 'everyday' is defined as 'happening or used every day; daily', 'commonplace'. 'Ordinary' as an adjective is defined as: 'with no special or distinctive features; normal', 'not interesting or exceptional; commonplace' (Oxford Dictionaries, 2018b). During fieldwork, I focused on the everyday as it is organized by the prison, and the everyday and the ordinary as created and lived by prisoners. This brought me to focus on routine activities and objects such as the staff's daily locking and unlocking of cell doors, cell furnishings, the prisoners' daily walks in the courtyard or ways of passing time—that is, the rudiments of prison life. This methodological shift from the 'spectacular' to the (at least at first glance) 'unspectacular' aspects of prison life allowed me to study prisoners' ways of *being* and *doing* indefinite time by remaining empirically grounded, and to capture their diverse modes of engagement in different everyday situations, all contextually embedded.

The association of normalcy and ordinariness with imprisonment was also expressed by the prisoners I met. Many of the long-term prisoners who had already spent more than half of their lives in prison told me that that they have 'lost the feeling for the outside world' (Kurt, 3.5.2016), so that 'this is now normal life' and 'everything else would be abnormal' (Marco, 10.9.2013) or exceptional. Moreover, for long-term prisoners who may remain in prison for the rest of their lives, to perceive imprisonment as their 'normal life' may also allow them 'to regain mental free spaces', to 'feel safe' and 'comfortable' and to go about their lives (Marco, 4.5.2016). Yet, this does not mean that the pain or sense of loss disappears automatically. I would like to insist, therefore, that in approaching the prison and imprisonment through the lens of the ordinary and the everyday, my aim is not to neglect the suffering of prisoners. Drawing on Vigh (2008), I understand the ordinary or the normal not in the sense of 'how things should be', but in terms of 'what there is most': 'normalising' imprisonment is not about 'indifference' but rather involves looking at it as a 'frame of action' (Vigh, 2008, p. 11). Although they may not be in a position to change the forces that affect their lives in a negative way, prisoners remain able to act and live within this context and are free to 'choose' their attitude (O'Donnell, 2014, p. 277).

'Normalising' the Prison Context

Approaching the prisoners as people living an ordinary, everyday life in this particular place also fosters trust. Of course, a (female) researcher coming from the outside is per se something *extra*ordinary. Yet, participating in everyday life over a longer period of time automatically leads to jointly constructed modes of daily interaction and thus also to some degree of 'normalcy' between researcher and research participants, as we simply got used to each other's presence. Here, by 'normalising' I also, and above all, mean actively and jointly 'dampening' the effects of the institutional context that ascribes (oppositional) roles, statuses and positions to individuals—such as *prisoners* and *independent researchers* from the outside—and dampening the specific form of epistemological violence already inscribed in the prison context, in order to facilitate moments and conditions for encounters between simple 'human beings' (Hostettler et al., 2016; Marti & Hostettler, 2018, 2016). I wish therefore to nuance the often-repeated argument regarding the necessity of taking sides, by considering the establishment of trust between researcher and research participants as a relational and situated interpersonal process. In sum, I believe it is possible to gain access to 'both sides' (prisoners and employees) without simultaneously rendering a relationship with the 'other side' impossible.

More concretely, I understand moments where 'normalcy' is established as special space–time–actor constellations. These can be the making and holding of an appointment, such as having a cup of coffee together, where mutual respect and recognition are foregrounded through the negotiation of time and place and a consideration of the other party's interests and obligations, rather than their role or status. The process of co-creation, through activities such as working together, making music, creating something together or even just playing games, where each faces the other as a game partner, can also promote moments of mutual acceptance, openness and trust. Finally, all situations allow for the redefinition and neutralization of symbols of power, such as holding and using a key, which, while it might a priori seem to foster distance between the researcher and prisoners, also offers opportunities for personal communication (for a more detailed description of these three moments see Marti & Hostettler, 2016).

On a more general level, I also tried to establish some degree of 'normalcy' by shaking the prisoners' hands when meeting them, not if I was present for several weeks without interruption, but during my day trips. Through this action, I broke the internal rule according to which prison officers and prisoners must (for security reasons) keep physical distance and not touch each other, the exceptions to which (emergency situations or body searches) only highlight the power relations at the base of the prison system. However, this ordinary gesture of normalcy also provoked confusion on both sides: on two occasions a prisoner held my hand for too long (for a common handshake) and in a way I did not feel comfortable with. The fact that this happened both times in a surveillance camera blind spot suggests that both prisoners were well aware of what they were doing. In contrast, I also met prisoners who tried to avoid *any* physical contact with me. This led to clumsy situations, when handing over the birdie during badminton, for instance.

There were several prisoners who explicitly told me that I was 'human' and 'normal', that I was bringing the 'human' into prison, and that spending time with me made them feel 'good' and 'normal':

> Playing parlour games or sports with prisoners always offered nice opportunities for the fading out of the prison context. [...]. During a game, we faced each other as equal partners. Not necessarily in terms of personal talents and skills, but for sure in terms of status. Simon, with whom I used to play table tennis, once mentioned that he 'always felt normal' and 'like a human being' when we played table tennis together. (Fieldnotes, 18.8.2013)

> You are a sincere, honest woman. [...] You have the human inside you, which I miss so much in here. Although you came here first of all for your work, the fact that you decided to talk to us shows true interest, courage and sincerity. (Letter from a prisoner, 12.11.2017)

Such interactions generally took place after a certain period of time. Thus, (successful) 'normalisation' (i.e. the dimming of institutional effects) requires time. Furthermore, it also depends on the particularity of the context in which the interaction takes place. For instance, I spent time with both prisoners mentioned in the examples above during their leisure time, playing games or doing sport together, either in the courtyard or in the sports hall. These are places where they (and I) were less observed by prison staff and granted more autonomy.

However, there are also limits to this approach. For instance, the intention to 'normalise' the prison may not always be welcomed in the same way by the two partners in the interaction. I met prisoners for whom it was important to emphasize that from their perspective the prison is everything but normal, and that they could not be the person they 'normally' were. There are other potential limits to emphasize regarding this approach. For instance, for security reasons I tried to not disclose any personal information to prisoners. This of course leads to the question of whether 'real' and 'simple' encounters between 'human beings' can really be established. According to Oakley, during in-depth interviews, there is 'no intimacy without reciprocity' (Oakley, 1981, p. 41). Indeed, while this was never an issue during my first fieldwork trip in 2013, it increasingly became one—on both sides—during fieldwork for the PhD. While prisoners generally showed the need to talk about themselves and were grateful for my sympathetic ear, it also happened, though rarely, that they wanted to know personal things about me, for instance, whether I was in a relationship or married. I always evaded these questions (as recommended by prison staff) because I feared further intimate questions.

Generally, the prisoners who asked me such questions did not express astonishment about my reaction, probably because they were already used to this behaviour from prison staff. However, I always felt uncomfortable during such situations. I became particularly aware of the one-sidedness of the relationships I established and maintained with prisoners when one prisoner explicitly asked me in the presence of other prisoners, during an informal gathering, to finally 'come out of my shell'. However, although I was aware from the beginning that the only thing I would offer them was an opportunity to talk, the need to *not* disclose personal information (in a way far beyond the general researcher's need to maintain a certain 'neutrality' or critical distance from his or her research participants), especially during informal discussions, increasingly became an issue for me. It also made me aware of the fact that—in contrast to common assumptions—ethnographic research, depending on the context, does not necessarily increase in quality the longer we remain in the field.

Finally, there were also moments where I failed or did not want to 'normalise' the prison, due to my personal and ambivalent feelings towards the prison and the prisoners. These feelings sometimes came up and shook my professional sense of self, as illustrated by the following extract from my fieldnotes:

> Right now, I would prefer to stop everything. I don't remember why I wanted to do this at all [...] I think I am struggling to find the right

balance between closeness and distance. I am too involved emotionally, too open, in search of interpersonal connections, trust, etc. But at the same time, I should, however, face them [the prisoners] with suspicion (you never know …). Already this creates tension, which is difficult to handle. Then, I hear these horrible stories about all these cruel offenses, and at the same time I see and feel how degradingly prisoners are treated, what long-term imprisonment can do to a human being – another field of tension. Right now, I just want to leave, and not to return to this place. What would the victims and their relatives think of my work if they knew about it? This was going through my head today as well. (Fieldnotes, 12.2.2016)

As this example shows, there were moments in which the prison for me was simply and above all a 'bad' place and my interview partners 'bad' people. What I could not and did not want to 'normalise' included both the degrading treatment by prison staff and the offences these prisoners had committed—two elements that were, however, irrelevant to my research questions.

The fact that my research participants had been labelled as 'dangerous' and sentenced to indefinite incarceration (whether this was right in every case is, again, a separate question) and the general distrust the prison shows towards them (expressed in prison architecture, infrastructure, norms and rules) made me careful and cautious. For instance, whenever I entered the prison, I immediately switched on all my sensors. Certain prisoners themselves expressed an awareness of the label they were carrying and the general distrust they aroused. Especially during interactions that occurred in situations less directly surveilled by prison staff, some prisoners expressed their anticipated concerns and possible institutional reactions. Their statements worked as constant (although passing) reminders of the context in which we found ourselves. For instance, when one prisoner invited me to visit him in his cell, he immediately added that 'of course' the door would remain open all the time (Fieldnotes, 15.2.2016). Another prisoner was concerned about us being out of sight of the prison officers' lens:

While searching for an appropriate place to have an undisturbed conversation with one of the prisoners during their break [that they generally

> spend outside in the courtyard], I proposed the bench that was furthest away. He agreed but expressed his concerns: he wanted to know whether it was 'not too far' for me to go there. Of course, he wasn't referring to the geographical distance, since it was a matter of several meters only, but to security issues. (Fieldnotes, 21.4.2016)

Yet another prisoner made use of the cracks offered by such situations by playing with his label of being 'dangerous' in a provocative way:

> Today, the same prisoner as yesterday approached me during one of these short moments when I was sitting alone in the prison officers' office (which is not monitored) with the staff all far away. Standing on the doorstep, he asked me in a provocative way if I was not afraid of being here in this unit, among all these 'monsters'. I indeed felt uncomfortable but tried to remain calm and friendly. (Fieldnotes, 13.5.2013)

At the same time, I also created situations in which prisoners' label implicitly became an issue. During my visits to prisoners in their cells, I sometimes entered them (for which I needed approval by staff), but more often I remained on the doorstep, which did not require any permission and made me feel more comfortable as well. A couple of times, prisoners asked me to enter, adding that they 'would not do me any harm'. I generally responded to this remark with a smile, saying that I appreciated the offer but preferred to remain outside. By not wanting to enter a prisoner's 'home' as a 'guest', I of course stressed the fact that visiting them in their cells was not a 'normal' meeting, but an encounter between a 'harmless' citizen coming from the outside and a 'dangerous' offender held in prison. The supposed dangerousness was implicitly also an issue (for both sides) during the situation illustrated in the following extract from my fieldnotes, in which my intuitive and non-verbally expressed mistrust provoked an immediate reaction by a prisoner:

> This afternoon, as we agreed in the morning, I had quickly visited [a prisoner] in his cell. He wanted to give me a document he had mentioned. Together with a security officer, I went to [his] cell. [...] He gave me the document and asked the officer if he could briefly have a chat with me. The officer agreed but wanted us to remain in the hall. So we remained

in the hall, at the entry of his cell. [...]. At some point, I inquired about the time saying that I probably should go now. He handed me a small bottle of mineral water, which he had put into the water-filled *lavabo* for cooling, asking me if he could offer it to me for my way home. I hesitated for a moment, which he seemed to notice, he said: 'There is nothing in it, just water', I took it and thanked him. With my fingers, I instinctively checked whether the cap was untouched. We said good-bye and he thanked me for the visit. [...] The first thing I did after I had left the prison was to throw the bottle in the dustbin and wash my hands. (Fieldnotes, 1.9.2016)

Some Thoughts on Gender

While gender probably matters in any ethnographic research, it certainly has particular significance when a female researcher conducts fieldwork in prisons for male offenders. At least, this is what I was told again and again. I encountered many situations (at academic conferences and seminars, during get-togethers with friends and family members) where the fact of me being a 'woman' (above all, as I was often told, a 'small and slender' one) doing research with ('dangerous') 'men' (among whom were numerous sex offenders), in prison where they deal with the deprivation of (hetero-)sexual encounters, provoked numerous concerns and questions. It was also an issue that was taken up by the media. I received several inquiries from newspapers interested in publishing a story about 'the female researcher in a male prison'; I rejected almost all of them on the grounds that this strong focus on gender distracted from the content and main goals of my research project. I do not claim that gender does not matter in my research. However, from my experience it was much more an issue for the people in the outside world than for the prisoners. Nevertheless, of course the particular context of the prison, a male-dominated area, *did* shape my research practice.

That I was a woman researcher entering a men's prison was first taken up by the prison management, who formulated specific codes of conduct regarding my physical appearance. A few weeks before starting my fieldwork, I received a message from the prison management which, among other things, asked me to wear clothes that were 'appropriate' to the locality, in the sense that 'shoulders must be covered. Not allowed are tank tops, belly shirts, short trousers or skirts' (letter, JVA Lenzburg, 16.4.2013, my translation). I believe I would have dressed like this anyway, since I expected this dress code from an institution where the staff wear uniforms, and I did not pay special attention to this remark at the outset. However, the issue of clothing turned out to be a permanent preoccupation. Interestingly, clothing was never an issue for one of my male colleagues who also conducted ethnographic prison research—either on the part of the institution or for himself. My constant concern was that my female body would, through inappropriate clothing, become an issue. For this reason, in addition to following the prison's request, which basically boiled down to not showing too much skin, I tried not to wear clothing that accentuated those parts of my body that are commonly perceived as female. For example, I never wore tight trousers or a tight blouse. Even when I went jogging with prison staff over lunch time, I avoided wearing tight or short sport pants. I also never wore bright or striking colours (commonly ascribed to women) but preferred black, blue and grey. My intention was to somehow preventively 'neutralize' gender (Hirschauer, 2001) by 'reducing' my femininity (Sloan & Wright, 2015, p. 152) through my appearance, in order to render gender differences as *irrelevant* as possible during the research process. I found this important in order to gain and maintain my professional credibility as a researcher but also to avoid endangering my reputation as a ('serious') woman in this particular male-dominated research context.

To the extent that I could comprehend it, from the prisoners' point of view, the fact that I was a woman—one who was not a prison officer—mattered in the sense that it allowed them to experience and to perform masculinity in a way that was most likely rare for them. Hence, while I generally tried to 'neutralize' gender, during our interactions inmates did mobilize gender as a 'relational category' (Hirschauer, 2001) of difference that allowed them to establish gendered relations between us. For instance, there were several prisoners who openly expressed appreciation for the possibility my presence gave them to 'finally talk to a woman again'. There was one prisoner who added that he had 'almost forgotten how to talk to a woman' (Fieldnotes, 16.2.2016). Although there were female officers (although few in number), this statement made clear that my status as a penal system outsider was of particular importance—indeed, it was the most important aspect as it connected to the experience of some degree of 'normalcy', as mentioned above. Moreover, interacting with me also allowed prisoners to play various masculine roles, such as the role of the 'gentleman' who protects me from 'rude' fellow prisoners and 'cruel' male conversation. For others, it was possibly an opportunity to express certain feelings and show their 'weak' side, which, as I was told, is often difficult in prison, a 'homosocial institution' (Crewe, 2014, p. 431) where prisoners generally 'mask' emotional expression and put on 'fronts' of bravado and aggression (Crewe, 2014, p. 430), as signs of weakness may identify prisoners as 'vulnerable' (Fieldnotes, 16.2.2016). I noticed, furthermore, that some prisoners were strongly perfumed when meeting me. Maybe this was part of their daily routine, or perhaps it was part of their 'impression management' (Largey & Watson, 2006 [1972], p. 35) when meeting a woman—more specifically a woman not part of the penal system. All these experiences taken together led me to assume that meeting a female researcher from the outside was basically a welcome change in the prisoners' everyday lives. Yet, given the deprivation of heterosexual relationships in prison, it is possible that some saw in me a 'projection surface' for personal (sexual) desires and fantasies. If this was the case, these were not disclosed to me.

On a different note, a few times prisoners (as well as staff members) tried to benefit from my presence to (re)live the experience of flirting. While some studies describe flirting (or sexuality in general) as an inherent part of fieldwork, I never considered 'playing' (Kaspar & Landolt, 2016, p. 108) with my sexuality during fieldwork—especially not in prison. Nonetheless, I had to deal with some attempts at flirting during my research encounters. As pointed out by Kaspar and Landolt (2016, p. 116), such unexpected moments can be experienced as 'both threatening and pleasant; [they] can facilitate data collection or impede it; it can balance power relations or enforce or reverse the asymmetry'.

During fieldwork, I experienced both implicit and explicit demonstrations of interest. One prisoner once tried to flirt with me by redefining the interview situation as a date. He managed to 'smuggle' (although it was probably allowed) a Coke, two cups, and cookies into the room, and brought with him a lot of pictures of his family which he had been hiding under his sweater. In the middle of the interview he suddenly interrupted me and asked:

> *Simon*: But tell me, what did you actually think when you saw me for the first time?
> *Irene*: (laughing)
> *S*: Honestly, I always see you with a smiling face, I don't know, whenever I see you, whenever we play table tennis, you always smile at me (laughing), you always bring sunshine to me.
> *I*: I don't know; you obviously make me laugh.
> *S*: Really?
> *I*: So, what do you think about prison officers, how do you get along with them? (Simon, 11.9.2013)

At the end of the interview, he repeated his questions and I hastily switched off the recording device. Even though I did not experience the prisoner's behaviour as particularly obtrusive, I was unsettled by his 'reframing' of our encounter, obviously aimed at creating intimacy between us in a way that did not correspond to my professional demeanour in prison. Moreover, given that this situation happened during an early stage of my research, I also worried about not receiving 'proper' answers to my questions (see also Kaspar & Landolt, 2016, p. 115). When handing the audio file to the student assistant hired to transcribe interviews for the end-of-life project, I somehow felt embarrassed knowing that she would hear that a prisoner tried to flirt with me, and I worried about her impression regarding my professional credibility.

The following extract from my fieldnotes illustrates an attempt to flirt that not only depicts the importance and influence of the prison context, but also the prisoners' (possible) confusion about my interest in their lives:

> In the afternoon, I went to [a workshop] where I met [a prisoner] again; I was sitting next to him, helping him fold envelopes. We were talking about this and that [...] Then, he started flirting. He came physically close to me whenever he had to get up and get something. He told me that for the past 23 months he had been in prison, I was the first woman

that came that close to him [I guess he meant physically], that he didn't receive any visitors, and that this was a special feeling for him. He said he didn't know whether it was the 23 months or me, but he thought that I was nice – 'you are nice, aren't you?' he asked. I was embarrassed and replied, while laughing, 'Yes, I think I'm nice'. He wanted to know if I want to have kids. He said that he knew that I didn't have any [which was true at that time] because I didn't wear a ring. I replied that 'maybe I wouldn't wear it in here, even if I had one'. This confused him. Why should I want to keep this secret? I didn't give a clear answer and changed the topic of conversation. The same applied to the disclosure of my first name. When he asked me about it, I felt uncomfortable and quickly replied 'just call me Ms. Marti'. He was even more confused. (Fieldnotes, 16.2.2016)

During qualitative research, and in particular during ethnographic fieldwork, the generation of rich data is strongly dependent on the researcher's ability to create a friendly atmosphere. However, as this example illustrates, this can also cause confusion among research participants who may mis- or over-interpret the researcher's intention. Although the encounter with this prisoner was generally a pleasurable moment which allowed us to co-construct some kind of 'normalcy' (as described above), his attempt to create intimacy between us led me to 're-position' us again as prisoner and researcher. This became visible in my refusal to disclose any personal information, even information I easily share with non-prisoners.

More frequent were the occasions when prison officers would flirt with me. Interestingly, even though it was unexpected, it was much easier for me to handle this than when prisoners were involved. Although I tried to avoid such situations as well, no pre-defined images and stereotypes about these men framed these interactions. I was therefore much more relaxed and saw it more as a game. I felt 'safer' than with prisoners and less concerned about data collection.

To conclude, the question of gender was certainly a concern from an external perspective, and from the point of view of prison management. For me, it was an issue precisely because I did not want it to be one. Finally, for the prisoners it was also an issue, as encountering a person of the opposite sex provided them with a welcome change in their daily lives. However, in the end I think what was equally if not more important was the fact that I was a person from the outside world, interested in their lives and not interwoven with the penal system.

1.1.2 Face-to-Face Interviews

After completing my fieldwork, I conducted semi-structured interviews with prisoners, a few staff members and a small number of representatives of the penal enforcement authorities. My choice of interview partners among prisoners was mainly driven by the connections that I was able to establish during fieldwork. Almost all the prisoners I met were, in the end, willing to be interviewed; the three who refused stated that that they had already shared a lot of information with me during our informal discussions. A few more interview partners were organized by prison staff, and one prisoner asked his mate to let me interview him. I tried to provide those who agreed with as much autonomy as possible, meaning that I let them decide on the day and time of the interview (which of course still had to fit within the prison schedule).

All the interviews took place in a room provided by the prison—either in a social worker's office or a room where prisoners receive visitors, such as the chaplain or psychotherapist's room. In every prison, the management wanted me to carry an alarm device. I tried to handle this device with as much discretion as possible. For instance, I tried to avoid attaching it to my belt in front of the prisoners and to do so in the prison officers' office instead. During the interviews, I tried to create a friendly atmosphere as much as possible, by not sitting down facing the prisoners, for instance, to avoid an arrangement similar to an interrogation. Moreover, whenever possible, I offered them some water to drink.

Between 2016 and 2017, I met with a total of 32 prisoners sentenced to indefinite confinement. I conducted in-depth formal interviews with 18 of these prisoners, ten prison staff members (including representatives of management, social and security services, as well as workshop foremen) and five members of penal enforcement authorities. For my analysis, I also included portions of the data that our research group gathered in the context of the previous project on end-of-life situations in Switzerland. These data included in-depth interviews with 17 prisoners (seven of whom I interviewed again in the context of the PhD project), 27 prison staff members and three members of penal enforcement authorities. I asked my interview partners to complete and sign an informed consent form before the interview. The interviews lasted approximately 90 minutes (the shortest 30 minutes and the longest three hours). All the interviews were recorded and transcribed and later coded and analysed. Before beginning the analysis, I gave a copy of each interview transcript to the prisoners. The intention behind this was not only to give my research participants the possibility to retract statements, but also to create a symbolic gesture of reciprocity in a context where all I could offer them was 'a non-judgmental ear and an opportunity to talk' (Waldram, 2009a, p. 5).

After an initial analysis of my data, I decided to collect additional materials that more explicitly investigated the prisoners' relations to the various spatial settings in situ in order to extend and deepen my knowledge of their everyday experience of the various carceral contexts.

1.1.3 Walking Interviews[10]

Inspired by Kusenbach (2003), I decided to conduct individual 'walking interviews' or so-called 'go-alongs' with some of the prisoners I had already interviewed. Conducting individual walking interviews at the final stage of my fieldwork was particularly useful to explore systematically, in situ and *in real time*, prisoners' perceptions of the various everyday prison contexts as well as their sensory memories and imaginations (Pink, 2009).[11] In contrast to the 'classical' semi-structured interviews that I conducted sitting at a table in a room provided by prison management and talking about particular places and activities while being somewhere else, in these follow-up interviews, I explored

[10] Parts of this section have been published as Marti (2021): Sensing freedom: Insights into long-term prisoners' perceptions of the outside world, Incarceration SAGE, Vol. 2(2): 1–20.

[11] As explored by Herrity et al. (2021, p. xxiii), 'penality has an inherent sensory component'. The sensory experience of prisoners as a source of insight, however, is only rarely considered in the criminological literature on prison life.

prisoners' relations to the various carceral contexts by letting them give me 'guided tours' through *their* prison.

Conducting walking interviews in prison of course required permission from prison management, which I obtained from only one prison. In agreement with management, I was allowed to select the prisoners and to ask them in person to determine the time and the exact route for the walking interview. However, these details had to be approved by the management in advance. Fortunately, no changes were necessary, and we could conduct the prison tours as planned by the prisoners, under the condition that we were accompanied by a member of the staff. The reason for this arrangement was to guarantee my safety but also to have someone with us who was authorized to carry keys and unlock doors for us. In a preliminary meeting with the prison officer in charge, I asked him to keep, if possible, a certain distance during the interviews, to which he fully agreed. The duration for each interview was limited by management to 90 minutes. In total, I conducted six walking interviews. Again, all the interviews were recorded and later transcribed, coded and analysed.

During the walking interviews, as suggested by Kusenbach (2003), I tried to give the prisoners as little direction as possible. I sometimes let them comment on whatever came to mind while looking at or being in a particular place. I also made comments on things that struck me and asked them for their opinion or feelings about it. The prison management also allowed me to take a camera with me and to ask the prisoners to take pictures during the walking interview of things or places they found relevant. Inspired by a method called photo-elicitation (Rose, 2012), I wanted them to take pictures to sharpen their awareness and to make them look at their familiar environment in a new way. Also, the pictures they took and the conversations we had about them in situ provided me with additional information about their experiences. Finally, it offered them the opportunity to produce visual material, which I could later use as illustrations in my thesis. All the interviews were audio recorded and later transcribed. I decided to not take notes during the interviews, in order to create a more informal and relaxed ambiance. I noted my observations and reflections in my field notebook immediately after each interview.

As I discovered, using the walking interview as a research tool is particularly well suited to normalizing the prison context. Despite the limits set by the prison management, walking interviews allowed prisoners a certain degree of self-determination (regarding date and time as well as the route we took), something they very rarely experience in their daily lives. Specifically, during the walking interviews we generally visited places at unusual times (e.g. the courtyard in the morning instead of the afternoon) and for an unusual duration. We also took routes from one place to another that the prisoners are usually not allowed to follow (e.g. taking a shortcut generally only used by prison staff). Thus, walking interviews interrupted the ordinariness of prison life and let prisoners experience change and something exceptional. Finally, the possibility of creating a rather informal atmosphere during the walking interviews, remaining open and letting the conversation develop as spontaneously as possible, also helped to normalize (and maybe also humanize) the institutional context of the prison for a moment. As Leo suddenly said while we were walking around the courtyard together: 'As long as I look upwards [to the sky], I actually feel free, or let's say less imprisoned'. He laughed and added: 'Or right now, when I can walk around like this, not knowing when exactly I have to go back in again or having an appointment at a particular time … when I can move a bit more freely than usual' (Leo, 31.8.2017).

1.1.4 Documents

Finally, I also used a wide range of documents to generate data. These documents included official organizational documents produced by the prison and enforcement authorities (e.g. the prisons' house rules and annual reports, or cantonal recommendations) that allowed me to grasp the institutional framework. They also included everyday internal prison documents, such as the planning of the inmates' stays or staff reports, to get a better understanding of the prison norms and routines and the institutional handling of the prisoners. Finally, I also included private documents—that is, letters and writings the prisoners gave me.

1.2 Structure of the Book

Chapter 2 starts with a description of the legal definition of indefinite confinement—that is, indefinite incarceration and in-patient therapeutic treatment of mental disorders, and provides insight into penal policy. It further explores the perspective of the three groups of actors who most directly organize and shape prisoners' everyday lives: penal enforcement authorities, prison management and prison staff. This section presents these actors' formal tasks in the enforcement of indefinite confinement as well as their individual experiences and attitudes regarding these prisoners. Finally, I establish the two main features of life in indefinite confinement, namely indeterminacy and an institutionally established present, viewed from the perspective of those directly concerned: the prisoners. In Chapter 3, I present my theoretical framework. In this book, I analytically grasp the prison and the experience of imprisonment by using space, time and embodiment as key concepts.

Chapters 4–6 serve as the core of the book: they are entirely devoted to the prisoners' lived experiences of prison life and their individual ways of *doing indefinite time*. Chapter 4 examines prisoners' experiences of and in the prison cell. It starts with a description of the legal and institutional norms regarding the design, materiality and furnishing of the cell. It then explores the various meanings prisoners attribute to their cells, their individual experiences of being inside, and their ways of arranging their cells and doing time in this place where they spend most of their time, almost always alone. Chapter 5 is dedicated to prisoners' experiences at work. It also begins with a short description of the legal and institutional framework of work in Swiss prisons and, specifically, in the prisons where I conducted fieldwork. I then explore prisoners' experiences of these different work contexts and how this affects their corporal and spatial experience of imprisonment. I also shed light on prisoners' various temporal experiences at work and the ways they rearrange institutionally established work rhythms according to their individual needs. Finally, I delve into the experiences of being a worker and how this affects prisoners' sense of self. Chapter 6 focuses on leisure time. More concretely, it explores prisoners' spatial, temporal and embodied experiences of and during the particular moment of the day that is labelled and organized by the prison as 'leisure time', taking place in a wide range of contexts where various temporalities and rhythms are produced. After a brief description of the legal and institutional norms regarding leisure time in Swiss prisons and a presentation of the internal rules and available leisure time activities in the prisons where I conducted fieldwork, I present the prisoners' multiple approaches to *doing* leisure time, during which they have various opportunities to encounter the outside world.

References

20 Minuten (2016, January 25). Verwahrter Mörder. «Ein Monster, das eine gütige Seite hat». *20 Minuten.* https://www.20min.ch/schweiz/news/story/-Ein-Monster--das-eine-guetige-Seite-hat--29337078. Accessed 10 December 2019.

Amt für Justizvollzug Kanton Zürich. (2019a). *Justizvollzugsanstalt Pöschwies.* https://justizvollzug.zh.ch/internet/justiz_inneres/juv/de/ueber_uns/organisation/jva.html. Accessed 10 December 2019.

Amt für Justizvollzug Kanton Zürich. (2019b). *Justizvollzugsanstalt Pöschwies.* Abteilung Alter & Gesundheit. https://justizvollzug.zh.ch/internet/justiz_inneres/juv/de/ueber_uns/organisation/jva/bereiche/betreuung-sicherheit/alter-gesundheit.html. Accessed 10 December 2019.

Annison, H. (2018). Tracing the Gordian knot: Indeterminate-sentenced prisoners and the pathologies of English penal politics. *The Political Quarterly*, 1–9. https://doi.org/10.1111/1467-923X.12462

Baechtold, A., Weber, J., & Hostettler, U. (2016). *Strafvollzug: Straf- und Massnahmenvollzug an Erwachsenen in der Schweiz* (3rd ed., Kriminalität, Justiz und Sanktionen KJS: Vol. 17). Stämpfli Verlag.

Banister, P., Smith, F. V., Heskin, K., & Bolton, N. (1973). Psychological correlates of long-term imprisonment: I Cognitive variables. *The British Journal of Criminology, 13*, 312–323. https://doi.org/10.1093/oxfordjournals.bjc.a046480

Blick (2018, September 11). Die Bestie von Rupperswil. Er missbrauchte den jüngsten Sohn - dann tötete er alle! *Blick.* https://www.blick.ch/news/schweiz/mittelland/polizei-informiert-heute-nachmittag-durchbruch-im-fall-rupperswil-id5027357.html. Accessed 10 December 2019.

Bouillon, F., Fresia, M., & Tallio, V. (Eds.). (2006). *Terrains sensibles. Expériences actuelles de l'anthropologie*. École des Hautes Études en Sciences Sociales.
Brown, A. (1998). 'Doing time': The extended present of the long-term prisoner. *Time & Society, 7*, 93–103. https://doi.org/10.1177/0961463X98007001005
Bundeskanzlei BK. (2019). *Eidgenössische Volksinitiative 'Todesstrafe bei Mord mit sexuellem Missbrauch'*. Bundeskanzlei BK. https://www.bk.admin.ch/ch/d/pore/vi/vis392.html. Accessed 10 December 2019.
Clemmer, D. (1958 [1940]). *The prison community*. Holt, Rinehart & Wilson.
Cohen, S., & Taylor, L. (1972). *Psychological survival: The experience of long-term imprisonment*. Penguin Books.
Cope, N. (2003). 'It's no time or high time': Young offenders' experiences of time and drug use in prison. *The Howard Journal of Criminal Justice, 42*, 158–175. https://doi.org/10.1111/1468-2311.t01-1-00273
Council of Europe. (1967). *Resolution 67(5), adopted by the Minister's Deputies on 4th March 1967: Research on prisoners considered from the individual angle, and on the prison community*. https://search.coe.int/cm/Pages/result_details.aspx?ObjectID=09000016804bb8e0. Accessed 11 May 2021.
Coyle, A. (2005). *Understanding prisons: Key issues in policy and practice*. Open University Press.
Crewe, B. (2006). Prison drug dealing and the ethnographic lens. *The Howard Journal, 45*, 347–368.
Crewe, B. (2009). *The prisoner society: Power, adaptation and social life in an English prison*. Oxford University Press.
Crewe, B. (2014). Not looking hard enough: Masculinity, emotion, and prison research. *Qualitative Inquiry, 20*(4), 426–437.
Crewe, B., Hulley, S., & Wright, S. (2016). Swimming with the tide: Adapting to long-term imprisonment. *Justice Quarterly, 34*, 1–25. https://doi.org/10.1080/07418825.2016.1190394
Crewe, B., Hulley, S., & Wright, S. (2017). The gendered pains of life imprisonment. *The British Journal of Criminology, 57*, 1359–1378. https://doi.org/10.1093/bjc/azw088
Crewe, B., Hulley, S., & Wright, S. (2020). *Life imprisonment from young adulthood: Adaptation, identity and time* (Palgrave studies in prisons and penology). Palgrave Macmillan.
Cunha, M. I. (1997). Le temps suspendu. Rythmes et durées dans une prison portugaise. *Terrain* (29), 59–68.

Cunha, M. I. (2016). Une prison à l'épreuve du temps. Temporalités carcérales d'hier et d'aujourd'hui. *Rhuthmos* (27), 1–7.
Drake, D. H., Earle, R., & Sloan, J. (Eds.). (2015). *The Palgrave handbook of prison ethnography: Palgrave studies in prisons and penology*. Palgrave Macmillan.
Drake, D. H., & Harvey, J. (2013). Performing the role of ethnographer: Processing and managing the emotional dimensions of prison research. *International Journal of Social Research Methodology, 17*, 489–501. https://doi.org/10.1080/13645579.2013.769702
Drenkhahn, K. (2013). Secure preventive detention in Germany: Incapacitation or treatment intervention? *Behavioral Sciences and the Law, 31*, 312–327.
Eriksen, T. H. (2015 [1995]). *Small places, large issues: An introduction to social and cultural anthropology*. Pluto Press.
European Court of Human Rights. (2019). *Life imprisonment: Factsheet—Life imprisonment*. https://www.echr.coe.int/documents/fs_life_sentences_eng.pdf. Accessed 11 May 2021.
Feldmann, A. (1991). *Formations of violence: The narrative of the body and political terror in Northern Ireland*. University Chicago Press.
Flanagan, T. J. (1980). The pains of long-term imprisonment: A comparison of British and American perspectives. *The British Journal of Criminology, 20*, 148–156. https://doi.org/10.2307/23636693
Flanagan, T. J. (1981). Dealing with long-term confinement: Adaptive strategies and perspectives among long-term prisoners. *Criminal Justice and Behavior, 8*(2), 201–222.
Fleisher, M. S. (1989). *Warehousing violence*. Sage.
Flick, U. (2014). *An introduction to qualitative research* (5th ed.). Sage.
Galli, F. (2016). Einen altersgerechten Vollzugsplatz anbieten: Die Seniorenabteilung der JVA Lenzburg stellt sich den Herausforderungen der Zeit. *Information zum Straf- und Massnahmenvollzug – info bulletin, 41*(2), 13–16.
Garin, V. (2012). Social instability and reaction to deviance: A multilevel analysis of the Swiss lifelong detention initiative. *Punishment & Society, 14*, 289–314. https://doi.org/10.1177/1462474511427516
Garland, D. (2001). *The culture of control: Crime and social order in contemporary society*. Oxford University Press.
Greer, C., & Jewkes, Y. (2005). Extremes of otherness: Media images of social exclusion. *Social Justice, 32*(1), 20–31.
Hassine, V. (2009). *Life without parole: Living in prison today*. Oxford University Press.

Heather, N. (1977). Personal illness in "lifers" and the effects of long-term indeterminate sentences. *British Journal of Criminology, 17*, 378–386.

Herrity, K., Schmidt, B. E., & Warr, J. (Eds.). (2021). *Sensory penalities: Exploring the senses in spaces of punishment and social control*. Emerald Publishing Limited.

Hirschauer, S. (2001). Das Vergessen des Geschlechts: Zur Praxeologie einer Kategorie sozialer Ordnung. *Kölner Zeitschrift für Soziologie und Sozialpsychologie* (41), 208–235.

Hostettler, U. (2012). Exploring hidden ordinariness: Ethnographic approaches to life behind prison walls. In M. Budowski, M. Nollert, & C. Young (Eds.), *Delinquenz und Bestrafung* (pp. 158–166). Seismo.

Hostettler, U., Marti, I., & Richter, M. (2016). *Lebensende im Justizvollzug. Gefangene, Anstalten, Behörden*. Stämpfli Verlag.

Hulley, S., Crewe, B., & Wright, S. (2015). Re-examining the problems of long-term imprisonment. *The British Journal of Criminology, 56*, 769–792. https://doi.org/10.1093/bjc/azv077

Jack, A. (1988). Working in a prison organization. *NAPANAPA Bulletin, Special Issue: Mainstreaming Anthropology: Experiences in Government Employment, 5*(1), 16–27.

Jacobson, J., & Hough, M. (2010). *Unjust deserts: Imprisonment for public protection* (Project Report). Prison Reform Trust.

Jewkes, Y. (2002). *Captive audience: Media, masculinity and power in prisons*. Willan Publishing.

Jewkes, Y. (2005). Loss, liminality and the life sentence: Managing identity through disrupted lifecourse. In A. Liebling & S. Maruna (Eds.), *The effects of imprisonment* (pp. 366–388). Routledge.

Jewkes, Y. (2012). Autoethnography and emotion as intellectual resources: Doing prison research differently. *Qualitative Inquiry, 18*, 63–75. https://doi.org/10.1177/1077800411428942

Jewkes, Y. (2014). An introduction to "Doing prison research differently." *Qualitative Inquiry*. https://doi.org/10.1177/1077800413515828

Jewkes, Y. (2015). Foreword. In D. H. Drake, R. Earle, & J. Sloan (Eds.), *The Palgrave handbook of prison ethnography: Palgrave studies in prisons and penology* (pp. ix–xiii). Palgrave Macmillan.

Jose-Kampfner, C. (1990). Coming to terms with existential death: An analysis of women's adaptation to life in prison. *Social Justice, 17*(2 [40]), 110–125.

JVA Lenzburg. (2012). *Justizvollzugsanstalt Lenzburg. Jahrbuch 2010/2011.*

JVA Lenzburg. (2014). *Justizvollzugsanstalt Lenzburg. Jahrbuch 2012/2013* .

JVA Pöschwies. (2014). *Justizvollzugsanstalt Pöschwies. Jahresbericht 2014* .

Kanton Aargau. Departement Volkswirtschaft und Inneres. (2020). Justizvollzugsanstalt Lenzburg. https://www.ag.ch/de/dvi/strafverfolgung_strafvollzug/jva_lenzburg/jva_lenzburg.jsp. Accessed 14 January 2020.

Kaspar, H., & Landolt, S. (2016). Flirting in the field: Shifting positionalities and power relations in innocuous sexualisations of research encounters. *Gender, Place & Culture, 23*, 107–119. https://doi.org/10.1080/0966369X.2014.991704

King, R. (2005). Effects of supermax custody. In A. Liebling & S. Maruna (Eds.), *The effects of imprisonment* (pp. 118–145). Routledge.

Kinzig, J. (2008). *Die Legalbewährung gefährlicher Rückfalltäter. Zugleich ein Beitrag zur Entwicklung des Rechts der Sicherungsverwahrung* (2nd ed.). Duncker & Humblot.

Kuhn, A. (2017). Droit suisse des sanctions: de l'utopie à la dystopie. *Revue Pénale Suisse, 135*(3), 235–255.

Kunz, K.-L., & Moser, R. (Eds.). (1997). *Innere Sicherheit und Lebensängste: Referate einer Vorlesungsreihe des Collegium Generale der Universität Bern im Sommersemester 1996*. Bern.

Künzli, J., Eugster, A., & Schultheiss, M. (2016). *Haftbedingungen in der Verwahrung: Menschenrechtliche Standards und die Situation in der Schweiz*. Bern.

Kusenbach, M. (2003). Street phenomenology: The go-along as ethnographic research tool. *Ethnography, 4*, 455–485. https://doi.org/10.1177/146613810343007

Largey, G., & Watson, R. (2006 [1972]). The Sociology of Odors. In J. Drobnick (Ed.), *The Smell Culture Reader*. Berg.

Leigey, M. E., & Ryder, M. A. (2015). The pains of permanent imprisonment: Examining perceptions of confinement among older life without parole inmates. *International Journal of Offender Therapy and Comparative Criminology, 59*, 726–742. https://doi.org/10.1177/0306624X13517868

Liebling, A. (1999). Doing research in prisons: Breaking the silence? *Theoretical Criminology, 3*, 147–173.

Liebling, A. (2001). Whose side are we on?: Theory, practice and allegiances in prison research. *British Journal of Criminology, 41*, 472–484.

Liebling, A. (2014a). Moral and philosophical problems of long-term imprisonment. *Studies in Christian Ethics, 27*, 258–269. https://doi.org/10.1177/0953946814530219

Liebling, A. (2014b). Postscript: Integrity and emotion in prisons research. *Qualitative Inquiry, 20*, 481–486. https://doi.org/10.1177/1077800413516273

MacKenzie, D. L., & Goodstein, L. (1985). Long-term incarceration impacts and characteristics of long-term offenders: An empirical analysis. *Criminal Justice and Behavior, 12*, 395–414. https://doi.org/10.1177/0093854885012004001

Marti, I. (2021). Sensing freedom: Insights into long-term prisoners' perceptions of the outside world. *Incarceration, 2*. https://doi.org/10.1177/26326663211013703

Marti, I., & Hostettler, U. (2016). Feldforschung im Justizvollzug: Erfahrungen und Überlegungen zu Fragen des Zugangs zum Feld und zu den Forschungsteilnehmenden. *Tsantsa, 21*, 137–143.

Marti, I., & Hostettler, U. (2018). Hinter den Mauern. Einblicke in die ethnografische Gefängnisforschung. *Bulletin de la Société suisse de sociologie* (153), 28–32.

Marti, I., Hostettler, U., & Richter, M. (2014). Sterben im geschlossenen Vollzug: Inhaltliche und methodische Herausforderungen für die Forschung. *Schweizerische Zeitschrift für Kriminologie, 13*(1), 26–43.

Marti, I., Hostettler, U., & Richter, M. (2017). End of life in high-security prisons in Switzerland: Overlapping and blurring of "care" and "custody" as Institutional Logics. *Journal of Correctional Health Care, 23*, 32–42. https://doi.org/10.1177/1078345816684782

Mathiesen, T. (1965). *The defences of the weak: A sociological study of a Norwegian correctional institution*. Tavistock Publications.

Mayring, P. (2010). *Qualitative Inhaltsanalyse: Grundlagen und Techniken* (11th ed.). Beltz Verlag.

Mitchell, B. (1990). The management of life sentence prisoners in England and Wales. *The Prison Journal, 70*, 96–108. https://doi.org/10.1177/003288559007000110

Moran, D., Turner, J., & Schliehe, A. K. (2018). Conceptualizing the carceral in carceral geography. *Progress in Human Geography, 42*, 666–686. https://doi.org/10.1177/0309132517710352

Oakley, A. (1981). *Subject women: Where women stand today—Politically, economically, socially, emotionally*. Pantheon Books.

O'Donnell, I. (2014). *Prisoners, solitude, and time*. Oxford University Press.

Oxford Dictionaries. (2018a). Everyday. https://en.oxforddictionaries.com/definition/everyday. Accessed 29 June 2018.

Oxford Dictionaries. (2018b). Ordinary. https://en.oxforddictionaries.com/definition/ordinary. Accessed 29 June 2018.

Paluch, J. A. (2004). *A life for a life: Life punishment (America's other death penalty)*. Roxbury.

Piché, J., & Walby, K. (2010). Problematizing carceral tours. *British Journal of Criminology, 50*, 570–581. https://doi.org/10.1093/bjc/azq014
Pink, S. (2009). *Doing sensory ethnography*. Sage.
Queloz, N. (2013). Les dérives des politiques pénales contemporaines. La fin de l'ultima ratio du droit pénal? *Revue Suisse de Criminologie* (2), 3–8.
Rasch, W. (1981). The effects of indeterminate detention: A study of men sentenced to life imprisonment. *International Journal of Law and Psychiatry, 4*(3–4), 417–431.
Reiter, K. (2014). Making windows in walls: Strategies for prison research. *Qualitative Inquiry*. https://doi.org/10.1177/1077800413515831
Rhodes, L. A. (2001). Toward an anthropology of prison. *Annual Review of Anthropology, 30*, 65–83.
Rhodes, L. A. (2004). *Total confinement: Madness and reason in the maximum security prison*. University of California Press.
Richards, B. (1978). The experience of long-term imprisonment: An exploratory investigation. *The British Journal of Criminology, 18*, 162–169. https://doi.org/10.2307/23636608
Rose, G. (2012). Making photographs as part of a research project: Photo-elicitation, photo-documentation and photo-essays. In G. Rose (Ed.), *Visual methodologies: An introduction to researching with visual materials* (3rd ed., pp. 297–327). Sage.
Rowe, A. (2014). Situating the self in prison research: Power, identity, and epistemology. *Qualitative Inquiry, 20*, 464–476. https://doi.org/10.1177/1077800413515830
Sapsford, R. (1983). *Life sentence prisoners: Reaction, response and change*. Open University Press.
Schatzman, L., & Strauss, A. L. (1973). *Field research: Strategies for a natural sociology*. Prentice-Hall.
Schinkel, M. (2014). *Being imprisoned: Punishment, adaptation and desistance* (Palgrave studies in prisons and penology). Palgrave Macmillan.
Scott, D. (2014). Prison research: Appreciative or critical inquiry? *Criminal Justice Matters, 95*, 30–31. https://doi.org/10.1080/09627251.2014.902207
Simmler, M. (2016). Sieben enttäuschte Hoffnungen? - Zur statistischen Überprüfung der realen Folgen der AT-Revision. *ZStrR, 134*(1), 73–99.
Sloan, J., & Wright, S. (2015). Going in green: Reflections on the challenges of "getting in, getting on, and getting out" for doctoral prisons researcher. In D. H. Drake, R. Earle, & J. Sloan (Eds.), *The Palgrave handbook of prison ethnography: Palgrave studies in prisons and penology* (pp. 143–163). Palgrave Macmillan.

Staerklé, C., Delay, C., Gianettoni, L., & Roux, P. (2007). *Qui a droit à quoi ? Représentations et légitimation de l'ordre social*. PUG.

Sykes, G. M. (1971 [1958]). *The society of captives: A study of a maximum security prison.* Princeton University Press.

Teo, T. (2010). What is epistemological violence in the empirical social sciences? *Social and Personality Psychology Compass, 4*, 295–303. https://doi.org/10.1111/j.1751-9004.2010.00265.x

Thornton, P. H., Ocasio, W., & Lounsbury, M. (2012). *The institutional logics perspective: A new approach to culture, structure, and process.* Oxford University Press.

Toch, H. (1996 [1977]). *Living in prison: The ecology of survival*. Princeton University Press.

Tynan, R. R. (2019). *Young men's experiences of long-term imprisonment: Living life* (Routledge advances in ethnography). Routledge.

Vigh, H. (2008). Crisis and chronicity: Anthropological perspectives on continuous conflict and decline. *Ethnos: Journal of Anthropology, 73*(1), 5–24.

Wacquant, L. (2002). The curious eclipse of prison ethnography in the age of mass incarceration. *Ethnography, 3*, 371–398.

Waldram, J. B. (2009a). Challenges of prison ethnography. *Anthropology News, 50*, 4–5. https://doi.org/10.1111/j.1556-3502.2009.05014.x

Waldram, J. B. (2009b). It's just you and Satan, hanging out at a pre-school: Notions of evil and the rehabilitation of sexual offenders. *Anthropology and Humanism, 34*(2), 219–234.

Walker, S., & Worrall, A. (2000). Life as a woman: The gendered pains of indeterminate imprisonment. *Prison Service Journal, 132*, 27–37.

Young, C. (2018). *Narrative im Justizvollzug. Identitäten von Mitarbeitenden, medialer Diskurs und historischer Kontext*. Seismo.

Zamble, E. (1992). Behavior and adaptation in long-term prison inmates: Descriptive longitudinal results. *Criminal Justice and Behavior, 19*, 409–425. https://doi.org/10.1177/0093854892019004005

Zamble, E., & Porporino, F. J. (1988). *Coping, behavior, and adaptation in prison inmates*. Springer-Verlag.

2

Indefinite Confinement in Switzerland

The Swiss Criminal Code (SCC) distinguishes between prison sentences and measures, as the duration of the latter is not linked to the guilt of the offender but to the intended purpose of the measure, which could be to provide therapy or to ensure public security. Courts order such measures in addition to a sentence. In principle, these (preventive-oriented) measures should only last as long as is necessary to avert the risk of reoffending (Art. 56 SCC). In this book, I am interested in the two particular measures that entail indefinite duration: *indefinite incarceration* (Art. 64 SCC) and *in-patient therapeutic treatment of mental disorders* (Art. 59 SCC).

I. Marti, *Doing Indefinite Time*, Palgrave Studies in Prisons and Penology,
https://doi.org/10.1007/978-3-031-12590-4_2

2.1 Legal Framework and Penal Policy

2.1.1 Article 64 and Article 59: Indefinite Confinement in the Swiss Criminal Code

According to Art. 64 of the SCC, the court shall order **indefinite incarceration** (*Verwahrung*) if the offender has committed murder, intentional homicide, serious assault, rape, robbery, hostage taking, arson, life endangerment *or* another offence that carries a maximum sentence of five or more years by which he has caused or intended to cause serious detriment to the physical, psychological or sexual integrity of another person (Art. 64 para. 1. SCC), *and* if a high risk of reoffending has been identified due to a) the personality traits of the offender, the circumstances of the offence, and his or her general personal circumstances, or b) a permanent or long-term mental disorder that played a role in the offence, and it is expected that imposing a therapeutic measure in accordance with Art. 59 SCC will not be successful (Art. 64 para. 1 SCC).

Until 2007 indefinite incarceration could only be ordered in the case of habitual offenders (Art. 42 of the former SCC) or mentally disturbed first-time offenders (Art. 43 of the former SCC); however, after the revision of the SCC in 2007, it could also be ordered in the case of first-time ('dangerous') offenders—with or without a (diagnosed) mental disorder. However, in contrast to the old law, indefinite incarceration today can only be ordered if a mentally disturbed offender is—in accordance with an assessment conducted by an expert—categorized as 'untreatable' (Art. 64 para. 1 let. b SCC). When a chance of recovery exists but the offender is nevertheless labelled 'dangerous', the offender shall be treated in a secure institution according to Art. 59 para. 3 SCC (Simmler, 2016, p. 94). Moreover, since 2007, the execution of the custodial sentence takes priority over indefinite incarceration, and provisions on parole (which is commonly granted after the offender has served two-thirds of the sentence, ordered by the competent penal authority) in relation to the custodial sentence do not apply (Art. 86–88 SCC). Yet, as soon as it is determined that the offender will be able to live life without reoffending again, he or she must be conditionally released, either during the execution of the preceding prison sentence (Art. 64 para. 3 SCC) or indefinite incarceration (Art. 64a para. 1 SCC).[1] In accordance with Art. 75a SCC, with a view to the authorization of *any* relaxation of the execution of indefinite incarceration (e.g. transfer to an open prison, the granting of release on temporary licence), the competent authority shall reach its decision based on the recommendation of an expert committee on risk assessment (Art. 62d para. 2 SCC). According to the law, prisoners sentenced to indefinite incarceration have to be housed in a secure therapeutic or penal institution (or a secure section thereof) in order to guarantee public safety (Art. 64 para. 4 SCC).

According to Art. 59 of the SCC, the court may order **in-patient therapeutic treatment of mental disorders** (*stationäre therapeutische Massnahme zur Behandlung von psychischen Störungen*) if the offender is suffering from a 'serious mental disorder' and if a) the felony or misdemeanour is related to his or her mental disorder and b) it is expected that the measure will reduce the risk of further offences in which his or her mental disorder is a factor (Art. 59 para. 1 SCC). In contrast to Art. 64 SCC, the implementation of the measure outlined in Art. 59 SCC takes precedence over a prison sentence, which is imposed at the same time (Art. 57, para. 2 SCC), and the deprivation of liberty associated with the measure must be considered when determining the penalty (Art. 57 para. 3 SCC). The deprivation of liberty associated with in-patient treatment according to Art. 59 SCC normally lasts for a maximum of five years. However, at the request of the competent penal authority, the court may order an extension of the measure for one or more five-year periods, if the requirements for release are not met after this period of time (Art. 59 para. 4 SCC). If the treatment does not promise any success and the offender is still considered dangerous, Art. 59 SCC can be converted into Art. 64 SCC (Art. 62c para. 4 SCC). Prisoners sentenced to in-patient therapeutic measures according to Art. 59 SCC should be placed in an 'appropriate' psychiatric institution or a therapeutic institution (Art. 59

[1] Furthermore, if the offender has been assessed as 'being permanently untreatable', as the treatment offers 'no long-term prospect of success', the court shall order lifelong incarceration (Art. 64 para. 1bis SCC). However, as noted by Simmler (2016, p. 95), legal experts doubt that it will be possible to find specialists who will diagnose permanent therapy resistance. Indeed, so far only one person has been sentenced according to Art. 64 para. 1bis SCC (NZZ (2010).

para. 2 SCC). If there is a risk that the offender could escape or commit further offences, he or she may also be treated in a secure institution, such as a penal institution, if the required therapeutic treatment can be provided there (Art. 59 para. 3 SCC). Due to the possibility of extension and the fact that in-patient therapeutic measures for the treatment of mental disorders are increasingly executed in secure penal institutions, these measures have come to be known as 'small indefinite incarceration' (*kleine Verwahrung*) (Weber et al., 2016, p. 20).

According to Art. 56 SCC, these measures should only be ordered if a prison sentence alone is considered insufficient to counter the risk of further offending, if the offender requires treatment, or if treatment is required in the interest of public safety (Art. 56 para. 1 SCC).[2] Furthermore, the ordering of a measure must be consistent with the principle of proportionality: the effect of the related intervention on the personal rights of the offender must not be unreasonable in relation to the probability and seriousness of additional offences (Art. 56 para. 2 SCC). Finally, in ordering Art. 59 or Art. 64 SCC, the court shall base its decision on an expert assessment, which must provide an opinion on the necessity and prospect of success of any treatment of the offender, the nature and probability of possible additional offences, and the ways in which the measure may be implemented (Art. 56 para. 3 SCC).

Due to the fact that, since the revision of the SCC, indefinite incarceration can only be ordered in cases of 'dangerous' offenders who are considered 'untreatable', the courts today sentence fewer people to indefinite incarceration but many more to in-patient therapeutic treatment for mental disorders; as mentioned, these sentences can be extended (for additional five-year periods) (Art. 59 para. 4 SCC) or even converted into indefinite incarceration (Art. 62c para. 4 SCC). By the end of 2018, of the approximately 7,000 prison inmates in Switzerland (of which 1,843 were in pre-trial detention), 731 people were serving a sentence with no concrete date of release (Bundesamt für Statistik, 2019a) (see Fig. 2.1).

[2] In addition to Art. 59 and Art. 64 SCC, Swiss criminal law lists three other therapeutic measures that can be ordered by the court and for which the provisions of Art. 56 SCC apply as well: Art. 60 SCC (in-patient 'treatment of addiction'), Art. 61 SCC (in-patient 'measures for young adults') and Art. 63 SCC ('out-patient treatment' for offenders who are suffering from serious mental disorders or are dependent on addictive substances).

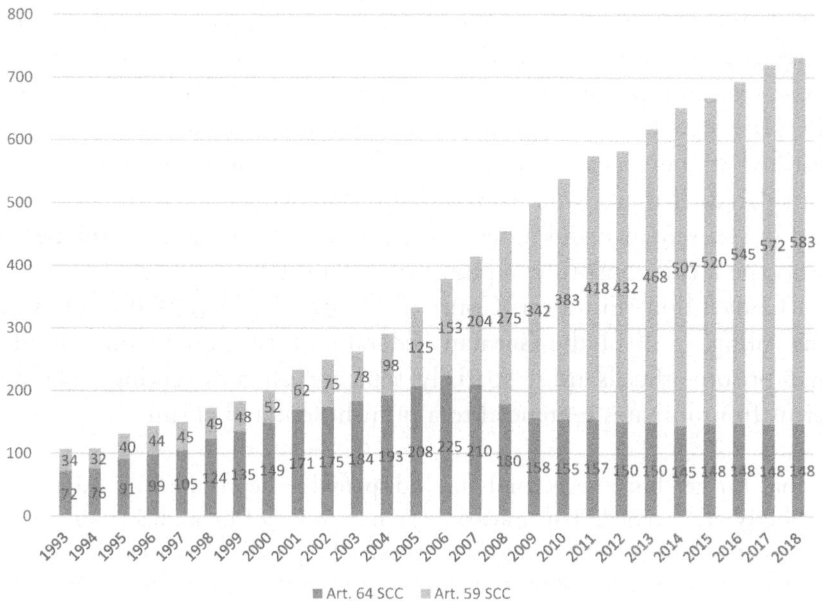

Fig. 2.1 Average number of inmates sentenced according to Art. 64 SCC or Art. 59 SCC (1993–2018)[3] (*Source* Author, based on data from the Swiss Federal Statistical Office [04.11.2019])

According to international and European human rights requirements, indefinite incarceration can only be considered legitimate if its application clearly differs from that of a regular prison sentence. In its General Comment on Article 9 of the UN Pact II, the UN Human Rights Committee calls for explicit consideration of the non-punitive character of indefinite incarceration (or 'preventive detention' as it is termed by the UN). It further states that the conditions of such detention must be distinct from the conditions for prisoners serving a punitive sentence and aimed at prisoners' rehabilitation and reintegration into society (UN Human Rights Committee, 2014). In 2009, in the case *M. v Germany*,

[3] Before the revision of the SCC in 2007, those held in indefinite incarceration for security reasons were 'habitual offenders' sentenced according to Art. 42 of the former SCC. 'Mentally disturbed' offenders were sentenced following Art. 43 para. 2 of the former SCC.

based on the fact that the regime of detention for prisoners held in indefinite incarceration in Germany did not differ materially from that for those serving a prison sentence, the European Court of Human Rights (ECHR) stated that, in principle, indefinite incarceration can only be justified if the special character of the encroachment it constitutes is considered. If there is no 'substantial difference' between the execution of a prison sentence and indefinite incarceration in favour of the person concerned, this constitutes a punishment in the sense of Art. 7 para. 1 of the Convention (European Court of Human Rights, 2010). Following this ruling, in 2011 the German Federal Constitutional Court decided that prison officials must spatially separate inmates serving indefinite terms from inmates sentenced to a punishment and ensure,

> that further burdens beyond the indispensable deprivation of 'external' liberty are avoided. This must be taken account of by a liberty-oriented execution aimed at therapy which makes the purely preventive character of the measure plain both to the detainee under preventive detention and to the general public. The deprivation of liberty must be designed in such a way – at a marked distance from the execution of a custodial sentence ('distance requirement', see BVerfGE 109, 133 <166>) – that the prospect of regaining freedom visibly determines the practice of confinement. (BVerfG, 2011)

This decision has been legally anchored in the German Penal Code (§ 66c) under the concept of *Abstandsgebot* (the 'distance requirement'). In Switzerland, while a debate on this topic is emerging, the situation of prisoners held in indefinite incarceration has yet to be officially considered, either on a legal or practical level; the regime of detention is the same for prisoners experiencing indefinite incarceration as for those serving finite sentences (Künzli et al., 2016, p. 23).

2.1.2 High-Risk Offenders: Identifying Individuals Posing a 'Danger to the Public'

As demonstrated by Holmes and Soothill (2007), the concept of dangerousness and the imprisonment of 'dangerous' individuals in so-called

Western societies is nothing new from a historical perspective. However, as a relative concept that is socially constructed and influenced by public values and attitudes towards crime and punishment as well as the legal framework, the definition of what constitutes dangerousness, what can be regarded as dangerous, and how society should deal with danger, has constantly shifted. Yet, '[t]hose classified as dangerous [...] have all represented similar threats to the values of normal society' (Holmes & Soothill, 2007, p. 591)—they are the 'ungovernables' (Pratt, 1997, p. 97) over whom the state needs to introduce 'special powers of control'.

In the late nineteenth and early twentieth centuries, in Switzerland and elsewhere, the 'ungovernables' included habitual criminals, namely 'petty property offenders' and 'vagrants'—that is, 'those people who lived by robbery and thieving' and therefore threatened the population's standard of living (Holmes & Soothill, 2007, pp. 591–592). As a response, many countries introduced indeterminate sentences in order to protect the general public, who were put at risk by these repeat offenders (Holmes & Soothill, 2007, p. 592). In Switzerland, with the introduction of the SCC in 1942, indefinite incarceration was also ordered for offenders who were considered 'work-shy' or having 'a tendency towards dissipatedness' (Art. 42 of the former SCC) (Die Bundesversammlung der schweizerischen Eidgenossenschaft, 1937, my translation).

As further explained by Holmes and Soothill (2007), together with a shift in the political rationality from classical liberalism towards welfarism and a strengthening of psychiatry in the second half of the twentieth century, these 'habituals' were more often placed in 'corrective' mental health institutions than prisons and therefore were no longer considered dangerous but rather 'inadequate' (Holmes & Soothill, 2007, p. 593). In Switzerland, this development led to the introduction in 1971 of the 'mentally disturbed offender' (Art. 43 of the former SCC) (Bundesversammlung der Schweizerischen Eidgenossenschaft, 2001, my translation), for whom rehabilitation would be provided through therapy in a psychiatric institute rather than imprisonment. Yet, indefinite incarceration was still an option in the case of an offender who was considered to pose a risk to the public (Art. 43 para. 1 Section 2.2 of the former SCC) (Bundesversammlung der Schweizerischen Eidgenossenschaft, 2001). Since the shift to neoliberalism and changes in values in the late 1960s, dangerousness has increasingly been defined with reference to the body. As a result, sex and violent offenders came to represent danger. Moreover, there was an increased focus on the risk offenders may pose—that is, 'the crimes they might commit in the future' (Holmes & Soothill, 2007, p. 594). Today, as mentioned in the introduction, they are often represented in the media and public discourse as 'monsters' or 'beasts', and are thus categorized as 'evil and sub-human' (Waldram, 2009, p. 4). They hence constitute today's 'absolute others', not only physically excluded from society through imprisonment, but also completely detached from 'the social, moral, and cultural universe of ordinary, decent people' (Greer & Jewkes, 2005, p. 21).

In Switzerland, the systematic identification and labelling of sex and violent offenders as 'dangerous' can be traced back to a 1993 incident in which a young woman was killed by an offender on prison leave who had been sentenced to life imprisonment. This incident marked a turning point in criminal law and penal policy (Schneeberger Georgescu, 2009). First, the term 'dangerous convict' found its way into cantonal law and enforcement practices (Baechtold et al., 2016, p. 247). Second, between 1994 and 1997, six cantonal or regional expert committees were established to assess the 'dangerousness' of offenders and to advise the enforcement authorities responsible for placing the offenders, retaining the ability to loosen the regime of detention after some time (Baechtold et al., 2016, p. 248). With the revision of the Criminal Code in 2007 (and the restructuring of indefinite incarceration), the term 'dangerous convict' finally became anchored in Swiss national law, and the establishment of expert committees (Art. 62d para. 2 SCC) was declared compulsory (Baechtold et al., 2016, p. 249). Today, following Art. 75a para. 3 of the SCC, prisoners are considered to pose a 'danger to the public', 'if there is a risk that the prison inmate will abscond and commit a further offence that severely prejudices the physical, psychological or sexual integrity of another person'. The committees, which at a minimum consist of representatives of the prosecution services, enforcement authorities and psychiatric professionals (Art. 62d para. 2 SCC), have to assess the danger an offender may pose to the public a) whenever he or she has committed a crime in terms of Art. 64 para. 1 SCC, and b) when the cantonal penal authority cannot satisfactorily answer the question of dangerousness. Generally, as mentioned above, the assessment of dangerousness is carried out with a view towards easing the regime for the deprivation of liberty, such as a transfer to an open prison, the granting of release on temporary licence, the authorization of day release employment or of external accommodation, or the granting of parole (Art. 75a para. 2 SCC).[4] Since the 1990s, the number of individuals in indefinite incarceration has increased rapidly. As mentioned above, this stems not from an exceptional rise in condemnations but, more particularly, from increasingly severe practices with respect to the release of these so-called high-risk offenders. For example, between 2008 and 2018, a total of 40 persons sentenced to indefinite incarceration (Art. 64 SCC) were released. In 2017, not a single prisoner was released, and only three were released in 2018 ($N = 148$) (Bundesamt für Statistik, 2019b) (see Fig. 2.2).

While it has been argued that the systematic classification of offenders has increased the identification of dangerous offenders and so far has successfully helped to prevent further crimes of the same type, the committees' work has also been criticized (Baechtold et al., 2016, p. 248). In particular, criticism was voiced, first, over the lack of participatory rights for offenders in terms of the classification procedure, which has been described as clandestine and non-transparent; second, that the offenders concerned have no legal remedy against the classification made by the expert committees; third, that the activities of the expert committees are not subject to any scientific assessment; and, finally, that today the label 'dangerous' is too often ascribed to offenders in order to avoid the risk of a person wrongly being classified as 'harmless' and then

[4] As pointed out by Baechtold et al. (2016, pp. 247–248), early experiences with the expert committees, however, have shown that although they used the same catalogue of criteria developed by forensic psychiatrists, they often applied them differently. As a result, in 2004, in the canton of Zürich, four times more offenders were labelled dangerous than in the canton of Bern. In order to strengthen coherence within the Swiss practice of risk assessment, between 2010 and 2013 the Federal Office of Justice supported a pilot project for a risk-oriented penal system (*Risikoorientierter Sanktionenvollzug ROS*) with the aim to implement a systematic and standardized instrument that integrates all phases of sentence enforcement (see Amt für Justizvollzug Kanton Zürich (2014). The project was tested and later implemented in four Swiss cantons and in all other German-speaking cantons between 2016 and 2018 (see Amt für Justizvollzug Kanton Zürich, 2019).

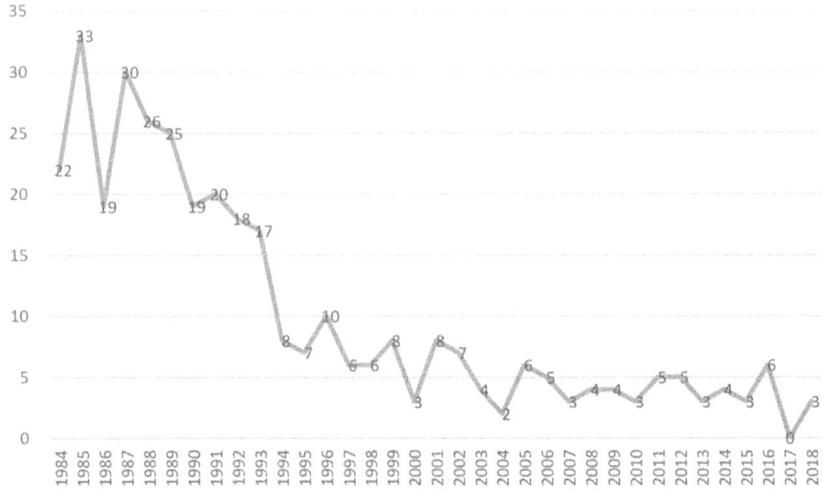

Fig. 2.2 Release of inmates sentenced under Art. 64 SCC (1984–2018)[5] (*Source* Author, based on data from the Swiss Federal Statistical Office [04.11.2019])

committing further crimes (i.e. a 'false negative'). The error rate of so-called 'false positives' is estimated to be 60 to 70% (Baechtold et al., 2016, p. 248). Those who are wrongly classified as 'dangerous' are offered no chance to disprove this judgement, as they—due to their label—can rarely be released (Baechtold et al., 2016, pp. 248–249).

2.1.3 Institutional Placement and Handling of 'Dangerous' Offenders

Similar to regular prison sentences, indefinite incarceration or in-patient measures for the treatment of mental disorders are ordered by the court. The cantonal enforcement authorities and institutions are responsible for their enforcement and for the management of the prisoners. They must

[5] It should be noted that before the revision of the SCC in 2007, people held in indefinite incarceration were either 'habitual criminals' sentenced according to Art. 42 of the former SCC, or 'mentally disturbed' first offenders following Art. 43 para. 2 of the former SCC. All inmates detained according to Art. 42 and Art. 43 of the former SCC were further re-evaluated in 2007 in order to keep them in prison following Art. 59 or 64 SCC.

orient themselves using the relevant provisions of the SCC that are based on two constitutional principles: (1) respect for 'human dignity' and (2) the freedom of prison inmates to exercise their legal rights, as their rights may only be limited to the extent required for the deprivation of their liberty and their co-existence in the penal institution (Art. 74 SCC). Additional principles regarding the execution of sentences and measures include preventing reoffending after release, making institutional life as normal as possible, combating the harmful effects of spending time in detention, and the duty to provide proper care and to prevent offending while in detention (Art. 75 para. 1 SCC). These principles apply to the enforcement of all forms of prison sentences and measures. There is no specific (additional) legal basis regarding the conditions of detention for prisoners sentenced to a measure of indefinite duration. As mentioned above, the in-patient therapeutic treatment of mental disorders according to Art. 59 SCC should principally be executed in a psychiatric or therapeutic institution (Art. 59 para. 2 SCC), and only in a secure institution if there is a risk that the offender could escape or commit further offences (Art. 59 para. 3 SCC); however, due to a lack of appropriate facilities (and increasing prisoner rates), people sentenced under Art. 59 SCC are mostly housed in a secure prison (Weber et al., 2016, p. 44). According to the most recent survey conducted by the *Conference of the Cantonal Heads of the Departments of Police and Justice (KKJPD)*, in Switzerland there are deficits of approximately 280 places in forensic psychiatric facilities and 90 places in secure penal institutions for offenders with 'mental disorders' (KKJPD, 2017a, p. 15).

As mentioned above, prisoners sentenced to indefinite incarceration must by law be housed in a (secure) therapeutic or penal institution (Art. 64 para. 4 SCC). As shown by the KKJPD, in 2016 85% of the prisoners who were sentenced to indefinite incarceration were held in a secure penal institution and therefore in the same conditions as prisoners serving a regular sentence (KKJPD, 2017b). However, in accordance with international human rights requirements, several national and cantonal recommendations call for an improvement in the living conditions for offenders sentenced to indefinite incarceration. As early as 2008, the Concordat of the execution of sentences in Eastern Switzerland recommended taking into account the 'special situation' of these prisoners and granting them 'as much freedom as possible' within the prison as 'the lack of perspective may lead them to put themselves or others in danger, because they do not see any purpose in life or have nothing left to lose' (Ostschweizer Strafvollzugskommission, 2008, my translation). In 2013, within the framework of the inter-cantonal planning of prison facilities (*Anstaltsplanung der Strafvollzugskonkordate*), it was argued that it would be appropriate to create special (secure) units for this prisoner population (Strafvollzugskonkordate der Schweiz, 2014). Finally, in 2016, the Federal Office of Justice recommended the provision of larger cells (i.e. more than 12 m^2) for those held in indefinite incarceration (Bundesamt für Justiz BJ, 2016). However, as mentioned above, the living conditions today remain the same for these prisoners as for those serving a regular sentence. Prisoners held in indefinite incarceration are placed and handled in the same way as 'ordinary' prisoners. They receive no benefits despite their different status as prisoners who have already served their sentences (Künzli et al., 2016, p. 23). Yet, as they all at some point belong to the ill and elderly category, they are often placed in special units, such as the *60plus* unit or the *AGE*. Therefore, some of these prisoners do benefit from a more relaxed prison regime (Künzli et al., 2016, p. 23).

2.2 Key Actors

In this section, I provide insight into the perspectives and experiences of the key actors most directly involved in the enforcement of indefinite confinement and concrete handling of the prisoners. I start with those who are furthest away from the prisoners—not only physically but also regarding the amount of time they spend directly with them—but whose decisions are most important: the penal enforcement authorities. In the subsequent section, I present the perspectives of prison management. Finally, I explore the experience of the prison staff, those who deal with these prisoners most directly and on a daily basis (see Fig. 2.3).

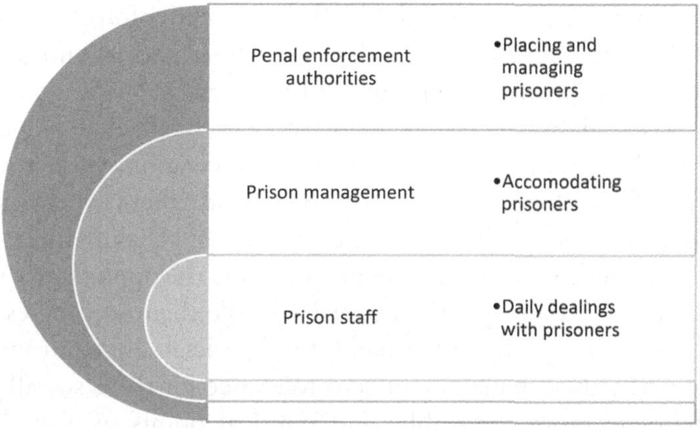

Fig. 2.3 Key actors in the enforcement of indefinite confinement (*Source* Author's own graph)

2.2.1 Penal Enforcement Authorities: Placing and Managing Prisoners

The cantonal penal enforcement authorities (hereinafter enforcement authorities) are in charge of the placement of convicted offenders in a suitable penal institution, which, as mentioned above, is generally considered to be a secure prison. Moreover, in accordance with Art. 64b para. 1 SCC and in reference to public safety, enforcement authorities are responsible for the periodic examination of the prisoners' situations and the possibility of relaxing their conditions of incarceration, such as the annual examination of conditional release from indefinite incarceration, or the biennial examination of the possibility of converting Art. 64 SCC into Art. 59 SCC—or, in case of offenders sentenced to Art. 59 SCC, the extension of the measure or its conversion into Art. 64 SCC (according to Art. 62c para. 4 SCC). In order to investigate the future prospects of prisoners sentenced to indefinite incarceration, following Art. 64b para. 2 SCC, the enforcement authorities reach their decision on the basis of a report from prison management, the opinion of an independent expert (forensic-psychological assessment) and recommendations by an expert committee. They also must grant the offender a hearing. Finally, as explained above, the cantonal enforcement authorities also have the ability to formulate guidelines and recommendations regarding the institutional handling of prisoners.

As I was told by the enforcement officials I talked to, in terms of managing those sentenced to indefinite incarceration, they find themselves in a fraught position. On the one hand, they are charged with working with these prisoners for the purpose of rehabilitation. By law, enforcement authorities have to grant prisoners the opportunity to prove that they have changed for the better to enable them to progress within the penal system. On the other hand, these officials are confronted with political and public demands for zero tolerance for these so-called high-risk offenders. From the public and political points of view, 'nothing must happen' (Penal authority representative C., 15.3.2018). As a consequence, enforcement authorities today are more cautious regarding the loosening of the penal regime (e.g. by granting temporary prison leave) in the case of offenders sentenced to indefinite incarceration. For prisoners, the fields to prove themselves can therefore 'almost only be created within the prisons' walls' (Penal authority representative C., 15.3.2018) and not in public. Moreover, as mentioned, public pressure has also led to stricter practices related to (conditional) release. This change in the handling of high-risk offenders has contributed to an increase in the number of long-term prisoners who not only have to stay behind bars for the rest of their lives, but also spend the end of their lives in a carceral setting (Hostettler et al., 2016). This also leads to critical remarks from both the public and academia, generally with reference to medical, legal and ethical issues and based on the assumption that dying in prison is per se 'inhumane' and 'undignified' (Handtke et al., 2012; Kinzig, 2012; Wulf & Grube, 2012).

As a result, the enforcement authorities and, in particular, decision makers are under constant observation. This puts a lot of pressure on them: 'You always have to justify yourself, that's exhausting' (Penal authority representative C., 15.3.2018). They feel they are principally 'measured by the failures'—when things are going well, which is usually the case, 'it's not recognized' (penal authority representative C., 15.3.2018). However, whenever an incident occurs, the media—'always in search of a story' (Penal authority representative G., 27.1.2015)—immediately exploits the 'scandal' (Young, 2018). Moreover, such (rare) incidents typically have severe consequences—not only at the staff level but often also for all the other prisoners held in indefinite incarceration, of whom the authorities are in charge:

> If an inmate [for whom we are responsible] kills someone on a vacation, [this is a] meltdown. […] [F]or the relevant executive council or head official, and of course the staff, [it's] an incredible meltdown. And then it's about proving to the public that you're doing something. And this action is mostly to stop everything [all the prison leaves that have been granted] for everyone. We've already had that in the past. And until this is relaunched, the impact this has for all other inmates who are affected by this stop is of course dramatic. (Penal authority representative F., 28.5.2014)

Furthermore, today the prisoners' potential 'way out', including the granting of temporary prison leave, almost exclusively leads through psychotherapy, which has been further developed and professionalized since the 1990s. In other words, progression within the penal system is nearly impossible without therapy. Although offenders sentenced to indefinite incarceration are by law defined as 'untreatable', if the potential for personal development and the possibility of converting Art. 64 SCC into Art. 59 SCC are identified by forensic psychiatrists, therapy can be provided. At the core of the treatment is the prisoner's offence(s), which is therefore seen as the key feature of the convicted person:

> In order to be able to assess possibilities for loosening the regime, we need to know something about the person, and so he or she has to work on the offense. There is an obligation to cooperate, […] but some refuse. So [in these cases] we cannot judge [regarding the loosening of the regime]. If there is any doubt […] we decide in favour of security. (Penal authority representative C., 15.3.2018)

As this excerpt suggests, the contemporary focus on prisoners' offences in rehabilitative treatment, which is also present in other countries, is therefore oriented mainly towards public security. Crewe (2009) understood this development as a direct result of the punitive turn: 'prisoners' psychological "needs" [are] narrowly defined according to what is deemed to be desirable for the public rather than what prisoners might require to enhance their psychological wellbeing or address their social needs' (Crewe, 2009, p. 115). While the majority of the official representatives I talked to agree with the therapeutic approach, a few of my interview partners also questioned this strong and paramount focus on the offence in a way similar to Crewe. They argued that socio-pedagogical support should also be offered, in order to grant prisoners the opportunity for individual development and 'room for their competence' (Penal authority representative A., 20.3.2018). From this point of view, the system as a whole should shift its main focus from the offence to the person—that is, to 'his resources and ways of coping with everyday life', 'social relations', 'professional identity' and 'personal health'—considering all the related and observable changes in the risk assessments (Penal authority representative A., 20.3.2018). Therefore, while the current approach places responsibility for successful rehabilitation mainly on the offender, from which personal engagement is expected (showing remorse and undergoing psychotherapy; see also Sect. 2.3.1), from this critical perspective, the institution should also make a contribution by supporting the prisoner—that is, the person—as a whole.

Regarding the inter-cantonal recommendations that propose separation and the improvement of these prisoners' living conditions, to some extent similar to the *Abstandsgebot* implemented in Germany (i.e. a differently designed system for indefinite incarceration, including strict separation of these prisoners from the rest of the prisoner population), my interview partners all rejected the idea of a complete spatial separation of these prisoners from the rest of the prisoner community. They argued that this would lead to 'ghettoization' (Penal authority representative C., 15.3.2018) and cut off important social relations that had been established over time between prisoners and prison staff members (Penal authority representative B., 20.3.2018). They generally support the status quo by emphasizing that the 'Swiss standards' in the penal system are generally 'already high', and certainly higher than in other countries. By contrast, one representative I talked to argued that the current carceral regime in Switzerland mainly ensures 'peace and order', which, in the long term, not only hinders any progress but may even have damaging effects on the prisoners, as it may lead to 'regression' (Penal authority representative A., 20.3.2018):

> The question arises whether the execution of indefinite incarceration is currently organized in a way that promotes the resources of the person. How is the execution concretely organized? Is it all about peace and order or is it focused on [the prisoners'] resources? They [prisoners sentenced to indefinite confinement] too should have a perspective. The current practice doesn't convince me. [...] Today, people are breaking down, becoming stunted. We have calm and adjusted inmates, who have been prisonised. In the end, we perhaps hold persons in indefinite incarceration who do not even belong there. (Penal authority representative A., 20.3.2018)

Despite general support for the status quo, all of my interview partners supported, in principle, the idea of granting these prisoners more freedom and opportunities within the prison walls, such as more diverse leisure time activities or the possibility to keep pets. Yet, from their perspective, a lack of resources and public acceptance makes this endeavour impossible, at least for now.

Regarding their vision for potential improvements, the separation of these prisoners was nonetheless considered conceivable, but only within the prison, for instance by establishing a special unit. As one of my interview partners explained, such an arrangement—an 'island within the prison' (Penal authority representative A., 20.3.2018)—would allow an internal loosening of the regime (e.g. longer opening hours of the cell doors) 'without disturbing the system' and while maintaining a high level of security. Yet, it would require 'professionalism and structures' specialized in handling this particular population in order to establish a 'counter-program to prisonisation' (Penal authority representative A., 20.3.2018) or, to put it in the words of Liebling, to allow prisoners to 'flourish' (Liebling, 2014). From the perspective of my interview partner, this would include hiring additional staff trained in social pedagogy and care professions as well as professional handling and quality management, as is the case for institutions in charge of caring for disabled people.

Others find it difficult to imagine concretely what should or could be improved. They emphasized that some prisoners held in indefinite incarceration do not want and would not support any changes, in particular those who had 'found a good daily routine' (Penal authority representative D., 15.6.2018), those having one of the 'popular jobs with responsibility' (Penal authority representative E., 15.6.2018), and those with 'important persons of reference' (Penal authority representative C., 15.3.2018) inside the prison who 'treat them very humanely' (Penal authority representative D., 15.6.2018). It was suggested that the separation of these prisoners makes sense principally in cases of illness and old age, as is currently the case in the prisons of Lenzburg and Pöschwies.

> For me, it's unclear what precisely should be changed. Do we need to provide more assistance, does this really help? Often the prisoners do not want to undergo therapy, and we do not force anyone to do therapy; it's an offer. […] It's difficult. You have to look at each case individually. Many do not want anything else. And others, due to mental health issues, cannot be housed together with the general population, because there are too many stimuli and stressors. I think a lot of criticism comes from mobilising the human rights discourse in Switzerland at a very high level. […]. The demands are often unrealistic. Especially if one considers the fact that [for these prisoners] the way they are treated by staff is the most important aspect. And prison staff in Switzerland are doing very well: they treat these prisoners with respect and very humanely. (Penal authority representative D., 15.6.2018)

Yet, it was also emphasized that pressure to make improvements in these prisoners' living conditions was certainly expected to increase, not only from human rights organizations and experts, but also from the prisoners themselves and their lawyers. However, from the perspective of most of the authorities I interviewed, changes should be initiated from the bottom up by prison management, because they are the ones who deal with these prisoners on a daily basis and can best evaluate what changes would be reasonable to implement and worthwhile to improve within the existing structures and with the financial resources available. This could then lead to the formulation of new (inter)cantonal guidelines, which would further influence jurisprudence and, perhaps, eventually lead to legal changes (Penal authority representative B., 20.3.2018).

2.2.2 Prison Management: Accommodating Prisoners

Framed by the institutional logics of punishment and rehabilitation, the prisons are in charge of carrying out the deprivation of liberty, while also providing care and support, work, training and further education as part of a prisoner's sentence management plan (Art. 75 para. 3 SCC), as well as preparing prisoners for release (Baechtold et al., 2016, p. 155). Similar to enforcement authorities, the prison management team (including the prison director and department heads) is judged by the public regarding the security and safety it provides—that is, the prevention of escape and further criminal incidents, inside as well as outside the prison.

Prisons have always accommodated prisoners who were meant to be incarcerated for an undetermined duration. However, while they were generally released after ten or 15 years, today 'they stay longer and grow old' inside prison (Prison management member B., 18.10.2016). Moreover, while previous prison populations consisted of 'habituals', property offenders and vagrants, as mentioned above, offenders sentenced to indefinite incarceration today are generally sexual and violent offenders, all labelled 'dangerous'.

The prison management team members I interviewed emphasized, first of all, that the majority of these prisoners—although they designated them as 'not normal', having 'serious disorders' (Prison management member B., 18.10.2016) or 'special personalities' (Prison management member A., 19.10.2016), and as being 'stubborn and incorrigible' people (Prison management member D., 4.11.2016)—do not generally stand out within the prison community. This means, for them, that 'they pose few to no problems' (Prison management member A., 19.10.2016). My interview partners advanced a number of reasons for this. First, these prisoners are few in number and hence constitute a minority in prison. At the time of my fieldwork, as I was told by the two directors, the *JVA Lenzburg* accommodated a total of 24 prisoners sentenced to indefinite incarceration, while the *JVA Pöschwies* had 40. Second, it was noted that long-term prisoners generally show conformist behaviour because, over time, they get to know how the system works. Furthermore, as these prisoners will stay for a longer period of time than short-term prisoners, or even for the rest of their lives, it was argued that they are generally interested in having 'steady and quiet' living conditions (Prison management member A., 19.10.2016) and therefore avoid behaviour or activities that might get them into trouble and lead to sanctions or further restrictions. This coincides with the expectations of the prison management and staff who are also interested in a calm and smooth daily routine, which leads, to some extent, to mutual dependency. As explained by one of my interview partners: 'one's more concerned about the other because we're both [staff and prisoners] in here, right? One will maybe still working [here] for 20 years, the other one will be doing time for 20 years' (Prison management member A., 19.10.2016). The fact that these prisoners do not particularly stand out—that is, cause problems—was therefore also seen as an 'indicator that allows you to say: the way it is now [the way these prisoners are treated] is probably not that bad' (Prison management member C., 27.10.2016). However, as (self-)critically added by another interview partner, certainly this is not only the result of good staff–prisoners relations, but also linked to the restricted institutional environment of secure penal institutions that gives prisoners little room for manoeuvre:

> The secure [penal] institutions are not struggling with prisoners sentenced to indefinite incarceration. Why not? Because [...] the secure institutions are mainly measured by the fact that [they] are running [without incident], and to keep something, to store something, that for me implies [...] that it is a quiet story. And we are actually very good at this. [...] This is actually one of our core competencies: having 180 men in one place, more or less orderly and quiet. And prisoners sentenced to indefinite incarceration fit in perfectly, so from this point of view, market-technically speaking, it is a client segment that fits very well in our

> range. They do not actually cause us any problems. (Prison management member E., 7.7.2016)

Yet, as I will show, some of these prisoners nevertheless do clearly stand out within the prison community: those who cause extraordinary trouble and those who are particularly well integrated and benefit from some privileges inside the prison.

Relatedly, I was told that there are certain prisoners from this particular prison population, although very few, who 'push the system to its limits' (Prison management member B., 18.10.2016): they do not respect the 'house rules', no matter how harshly and often they are sanctioned. From the prison management's perspective, such prisoners are very complicated to handle and can even make the whole system (temporarily) 'unable to act' (Prison management member B., 18.10.2016). Due to the long-term nature of these prisoners' stays and the prison's obligation to provide adequate care and support, solutions must be found to achieve compliance, or, to put it in the words of one of my interview partners, 'to make them willing to cooperate' (Prison management member B., 18.10.2016). Such solutions include the (generally temporary) relocation of the prisoner to the high-security unit or another institution, the granting of exceptions, and situational negotiation between prison staff and the prisoner instead of a strict application of the rules.

> One [prisoner] bangs his head against the wall until he becomes unconscious. And you have to stay with him; otherwise he gets a cerebral haemorrhage and dies. He is in our care, even when he puts pressure on us. [...] In such situations [it is very challenging to find a solution]. You cannot be there [with him] for 24 hours, we cannot [are not allowed to] tie him up ... so we have to hospitalise him. And then, when the acute phase is over, he is returned to us. So if a prisoner doesn't cooperate, it's very time consuming for us. That's why we seek relative peace and togetherness so that we can get along with the resources we have. (Prison management member B., 18.10.2016)

Far more often than causing extraordinary trouble, however, these prisoners are remarkably well integrated into the prison routine and therefore are allowed to carry out work that is based on trust—such as running the prison's library or cleaning areas that are generally only accessible to prison staff. As a result, the majority of my interview partners mentioned that they generally have much more contact with these prisoners than with those serving regular sentences and thus know them personally. However, my interview partners added that this kind of integration into the prison routine—and, more generally, the long-term nature of these prisoners' stays—can also cause problems, especially for prison staff, as it automatically leads to the development of a sense of trust as well as normalcy. It is hence important not to abandon a critical attitude and maintain a professional distance.

Generally, from the point of view of prison management, severe problems and challenges with this prison population mostly arise when these prisoners grow older, become frail and ill, and eventually require special care:

> As long as [they haven't reached] a certain age, [lost] a certain mobility, [have severe health [issues], I think it is actually easy [to handle them]. I think problems arise especially when someone becomes immobile, when he is particularly ill, or when he is very old [...] [and] needs special care. (Prison management member C., 27.10.2016)

As presented in Sect. 2.2.1, regarding the current debate around the institutional handling of this prison population, the members of the enforcement authorities I talked to agreed, in principal, that they should consider these prisoners' special status and grant them more freedom and opportunities, but only within the secure penal institutions and when doing so is cost-neutral. As far as the prison management team members' point of view, my interview partners also agreed that a strict spatial separation of these prisoners from the rest of the prison population would not make sense. Like the representatives of the enforcement authorities, they pointed to the small number of these prisoners, the already high standards required of Swiss penal institutions, insufficient financial resources and a lack of acceptance by the public as well as by most of the enforcement authorities. Moreover, my interview partners declared themselves to be in favour of mixing the prisoners, as this corresponds much more closely to the outside community, which also consists of people from different 'classes, cultures, [with] different levels of education' (Prison management member C., 27.10.2016), young people and elders—and thus meets the principle of normalization according to Art. 75 para. 1 SCC. From their point of view, it is clear that separation only makes sense in the case of illness and old age, which is already being implemented.

Nevertheless, ideas and plans are circulating (and currently being discussed) among my interview partners to grant these prisoners more privileges, freedom and individuality within the secure penal institution, such as systematically placing them (if they wish) in the few larger cells already available in these two prisons, equipping their cells with a fridge, and allowing longer cell opening hours, better remuneration and generally a more individualized and supportive approach by prison staff to provide them more autonomy and perspective inside the prison. This, however, would eventually require a separation of these prisoners within the prison, and the installation of a special unit for prisoners sentenced to indefinite incarceration (not least to avoid conflicts with prisoners serving standard sentences). Those who question the idea of granting them more privileges stressed that these prisoners are not the ones whom the prison has to prepare for reintegration into society and hence to ensure that they do not 'unlearn' life. This leads to particular reflections and questions, such as why they—and not those serving short sentences—should be allowed to cook their own food, or why these prisoners should have the ability to go on prison leave when they have only the smallest chance of being released.

Finally, from their perspective, many of these prisoners do not actually wish for changes or more freedom within the prison walls, or they have requests that are not feasible due to the current political and public attitudes towards them, such as access to the Internet or unaccompanied release on temporary license. Finally, it was also stressed to me that many of these prisoners do not take advantage of the offers and programmes that are currently available, and that it is difficult to motivate them to set goals for personal development, as they prefer to spend time in their cells—since they are not 'normal' people:

> Not everyone is like you and me, so that you can say: learn Chinese!, because they have never done anything else other than reading *Blick* [a daily tabloid newspaper] and watching TV. So what do you want [to do] with someone like this? (Prison management member B., 18.10.2016)

> For instance, we could offer yoga classes for prisoners held in indefinite incarceration, not only once a week, as today, but twice. [...] I think from the ten prisoners who participate today, two of them are sentenced to indefinite incarceration. But I suspect there wouldn't be more than the two who already participate ... I fear that this probably wouldn't make a difference. [Much like] [t]he gymnastics for elderly prisoners [offered in the unit for ill and elderly prisoners], there are three or four who participate. Actually, probably [all of the prisoners] there need it. But we do not want to force them: this would be stupid. And that's where they [staff working in this unit] are a bit frustrated sometimes: you propose an offer and it's not used. (Prison management member A., 19.10.2016)

2.2.3 Prison Staff: Daily Dealings with Prisoners

Prison staff members are those who deal directly with these prisoners on a daily basis. They are in charge of the implementation of prison norms, rules and regulations. They are responsible for the care, custody and control of the prisoners. Regarding long-term prisoners sentenced to indefinite incarceration, prison staff have no specific assignment and there are no additional resources available. They have to work within the given structures and instruments, such as the execution plan framed by the principle of rehabilitation, although this—release and reintegration into society—is not a realistic perspective for the majority of these prisoners. Given this particular situation, indefinite incarceration poses various challenges for prison staff.

The long-term nature of these prisoners' stays is not primarily an issue for staff members working in the security service. As they mention, these prisoners provide them with 'hardly any work' (Security officer A., 2.9.2016). They are almost invisible, as they are the ones who generally follow the rules:

For us, they are just those, with a few exceptions, with whom we have nothing to do. You may have to empty their cell at some point once a year. Because this is their life, everything they have in there is somehow, that's what they have. And they don't have much more. That's maybe the interesting thing. But otherwise, it's actually … from the point of view of the security service, I can say, we have very, very little to do with them, we don't really deal with them much. They are not the ones we have to sanction, those to whom we have to keep saying in the evening at eight: you have to be standing in front of the cell or inside now. That just works. (Security officer A., 2.9.2016)

While these prisoners do not appear on the radar screen of the security officers, staff members from other services, such as social assistants, foremen, chaplains and prison officers who are not only assigned to provide security but also care (in the units for ill and elderly prisoners), face a wide range of challenges in their everyday handling of these prisoners.

These challenges mainly result from the fact that, for these prisoners, rehabilitation is no longer a realistic goal. One of my interview partners compared indefinite incarceration to an incurable illness—a dramatic disruption in someone's life course whereby 'common-sense models' that used to provide meaning in their lives lose their significance:

Indefinite incarceration, even if it is re-evaluated, it is 99 percent sure that you will never be released. […] Therefore questions about one's own existence and its finite nature emerge in a different way than they do outside. It is like you get the diagnosis of an incurable disease. Although you still have five years to live, the common-sense models that used to give meaning to your life start to lose their significance. You have to find new ones. (Chaplain D., 4.2.2014)

Most of the prison employees with whom I spoke felt that many of these prisoners suffer from a lack of perspective and indeed have difficulty finding meaning in their lives. They further referred to the fact that these prisoners have to arrange themselves within a context characterized by routine and coercive structures, which almost completely deprives them of the ability 'to create' their own lives:

> You really do not have to think of anything, you know exactly: the door opens, you go out, now the boss says: [work is] done, [you go] back. In the evening: sports, telephone time … everything is predetermined. This takes away independence, or the possibility to create your own life. (Social assistant B., 27.6.2016)

From the point of view of the staff, different prisoners respond differently to this situation. Some become restless, others give up and completely 'let themselves go' (Social assistant A., 13.2.2014). Still others seem to have decided to live in their 'own world […] not in reality' (Foreman A., 27.6.2016), or settle in prison and 'find security in the structures' (Foreman C., 7.7.2016). For some staff members, these prisoners seem to merge into the routine since not only is daily life 'always the same', but the prisoners become 'always the same' as well (Security officer A., 2.9.2016).

Generally, working with prisoners who do not have any concrete perspective was described as a challenging task:

> I find it very difficult to deal with […] the prisoners held in indefinite incarceration, to deal with this situation. I find that very difficult. This is a tremendous challenge. [But] I'm convinced that there are perspectives. I just don't know which ones yet. But I believe that there are perspectives in any situation of life. I am convinced of that. (Chaplain A., 8.4.2014)

As these prisoners have no perspective and are also not granted much room to prove themselves (e.g. through temporary prison leaves), it is difficult to develop future plans and goals with them, which is the formal task of the social assistants. I was told that with the younger prisoners it is sometimes possible to agree on goals such as education, therapy or abstinence from drugs. With the older ones, however, this was described as being difficult, often because they do not wish to think about or make any agreements regarding future steps (Fieldnotes, 22.2.2016). As a result, in the prisoners' sentence management plans, I often found statements such as the following: '[To] continue to work in our firm framework and maintain the positive overall impression. It would be nice if [name of a prisoner] would be more physically active' (Analysis of inmate files, 6.4.2106, my translation); '[Name of a prisoner] makes an open and sociable impression. Maintaining a good and positive impression; the possible improvement of his health is desirable' (Analysis of inmate file, 6.4.2106, my translation).

In addition to the social assistants who try to create perspective for these prisoners inside prison by finding out 'what they still enjoy' or 'what can still motivate them' (Social assistant A., 13.2.2014), prison staff in general mentioned these inmates' special situation and thus—within their scope of discretion regarding the implementation of prison rules—try to support them individually in finding perspective within the prison walls. Some also try to make their days a bit livelier, for instance by providing them with variety and change (e.g. at the workplace), or with as much autonomy as possible, for example by giving them freedom of choice (e.g. regarding the fulfilment of obligations, such as the timing of cleaning their cells). In this regard, some prison officers apply certain rules a bit less strictly, especially in the units for ill and elderly prisoners:

> For example, usually you [as a prisoner] are not allowed to go out and smoke [in the courtyard] or do anything else during work or say: I will quickly go to my cell and so on. Some [employees] in here are very strict. They then say: no, it's forbidden, now it's time to work [...]. I see it differently. Why shouldn't he be allowed to go and get something he needs out of his cell? Why not? Why isn't he allowed to go out [to the courtyard] now? 'Yes, go out, have a smoke!' Why not? He will be in here forever; he will die in here. Why shouldn't I let him out for a smoke or to do anything else? (Prison officer I., 21.11.2013)

In addition to the lack of perspective, another aspect that is increasingly debated and sometimes questioned regarding prisoners held in custody until the end of their lives is the interdiction of physical contact between staff and prisoners, which is primarily designed to protect employees and includes all forms of physical contact. This rule, however, becomes simply impossible to follow during the increasing number of situations in which prison officers have to provide (medical) care and support, especially in the units for ill and elderly prisoners (see also Hostettler et al., 2016). Moreover, I also met prison officers who consciously allowed some kind of physical contact during situations other than those requiring medical care, being aware that there is no one else around by whom they can expect to be physically touched.[6] As explained by one of the staff members:

> [w]e humans, we need touch and these people [the prisoners held in indefinite incarceration] are all of them, let's say, dried out regarding [physical] contact. […] For instance, he [a prisoner] wants to shake your hand every morning. […] When I am walking around with someone like [another prisoner], I consciously allow closeness, sitting next to him and giving him a nudge from time to time […] I'm not a *Töpli* [someone who easily and quickly touches others], this is dangerous, but when he's sitting next to me, maybe I'll say, 'now listen, […]', then I'll touch him here [on the shoulder]: 'hey, have you heard of that?' (Prison officer B., 8.10.2013)

Finally, some of the staff members also discussed creating some kind of 'free spaces' for these prisoners. These moments are in particular initiated by those responsible for spiritual or medico-therapeutic care. Free spaces are described as moments in which 'prison pressure is put in the background', when they can 'just be' (Social assistant B., 27.6.2016) or even 'let go' (Medical staff member C., 18.2.2014), or which allow them to experience 'the feeling of being at home' ('*Beheimatung*') (Chaplain C., 15.1.2014).

Although it is the penal enforcement authorities who divide the prisoners into categories (in particular regarding their degree of 'dangerousness' and treatability) and determine the course of action, prison staff have substantial influence as well. For example, they have to write daily and weekly reports regarding prisoners' behaviour that are later included in the prison reports for the attention of the enforcement authorities. Through these instruments, prison officers are forced to constantly observe and interpret the prisoners' behaviours and activities. These interpretations are not only shaped by their obligation to ensure order and security, but also filtered through their personal norms and moral values (see also Hostettler et al., 2016, p. 156). For example,

---

[6] The *JVA Pöschwies* has a so-called 'family room' where prisoners and their visitors can experience a bit more privacy and intimacy. However, among the prisoners with whom I spoke, no one benefited from this kind of visit (see also Sect. 6.3.1).

as I noted during fieldwork, some prisoners were categorized by staff members as 'extremely grubby' (Fieldnotes, 7.4.2016), or, in contrast, as having a 'mania for cleaning' (Fieldnotes, 5.4.2016); some were described as 'unfriendly', while others were reproached for displaying a 'friendliness' that is 'exaggerated and ingratiating' (Fieldnotes, 5.4.2016). These reports may have severe consequences for the prisoners (this also affects their everyday lives; see Sect. 2.3.1):

> In the office of the staff: an employee informed his colleagues from the late shift about the events of the day. Each prisoner was briefly discussed. [A prisoner] who had been visited by the social assistant today was discussed in detail. Apparently, a transfer does again not seem to be an issue, although the employees think that it would be best to place him in a retirement home […] The employee announced that the social assistant had told him it was noted in a report a year ago that [the prisoner] had been 'aggressive' and resisted instructions from the staff 'with all his bodily forces'. Given these statements, the commission would certainly come to a negative decision regarding the question of transfer. The employee reminded his colleagues of the importance of writing reports that are 'as value-free as possible ', and 'only to describe what happened'. An intense discussion ensued, and the employees didn't agree on this issue. (Fieldnotes, 19.8.2013)

Furthermore, over time, as these prisoners hardly ever get released, prison officers often become the prisoners' only remaining reference persons. This also means that they in some ways become a substitute for inmates' families, especially in the units for ill and elderly prisoners, where prisoners and staff have more time and opportunities for interaction. As the following quote illustrates, for most employees this is still a new and unfamiliar situation, which can also disturb the fragile balance between proximity and distance and lead to role conflicts among staff members.

> You spend much more time together with these people [compared to preventive detention], I mean much closer, you know […] you are the caregiver, you are the security officer, you are the prisoners' contact

> person; you are almost a family substitute. This sometimes creates a bit of a role conflict here [in this unit]. (Prison officer B., 8.10.2013)

Most of the prisoners sentenced to indefinite incarceration not only grow old but eventually die in prison or another carceral setting. This creates special challenges for the medical service in prison, which is not equipped to provide long-term geriatric or even palliative care, but also for the prison staff, as it further questions the curative- and prevention-oriented prison logic of care (see Marti et al., 2017). However, public care institutions are mostly unwilling to accommodate 'dangerous' offenders (see Hostettler et al., 2016).

Regarding the future handling of prisoners sentenced to indefinite incarceration, prison staff agree that their particular status should be considered, either in the frame of existing structures or through the creation of new ones. Issues mentioned regarding adjustments to the existing structures include the granting of more individuality, freedom and autonomy in the prisoners' daily lives (e.g. concerning the management of their wage, the possession of personal objects, the opportunity to cook their own food and do their laundry), fewer restrictions regarding social contact with the outside world but also within the institution (e.g. more generous cell opening times, organization and participation in social events inside prison) and more occupational opportunities (in addition to work), to shift the focus away from their crime and towards individual resources and to promote prisoners' creativity. Some officers also wished for the availability of more resources for the handling of this prison population, including more time, additional staff with training in fields such as social pedagogy or work and occupational pedagogy, as well as additional care staff. Prison staff also outlined their visions regarding the future enforcement of indefinite incarceration by creating new structures. For example, several officers brought up the idea of converting a farm for the accommodation of these prisoners, especially for those for whom, perhaps due to their advanced age, it may no longer be necessary to have the security standards of a secure penal institution.

As has become clear throughout these three sections, the lives of the prisoners sentenced to indefinite incarceration are organized and shaped by a wide range of institutional actors. These actors all have different responsibilities, attitudes and interests regarding the enforcement of indefinite incarceration and are thereby challenged in different ways. These challenges range from the difficulty of working with these prisoners towards rehabilitation without taking the smallest risk, to the responsibility of accommodating prisoners who increasingly grow old and become frail and ill in prison, to the everyday handling of prisoners who are suffering from a lack of perspective and to become their last remaining reference persons.

2.3 The Sentenced Prisoners

By the end of 2018, 583 persons were incarcerated according to Art. 59 SCC, and 148 persons were held in indefinite incarceration following Art. 64 SCC. A large majority of these prisoners are male offenders with Swiss citizenship (Bundesamt für Statistik, 2019c). More concretely, among those held in indefinite incarceration (Art. 64 SCC), by the end of 2018 there were 146 male and two female prisoners. Most of them had Swiss citizenship and were at that time older than 45 years of age. These characteristics have varied little over the past ten years (see Table 2.1).

Due to the legal and institutional frameworks, the everyday lives of the prisoners held in indefinite confinement (Art. 59 and 64 SCC) are, at a first glance, characterized by two key features: *indeterminacy* and an *ever-same present*. What this means for those directly concerned is addressed in the following two sections, investigated from a phenomenological perspective.

2.3.1 Facing Indeterminacy

As argued by Crewe (2011), prisoners sentenced to indeterminate sentences face particular 'pains of imprisonment', strongly related to feelings of uncertainty, dependence and disorientation. While the feeling of

Table 2.1 Average number of inmates (Art. 64 SCC) according to gender, nationality and age (2008–2018)

	Total	Gender		Nationality		Age				
		Male	Female	Swiss	Foreigner	<25	25–34	35–44	45–59	60+
2008	180	175	5	133	46	5	28	49	75	24
2009	158	154	4	112	45	4	21	43	72	18
2010	155	150	5	112	42	3	18	44	72	18
2011	157	153	4	114	43	2	16	43	72	23
2012	150	146	4	107	43	1	17	37	70	25
2013	150	146	4	106	44	0	18	33	71	28
2014	145	141	4	102	42	0	14	32	68	31
2015	148	145	3	104	44	0	16	27	72	34
2016	148	145	3	101	47	0	14	28	68	38
2017	148	145	3	101	46	0	9	30	64	45
2018	148	146	2	103	45	0	8	30	63	48

Source Author's own table, based on data from the Swiss Federal Statistical Office (18.11.2019)

uncertainty is probably, in one way or another, inherent to all imprisonment,[7] in the case of prisoners held in indefinite incarceration, it takes a particular shape, which relates both to their *future* and their *present*.

In light of the restrictive practice of release by enforcement authorities, the probability that these prisoners will remain in prison until the end of their lives has over the past decades become more and more certain. Yet, as mentioned above, as the possibility of release is legally anchored in *both* Art. 59 and 64 SCC, the prisoners' futures (i.e. whether they will take place inside or outside the prison) nevertheless remain uncertain. Their chances for having a future perspective (outside prison) depend on the decision of the courts and the enforcement authorities, who evaluate the prisoners' situations based predominantly on prison reports, psychiatric assessments and recommendations by committees of experts.

Prison reports in particular strongly impact the everyday lives of the prisoners who depend on positive reports in order to progress within the

[7] For example, prisoners in pre-trial detention may face uncertainty regarding sentencing; prisoners serving regular sentences may experience uncertainty in terms of their release date—for instance, whether or not they will be granted conditional release. Finally, returning to society is always accompanied by some degree of uncertainty since not all aspects of post-prison life can be anticipated.

system. As emphasized by Crewe (2011), this generally puts significant pressure on prisoners because 'whatever [the prisoner] does, it will be open to interpretation. If he explodes, his report may say that he cannot cope with frustration ... if he keeps his own counsel, the reports may say that he is withdrawn and cannot come to terms with his offence' (Crewe, 2011, p. 512). A similar statement comes from Paul, who told me the following:

> I sometimes have the feeling that you only have to function in here. You must not get sick: it will be punished. You must not break down: you will be punished. Because then they say: he is not strong enough, it will be written in the report, which has negative consequences in terms of release. So you cannot do anything. You only have to work, function, function, work, work, work and be locked up. (Paul, 29.3.2016)

The fact that prisoners' behaviour is reported also influences interactions between them. Lars, for instance, told me that he tries to avoid hanging around with the 'really tough guys' because this may create 'a bad impression' of him and be reported, even though he would actually prefer to spend time with them, as these long-term prisoners are the ones who are in the same situation and therefore do not include those who will leave the prison again soon (Fieldnotes, 9.2.2016). Given the fact that they must control their emotions, interactions among prisoners are generally framed by what Marco called 'superficial friendliness' (Marco, 3.5.2016). In this regard, another prisoner wrote to me that he 'misses the human [*das Menschliche*]' in prison and that although 'everyone is friendly', interactions are 'formal and rigid', which is why he sometimes does not 'feel' himself anymore (Letter from a prisoner, 21.11.2016).

In Sect. 2.2.1, I highlighted the importance of forensic-psychiatric assessments regarding these prisoners' futures. A chance for a future outside the prison can today almost exclusively be achieved through (successful) therapy and/or a positive psychiatric report. However, as prisoners sentenced according to Art. 64 SCC are by law classified as 'untreatable', they are generally not granted any future-oriented psychotherapy—that is, only if forensic psychiatrists see some potential for converting Art. 64 into Art. 59 SCC—and generally do not get the chance to prove that they have changed for the better, within the scope of temporary prison leave, for example. The prisoners I met were aware of the fact that without therapy and proof, their chances for release are close to zero. At the time of my fieldwork, of those prisoners sentenced under Art. 64 SCC, only a very small number gained access to therapy—some with the perspective of a possible conversion of Art. 64 SCC into Art. 59 SCC and some without:

> I can finally participate in an offense-oriented group therapy after a long struggle. Although I have no entitlement to get (intensive) therapy, I was able, together with my competent authority and with pressure from my lawyer, to enforce this. Since until now nobody has been really interested in rehabilitating me in some way, I had to act. I'm a perpetrator and not a victim they told me. (Letter from a prisoner, 27.6.2016)

Among those prisoners who were receiving therapy within the framework of Art. 59 SCC at the time I met them, some had bad and disturbing experiences and perceived the requirements necessary to (potentially) progress as unclear or unattainable, and therefore decided to stop. For instance, Louis had confusing experiences related to the evaluation of his therapeutically achieved progress:

> All that I had achieved therapeutically during these nine years, which was also all confirmed by the experts, was then defined as negative in [another prison], as wrong, not possible to be [...] Everything that was considered positive, the changes in my behaviour, the way I now address people, express myself, [...] everything I have learned from therapy was suddenly considered negative. And they wanted me to start again from the beginning. And then I said: No! I've been playing this game for over 18 years now. Every time, wherever I go [to another prison], this is not good, while this is good, I have to start again and again ... no! [...] And at some point you just have to say: Hey, now it's enough, now this has to stop. I then started to fight back a little bit and then I was transferred again, they brought me to [another prison] and there I stayed for a few months, and then they wanted to put me into [another prison] but I refused. I refuse to go to a therapeutic institution because why should I always start all over again? I was actually brought so far that I was ready to

> get out, now I'm virtually back in the hole, in the kennel. One is beaten on the mouth by the authorities or all together until the dog bites. So that one can say: look, this man is dangerous. (Louis, 22.3.2016)

Finally, some prisoners categorically refused the offer of therapy. They did not see any reason for therapy, as they did not consider themselves mentally ill or disturbed. Furthermore, only four of the prisoners I talked to were at that time benefitting from a couple of four- to eight-hour (accompanied) prison leaves per year (for more details, see Sect. 6.7). However, without therapy and proof that they have changed for the better, prisoners cannot get rid of the label 'dangerous' and may carry it until the end of their lives.

The results of the enforcement authorities' examinations, which, as I was told, do not in fact take place as regularly as they should (e.g. two prisoners told me that the last time they had been visited by the competent authority was in 2007), are frequently perceived as arbitrary and inconsistent, and sometimes even deeply confusing. The following quote comes from Rolf. As he told me, one particular aspect of his life, namely the fact that he has a large social network in the outside world, had once been evaluated as extremely positive, the next time as negative:

> All instances within the enforcement authority actually concluded that due to my big social network, I was well protected, and the risk of recidivism was considered to be minimal [...]. Release was therefore within reach [...] And then, one year later, just everything was messed up by the expert commission [...]. So the same authority [that assessed the big network as positive] then twisted the argument regarding my big and good social network out there in the pure opposite direction. It was argued that my big social network would actually foster my escape and the risk of recidivism. [...] And this shows how absurd the reasons set out sometimes are. Obviously it is only a matter of achieving something that seems more opportune because of a certain sentiment among the population, because of political agendas or whatever. That's why many of us see ourselves as political prisoners. (Rolf, 6.5.2016)

As the quotations from Louis and Rolf illustrate, changing and contradictory statements regarding the prisoners' personal attributes, behaviour or development can create confusion and additional uncertainty. Prisoners may lose orientation in their lives, not knowing anymore how to behave or where they stand. As argued by Crewe (2011, p. 513), this may lead to the experience of 'ontological insecurity' (Giddens, 1991) as these prisoners may face existential difficulties and lose faith in the reliability of the world beyond them.

In addition to the lack of orientation that would allow prisoners to 'navigate' their time in prison, without any concrete date of release, prisoners have 'no goal, no perspective, no horizon' (Louis, 22.3.2016). Following Tuan (2001 [1977], p. 123), the horizon, is—at least in so-called Western societies—a common image of the future. More concretely, phenomenologically speaking, it is the horizon of potentialities or 'the future world of the not-yet' that provides meaning to human existence (Meisenhelder, 1985, p. 42). Almost all the prisoners I talked to said that they accept the sentence they received, but struggle significantly with the lack of perspective that comes along with indefinite incarceration:

> I'm in a place where I have no prospects, no prospects for the future. I'm on a path without an end. The durability here is dateless. They can say: I'll keep you as long as I want. One is entangled in different feelings; one is angry, sad, depending on the condition, but mostly angry and sad. (Kurt, 3.5.2016)

Others described the condition of having no perspective as 'mental torture' (Rolf, 11.9.2013) or an 'inhumanly long-drawn-out death penalty' (Markus, 29.3.2016). Many of the prisoners said that they would prefer a 'real' life sentence or even the death penalty to indefinite incarceration. Prisoners serving undetermined sentences find themselves, in a certain sense, in a situation of 'chronic crisis' (Vigh, 2008) characterized by a lack of perspective and uncertainty regarding their future.

Given this situation, prisoners develop different attitudes towards or modes of *being with time* (Marti, 2017). Even though their chances are very small, I met prisoners who keep 'fighting' for their release. By continuously writing letters to the authorities, making complaints and objections, and imagining alternatives of what life in the future could be like, they keep hope alive. Their mode of being with time is concentrated on the future: they are constantly waiting for something that may happen—a visit by their lawyer, an appointment at the court, a transfer to a more open prison—and, possibly, their eventual release. However, as stressed by Marco, 'waiting makes time pass very slowly' (Marco, 4.5.2016). Moreover, because of their strong hope for change and their intense orientation towards the (uncertain) future, these prisoners are doing 'hard time' (Cohen & Taylor, 1972, p. 92). Without any concrete perspective, they are permanently suffering the 'pains of uncertainty and indeterminacy' (Crewe, 2011, p. 513) and have difficulty assigning meaning to their present life in prison. Moreover, for most of these prisoners, the idea of having a future outside of prison is connected to uncertainty as well. Some fear that, in the case of release, they would be too old to be integrated into the Swiss job market and that the pension they would be granted would be insufficient to live a decent life. Others fear that due to the crime they committed or simply because of their old age, they have lost the ability to establish any social relations. Finally, a lot of the places that used to be familiar to them no longer exist. Yet, as I show further below, some prisoners also imagine possible futures, often linked to the idea of starting a new life abroad.

Other prisoners, in contrast, try to concentrate on the present. According to Flanagan, this is indeed 'the most effective method to reduce the uncertainty and ambiguity of the future' (1981, p. 210). This mode of being with time is also illustrated in the following quote:

> Me, as an inmate sentenced to indefinite incarceration, I cannot hope to be released. I cannot wait, though. I take the days as they come. You have to adapt to a certain degree to the setting, to know the rules so that you don't ignore them and get into trouble, and to establish your own routine that makes you feel comfortable. Me, I feel safe and comfortable [...] I don't say time passes too slowly or too fast, I take it as it comes. I flow with the time, day after day. But this has nothing to do with simply living for the moment. It just helps me to protect myself and not to think too much about my situation. (Marco, 4.5.2016)

Prisoners who focus on the present generally told me that they try not to worry too much about their future but to accept the situation as it is.

Some of them mentioned that they also try to use their time in prison as constructively as possible. As argued by Crewe et al. (2016, p. 10), this is a typical pattern for long-term prisoners beyond the early sentence phase: they no longer experience the present as a form of stasis because life is no longer considered 'on hold' (in the past, or being lived elsewhere),[8] and the prison is now considered their 'home' and 'the only place where life could meaningfully be led'. By concentrating on the present instead of an uncertain future, I argue that long-term prisoners actively 'normalise' indefinite incarceration and thus transform it into a (potential) 'frame of action' (see Vigh, 2008, p. 11). To perceive imprisonment as their 'normal life' allows them to feel comfortable and to go about their lives. However, those who decide to make the best out of their situation feel the need not only to accept but also to engage themselves in their situation. As I was told, this changing attitude requires the development of a certain awareness 'of what this place can give you' (Fieldnotes, 2.5.2016). In concrete terms, prisoners talk about developing the capacity 'to take the day as it comes' and 'to appreciate the little things' (Darko, 6.5.2016). For some, it also requires that they cut off contact with the outside world, even with their loved ones, and let go of their (pre-prison) selves as it is emotionally too demanding and too painful to live in two worlds at the same time:

> I notice that the more I let go and just accept that I won't get out, I actually find it easier to feel comfortable [compared to] when I am constantly worrying if I will ever get out, if there may still be a possibility, [and] put pressure on myself. […] But this also means that I would need to give myself up. I just talked to someone, just yesterday, who is in exactly the same situation as I am. He has now resigned, has given up. He denies everything, therapy and all that, and yes, he said he felt extremely comfortable. (Leo, 23.3.2016)

[8] As Cunha (2016) showed, the feeling of stasis and experience of the prison as 'a world apart' is actually less pronounced in the narratives of prisoners who stay integrated into their (pre-prison) social networks, and in the case that family members, friends or neighbours are incarcerated as well, and therefore the 'past' as well as the 'future' are no longer equivalent to the 'outside', but part of the prison. This, however, does not apply to the prisoners I met because (as far as I know) all of them entered the prison alone. Yet, some of them knew each other already, as they had met in a prison where they were previously held.

> I don't read any newspapers anymore [...] I also gave away the television, where you anyway always see the same things [...] I actually built my own world in here. With painting, programming, my budgies, my mates [fellow prisoners] ... it's kind of my own world in here that I have. (Franz, 10.9.2013)

Finally, I also met prisoners who described their present-oriented mode of being with time, in a certain sense, more radically, namely as 'vegetating' (Patrick, 3.5.2016), or having no expectations anymore and being 'done with life' (Lorenzo, 23.11.2013).

Simply put, regarding their future, prisoners serving undetermined lengths of time face a kind of existential dilemma: to focus on the *future* and to continue to fight for release means, for some, resistance and keeping hope alive but at the same time suffering the pains of uncertainty; to concentrate on the *present* and to accept imprisonment allows for the building of a life inside prison, but it also means giving up hope, cutting bonds to the outside world, and maybe even letting go of one's former self, in order to create one's own world inside the prison. As I show throughout Chapters 4, 5 and 6, the prisoners' different attitudes and ways of dealing with the time-based indefiniteness of their incarceration—that is, their ways of being with time—are also expressed in their everyday practices, for instance in terms of the arrangement of their cells or organization of leisure time. However, as I noticed during fieldwork, many prisoners' mode of being with time is not stable, but rather shifting, depending upon the circumstances and their personal life situation (e.g. a positive prison report). As I show in the following, whether prisoners continue to hope for their release or to accept incarceration, they all have to deal with the particularity of everyday life in prison.

2.3.2 Living in an Ever-Same Present

Prison life is characterized by coercion and heteronomy and a high density of rules and repetition (Goffman, 1961) that allows little spontaneity and few contingencies. Unexpected interruptions are rare, which leads to feelings of boredom, dreariness and stasis. Indeed, as pointed out by Toch (1996 [1977], p. 29), 'the eventlessness of prison life over served time is a general stressor for inmates'. When nothing really happens, time seems to pass very slowly—or even to stand still:

> Sometimes it feels as if time stands still. Especially because of the visual and the acoustic: it does not change much. You notice day and night, the changing seasons, but not much more. (Marco, 3.5.2016)

At the same time, because each day is generally the same in prison, inmates feel that retrospectively, time has passed quickly and that they have lost (life)time (see also Jewkes, 2005; Matthews, 2009):

> I have lost many years by now that I cannot make up. Of course, someone who came in here 20 years ago, maybe already at age 19, has another problem. He is really missing something serious. But me, at least, I had a life before prison. (Darko, 24.9.2013)

From the point of view of the prisoners to whom I spoke, due to the unchanging rhythm created by the prison regime and the uneventful present, everyday life in prison leaves 'no traces' on individuals (Fieldnotes, 25.6.2013). In other words, it leaves 'no more than a bit of dust in the soul' (Serge, 1970, p. 101, cited in O'Donnell, 2014, p. 183), which can make inmates 'feel empty' (Jonathan, 24.9.2013).

The feeling of emptiness has significant impacts on inmates' social relations both within and outside of the prison because there is not much to share or talk about. As Heinz told me, 'in order to be able to talk about something, you must have experienced something. If you haven't experienced anything, you cannot say much' (Heinz, 3.5.2016). The same experience is described by Jonathan:

> You know, when you're here and someone is out there, these are two different worlds. The one outside is full of topics, and I am empty, I have nothing to say, what should I tell him, that I saw the foreman, that I ate a sausage? That's of no interest to those outside. I notice when I'm in contact with my relatives, they are full of stories, they can talk for hours. And me, I just can't think of anything, I'm kind of limited with experiences …. Me, I'm kind of empty. (Jonathan, 24.9.2013)

Moreover, as pointed out by O'Donnell, 'the currency of the [pre-prison] past is soon spent' (2014, p. 179). As explained again by Jonathan, 'sometimes we [he and a fellow prisoner] sit together in silence because there are no themes to talk about, everything has been said, discussed, from our past … our youth, sports, holidays, family …' (Jonathan, 24.9.2013).

Prisoners agree that the ever-same present has not only influenced their social relations but has also had harmful effects on their mental state. The younger prisoners in particular (both related to age and time served to the present) expressed their fears regarding mental deterioration and losing their sense of self (see also Leigey & Ryder, 2015). From their point of view, long-term imprisonment, combined with medication use and the fact that many prisoners 'have given up', has 'dulled' them (Leo, 23.3.2016) and made them look like 'zombies' (Anton, 24.3.2016), having lost all interest or ability to participate in interpersonal exchange:

> Many of the *Verwahrten* [prisoners held in indefinite incarceration] in here, they are just sitting stubbornly in their cells, they don't come out, have isolated themselves, cut themselves off. They are no longer interested in people, emotions, in having conversations as we have now. Many of them are like that. (Leo, 23.3.2016)

The ever-same present in prison—as well as the time-based indefiniteness of their incarceration—weighs heavily on prisoners. However, as I show in the following chapters, a closer look at their ways of *living* everyday prison life reveals that even though they are not able to change the forces that affect their lives in a negative way, these prisoners find new and individual ways to deal with time—as well as space.

2.4 Conclusion

While indefinite incarceration is nothing new (in Switzerland as elsewhere), the fact that sexual and violent offenders are today's 'ungovernables', who have been preventively locked up, is a relatively new phenomenon embedded in wider social and political processes. With the exclusion of these prisoners from society comes their inclusion in the prison world, where they have to live under the same conditions as prisoners who serve ordinary (finite) prison sentences.

There are different institutional actors in charge of these prisoners, all having different responsibilities, obligations and attitudes towards them. As shown in this chapter, due to public and political pressure and calls for more safety, the penal enforcement authorities are today more cautious regarding the loosening of the penal regime or the granting of conditional release for so-called 'high-risk' offenders. As a consequence, most of these prisoners will have to stay in prison for the rest of their lives and will most probably die in a carceral setting. From the point of view of prison management, long-term prisoners sentenced to indefinite incarceration are generally those who exhibit conformist behaviour or, in contrast, cause extraordinary trouble, although this is much less often the case. They appear on the radar screen of prison management in particular when they grow older or become ill or frail, and it is for these men that the units for ill and elderly prisoners were established a few years ago. However, the way these units are currently equipped and staffed does not allow for the provision of adequate care for these prisoners (see Hostettler et al., 2016). Given the fact that their numbers will increase, further investment is inevitable. Prison employees who work with these prisoners on a daily basis are particularly challenged and also directly affected by the prisoners' lack of perspective. Although they do not have any official mandate, many of the staff members try to consider these prisoners' special life situations and support them in finding meaning and perspective within the prison walls. Prisoners sentenced to indefinite incarceration might stay forever, and staff members therefore often become the prisoners' only remaining reference persons. This is still a new and unfamiliar situation that can lead to role conflicts among staff members. As I have shown throughout these three sections, among the key actors there is a broad spectrum of opinions regarding the future handling of this group of prisoners. Although there is general agreement that their special status should be considered, these actors do not necessarily agree on what in particular could or should be improved and how this should be implemented.

As noted in the last part of this chapter, the lives of prisoners sentenced to indefinite incarceration are generally framed by the time-based indefiniteness of their imprisonment and an institutionally organized daily life characterized by coercion and repetition as well as many rules and regulations. As my data indicate, this situation can have powerful effects on how the prisoners relate to themselves, others and to the world in general.

References

Amt für Justizvollzug Kanton Zürich. (2014). *Schlussbericht: Modellversuch. Risikoorientierter Sanktionenvollzug*. https://www.bj.admin.ch/dam/data/bj/sicherheit/smv/modellversuche/evaluationsberichte/ros-schlussber-d.pdf. Accessed 10 December 2019.

Amt für Justizvollzug Kanton Zürich. (2019). *ROS allgemein*. https://www.rosnet.ch/de-ch/ros-allgemein. Accessed 10 December 2019.

Baechtold, A., Weber, J., & Hostettler, U. (2016). *Strafvollzug: Straf- und Massnahmenvollzug an Erwachsenen in der Schweiz* (3rd ed., Kriminalität, Justiz und Sanktionen KJS: Vol. 17). Stämpfli Verlag.

Bundesamt für Justiz BJ. (2016). *Handbuch für Bauten des Straf- und Massnahmenvollzugs: Einrichtungen Erwachsene*. https://www.bj.admin.ch/dam/data/bj/sicherheit/smv/baubeitraege/hb-erwachsene-d.pdf. Accessed 10 December 2019.

Bundesamt für Statistik. (2019a). *Kriminalität und Strafrecht*. Justizvollzug. Inhaftierte Erwachsene. https://www.bfs.admin.ch/bfs/de/home/statistiken/kriminalitaet-strafrecht/justizvollzug/inhaftierte-erwachsene.html#-1879612962. Accessed 27 February 2020.

Bundesamt für Statistik. (2019b). *Massnahmenvollzug: Entlassungen nach Art der Massnahme*. https://www.bfs.admin.ch/bfs/de/home/statistiken/kriminalitaet-strafrecht/justizvollzug/inhaftierte-erwachsene.assetdetail.10827157.html. Accessed 27 February 2020.

Bundesamt für Statistik. (2019c). *Massnahmenvollzug: Mittlerer Insassenbestand mit Verwahrung (Art. 64 StGB) nach Geschlecht, Nationalität und Alter*. https://www.bfs.admin.ch/bfs/de/home/statistiken/kriminalitaet-strafrecht/justizvollzug/inhaftierte-erwachsene.assetdetail.10827111.html. Accessed 27 February 2020.

Bundesversammlung der Schweizerischen Eidgenossenschaft. (2001). *Schweizerisches Strafgesetzbuch vom 21.* Dezember 1937 (Stand am 18. Dezember 2001). Bundesversammlung der Schweizerischen Eidgenossenschaft. https://www.admin.ch/opc/de/classified-compilation/19370083/200201010000/311.0.pdf.

BVerfG. (2011). Judgment of the Second Senate of 04 May 2011 - 2 BvR 2365/09 -, paras. (1–178). https://www.bundesverfassungsgericht.de/SharedDocs/Entscheidungen/EN/2011/05/rs20110504_2bvr236509en.html-;jsessionid=04C0C84714A8B799C629BCEB936ABD87.2_cid394. Accessed 10 December 2019.

Cohen, S., & Taylor, L. (1972). *Psychological survival: The experience of long-term imprisonment*. Penguin Books.

Crewe, B. (2009). *The prisoner society: Power, adaptation and social life in an English prison*. Oxford University Press.

Crewe, B. (2011). Depth, weight, tightness: Revisiting the pains of imprisonment. *Punishment & Society, 13*, 509–529.

Crewe, B., Hulley, S., & Wright, S. (2016). Swimming with the tide: Adapting to long-term imprisonment. *Justice Quarterly, 34*, 1–25. https://doi.org/10.1080/07418825.2016.1190394

Cunha, M. I. (2016). Une prison à l'épreuve du temps. Temporalités carcérales d'hier et d'aujourd'hui. *Rhuthmos* (27), 1–7.

Die Bundesversammlung der schweizerischen Eidgenossenschaft. (1937). Schweizerisches Strafgesetzbuch: (Vom 21. Dezember 1937). *Bundesblatt, 89*(III), 625–736.

European Court of Human Rights. (2010). M. vs Germany (App 19359/04). https://hudoc.echr.coe.int/eng#{%22fulltext%22:[%2219359/04%22],%22documentcollectionid2%22:[%22GRANDCHAMBER%22,%22CHAMBER%22],%22itemid%22:[%22001-96389%22]}. Accessed 10 December 2019.

Flanagan, T. J. (1981). Dealing with long-term confinement: Adaptive strategies and perspectives among long-term prisoners. *Criminal Justice and Behavior, 8*(2), 201–222.

Giddens, A. (1991). *Modernity and self-identity: Self and society in the late modern age*. Stanford University Press.

Goffman, E. (1961). *Asylums: Essays on the condition of the social situation of mental patients and other inmates*. Anchor Books, Doubleday & Co.

Greer, C., & Jewkes, Y. (2005). Extremes of otherness: Media images of social exclusion. *Social Justice, 32*(1), 20–31.

Handtke, V., Bretschneider, W., Wangmo, T., & Elger, B. (2012). Facing the challenges of an increasingly ageing prison population in Switzerland: In search of ethically acceptable solutions. *Bioethica-Forum, 5*(4), 134–141.
Holmes, K., & Soothill, K. (2007). Dangerous offenders and dangerousness. In Y. Jewkes (Ed.), *Handbook on Prisons* (pp. 589–607). Willan Publishing.
Hostettler, U., Marti, I., & Richter, M. (2016). *Lebensende im Justizvollzug. Gefangene, Anstalten, Behörden.* Stämpfli Verlag.
Jewkes, Y. (2005). Loss, liminality and the life sentence: managing identity through disrupted lifecourse. In L. Alison & S. Maruna (Eds.), *The effects of imprisonment* (pp. 366–388, The effects of imprisonment). Routledge.
Kinzig, J. (2012). Sterben in geschlossenen Einrichtungen des Massregelvollzugs. In M. Anderheiden & W. U. Eckart (Eds.), *Handbuch Sterben und Menschenwürde* (pp. 1595–1617). de Gruyter.
KKJPD. (2017a). *Kapazitätsmonitoring Freiheitsentzug 2016: Ergänzender Bericht zur Unterbringung, Behandlung und Betreuung psychisch gestörter und kranker Straftäter.* https://www.kkjpd.ch/files/Dokumente/News/vor%202018/170831%20Kapazitätsmonitoring%20ergänzender%20Bericht%20psychisch%20gestörter%20und%20kranker%20Straftäter%20d.pdf. Accessed 10 December 2019.
KKJPD. (2017b). *Fachgruppe «Kapazitätsmonitoring Freiheitsentzug»: Bericht zur Datenerhebung 2016*. https://www.kkjpd.ch/files/Dokumente/Themen/Strafvollzug/170731%20Bericht%20Kapazit%C3%A4tsmonitoring%202016%20d.pdf. Accessed 10 December 2019.
Künzli, J., Eugster, A., & Schultheiss, M. (2016). *Haftbedingungen in der Verwahrung: Menschenrechtliche Standards und die Situation in der Schweiz.* Bern.
Leigey, M. E., & Ryder, M. A. (2015). The pains of permanent imprisonment: Examining perceptions of confinement among older life without parole inmates. *International Journal of Offender Therapy and Comparative Criminology, 59*, 726–742. https://doi.org/10.1177/0306624X13517868
Liebling, A. (2014). Moral and philosophical problems of long-term imprisonment. *Studies in Christian Ethics, 27*, 258–269. https://doi.org/10.1177/0953946814530219
Marti, I. (2017). Doing (with) Time: Dealing with Indefinite Incarceration in Switzerland. *Tsantsa* (22), 68–77.
Marti, I., Hostettler, U., & Richter, M. (2017). End of life in high-security prisons in Switzerland: Overlapping and blurring of "care" and "custody" as Institutional Logics. *Journal of Correctional Health Care, 23*, 32–42. https://doi.org/10.1177/1078345816684782

Matthews, R. (2009). *Doing time: An introduction to the sociology of imprisonment*. Palgrave Macmillan.
Meisenhelder, T. (1985). An essay on time and the phenomenology of imprisonment. *Deviant Behavior, 6*, 39–56. https://doi.org/10.1080/01639625.1985.9967658
NZZ. (2010, October 7). Erstmals lebenslängliche Verwahrung angeordnet. *NZZ - Neue Zürcher Zeitung*. https://www.nzz.ch/lebenslaengliche_verwahrung_nach_toetung_eines_callgirls-1.7884669. Accessed 13 January 2019.
O'Donnell, I. (2014). *Prisoners, solitude, and time*. Oxford University Press.
Ostschweizer Strafvollzugskommission. (2008). *Empfehlung für den Vollzug der Verwahrung und der vorangehenden Freiheitsstrafe vom 4. April 2008*. https://justizvollzug.zh.ch/dam/justiz_innern/juv/amtsleitung/osk/richtlinien/richtlinien_vollzug/Empfehlung_OSK_Verwahrungsvollzug_KK_04.04.2008.pdf.spooler.download.1386230816651.pdf/Empfehlung_OSK_Verwahrungsvollzug_KK_04.04.2008.pdf
Pratt, J. (1997). *Governing the dangerous: Dangerousness, law and social change*. Federation Press.
Schneeberger Georgescu, R. (2009). Im schweizerischen Freiheitsentzug altern: Nicht der Alterskriminelle prägt das Bild des alten Insassen, sondern der langjährige Insasse im Massnahmenvollzug. *Forum Strafvollzug. Zeitschrift für Strafvollzug und Straffälligenhilfe* (58), 124–127.
Simmler, M. (2016). Sieben enttäuschte Hoffnungen? - Zur statistischen Überprüfung der realen Folgen der AT-Revision. *ZStrR, 134*(1), 73–99.
Strafvollzugskonkordate der Schweiz. (2014). *Anstaltsplanung 2013 (Version 12.06.2014)*. https://www.konkordate.ch/anstaltsplanung
Toch, H. (1996 [1977]). *Living in prison: The ecology of survival*. Princeton University Press.
Tuan, Y. F. (2001 [1977]). *Space and place: The perspective of experience*. University of Minnesota Press.
UN Human Rights Committee. (2014). *International Covenant on Civil and Political Rights: General comment No. 35*. https://tbinternet.ohchr.org/_layouts/15/treatybodyexternal/Download.aspx?symbolno=CCPR%2fC%2fGC%2f35&Lang-=en. Accessed 10 December 2019.
Vigh, H. (2008). Crisis and chronicity: Anthropological perspectives on continuous conflict and decline. *Ethnos: Journal of Anthropology, 73*(1), 5–24.
Waldram, J. B. (2009). Challenges of prison ethnography. *Anthropology News, 50*, 4–5. https://doi.org/10.1111/j.1556-3502.2009.05014.x

Weber, J., Schaub, J., Bumann-Pacozzi, C. M., & Sacher, K. (2016). *Anordnung und Vollzug stationärer therapeutischer Massnahmen gemäss Art. 59 StGB mit Fokus auf geschlossene Strafanstalten bzw. geschlossene Massnahmeneinrichtungen. Studie zuhanden der Nationalen Kommission zur Verhütung von Folter (NKVF)*. Bern.

Wulf, R., & Grube, A. (2012). Sterben im Gefängnis - Menschenrechtliche, ethische und praktische Aspekte. In M. Anderheiden & W. U. Eckart (Eds.), *Handbuch Sterben und Menschenwürde* (pp. 1571–1594). de Gruyter.

Young, C. (2018). *Narrative im Justizvollzug. Identitäten von Mitarbeitenden, medialer Diskurs und historischer Kontext*. Seismo.

3

Space, Time, Embodiment

3.1 The Prison as an Inhabited Time–Space

To explore long-term prisoners' ways of *being* and *doing* indefinite time, I propose refocusing the lens of prison studies away from the frequently used framework of power and resistance and using space, time and embodiment as key concepts instead. The main focus of the research thus shifts from human actors to the (most fundamental) non-human actors that structure all of our (embodied) experiences—whether we live in prison or any other condition—namely space and time.[1]

In the prison context, space and time are particularly important. Firstly, space and time are the main elements on which the 'modern' penal system, developed in the late eighteenth century, is built: the offenders are segregated in a particular place—the prison—from the rest of society for a certain period of time (see Foucault, 1975). Secondly, prison life is to a great extent characterized by spatial deprivation, in particular the restricted liberty of movement and mobility within the

[1] Parts of this section have been published as Marti (2021): 'Sensing freedom: Insights into long-term prisoners' perceptions of the outside world', Incarceration SAGE, Vol. 2(2): 1–20.

I. Marti, *Doing Indefinite Time*, Palgrave Studies in Prisons and Penology,
https://doi.org/10.1007/978-3-031-12590-4_3

prison, limited connections to the outside world and separation of prisoners by sex (Milhaud, 2009, p. 146). Disciplinary sanctions are also primarily spatial in nature (e.g. solitary confinement, additional exclusion in the cell). Furthermore, as stressed by Matthews (2009, p. 38), 'although imprisonment is in essence about time', due to institutional constraints and the many prison rules, prisoners experience it 'as a form of timelessness, with prison terms often described as "doing" or "killing time"'. This is also linked to the sensory qualities of prison spaces in terms of their materiality, general lack of variation in colour and light (see also Cohen & Taylor, 1972, pp. 61–62) and typical (repetitive) sounds (Herrity, 2019).

Cohen and Taylor (1972, p. 87) point to a particular meaning of time for long-term prisoners, arguing that for these prisoners, time is basically 'a problem' because they have been given 'time as a punishment' (for long-term prisoners in the early phases of their sentence, see Wright et al., 2017, pp. 232–234). Therefore, in contrast to the outside world, where time is considered a resource, for long-term prisoners, time becomes 'a controller, it has to be served rather than used' (Cohen & Taylor, 1972, p. 89). However, Crewe et al. (2016, 2020) argue that prisoners—especially those who are further along in a long sentence—may find ways to use their time in prison constructively by actively managing the future and casting themselves beyond the immediate present (see also Flanagan, 1981). As I show throughout this book, the situation is slightly different for long-term prisoners sentenced to *indefinite* incarceration, who are preventively held in prison after having served their custodial sentence. Although release is possible, due to the punitive turn in most so-called Western countries since the 1990s mentioned above—and the more restrictive practice of release in the case of those designated as 'high-risk' offenders—it is possible that these prisoners will stay behind bars for the rest of their lives. Therefore, this prison population is suffering very particular 'pains of imprisonment' (Sykes, 1971 [1958]) and basically has to find new ways to deal with time—as well as space.

In this book, I explore the experience of long-term prisoners sentenced to indefinite incarceration by considering both space *and* time—that is, thinking about them together—to shed light on how space (and more precisely the various spaces constituting 'the prison') affects perceptions of and ways of dealing with time, and on how time affects perceptions and ways of appropriating space for prisoners held in indefinite incarceration. Inspired by Moran (2012), I start from the idea that anything prisoners think or feel about the past or the future takes place in the present, in 'each successive now', and in the context of what the present is like. The 'now' comprises, therefore, both 'the time *and* the space—the TimeSpace—of incarceration, and is bound up with the corporeality of the individual whose now is being experienced' (Moran, 2012, p. 310). This means that the embodied experience of time is inseparably bound up with the embodied experience of space and vice versa. Being physically present in a carceral context hence determines the nature of the 'now', which further shapes prisoners' perceptions of the past, present and future, of the passage of time and of their sense of self.

While geographers in particular have long been inherently concerned with the relationship between time and space (Dodgshon, 2008; May & Thrift, 2001), as noted by Moran (2012), in the field of prison studies, criminologists and prison sociologists tend to look exclusively at the temporal dimension of incarceration, while carceral geographers primarily focus on the spatial dimension.[2] In looking at prisoners' lived

[2] Moran (2012) shows that criminological studies dealing with time mainly focus on time as a given constant and axis of differentiation, for example regarding changes over time in terms of imprisonment rates or levels of overcrowding Jacobs and Helms (1996) as well as studies dealing with the individual experience and adjustment over time (Crewe et al., 2016; Zamble, 1992; Warren et al., 2004). Time has also been mobilized to look at imprisonment as a specific period in someone's life course, as a variable to explore the effect of the length of a sentence Aebi and Kuhn (2000) as well as prisoners' experience of the passage of time at different stages of their life course Biggam and Power (1997), and Aday (1994). Finally, there are studies that deal, among other topics, with the individual perception of time in prison, and prisoners' ways of coping with time (Cohen & Taylor, 1972; Cope, 2003; O'Donnell, 2014; Crewe et al., 2020). In contrast to this body of literature, the issue of space has so far mostly been researched by carceral geographers. Inspired by Foucault's (1975) work, some studies deal with the prison as a particular institution that regulates space and the 'docility' of bodies as well as prisoners' resistance and reclamation of space (see e.g. Baer, 2005; Dirsuweit 1999, and Sibley & van Hoven 2009). There are also studies focused on 'the distributional geographies of incarceration' (Moran, 2012, p. 306) and its effects on the experience of carceral spaces themselves, for example in terms of distance from home (Moran et al., 2011), as well as on the outside communities, for example regarding economic development Che (2005), and Glasmeier and Farrigan (2007). There is a smaller body of anthropological work regarding space and time in the carceral context. Some studies focus on the 'peri-carceral space of the institution' (Cunha, 2014, p. 222) and the effects of the 'penal stigma' of prison on the immediate spatial vicinity in the French context (see e.g. Combessie, 2002; Marchetti & Combessie, 1996). Cunha's research,

experiences by considering both space and time, I join scholars who wish to build a bridge between studies in carceral geography and criminology (see e.g. Crewe et al., 2020).

3.1.1 The Prison Regime: A Formal Set of Arrangements of Space and Time

From an institutional perspective, everyday life in Swiss prisons is divided into three basic entities or *time–spaces*: 'work time', 'resting time' and 'leisure time' (Art. 77 SCC) (see Fig. 3.1).[3,4] Yet, the prison's formal organization of daily life is shaped by the prison system's 'institutional logics' (Thornton & Ocasio, 2008; Thornton et al., 2012), which are profoundly contradictory, as prisons are subject to two conflicting goals, namely punishment and rehabilitation (Marti et al., 2017). The logic of punishment refers to the deprivation of a person's liberty and includes the principle of security (within and outside the prison). This logic is visibly expressed in the prison's architecture and design, for instance in its barred windows and steel doors, but also in its rigid daily schedule. The logic of rehabilitation is strongly linked to the principle of 'normalisation'. According to the law,

> [t]he execution of sentences must encourage an improvement in the social behaviour of the prison inmates and in particular their ability to live their lives without offending again. The conditions under which sentences are

carried out in Portugal, centred on prisoners' experiences and representations of time in prison during different stages of imprisonment (Cunha, 1997) as well as on the networks between prisoners and people on the outside and how these relationships synchronize prison temporality with the rhythms of the outside world (Cunha, 2002, 2008). More recently, Chassagne (2017, 2019) and Chassagne (2017) have explored the experience of ageing and time among older prisoners in French institutions.

[3] The daily structure in the units inhabited by elderly and ill prisoners is slightly different: prisoners have shorter workdays and can spend more time outside their cells and in the courtyard.

[4] During weekends, prisoners are served breakfast at 7.45 am (Saturday) and 9.15 am (Sunday). On Saturday morning from 8.20 am to 11 am and in the afternoon from 11.30 am to 8 pm, the prisoners are allowed to spend time outside the cell. On Sunday, the cells are locked at 4.55 pm (JVA Lenzburg, 2010).

executed must correspond as far as possible with those of normal life. (Art. 75 para. 1 SCC)

The principle of 'normalisation' is inscribed in contemporary prison philosophy not only in Switzerland, but also in other European countries (although implemented in varied forms and to different degrees). At its core is the idea that 'prisons should [...] aim to reduce the gap between the inside and the outside worlds and to mirror free society in central aspects of human existence (from civic to sexual aspects)' (Cunha, 2014, p. 221).

According to this system, work, leisure and resting time in prison should, on the one hand, be organized to correspond to 'normal life'; on the other hand, everyday life in prison is highly regulated and constrained

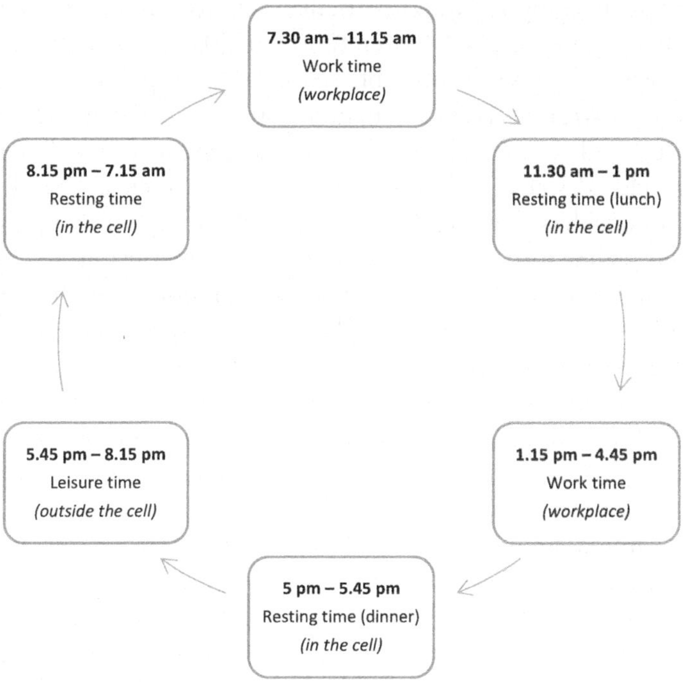

Fig. 3.1 The prison's daily routine (*Source* Author)

in the name of security. The prison hence imposes a particular *everyday life regime*.

The term 'prison regime' is commonly used to define the 'formal elements' of a prison environment, such as security measures, prisoners' programmes, medical and social services and the policies guiding staff–prisoner interactions (Sparks et al., 1996). In this book, however, I identify the prison regime as the institutional organization of everyday life, and more generally, as a formal *set of arrangements of space and time* through which a particular *spatio-temporal order* is established. This means that I conceive of the three entities—work time/resting time/leisure time—as particular arrangements of space and time that each organize the prisoner's body in a specific way and restrict his or her freedom of movement and autonomy (e.g. when he or she has to be in a particular location and for how long, with whom, under which conditions, engaging in which particular activity, etc.). This echoes the definition by Sibley and van Hoven (2009, p. 201), for whom the prison's carceral regime is 'a set of inflexible spatial and temporal routines which take place in strongly classified material spaces – cells, gated corridors, workshops, and so on' and therefore an instrument to 'regulat[e] movements in closed spaces'. However, in contrast to their approach, which primarily considers the spatial realm, I take the temporality produced by the prison regime into equal consideration by using the notion of *rhythm*, inspired by Lefebvre (2014). This allows me to look at the concrete realization of routines and their multiple forms of expression. For example, according to the prison schedule, the prisoners are locked in their cells at around 8.15 pm. Yet, as I was told by prisoners, some officers close the doors carefully, while others slam them shut. Some officers also use this moment of the day to have a chat with the prisoner he is about to lock in his cell, while others do not exchange a word with the inmates, or only what is required, and rush from cell to cell. Therefore, prison staff create different rhythmic variations and dynamics while carrying out the daily routine of locking the doors, strongly shaping prisoners' experiences of this particular moment of the day. After the nightly locking-up, there is a final inspection or walkthrough during which prison officers have to verify one last time the prisoners' presence in their cells. The implementation of this routine varies from one prison officer to another, in particular with regard to the starting point. This final routine of the day also affects the experience and, more concretely, the activities of the prisoners, who can hear very well what goes on outside their doors. As I was told by prisoners, at some point they come to recognize the officers' individual routes and routines, and therefore schedule their private activities, such as using the toilet, accordingly.

The prisoners' everyday lives are therefore embedded in various (material and social) contexts, all shaped by the prison's spatio-temporal order. However, as I explain in more detail in the following, moulded by their individual and embodied perceptions of these contexts, prisoners also make use of time and spatial elements and thereby *rearrange* them during everyday situations.

3.1.2 Inhabiting the Prison: Prisoners' Lived Experiences

In order to grasp these prisoners' embodied experiences of space and time analytically, I use the concept of 'inhabiting', inspired by two theoretical approaches in particular. On the one hand, I draw on Merleau-Ponty's (1962) phenomenological theory, which allows me to explore 'the prison' from the prisoners' perspective, through their emplaced and embodied experiences. On the other hand, the pragmatist perspective developed by Lussault and Stock (2010) allows me to explore prisoners' multiple ways of dealing with various contexts through their everyday practices.

3.1.2.1 Bodily Experiences of Space and Time

First, I analyse prisoners' ways of inhabiting the prison by examining their subjective *perceptions* and ways of making sense of the prison context, including things as well as other human beings and themselves, drawing on phenomenological theory. This perspective allows me to explore prisoners' lived experiences detached from (my own) pre-defined assumptions and concepts about imprisonment.

I am especially inspired by approaches that draw on Merleau-Ponty's phenomenological theory, which emphasizes the role of the body in the human experience of the world—the bodily being-in-the-world. From Merleau-Ponty's (1962) perspective, the core of our being-in-the-world is *perception*, which he conceives of as a non-mental phenomenon; it is neither grounded in sensations (as argued by empiricists) nor a function of judgement (as argued by intellectualists), but a bodily phenomenon. As he argues, '[m]y body is the fabric into which all objects are woven, and it is, at least in relation to the perceived world, the general instrument of my "comprehension"' (Merleau-Ponty, 1978 [1962], p. 235). According to Merleau-Ponty, 'the world is what we perceive' (1978 [1962], p. xvi) through sensory experience, such as hearing and seeing – whereby 'synaesthetic perception is the rule' (Merleau-Ponty, 1978 [1962], p. 229), but also through corporal movement and activity. Hence, from this perspective, the body is the 'existential null point' (Simonsen, 2007, p. 169) from which we engage with and understand the world, things, others and ourselves—it is 'our general medium for having a world' (Merleau-Ponty, 1978 [1962], p. 146).

In Merleau-Ponty's thinking, the body is not *in* space; it 'inhabits' space (Merleau-Ponty, 1978 [1962], p. 139). Space is not conceived as 'the setting (real or logical) in which things are arranged, but the means whereby the position of things becomes possible' (1978 [1962], p. 243). The same goes for time. As Merleau-Ponty argues, '[m]y body takes possession of time; it brings into existence a past and a future for a present, it is not a thing, but creates time instead of submitting to it' (1978 [1962], p. 240). In sum, according to the author, 'I am not in space and time, nor do I conceive space and time; I belong to them, my body combines with them and includes them' (1978 [1962], p. 140).

Drawing on Merleau-Ponty, Casey (1996) emphasizes the role of *place* and our *emplacement* as the starting point for our understanding of space and time. More concretely, it is through our experience of place that space and time arise. Therefore, space and time are 'contained in place rather than vice versa' (Casey, 1996, pp. 43–44). As Casey argues, place is nothing static; it is an 'event'—constantly changing but sufficiently coherent to be 'considered as the *same* (hence to be remembered, returned to, etc.)' and to be classified into certain 'types' (workplace, home, etc.). These types of place often become the locations for, or the subjects or objects of, ethnography (Casey, 1996, p. 44)—as in the present book.

To conclude, a phenomenological perspective allows me to grasp *the prison* through prisoners' emplaced and embodied experiences. As Merleau-Ponty has argued, 'the world'—and the prison—'is not what I think, but what I live through' (1978 [1962], pp. xvi–xvii).

3.1.2.2 Doing with Space and Time

In addition to this perspective, I am interested in prisoners' ways of *arranging* their daily lives. I start from the idea that prisoners' everyday lives are never fully determined by the institutional order, but that they use, appropriate and constantly (re)arrange the institutional spatio-temporal order through individual practices. Such practices allow them to attribute (new) meanings and values to various prison contexts, create personal and intimate spaces and redefine carceral rhythms.

Inspired by the pragmatist approach of geographers Lussault and Stock, inhabiting is here understood as both a general *relation to the world*, expressed through practice, and a way of concretely *residing* (Stock, 2006) in prison. Like Merleau-Ponty, Lussault and Stock challenge Heidegger's definition of being-in-the-world. From their perspective, being in the world is not (only) about 'being on Earth' or 'being in space' but about 'coping with space' (Lussault & Stock, 2010; Stock, 2015, p. 430). They argue that the expression 'in' (or 'within') space suggests that there is a 'pre-existent spatial volume or *res extensa*, a conception of space as container or as a substance'—completely separate from the practices of individuals (Lussault & Stock, 2010, p. 14). Indeed, the authors prefer the terminology 'doing with' instead of 'coping with' space; from their perspective, the expression 'to cope with space' makes sense when space is considered a problem, which is certainly not always the case. The authors propose a shift away from the idea of 'being in space' towards that of 'doing with space', arguing that (individual as well as collective) actors may encounter and mobilize space either as a 'problem' or as 'empowerment' (Lussault & Stock, 2010, p. 13).

Thus, this perspective allows me to look at prisoners' practical engagement or ways of dealing with imprisonment without necessarily labelling these 'resistance', 'coping' or 'adaptation' to the prison context, as other research often does (Cohen & Taylor, 1972; Crewe, 2009; Ugelvik, 2014).

More concretely, following Lussault and Stock (2010), by encountering places, actors make use of spatial elements and thereby get 'playfully or in a constrained way [...] over distances, transgress boundaries and [...] arrange and [...] rearrange things, and, through discourses and other kinds of acts shape the quality of places' (Lussault & Stock, 2010, p. 15). Space is therefore both a *condition* and a (material as well as immaterial) *resource* for practices (Lussault, 2007, pp. 215–218). Individuals' approaches to space are thereby strongly linked to the different 'competences' (perceptive, cognitive, linguistic, technological and relational) that they mobilize in order to deal with space (Lussault & Stock, 2010, p. 16). Lussault and Stock further argue that space and action are co-constructed. On the one hand, practices create spatial arrangements and define qualities of places. On the other hand, spatial discourses and imaginaries with spatial content as well as spatial elements (e.g. physical accessibilities and limits) are present in individual practices (Lussault & Stock, 2010, p. 16). However, as later added by Di Méo (2014), who draws on phenomenology, actors not only deal with *space*, but also with *time*, as 'every emplacement corresponds to a position in time, in a particular present, in a singular moment of duration' (Di Méo, 2014, p. 64, my translation).

Lussault and Stock's (2010, pp. 11–13) 'pragmatics of space' approach is anchored in four different theoretical approaches. First, it is inspired by de Certeau's (1990 [1980]) theory of '*arts de faire*' (arts of doing) that focuses on individual counter-hegemonic 'tactics' for coping with space. Second, it incorporates Foucault's (2001) approach that emphasizes the social as spatial ordering in order to perform discipline and surveillance. Of particular importance is the argument that 'in order to get things done', it is necessary to use space. Third, it draws on Schütz's (1932) phenomenological approach to conceptualize practice not as a purely corporal engagement but to understand the multiplicity of relationships present in action—not only the bodily co-presence of actors (here the authors reference Schütz's notions of '*Mitwelt*', '*Umwelt*' and '*Nachwelt*')—as well as the engagement of different 'competences' within a situation. Finally, it mobilizes a 'situated action' approach (Goffman, 1963, 1964; Popper, 1972; Thomas, 1927). The situation is thus the unit of analysis. Yet, in contrast to authors who use this concept exclusively to examine face-to-face interaction on the micro-level, Lussault and Stock's (2010, pp. 13, 17) definition of the situation takes into account 'the mobilisation of elements that are physically absent', i.e. those other spaces to which individuals are connected, by tools or imagination. Therefore, as the authors argue, to look at situated actions allows for the detection of ephemeral 'assemblages' (Latour, 2005) that are constructed within a situation and then deconstructed. I use the situation as my unit of analysis as well. I consider *situations* to be meaningful moments in prisoners' everyday lives, always embedded in a particular *carceral (material and social) context* and framed by the *prison regime*. Yet, as I actively engaged in prison life through participant observation, I also defined (or tried to define) situations during prisoners' everyday lives.

3.1.3 Conclusion

Combining a phenomenological and pragmatist approach allows us (1) to understand the prison not as a space in the sense of a (predefined) static container that holds people, but as a formally established 'set of arrangements of space and (clock) time' that is *lived*—that is, individually perceived, used, appropriated and (re)arranged. Further, it enables (2) the exploration of prisoners' embodied, agentic and practical engagement with imprisonment without necessarily labelling it 'resistance', 'coping' or 'adaptation' to the prison environment, as has often been done in previous research (Cohen & Taylor, 1972; Crewe, 2009; Ugelvik, 2014). As mentioned above, from a pragmatist perspective, space and time can not only constitute a 'problem' but also be mobilized as a 'resource' (Lussault & Stock, 2010, p. 15). Finally, it also allows for (3) consideration of the apparently insignificant and banal aspects of everyday prison life, which are perhaps less 'spectacular' but by no means less existentially important for these prisoners' lives. This facilitates a broader understanding of 'the prison' that takes into account not only its materiality, regime or culture, but also the 'ambiance' (Thibaud, 2011) produced by its (social) environment, everyday routines and rhythms, as well as its surroundings.

References

Aday, R. (1994). Aging in prison: A case study of new elderly offenders. *International Journal of Offender Therapy and Comparative Criminology, 38*, 79–91. https://doi.org/10.1177/0306624X9403800108

Aebi, M. F., & Kuhn, A. (2000). Influences on the prisoner rate: Number of entries into prison, length of sentences and crime rate. *European Journal on Criminal Policy and Research, 8*, 65–75. https://doi.org/10.1023/A:1008753330678

Baer, L. D. (2005). Visual imprints on the prison landscape: A study on the decorations in prison cells. *Tijdschrift voor economische en sociale geografie, 96*, 209–217. https://doi.org/10.1111/j.1467-9663.2005.00451.x

Biggam, F. H., & Power, K. G. (1997). Social support and psychological distress in a group of incarcerated young offenders. *International Journal of Offender Therapy and Comparative Criminology, 41*, 213–230. https://doi.org/10.1177/0306624X97413002

Casey, E. S. (1996). How to get from space to place in a fairly short stretch of time: phenomenological prolegomena. In S. Feld & K. H. Basso (Eds.), *Senses of place* (School of American Research advanced seminar series, pp. 13–52). School of American Research Press.

Certeau, M. d. (1990 [1980]). *L'invention du quotidien 1. Arts de faire.* Gallimard.

Chassagne, A. (2017). Les temporalités de la vieillesse en prison. Le temps oublié des « vieux » détenus ». *ethnographiques.org* (35), [en ligne].

Chassagne, A. (2019). *Soins et prison. Enquête auprès de détenus gravement malades*. Érès.

Che, D. (2005). Constructing a prison in the forest: Conflicts over nature, paradise, and identity. *Annals of the Association of American Geographers, 95*, 809–831. https://doi.org/10.1111/j.1467-8306.2005.00488.x

Cohen, S., & Taylor, L. (1972). *Psychological survival: The experience of long-term imprisonment*. Penguin Books.

Combessie, P. (2002). Marking the carceral boundary: Penal stigma in the long shadow of the prison. *Ethnography, 3*, 535–555. https://doi.org/10.1177/146613810200300401 9

Cope, N. (2003). 'It's no time or high time': Young offenders' experiences of time and drug use in prison. *The Howard Journal of Criminal Justice, 42*, 158–175. https://doi.org/10.1111/1468-2311.t01-1-00273

Crewe, B. (2009). *The prisoner society: Power, adaptation and social life in an English prison.* Oxford University Press.

Crewe, B., Hulley, S., & Wright, S. (2016). Swimming with the tide: Adapting to long-term imprisonment. *Justice Quarterly, 34*, 1–25. https://doi.org/10.1080/07418825.2016.1190394

Crewe, B., Hulley, S., & Wright, S. (2020). *Life imprisonment from young adulthood: Adaptation, identity and time* (Palgrave studies in prisons and penology). Palgrave Macmillan.

Cunha, M. I. (1997). Le temps suspendu. Rythmes et durées dans une prison portugaise. *Terrain* (29), 59–68.

Cunha, M. I. (2002). *Entre o Bairro e a Prisão: Tráfico e trajectos.* Etnográfica Press.

Cunha, M. I. (2008). Closed circuits: Kinship, neighborhood and incarceration in urban Portugal. *Ethnography, 9*, 325–350. https://doi.org/10.1177/1466138108094974

Cunha, M. I. (2014). The ethnography of prisons and penal confinement. *Annual Review of Anthropology, 43*, 217–233. https://doi.org/10.1146/annurev-anthro-102313-030349

Di Méo, G. (2014). *Introduction à la géographie sociale.* Armand Colin.

Dirsuweit, T. (1999). Carceral spaces in South Africa: A case study of institutional power, sexuality and transgression in a women's prison. *Geoforum, 30*, 71–83. https://doi.org/10.1016/S0016-7185(98)00030-X

Dodgshon, R. A. (2008). Geography's place in time. *Geografiska Annaler: Series B, Human Geography, 90*, 1–15. https://doi.org/10.1111/j.1468-0467.2008.00272.x

Flanagan, T. J. (1981). Dealing with long-term confinement: Adaptive strategies and perspectives among long-term prisoners. *Criminal Justice and Behavior, 8*(2), 201–222.

Foucault, M. (1975). *Surveiller et punir, naissance de la prison.* Gallimard.

Foucault, M. (2001). *Dits et écrits.* Gallimard.

Glasmeier, A. K., & Farrigan, T. (2007). The economic impacts of the prison development boom on persistently poor rural places. *International Regional Science Review, 30*, 274–299. https://doi.org/10.1177/0160017607301608

Goffman, E. (1963). *Behavior in public places; notes on the social organization of gatherings*. Free Press of Glencoe.
Goffman, E. (1964). The neglected situation. *American Anthropologist* (66), 133–136.
Herrity, K. (2019). *Rhythms and routines: Sounding order in a local men's prison through aural ethnography* (PhD thesis). University of Leicester, Leicester.
Jacobs, D., & Helms, R. E. (1996). Toward a political model of incarceration: A time-series examination of multiple explanations for prison admission rates. *American Journal of Sociology, 102*(2), 323–357.
JVA Lenzburg. (2010). *Orientierung an die Gefangenen.*
Latour, B. (2005). *Reassembling the social: An introduction to actor-network-theory*. Oxford University Press.
Lefebvre, H. (2014). *Rhythmanalysis: Space, time and everyday life*. Bloomsbury.
Lussault, M. (2007). *L'homme spatial: la construction sociale de l'espace humain.* Édition du Seuil.
Lussault, M., & Stock, M. (2010). "Doing with space": Towards a pragmatics of space. *Social Geography, 5*, 11–19. https://doi.org/10.5194/sg-5-11-2010
Marchetti, A.-M., & Combessie, P. (1996). *La prison dans la cité*. Desclée de Brouwer.
Marti, I., Hostettler, U., & Richter, M. (2017). End of life in high-security prisons in Switzerland: Overlapping and blurring of "care" and "custody" as Institutional Logics. *Journal of Correctional Health Care, 23*, 32–42. https://doi.org/10.1177/1078345816684782
Matthews, R. (2009). *Doing time: An introduction to the sociology of imprisonment*. Palgrave Macmillan.
May, J., & Thrift, N. J. (Eds.). (2001). *Timespace: Geographies of temporality* (Critical geographies, Vol. 13). Routledge.
Merleau-Ponty, M. (1962). *Phenomenology of perception.* Routledge and Kegan Paul.
Merleau-Ponty, M. (1978 [1962]). *Phenomenology of perception.* Routledge and Kegan Paul.
Milhaud, O. (2009). *Séparer et punir. Les prisons françaises: mise à distance et punition par l'espace* (PhD thesis). Université Michel de Montaigne - Bordeaux III, Bordeaux. https://tel.archives-ouvertes.fr/tel-00441473
Moran, D. (2012). "Doing time" in carceral space: TimeSpace and carceral geography. *Geografiska Annaler: Series B, Human Geography, 94*, 305–316. https://doi.org/10.1111/geob.12000

Moran, D., Pallot, J., & Piacentini, L. (2011). The geography of crime and punishment in the Russian Federation. *Eurasian Geography and Economics, 52*, 79–104. https://doi.org/10.2747/1539-7216.52.1.79
O'Donnell, I. (2014). *Prisoners, solitude, and time*. Oxford University Press.
Popper, K. (1972). *Objective knowledge*. Clarendon Press.
Schütz, A. (1932). *Der sinnhafte Aufbau der sozialen Welt. Eine Einleitung in die verstehende Soziologie*. Springer.
Sibley, D., & van Hoven, B. (2009). The contamination of personal space: Boundary construction in a prison environment. *Area, 41*, 198–206. https://doi.org/10.1111/j.1475-4762.2008.00855.x
Simonsen, K. (2007). Practice, spatiality and embodied emotions: An outline of a geography of practice. *Human Affairs, 17*, 168–181.
Sparks, R., Bottoms, A., & Hay, W. (1996). *Prisons and the problem of order* (Clarendon studies in criminology). Clarendon Press.
Stock, M. (2006). Pratiques des lieux, modes d'habiter, régimes d'habiter: pour une analyse trialogique des dimensions spatiales des sociétés humaines. *Travaux de l'institut de Géographie de Reims, 115–118*, 213–230.
Stock, M. (2015). Habiter comme "faire avec l'espace". Réflexions à partir des théories de la pratique. *Annales de géographie, 704*, 424–441. https://doi.org/10.3917/ag.704.0424
Sykes, G. M. (1971 [1958]). *The society of captives: A study of a maximum security prison*. Princeton University Press.
Thibaud, J.-P. (2011). The sensory fabric of urban ambiances. *Senses and Society, 6*(2), 203–215.
Thomas, W. I. (1927). The behavior pattern and the situation. *Publications of the American Sociological Society, 22*, 1–14.
Thornton, P. H., & Ocasio, W. (2008). Institutional logics. In R. Greenwood, C. Oliver, R. Suddaby, & K. Sahlin-Andersson (Eds.), *Handbook of organizational institutionalism* (pp. 99–129). Sage.
Thornton, P. H., Ocasio, W., & Lounsbury, M. (2012). *The institutional logics perspective: A new approach to culture, structure, and process*. Oxford University Press.
Ugelvik, T. (2014). *Power and resistance in prison: Doing time, doing freedom*. Palgrave Macmillan.
Warren, J., Hurt, S., Loper, A., & Chauhan, P. (2004). Exploring prison adjustment among female inmates: Issues of measurement and prediction. *Criminal Justice and Behavior, 31*, 624–645. https://doi.org/10.1177/0093854804267096

Wright, S., Crewe, B., & Hulley, S. (2017). Suppression, denial, sublimation: Defending against the initial pains of very long life sentences. *Theoretical Criminology, 21*, 225–246. https://doi.org/10.1177/1362480616643581
Zamble, E. (1992). Behavior and adaptation in long-term prison inmates: Descriptive longitudinal results. *Criminal Justice and Behavior, 19*, 409–425. https://doi.org/10.1177/0093854892019004005

4

In the Prison Cell

Leo: This is my cell (we are standing in front of it; the prison officer who accompanies us during the walking interview is unlocking the door for us).

Irene: You've been here [in this particular cell] for a while now, haven't you?

L: Yes, yes. I was first in the 5, wing 5. Then, during the renovation of wing 2, we had to move over [to another wing] for half a year. We were obliged to go there. But I prefer to be here [in wing 3] because it has fewer cells. Only seven, instead of 11 or 12 on a row, which is a relief.

I: Is it therefore quieter?

L: Yes. But of course, it depends on the people, on their personality, on how they are. But generally, it is quieter. There is just more air, because you have a certain distance from cell to cell, while the others [in the other wing] are quite close to one another. And yes, I find it comfortable here especially because of the view [from the window].

I: And when you say there is more air, do you also notice that while you are inside [the cell]?

L: Yes, of course it [the cell] is bigger. [...] this is what suits me, and also the people here are more on their own. There are also

I. Marti, *Doing Indefinite Time*, Palgrave Studies in Prisons and Penology,
https://doi.org/10.1007/978-3-031-12590-4_4

many *Verwahrte* [prisoners sentenced to indefinite incarceration] here, or long-term prisoners. I have somehow settled down here. And yes, so this is my cell (he steps in).

I: May I come in?

L: Yeah, sure, now you're allowed (laughs) (I'm entering the cell). Yeah, so that's just … my little empire. (Leo, 31.8.2017)

As this quotation suggests, the experience of being and living in a prison cell is shaped by a wide range of elements: the size of the wing and the prisoners who live next door are just as important as the particular view one may have from the cell window. Before entering the prison cell, I propose we remain on the doorstep and have a brief look at the literature on this subject.

In general, prison scholars describe this particular place as ambiguous. On the one hand, they agree that the cell is probably the only place in the prison where prisoners can spend unobserved time and therefore experience (at least some degree of) privacy and relief from prison pressure (Cohen & Taylor, 1972; Toch, 1996 [1977]; Ugelvik, 2014). In contrast to other prison (common) spaces, such as the courtyard or the workplace, the cell is the place where prisoners usually sleep, get dressed, care for their personal hygiene, eat, watch TV, read and study, think and dream. Given these activities, the cell can be considered a 'private' and 'intimate sphere' (see also Ugelvik, 2014, p. 121). On the other hand, the cell is seen as not really 'their space' either, because 'nothing is theirs here [in the prison]' (Wacquant 2002, p. 378). The cell remains a domain that is highly controlled by the prison system (see also Foucault, 1975). For example, prison staff members can enter at any moment and without announcement, the cell is regularly searched, and prisoners may be transferred to another cell or prison at any time (see also Ugelvik, 2014, p. 118) This ambiguity is also experienced by the prisoners with whom I spoke. Jonathan summarized it spontaneously: 'The cell for me, it's an order. I must be there, regardless of whether I want to or not. But in the meantime, this is the place where I feel comfortable, where I can rest and find peace and quiet' (Jonathan, 2.5.2016).

A first look inside suggests that the prison cell is a very small and narrow place. In Switzerland, the size of a cell is generally 12m^2; possibilities for movement and activity are therefore very limited. If the prisoners are held in single cells (which is the case in *JVA Lenzburg* and *JVA Pöschwies*), when the doors are locked they have no opportunity for (direct) interpersonal communication. The cell is a place where they are forced to 'do time' alone, with themselves. Finally, according to the spatio-temporal regime of the prison, it is the place where they have to spend most of their time. Within the framework of the prison's daily structure, divided into work, leisure and resting time, the cell is the place where prisoners are supposed to rest.[1] However, as already indicated, the activities and actions carried out by the prisoners while locked in their cells obviously go beyond resting in a literal sense, meaning 'to relax, to sleep, or recover strength' (Oxford Dictionaries, 2018b). For instance, while some prisoners use the official resting time for (personal) work, others try to distract themselves as much as possible during this particular part of the day because they are suffering from being locked up. Either way, their time in the cell grants these prisoners a general break from their obligations concerning the activities and periods that take place in the prison's common rooms, namely work and leisure time.

The aim of this chapter is to take a closer look at prisoners' ambivalent attitudes towards the cell by 'entering' the prison cell with an ethnographic lens. As emphasized by Ugelvik, 'a cell is not necessarily a cell', because 'a room is never just a room' (2014, p. 116). In this sense, I aim to explore more deeply the meanings prisoners attribute to their cells, their individual experiences of being inside and their ways of doing time there.

As a first step into the prisoners' 'little empire', this chapter begins with a description of the legal and institutional norms regarding the design, materiality and furnishing of the cell in order to provide an initial impression of the cell from an outsider's perspective. This is followed by a description of the prisoners' perception of how it feels to be in a prison cell, based on the concept of 'ambiance' (Adey et al., 2013). As I will

[1] It is important to note here that being locked (for an additional period of time, e.g. during working hours) in the cell can also be part of a disciplinary measure JVA Lenzburg (2012, p. 70).

show in this section, the ambiance of the prison cell is not only a result of its materiality, but also of the prison (social) environment (inside) and its surroundings (outside). This is also expressed by Leo in the quote above, who is happy now that he is in a wing with fewer cells and a better view. In the subsequent section, I present the prison regime for the furnishing and maintenance of the cell, consisting of rules and regulations that are translated into practice by prison staff. I then provide insight into the prisoners' approaches to dealing with this particular place by looking more closely at their everyday practices, namely how they make use of spatial elements to create intimate and private spaces. The last section is dedicated to the prisoners' temporal experience and ways of dealing with time while being locked up alone in this very small place.

4.1 The Swiss Prison Cell

At the national level, no explicit rules exist regarding the material conditions of the prison cell in Switzerland (Baechtold et al., 2016, p. 159). However, the general guidelines for the execution of sentences and measures (Art. 74 and Art. 75 of the SCC) apply to the design and furnishing of the cell. On a cantonal level, again no common standards exist; they are mainly defined at the level of the individual institution. However, several cantonal guidelines suggest single cell occupancy as the norm. Since the revision of the SCC in 2007, the so-called 'principle of normalisation' has served as the point of reference for questions concerning the materiality of the cell. Thus, the material conditions of the cell must correspond to 'average living conditions' (*durchschnittliche Lebensgewohnheiten*). Based on this, there are minimal requirements regarding lighting, ventilation, sanitary facilities, furnishings and the size of the cell (Baechtold et al., 2016, pp. 159–160). In addition to the rather vague jurisprudence at the national level, the Federal Office of Justice has formulated explicit standards that come into force when authorities must decide on the subsidies to be allotted to new penal institutions (Bundesamt für Justiz BJ, 2016). For example, $12m^2$ has been determined as the minimum size required for a single cell (Baechtold et al., 2016, p. 160). In terms of lighting, heating and sanitary facilities, the norms should correspond to the rules concerning general housing construction in Switzerland. The cells should receive enough daylight so that the prisoner is able to read without artificial lighting during the day. Also, every cell must have access to running water—not necessarily warm water—and be naturally ventilated, heated to normal room temperature and equipped with a flush toilet. Every cell must be furnished with a bed, a chair, a table or desk, and a wardrobe or rack. Finally, the addition of personal objects, namely wall decorations, should be 'generously permitted' (Baechtold et al., 2016, p. 160).

In the *Strafanstalt* of *JVA Lenzburg*, the size of (the majority of) the cells, 7.86 m^2, does not meet today's standards, and they have recently been renovated in order to improve their condition (Lüthi, 2013). The windows were enlarged to augment the view and air circulation, and they now have access to hot water. However, the renovation also responded to security concerns. As the director of the prison explained, the ancient wooden windows could potentially have been unscrewed in order to hide something. Moreover, the floors, partially made of wood, tiles and linoleum, were worn-down and again potential hiding places for all kinds of objects. According to prison management, this is no longer possible with the resistant polyurethane coverings. Finally, the toilets are no longer installed in wooden cabinets, which also used to offer hiding places. In terms of furniture, the cells are equipped with a bed, a toilet, a cupboard with a sink, a table and chair, and a cupboard for storing clothes. The furniture is bolted in place (see Fig. 4.1).

In the *60plus* unit for ill and elderly prisoners at *JVA Lenzburg*, the size of the cells is 12.5 m^2. The basic material of the outside walls as well as the inner walls and floors is concrete. The furniture, including a bed, a table and a chair, a pin board, a cupboard, a toilet and a sink, is mostly fixed. While the architecture of the *60plus* unit is the same as for the units for prisoners on remand, some of the walls in this wing and the cells have been painted yellow, according to a member of the prison management, in order 'to improve the atmosphere' (fieldnotes, 14.3.2013).

The furniture in the cells in the *AGE* unit at *JVA Pöschwies* is basically the same as that at *JVA Lenzburg*. However, it is not fixed and is thus movable. The floors are made of wood.

Fig. 4.1 An empty prison cell (*Source* Photo by Andreas Moser)

4.2 Descriptions of the cell's Ambiance

Studies in the field of human geography argue that architectural space affects people, in that 'it can refine human feeling and perception [...] define [...] sensations and render them vivid' (Tuan, 2001 [1977], p. 102). Architectural spaces produce a particular 'ambiance'. The concept of ambiance emphasizes the affective and emotional resonances of spaces and the potential of an environment's 'material and sensory qualities' (Adey et al., 2013, p. 302) to touch human beings. However, 'it is not the ambiance that is perceived per se, but rather that it renders perception possible' (Thibaud, 2011, p. 213). In a nutshell, ambiance is 'a space–time qualified from a sensory perspective' (Thibaud, 2011, p. 203). It thus plays 'a major role in giving meaning to spaces in order to transform them into places' (Jones & Jam, 2016, p. 319). As emphasized by Thibaud (2002), ambiance does not exist without the presence of individuals. It is thus both 'what can be perceived and what can be produced' (2002, p. 185). It refers to 'the sorts of physical and moral surroundings of a person or as an "environmental quality", placing ambiance at the interface of the material and sensory qualities of the environment and individual and inter-subjective perception' (Adey et al., 2013, p. 302). Moreover, the prisoners' descriptions of their cell's ambiance are shaped by their 'perceptual filters' (Kusenbach, 2003), such as emotions, values and previous experiences, as well as their individual practices.

In the following, I provide insights into prisoners' sensory perception of their cells as expressed in their descriptions of the ambiance within—how it feels to be in them from the residents' point of view. As I show, the cell's ambiance is described with reference not only to the cell's materiality, but also to the prison environment (inside) as well as its surroundings (outside).

4.2.1 Architecture, Design and Furnishings

As mentioned above, in the *Strafanstalt* of *JVA Lenzburg*, the cells have recently been renovated. Almost all the prisoners agree that the renovation generally led to an 'improvement' of their material conditions. They described the renovated cells as 'modern, clean, bright, and easier to clean' (Fieldnotes). However, they did not agree on the degree of 'cosiness'. Some preferred the cells in their previous condition because of the greater number of wooden elements. These prisoners described the new ones—at least in their uninhabited state—as 'cold and dull' (Leo, 23.3.2016). Some prisoners also mentioned the enlargement of the window. They perceive this element as clearly increasing the level of cosiness, because 'it provides more daylight' (Hugo, 23.3.2016).

However, fastening the furniture in place (which, in the *Strafanstalt*, occurred with the renovation) has proven to be the most important issue, because it restricts the possibility of arranging the items according to personal needs.

> Everything is fixed now. Previously you could arrange the table, here the desk, over there the computer … you could really arrange it a bit like a home, your own … room or one-room apartment or whatever. And now everything is set in concrete and fixed. (Leo, 23.3.2016)

Fixing the furniture in place not only restricts further rearrangement. As mentioned by Tuan, 2001 [1977], p. 102), architectural space 'clarifies social roles and relations'; it provides people with an orientation regarding their status and behaviour. For instance, in the case of the prison cell, the bars in front of the windows remind the residents day after day that they are prisoners. Interestingly, however, the bars are something that most of the prisoners tend to ignore (see also Sect. 1.2.3). In contrast, they declared that the fixed furniture was a clear sign of heteronomy and a failure to recognize their status as prisoners who have already served their sentences and who are now preventively held in prison. Many prisoners associate this fixed arrangement of the cell with conditions that are common in pre-trial detention facilities, where security is privileged above all else in order to prevent vandalism and suicide (Bundesamt für Justiz BJ, 2016).

> It's like in pre-trial detention [*Untersuchungshaft*]: everything is fixed, everything on a concrete wall. You can't actually move anything. Before [in another prison], I could put the table across the cell, or put it in front of the bed. I could arrange the cell a little bit the way I wanted it. It's the same with the TV. Now I'm forced to have the TV behind me; I can't put it on the table, the way I want it. These are things that really annoy me a lot. Me as a *Verwahrter* [prisoner serving indefinite incarceration]! If I had only three, four years, a regular sentence, then I would say: ok. But as a *Verwahrter*, I don't see why I have to live like that. I don't see it! (Paul, 29.3.2016)

From Hugo's point of view, the fastening of the furniture fulfils one particular purpose above all: 'to make it easier for staff to search the cells' (Hugo, 23.3.2016). Similar to Paul, he wishes the cell were 'less prison-like':

> Yes, I already told the director, for people who have been in here for 10, 15 or 20 years now or who won't get out anymore, the room should be a bit bigger, and you should be able to arrange it in a way that you can feel at home or feel well. That there is a good atmosphere [in the cell]. Now it is just, just cell-like or prison-like and so on. This may be ok for people who will be released, but for people who are held in indefinite incarceration and have no chance at all [to ever be released], it's quite difficult. (Hugo, 23.3.2016)

This echoes Ugelvik's (2014, p. 118) argument that all the rules and limits regarding personalization of the cell are an expression of institutional power: 'the cell is a room that tells the prisoner who lives in it that "you are all the same to us"'.

Prisoners in the *60plus* unit described the fixed furniture principally in terms of health issues. Some said that they would like to adjust the level of the bed, which is considered to be 'too low' (François, 23.11.2013), as well as the height of the table, which—together with the chair, which is 'not a normal office chair' (David, 11.6.2013)—may cause back pain when sitting for long periods of time. Moreover, the concrete floor in the unit was described as 'uncomfortable' (David, 11.6.2013) for bare feet, and the windows as 'too small' and not providing enough daylight (Herbert, 5.6.2013). In addition, they pointed to the dominance of the colour grey in the cell (the floor, the walls), which, as one prisoner said, 'makes you sick' (David, 11.6.2013). According to David, the architecture and design of the prison cell is not 'species-appropriate' (David, 11.6.2013). In the *AGE* at *JVA Pöschwies*, the materiality of the cell was mentioned less frequently. However, the fact that the furniture is movable was often discussed, and prisoners explicitly emphasized that they make use of the (restricted) ability to move it and arrange the cell according to their wishes (see Sect. 1.4).

The prisoners' narratives regarding the materiality of the cell emphasize their desire for a personalized space in order to feel less like a prisoner and more like a 'normal' human being living in this particular place. As I show in the following section, in addition to the materiality and design of the cell, the wider (social) prison environment produced by both staff and prisoners also contributes to the ambiance of the cell.

4.2.2 Prison Environment

The relationship between staff and prisoners is 'at the heart of any prison' (Crewe, 2011b, p. 455). The prison staff's methods of exerting power and authority, their use of discretion and their approach towards care greatly influence the general climate of the prison (Bennett et al., 2008; Isenhardt et al., 2014; Liebling, 2000). To put it in the words of a prisoner, prison staff can put more or less 'pressure' on them (Marco, 4.5.2016). More concretely, the degree of pressure depends on the way officers treat prisoners: whether they 'see more than a prisoner' and 'the human side' (Herbert, 5.6.2013) of the person and express respect and maybe even helpfulness during their everyday interactions with prisoners, or whether they use 'every opportunity to harass and mentally destroy' them (Kurt, 3.5.2016).

These different staff attitudes reveal themselves, for example, when locking and unlocking a prisoner's cell—a routine that prison staff perform with different rhythmic variations and dynamics. Some officers knock before they open the door; others open it without warning. Some officers close the door carefully; others slam it. With these different attitudes, staff members grant prisoners more or less privacy (see also Sect. 4.2.2). Some officers behave in a way that gives prisoners the feeling that 'all they are interested in is to simply lock [prisoners] up and let [them] rot' (Hugo, 25.6.2013), while others use these moments of the day to have a chat, maybe make a joke or ask the prisoner how he is doing that day. Paul mentioned that making jokes with staff members in particular helps him to temporarily 'break out' of the strict daily routine (Paul, 29.3.2016). Thus, the locking and unlocking of the prison cell is a sensitive moment during which, depending on the officer's attitude and behaviour, prisoners may feel more or less respected as human beings.

The ambiance of the cell is further produced by the prison's sounds (see also Herrity, 2020). Even though the cell doors are made of steel, prisoners told me that they can still hear what goes on outside them. In the literature, the prison is generally described as a 'very noisy' place (Rice, 2016). Typical prison sounds include the 'banging' of cell doors when being shut; the 'rattle' of keys carried by staff members; their way of addressing prisoners in loud, 'gruff' and 'authoritative' voices; and sudden events, such as fights between prisoners or prisoners who become 'hysterical' and start screaming while in their cells (Rice, 2016, pp. 5–6). The elderly long-term prisoners I spoke to mentioned that they are generally sensitive to (prison) sounds and often experience them as 'noise'. They point to fellow prisoners who 'shout', especially during the day when the cells are open, or listen to 'too loud' music as a source of stress. Some prisoners stated that they had asked for a transfer to a wing that is supposed to be quieter (which, in the *Strafanstalt*, is the wing with mostly long-term prisoners) or to the unit for elderly and ill prisoners. These prisoners also appreciate the sound of silence that occurs immediately after the nightly lock-up. However, they still may live next to a 'noisy neighbour' or close to a main door that makes noise whenever it is used by a staff member.

While in the cell, one sound that makes inmates feel particularly uncomfortable is that of an approaching officer. One prisoner told me that whenever he is in his cell and hears footsteps on the wooden floor that seem to be getting closer, along with the sound of keys, he immediately feels tense because he always thinks: 'Now they are coming to my cell' (Fieldnotes, 24.2.2016)—even if there is no obvious reason for it. Because staff members are allowed to open the cell door and enter at any moment of the day, these particular sounds can strengthen the prisoners' perception that, in prison, 'one can never really relax' (Fieldnotes, 24.2.2016). As this same prisoner noted, the sound of an approaching prison or security officer always makes him feel 'interrupted'. Nonetheless, prison staff rarely enter a prisoner's cell after 8 pm, lock-up time. Most prisoners indicated that from that moment onwards, they can experience privacy and relief from prison pressure.

In the prison literature, quietude is generally described as a source of relief (Rice, 2016, p. 11). However, the lack of sound—silence—can also be a source of stress. As mentioned above, the units for elderly and ill prisoners are generally (not least because of the limited number of prisoners) described as 'quieter' than normal wings or units. While some perceive this as a welcome relief, for Marco this 'intense quietness' in the unit feels 'unnatural' because it does not correspond to the sounds of 'normal life' (Marco, 4.5.2016). Indeed, this particular ambiance makes him feel isolated. Jonathan said in this regard: 'It's like deserted, everyone closes his door, even when it is [unlocked]' (Jonathan, 24.9.2013). The predominance of silence that characterizes the ambiance in the cell after the nightly lock-up intensifies the experience of isolation and loneliness.[2] Many prisoners mentioned that after lock-up, they usually immediately switch on the radio or TV because they 'can't stand complete silence' (Markus, 28.9.2017). 'Whenever I enter the cell, I immediately switch on the TV. Not because I always watch it, but that there is a sound. Loneliness is thus less present' (Darko, 6.5.2016). By switching on the TV to make sound, prisoners drown out the loneliness produced by the lack of human presence and communication and thus create a lively ambiance:

> The TV sometimes also just runs in the background, so that I don't feel alone [...] especially when I write difficult letters I'm glad if it is on, especially when the door is locked. During the day [when the door is open], I often switch it off. Then I can concentrate better, because I know I'm not locked up, [I am] still in prison, but at least not confined in this narrow space [of the cell]. (Rolf, 6.5.2016)

As shown in this section, the ambiance of the prison cell and thus the feeling of being in it is not only created by the materiality of the cell,

---

[2] Some studies mention so-called 'window-to-window communication' between prisoners (see, among others, Rice (2016), Ugelvik, 2014). During my research, this form of communication was never mentioned to me, and I was also never able to hear prisoners talking with each other while in their cells. I assume that there are several reasons for this. First, long-term prisoners, at least in the prisons where I did research, know that window-to-window communication is not allowed, and they usually avoid breaking rules because they are as well aware of the consequences. Second, many of them mentioned that they had got used to being in their cells and did not necessarily feel the need to talk to fellow prisoners at that particular moment of the day.

the size of the window or the movability of the furniture, but also by the prison environment, the way the prison staff treat the prisoners during the locking and unlocking of their cells, and the prison's sounds—its noise as well as its silence. I argue that there is at least a third element: the prison's surroundings. While locked in their cells, prisoners are—at least physically—the most isolated from the outside world. However, each cell also has a window through which prisoners can get a glimpse of the outside world. How prisoners perceive and deal with this potential connection is also important.

4.2.3 Prison Surroundings[3]

Scholars agree that 'total institutions' are in general more permeable than as outlined by Goffman (1961). The idea of the 'totality' of prisons has been challenged by various scholars, who have pointed, for example, to prisoners' importation of gang patterns into the prison (Jacobs, 1977) and the penetration of the outside world through the media (Jewkes, 2002) or external visitors (Moran, 2013). Nonetheless, with the exception of a few studies in the field of carceral geography that challenge the idea of a distinct separation between the inside and outside of the prison (see e.g. Baer & Ravneberg, 2008; Turner, 2016), these studies remain focused on the inner world of the prison, on what happens *behind* the walls. In this section, I propose shifting the focus from the interior spaces to the exterior spaces of the prison, specifically to the prison surroundings. My aim is to trace the role of the prison surroundings by looking more closely at the prisoners' sensory perception of 'what goes on' *beyond* 'its high walls' (Coyle, 2005, p. xi) and how this affects their experience of imprisonment.

While the cells in a prison are generally all alike, the location and orientation of the cell window provide prisoners with different views and therefore potentially different sensory impressions and connections to the outside world. This strongly shapes the perceived 'ambiance' (Thibaud,

[3] Parts of this section have been published as Marti (2021): Sensing freedom: Insights into long-term prisoners' perceptions of the outside world, *Incarceration SAGE*, Vol. 2(2): 1–20.

2011) in the cell and thus how it feels to be in the cell as well as the experience of imprisonment in general (see also Turner et al., 2020). For instance, some prisoners told me that they could hear dogs barking or people laughing; others mentioned that they could hear birds chirping—or even have direct contact with them by feeding them—while in the cell. The location of the cell also influences whether the sun shines in at the time they are locked inside. A cell on the second floor may allow prisoners to look over the wall and obtain a glimpse of the 'free world' and maybe—depending on the surroundings of the prison—see a forest, a village, cars or even people. For example, Leo has recently moved to a cell on the second floor. This allows him to see 'more than the wall' and, as he said, 'to gaze into the distance' (Leo, 23.3.2016) (see Fig. 4.2). He can now see cars moving and sometimes people walking on the street. Of course, these views change with the seasons. As he told me, he sees 'a bit more of life out there' during winter, after the trees have lost their leaves (Leo, 6.9.2017). However, he has difficulty imagining 'that this is reality'; for him, looking out the window feels 'as if [he is] watching TV' (Leo, 23.3.2016).

Despite the difficulties in feeling that what they can see from the window is 'reality', some prisoners described the ability to peek at the outside world through the window of their cells as essential for their well-being. For some this means having the opportunity to see the blue sky or the green trees, to smell and feel the 'fresh air' (Leo, 23.3.2016); for others it means getting a glimpse of houses and cars—to see that 'normal life' (Leo, 6.9.2017) goes on. All of them mentioned that being able to gain sensory impressions of the outside world provides them with hope, makes them feel less isolated and (still) connected to the outside world (see also Jewkes, 2018; Moran, 2019).

> If I were inside a cell where I couldn't see green when I look out of the window, no sky and nothing, I would go crazy because I need that. This is what gives me back some energy and makes me keep going. (Hugo, 25.6.2013)

> [I]t's important for me to have this view, I can see a bit of green, the forest, I don't just see the wall, well I'm now up [on the second floor],

Fig. 4.2 A glance of the 'free world' through the cell's window (*Source* Photo by a prisoner)

> this gives you still a little feeling of freedom, and this is what matters to me [...] I'm often standing at the window, looking out into the forest, and simply enjoying it. It also calms me down. [...] This is important to me, to not be completely segregated, that I can still see the horizon. (Leo, 6.9.2017)

However, in contrast to prisoners who appreciate having a view, I also met prisoners who do not like to be confronted with the outside world, because they are constantly reminded of what they are missing (see also Jewkes, 2002, p. 91). Markus, a prisoner who wants to concentrate on the (prison) present instead of the (uncertain) future, told me that he avoids looking out his window, through which he can see a small town. As he explained to me while we were standing in his cell together, the outside world is just 'too close' (illustrated in Fig. 4.3):

> This is something I will not get used to: the view. I'm definitely not one of those ... there are many [prisoners] who are standing at the window in

> the evening, looking out while smoking a cigarette. Me, I don't do that. //Why?// I see houses and life //Yeah, they are very close actually// Yes. This is outside just next to the wall. I don't like that. It's nice to see, but it's depressing. For example, the house there with the two windows above [he is pointing a finger at it], //yes//, this is so close! (Markus, 28.8.2017)

Prison officers told me of one prisoner who used to stay in a cell that provided him with a view of the prison's open-air visiting area where certain prisoners can receive external visitors. After a while, he asked to move to another cell because, due to his paedophilic disposition, he could not bear to hear the voices of children.

As these examples suggest, sensing the outside world through the window of the cell constitutes a source of both well-being and discomfort. Having a sense of the outside world—which means for prisoners the possibility to gaze into the distance, see the open sky and the horizon, and be reminded visually and through sounds that 'normal life' goes on—thus does not increase prisoners' well-being *per se*, as is often

Fig. 4.3 Feeling 'too close' to the outside community (*Source* Photo by Irene Marti)

assumed (see also Turner et al., 2020). It can intensify as well as ease the pain caused by their social exclusion and spatial separation from the community.

Furthermore, the embodied experience of the prison cell as a particular space is inseparably bound up with the embodied experience of time (see Moran, 2012, p. 310). Everyday life in prison is characterized by its many rules, repetition and a high degree of 'eventlessness' (Toch, 1996 [1977], p. 29). Having access to the daily rhythms and routines of the outside community (e.g. in the shape of moving cars and people walking on the street) or the seasons, for instance in the form of a 'forest that changes its colours' (David, 18.10.2017), gives prisoners—especially those who have no concrete perspective and thus do not know if they will ever be released—a sense of the passage of time (see also Turner et al., 2020, p. 226). Moreover, as mentioned above, seeing the 'horizon' provides some prisoners with 'energy' and 'hope', which echoes Tuan's (2001 [1977]) reflections on time in experiential space. As he argues, distance is not a purely spatial concept: it also implies time. Therefore, the spatial experience of having a view of the open space and seeing the horizon—a common image of the future in so-called Western societies—may thus give prisoners, especially those who do not know if they will ever be released, a sense of the future, or at least of 'hopeful times' (Tuan, 2001 [1977], p. 123). However, since most of them have lost contact with their families and friends over time, and many of the places they used to know in the outside world have disappeared, their ideas about the future consist less of concrete plans and more of dreams and visions. Yet even though the future is difficult to imagine, many prisoners keep on 'fighting' against their situation in order to achieve their release.

Interestingly, what prisoners perceive through the window of their cells also depends on what they *want* to see or hear. Thus, to a certain extent, they also 'arrange' (Lussault & Stock, 2010) the view according to their sensibilities and interests. There are prisoners, like Patrick, who explicitly point to the prison infrastructure, such as 'the wall, the wire, the cameras … [that] everything is completely under control' (Patrick, 3.5.2016). Others told me that they 'don't see' these things anymore, especially the bars in front of the window, simply because they do not want to see them. They 'filter' their perception through their intention to disregard everything that reminds them of being in prison. Anton told me, 'from the window of my cell, I can see the castle, it has recently been renovated [...] they did a really good job. For me it is like this: the bars, I look through them, I just see what I want to see' (Anton, 24.3.2016). Some use the curtain for this. As I noticed, during the day many inmates would actually draw the curtains and turn on the light while in their cells. One of the prisoners explained to me that when he draws the curtain, not only does he not see the bars on the window anymore, he also does not notice when the weather is nice (Fieldnotes, 12.2.2016). As I was told by many prisoners, imprisonment is generally experienced as much harder on a sunny day. The curtain therefore helps prisoners to overlook the outside world and what they miss.

Sensing the outside world through the window of the cell is thus a source of both well-being and discomfort, as it can intensify as well as ease the pain caused by the deprivation of liberty, and it strongly shapes prisoners' lived experience of indefinite incarceration.

4.3 A 'Home' or 'a Place to Be, but not to Live'[4]

4.3.1 The prison's Accommodation Regime

While the previous sections described the materiality of the cell and the prisoners' experiences of being in them, this section sheds light on the accommodation regime established by prison management. In general, according to internal prison rules, the cells can be 'homely furnished' (JVA Lenzburg, 2011, p. 21, my translation) and they must be kept 'clean and tidy' (JVA Lenzburg, 2011, p. 22; JVA Pöschwies, 2017, p. 8, my translation). Through such internal norms and rules as well as through the prison staff's implementation practices, the prison instals

[4] Parts of this section were published as Marti, I. (2020). A 'home' or 'a place to be, but not to live': Arranging the prison cell. In J. Turner & V. Knight (Eds.), *The prison cell: Embodied and everyday spaces of incarceration* (pp. 121–142). London: Palgrave Macmillan.

a particular accommodation regime and thus constrains the prisoners' possibilities of 'doing with' the space of the cell.

4.3.1.1 The Right to Arrange the Cell in a 'Homely' Way

In Switzerland, according to the law, the furnishing of one's cell with personal objects, namely wall decorations, should be 'generously permitted' (Baechtold et al., 2016, p. 160).

Internal prison rules indicate that prisoners can furnish their cells in a 'homely' manner (JVA Lenzburg, 2011, p. 21) and have 'personal objects' (JVA Pöschwies, 2017, p. 8, my translation) in their cells. According to these rules, prisoners are authorized to hang pictures and photos on the wall. However, where these can (e.g. on the pin board) and cannot be put (e.g. on the door and the door frame) is clearly defined. Also, prisoners must use the specific fixing material that is provided by the prison (JVA Lenzburg, 2011, p. 22; JVA Pöschwies, 2016, p. 7). It is prohibited to hang pictures that are considered 'shocking', 'defamatory', political or religious, or photos and symbols that have a 'provocative' effect on others. Erotic images are allowed if they do not violate 'the morality of someone with normal sensitivity regarding sexual issues'; pornography is prohibited (JVA Lenzburg, 2011, p. 31, my translation).

Prison and security officers regularly have to 'search' the cells for prohibited objects that prisoners might have illicitly acquired. These so-called 'risk objects' include weapons, literature on weapons, escape tools and mobile phones (JVA Lenzburg, 2011, pp. 60–61). Objects that could be used for illegal purposes, but which are not illegal as such, fall into the same category. However, this is also a matter of interpretation. One day during my fieldwork, prison officers found a bent needle and a piece of wire with a small mirror attached to it in one of the cells. It was clear to the staff that this prisoner was hiding a SIM card, and that he used the needle and the mirror to locate it in its hiding place. Even though the prisoner denied this, he was sanctioned (Fieldnotes, 6.4.2016). As I noticed, prohibited objects are also something relational. For instance, posters showing semi-naked women in the cell of a prisoner who was sentenced for a sex crime are met with scepticism by some prison officers, and sometimes even with zero tolerance. The same applies to video games with children as key actors if the prisoner who wants to play them was sentenced for the sexual abuse of children. Objects that may 'potentially foster criminal fantasies' should, according to prison management, not be in a prisoner's cell (Fieldnotes, 3.2.2016).

The prisoners are allowed to buy additional furnishings, such as a carpet or a reading lamp (JVA Lenzburg, 2011, p. 21; JVA Pöschwies, 2016, p. 7). However, numbers and styles are limited, and they must generally fulfil specific standards (e.g. a specific size in the case of a carpet). They can buy plants from the prison garden, but it is forbidden to keep flowers in the cell. Stuffed animals are accepted if they are not bigger than 25 cm (JVA Pöschwies, 2016, p. 7). Moreover, it is prohibited to obstruct the view into the cell, by installing a curtain on the cell door, for example (JVA Lenzburg, 2011, p. 23; JVA Pöschwies, 2016, p. 7). It is also not permissible to use a towel as a tablecloth (JVA Pöschwies, 2016, p. 1). If the prison furniture is not fixed (which is today the case only in JVA Pöschwies), the prisoners can move it; however, they are not completely free to do so. For instance, it is prohibited to move furnishings to the so-called 'wet area' (where the toilet and the sink are installed), and they must be 'put on their legs' rather than placed upside-down (JVA Pöschwies, 2016, p. 1, my translation).

Finally, prisoners can be transferred at any time, and their personal items can be confiscated—with or without notification.

> I have never arranged the cell in a particular way. Because, I had to change cells six times … no: one, two, three, four, five … eight times in the course of 18 years. Of which two times were voluntary and six times the officers just packed my stuff … and so a whole range of books, my private duvet, pillow, stereo, they lost it all somewhere. And the worst is, I have complained and asked: when do you bring the second pallet with all my stuff?, and they said: you never had one (laughs). (Jonathan, 2.5.2016)

From my observation, in all three prisons, long-term prisoners generally have more objects in their cells compared to short-term prisoners. This is mainly the result of the informal loosening of the rules in the case of this particular prison population, based on the recognition that these prisoners may stay behind bars forever.

> [B]ut [concerning furnishing] we also negotiate, especially with these prisoners. I think exceptions are something dangerous, I think you can only allow exceptions when you can justify them […] But people like Clément, or Paul, who are here for a very long time, they may have a little bit more compared to the others. But this can be justified, we can say: he will stay for a longer period of time, or, you know, maybe he will never come out again. (Prison management member E., 7.7.2016)

> We [in the unit for ill and elderly prisoners] do not strictly apply the rules of order and [owing] things, so they can have relatively a lot in their cells actually, order and buy things. We simply have to be aware that many of them are there for a lifetime, it's not the same as someone who's in for two years or so. And indefinite incarceration is in the strict sense no longer a punishment, which is also something that you have to consider a little bit sometimes. (Prison officer H., 12.11.2013)

However, from the prison and security officers' point of view, there can also be 'too many objects' in a cell. 'Too many' refers both to the number of objects in general and the number of similar items (e.g. several bottles of shower gel or olive oil), but also to objects that have lost their initial function (parts of an old computer, a broken lamp). Cells with too many objects are often described as 'messy'. While this can refer to a lack of tidiness (as further described below), so-called 'messy cells' also complicate cell searches.

From the perspective of some prisoners, the management's individual-based handling of furnishing rules and the granting of additional personal objects is considered 'very vague'. 'One has got it [a particular object], the other doesn't; from another one it has been taken away […] this is also something that stresses me out' (Leo, 23.3.2016). At the same time, however, this also provides prisoners with room for negotiation (see Sect. 4.4.2).

4.3.1.2 The Obligation to Keep It 'Tidy and Clean'

In addition to the instructions regarding cell furnishings, there are several internal rules regarding the maintenance of the cell: 'The cell and its furnishing must be tidy and clean, and clearly arranged at all times. It should be lit by daylight' (JVA Lenzburg, 2012, p. 22, my translation). According to the Oxford Dictionaries, 'tidiness' refers to 'the state or quality of being arranged neatly and in order' (Oxford Dictionaries, 2018c). A lack of cleanliness indicates the presence of 'dirt', defined by the same source as '[a] substance, such as mud or dust, that soils someone or something' (Oxford Dictionaries, 2018a). However, as emphasized by Douglas, 'there is no such thing as absolute dirt: it exists in the eye of the beholder' (1966, p. 2). In prison, the order and tidiness of the cell is part of a regular assessment by prison officers or, depending on the prison, security officers, who are thus endowed with the power of definition.

During fieldwork, I noticed that some officers clearly distinguish between tidiness and cleanliness and define the latter as a reason to intervene:

> In the prison officers' office, we [a prison officer and I] were having a chat about the cell and the way he controls it. He told me that years ago he used to be much stricter, for example when someone hadn't made the bed. But now he thinks that those who haven't done it probably wouldn't do it either in the outside world. So he thinks that it should be as close to the outside world as possible. That's why he only makes a remark when the cell is 'really dirty'. Otherwise, he said that he 'doesn't care' about it. (Fieldnotes, 6.4.2016)

Others, however, intercede if, from their point of view, the cell is not tidy enough:

> [One of the prison officers] came back from cell inspection. In the office, he reported to his colleagues that the cell of [one of the prisoners] was 'messy'. Apparently, various bags were 'just standing around'. The staff was wondering whether he [the prisoner in question] was just too busy at his new job and therefore didn't care about the order in his cell or if he would tidy up later in the evening. The next day, it turned out that

> he had prepared these bags for an upcoming visit in a couple of days. One of the prison officers told him to store the bags in the cupboard. (Fieldnotes, 13.4.2016)

For others, tidiness and cleanliness go hand in hand, and both have to be judged:

> This morning, I accompanied two prison officers on their assignment to inspect some of the cells while the prisoners [those who are able] were at work. We began on the second floor, moving from cell to cell. Whenever a cell was in perfect order, they called it 'military'. According to [the first prison officer] this was 'especially the case with the Muslims'. [The second prison officer] said that 'especially the paedophiles' were, in contrast, 'extremely grubby'. As we came closer to the cell of [a prisoner] who is considered to have 'very strong' body odour, the two [officers] started to express disgust by making a wry face. Indeed, I could recognize a strong smell once they opened the cell door. While [the second prison officer] stepped back, [the first prison officer] went in with quick steps, pinching his nose with his fingers. He walked straight to the window and opened it. As they told me the day before, they had instructed the prisoner several times to open the window every morning, but he doesn't seem to follow the rule. [The second prison officer] started to swear while walking to the prisoners' dining room [located on the same floor] to open another window. A draught flowed through the floor, and the cell door banged loudly. The two officers continued on their way to the next cell, loudly swearing and complaining. One of the elderly prisoners came across and mumbled that there was no need to check his cell, another officer already did so earlier and 'anyway' he said, he was 'allergic' to this. We continued on our way. (Fieldnotes, 7.4.2016)

As this last example illustrates, officers' judgements of the prisoners' maintenance of their cells may range from 'extremely grubby' to 'military'—both being far beyond 'normal'. Obviously, such a perspective makes it almost impossible for prisoners to meet prison officers' demands. The discussion of a prisoner's body odour points to what I propose calling *invisible dirt*. Although it was a unique event during my fieldwork (and should probably also be interpreted as a performance by the prison officers that was influenced by my presence), the prisoners' body odours were discussed on a regular basis. As 'bad' body odour may be a sign of self-neglect or even point to illness, it makes sense from an institutional point of view to pay attention to it. In the incident recounted above, as far as I was informed, the prisoner in question was in good health and took care of his personal hygiene. His body odour, however, became a major issue for some prison officers, and they expressed discomfort whenever they had to interact with him or enter his cell. The prisoner's smell simply 'occupied' too much space. According to Pink (2009), who refers to Largey and Watson 2006 [1972]), body odours have communicative functions and can be seen as a form of 'impression management' through which individuals generally try to 'avoid moral stigmatization' by presenting an approved or appropriate 'olfactory identity' (Largey & Watson, 2006 [1972], p. 35). In a society where bodily odours and secretions in general are defined as a major cause of the 'disgust emotion' (Curtis & Biran, 2001, p. 21), the prisoner's decision—conscious or not—not to aerate his cell in order to reduce the negative effects of his body odour on the prison officers 'offends against the order' (Douglas, 1966, p. 2). Were it a conscious act, the prisoner's decision to expose prison staff to his body odour knowing that this provoked emotions of disgust could be interpreted as an 'everyday form of resistance' (Scott, 1986).

In line with Douglas' (1966) argument that 'absolute dirt' does not exist, these two examples show that whether a cell is kept 'tidy and clean' is always the result of a subjective assessment, shaped by the officers' views and stereotypes regarding certain offenders (e.g. the 'grubby paedophiles') and their ways of exerting authority (e.g. to make a remark only when the cell is 'really dirty'). In prison, however, these assessments have powerful consequences. They lead to notes in the prisoner's record—'cell order: sufficient. The cell is overloaded and chaotic' (Extract from a prisoner's record, my translation)—and immediate sanctions if it is decided that the cell order does not follow the rules.

The prisoners' experience of being in the cell is further shaped by the prison's internal rules regarding furnishing and maintaining the cell, which is the topic of the next section.

4.3.2 Arranging the Cell

As shown above, the furnishing and maintenance of a cell are highly constrained by the prison's accommodation regime. Internal rules and prison and security officers' practices restrict the number, type and arrangement of objects in the cell and define the degree of order and tidiness. However, the prisoners' ways of inhabiting the cell are never fully determined by the prison. As I show in the following, prisoners use, appropriate and (re)arrange the institutional spatio-temporal order that defines the prison cell through individual practices and thereby ascribe new meanings and values to the prison cell to create personal and intimate spaces.

4.3.2.1 Transforming the Cell into 'a Home'

During my fieldwork, I visited the cells of some of the prisoners with whom I had established closer connections. It began with an invitation from Clément, who was eager to show me his cell:

> In the afternoon, I went to Clément's cell. He welcomed me by saying: 'Welcome to my three-room-apartment, reduced to one room'. He smiled. His 'apartment' indeed looked quite cosy and is well furnished: there are two carpets on the floor, a TV, a stereo system, a computer, a wall clock, pictures on the wall, cooking utensils, and a lot of spices. We stepped in a little bit, and he explained to me how he arranged the three 'rooms' or areas (the cooking area, the wash corner, and the living area) and talked about his strategies in order to make the best out of this limited and highly controlled place: 'You have to use space to a maximum'. (Fieldnotes, 8.2.2016)

As this example suggests, the rigid accommodation regime installed by the prison does not prevent prisoners from transforming their cells into something else, for instance, as some said, into a 'home'. This arrangement can be carried out through a wide range of techniques: (1) narratives, (2) the arrangement and use of objects, (3) the application of domestic patterns of movement and activities and (4) the use of the senses.

Regarding prisoners' narratives about the cell, many explicitly refer to their cell as their 'home' or 'room'. 'I don't say cell, I say: This is my room, my studio (laughs)' (Darko, 6.5.2016). Also, they use the verb 'to live' (*leben/wohnen*) regarding their cell, which in German means far more than simply existing.

> Today was a busy day. In addition to the new face [a newly arrived prisoner] in the unit, the distribution of the two-week 'city purchase' had to be accomplished. At some point it became quite hectic, and suddenly one of the prisoners came out of his cell and complained, saying that 'now it's too loud and too turbulent for me', and, after all, he was the one who 'lives here' and that we were here in 'his house'. [One of the prison officers] and I looked at each other in amazement and then, after some seconds, [the prison officer] replied: 'Yes, that's true'. Without saying anything more, the prisoner then returned back to his cell and closed the door behind him. (Fieldnotes, 16.5.2013)

Narratives of the cell as a home might reflect what Tuan (2001 [1977], p. 32) considers a basic human need: the need to 'anchor' one's personality to objects and places. According to the author, 'all human beings appear to have personal belongings and perhaps all have the need of personal place, whether this be a particular chair in a room or a particular corner in a moving carriage' (Tuan, 2001 [1977], p. 32). For Tuan (2001 [1977], p. 144), a home involves emotions; it is an 'intimate place', a place where people feel a sense of attachment and rootedness, where they feel safe and cared for. Home is also related to familiarity. Through 'routine activity' people transform an 'unknown space' into a 'familiar place' (Tuan, 2001 [1977], p. 73). This also echoes Toch's idea of 'niches' in prison, which he defines as 'settings that provide a sense of belonging and of familiarity' (1996 [1977], p. 240).

These two aspects, the feelings of belonging (and linked to this the feeling of relief and security) and familiarity, also came out in the prisoners' narratives. Many prisoners said that the cell had become their 'favourite place' in prison because they could find peace and quiet there. The expression 'to have got used/accustomed to' was also used frequently during interviews. For instance, Jonathan explained: '[M]eanwhile, [the cell] is the place where I feel comfortable, where I can rest and find peace and quiet' (Jonathan, 2.5.2016). The statement that 'one gets used to it over time' was often followed by the expression that 'this is home now': 'I got used to it, I know everything now [how the prison functions] [...] I feel at home now, so to speak' (Erwin, 19.10.2017). By focusing on the narratives of the cell using Tuan's (2001 [1977) perspective, the transformation of the cell into a home appears to be the result of an almost 'natural' process, based on the very basic human need to belong somewhere, combined with a process of familiarization.

Leder (2004) sees a more active intention behind the transformation of the cell into a home, interpreting it as a 'reclamation of space' in order to 'humanize' the prison. 'If spatiality has become constricted, ruptured, disoriented, even reversed, [there are prisoners who] will do what is possible to reverse the reversals. [They] will make of [their] cell a home' (Leder, 2004, p. 58), not only through narratives, but also through furnishing. Indeed, in addition to the narrative of the cell as a home, the prisoners I talked to also made use of the spatial and material elements in the cell in order to transform it into a home (as illustrated in Figs. 4.4, 4.5, 4.6, and 4.7).

Even though the possibilities are limited, through the (re)arrangement and usage of particular objects they create what they consider a 'cosy ambiance'. They typically put carpets on the floor, buy plants, maybe keep birds (the only animal that is allowed in prison) and hang photos and posters on the wall.

> I want to furnish it so it doesn't look like a cell anymore, but rather a space where one sees that there is someone living in there: there lives a person, a human being, someone who also feels comfortable. So, I want to put a carpet, plants ... things like that. (Leo, 23.3.2016)

Leo's statement echoes Ugelvik, who defines the transformation of the cell into a home as a 'freedom-creating-action', whereby prisoners challenge their institutionally ascribed status and 'mak[e] themselves into something other than a prisoner' (2014, pp. 73–75). The personalization of the cell, especially through decoration, is also described as an effort to

Fig. 4.4 A homely furnished prison cell (*Source* Photo by Andreas Moser)

create 'the illusion of ownership, the feeling of private life' (Moran, 2013, cited in Ugelvik, 2014, p. 118), an attempt to express 'personal identity' and a way to 'manoeuvre within the space of the other' (Baer, 2005, p. 215). In a similar manner, Martel (2006, p. 602) describes keeping personal objects in the cell as a way to maintain 'a connection to one's past history' and to remember 'the self and its relation to others'.

I argue that by transforming the cell into a home through narratives, furnishings and decorations, prisoners not only personalize the space with the aim to 'humanize' the prison (Leder, 2004) and 'to leave their

Fig. 4.5 Plants in a prisoner's cell (*Source* Photo by a prisoner)

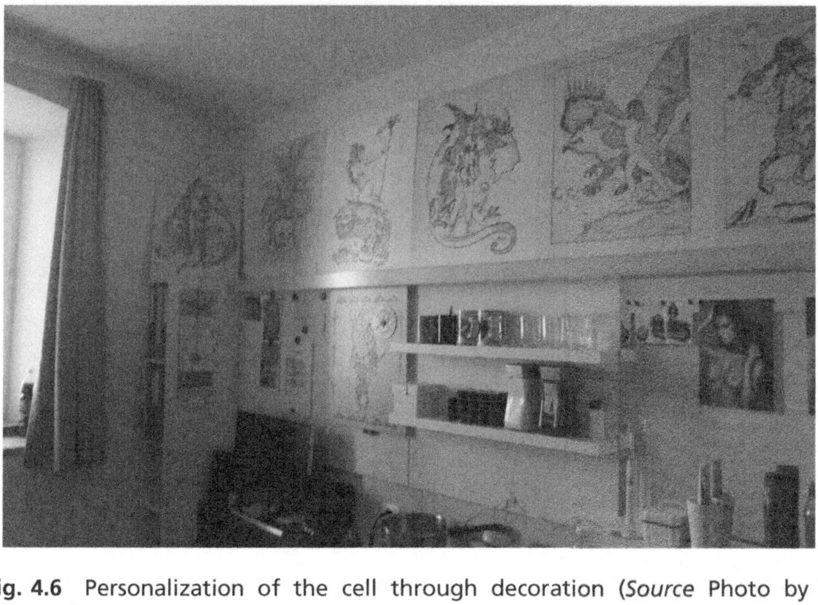

Fig. 4.6 Personalization of the cell through decoration (*Source* Photo by a prisoner)

Fig. 4.7 A prisoner's 'kitchen' (*Source* Photo by a prisoner)

Fig. 4.8 The computer: For many prisoners the most important tool for distraction (*Source* Photo by Irene Marti)

marks on the prison landscape' (Baer, 2005, p. 210), but also to manipulate their 'sense of size and spaciousness' (Tuan, 2001 [1977], p. 54). In addition to the acquisition and arrangement of objects, when furniture is not fixed, prisoners usually move it (within the frame of possibilities); for instance, David did so to create 'more space' and a friendlier ambiance:

> Yes, I moved the desk a little further down, closer to the window … and the cupboard, I pushed it closer to the bed, so, like this I have more space up there. Because the mates [fellow prisoners], when they come into my cell, they mostly sit on the bed, one on the chair, so if another one wants to join us then he has to bring his own chair or sit on the floor. So, it's practical to have a bit more space up there. (David, 2.5.2016)

By pushing the bed away from the corner, Darko created what he calls a 'resting oasis':

> So, my bed is not right there in the corner, I pushed it forward a little bit. So it is like an island, a resting oasis. If it were still there in the corner, it would be … so like dismissed, like: Go to the corner, that's where you belong! (Darko, 6.5.2016)

Through a particular arrangement of furniture and objects, Kurt transformed 'his room' in such a way that he sometimes even forgets that he is actually in prison:

> I have birds, which I got from a mate. […] And I bought plants, and on the floor I have put a carpet. And on the walls I hung a few pictures, and my flag, my country flag. Sometimes, when I come into my room, I don't know whether this is my house or prison (laughs). There is no difference at the moment, because I've been here for ten years, it feels like I was born here (laughs). (Kurt, 3.5.2016)

The creation of a homely ambiance can also be something temporary, by 'misusing' prison furniture and objects to transform them (temporarily) into something else. Very common is the dismounting of the cupboard door to create a table, big enough for four prisoners to enjoy a meal together. More of an exception is the story of a prisoner who told me that he transformed an object he (illicitly) 'borrowed' from his workplace into a grill to enjoy a barbecue with fellow prisoners (Fieldnotes, 22.3.2016).

As these last two examples suggest, the transformation of the cell into a home takes place through domestic patterns of movement and activities (see also Ugelvik, 2014, p. 118). One of the elderly prisoners told me that he lives 'like a family life' with two younger fellow prisoners, whom he has 'practically adopted' (Fieldnotes, 8.2.2016). They used to visit him in his cell, to lie on his bed and relax, watch a movie or listen to music together. These activities (watching TV together) and positions (lying down) emphasize 'comfort and domestic laziness' (Ugelvik, 2014, p. 118). Also, as he told me, he often cooks for them, usually once a week, after their sports lesson.[5] Sometimes he cooks everything by himself, but usually he uses the leftovers he keeps from prison meals, out of which he prepares 'a new meal' (Fieldnotes, 8.2.2016). Another prisoner told me how he and his 'best friend' in prison celebrated Christmas together by sharing a bottle of wine in his cell that they had illicitly bought from a fellow prisoner (Fieldnotes, 23.2.2016).

Prisoners in all the prisons I visited have permission to meet in the evening. In the *Strafanstalt*, prisoners are not only able to socialize during the evening (on a more spontaneous basis), but also in the context of so-called 'cell visits' during the weekends, which have to be organized and granted in advance. During these get-togethers, they usually cook and eat together, play games, have a chat or watch a movie, with the principle aims of creating a 'cosy' (Hugo, 23.3.2016) atmosphere and experiencing moments of 'peace' (Clément, 24.3.2016) and 'normality' (Louis, 22.3.2016). By engaging in domestic patterns of movement and activity, they make themselves *feel* at home. Although temporary (at least in prison), according to Tuan, human encounters are essential in the experience of home, because often 'the value of place [is] borrowed from the intimacy of a particular human relationship; place itself offer[s]

[5] Cooking is only possible for prisoners in the *60plus* unit that is equipped with a common kitchen, or in the *Strafanstalt*, where prisoners may have gas cookers in their cells. However, I also met prisoners who 'cook', or rather warm up food, such as sausages or a soup, with the steam that can be generated with a coffee machine.

little outside the human bond' (2001 [1977], p. 140). He argues that although for most people possessions and ideas are important, 'other human beings remain the focus of value and the source of meaning' (Tuan, 2001 [1977], pp. 138–139).

Finally, I claim that the transformation of the cell into a home also takes place through a particular use of the senses. As noted elsewhere, there are many prisoners who ignore or do not see the bars in front of the windows anymore. David uses a particular smell to create a homely ambiance, which at the same time provides a way to maintain memories of his past (and his previous home), invisible to others:

> From time to time I offer myself the luxury of buying a small bottle of eucalyptus oil from the medical service to put a few drops on my pillow. I tell them that this helps me to breathe better, but actually the reason is a sentimental one. [...] My wife used to put eucalyptus leaves in her pillow. [...] It smelled really good. (David, 2.5.2016)

Lastly, through music—for instance by playing the guitar or listening to their favourite music—prisoners transform the cell into a place where they can be immersed in their 'own world' (Leo, 23.3.2016) and transcend the prison context.

As I have shown in this section, prisoners' ways of transforming the cell into a home (as one way of inhabiting a cell) can be regarded as a 'natural' process linked to familiarization with the environment (see also Tuan, 2001 [1977]) and getting used to prison. It can also be defined as an attempt to express individuality and put a personal stamp on the prison landscape (Baer, 2005) or to challenge one's prisoner status (Ugelvik, 2014). I argue that transforming the cell into a home is also strongly rooted in the prisoners' intention to make the best of the situation and not to worry too much about their (uncertain) future. While showing me his cell, Erwin first of all pointed to his newly purchased coffee machine, his plants and the pictures he put on the wall and explained to me: 'This is where I live [...] and since I have to be in prison, I at least want to have it as nice as possible' (Erwin, 18.10.2017).

Markus made a similar argument. When I asked him whether the cell is a place he feels comfortable, he responded:

> Comfortable? Well … I feel good in this place, as far as you can say, because it is *my* place, it's my home. Of course, it is a prison cell, but since I haven't a home outside anymore and will never have one again, I got used to it. It's not a resignation, it's more … not an adaptation, you come to terms with it somehow: it's somehow a pragmatic decision to take that as your home. And it doesn't bother me. It's been a long time since I've been bothered by other people who came to close and lock the door. This doesn't bother me anymore. I don't even notice it anymore. (Markus, 28.8.2017)

As put forward by Crewe (2016), this is a typical pattern for long-term prisoners who have moved beyond the early sentence phase. The authors define it as a way of coping to make the problems of imprisonment more manageable over time: to accept the situation and use it in a positive way. As they argue, long-term prisoners who are further along in their sentences no longer experience the present as a form of stasis, because life is no longer considered 'on hold' (in the past, or being lived elsewhere); they now consider the prison their 'home' and 'the only place where life could meaningfully be led' (Crewe et al., 2016, p. 10). Similarly, I argue that transforming the cell into a home is also about 'normalising' incarceration and transforming it into 'a frame of action' (see Vigh, 2008, p. 11). It enables prisoners to feel comfortable and to go about their lives. However, as mentioned in Sect. 2.3.1, some prisoners told me that this requires giving up hope, letting go of their pre-prison selves and cutting their bonds to the outside world as it is too painful emotionally to live in two different worlds.

As I illustrate in the following, in contrast to prisoners who transform the cell into a home, I met prisoners who said that they would 'never' want a cell to be their home.

4.3.2.2 The Cell as 'a Place to Be, but not to Live'

Lars was one of the prisoners with whom I had frequent contact during my fieldwork. I spent several days with him and even helped him at work. At the end of our collaboration, I asked him if I might visit his cell, to which he agreed. We arranged an appointment for the following day:

> In the afternoon, after the prisoners' work hours had ended, I was waiting at the [security] pavilion [in the centre of the prison], until all the prisoners were locked in their cells. I then searched for a security officer who was willing to escort me to Lars. Once we arrived at his cell, the officer knocked at the door and, after a few seconds, opened it. Lars came to the doorstep and welcomed me. The officer offered to remain close to me, but I explained to him that there was no need for that and that I would not close the door completely. The officer agreed, I *stepped* in, and the officer pulled back the door – almost completely. So, here I was. I was surprised: the cell was almost empty! This was not at all what I expected, especially because Lars is one of the prisoners who will probably have to stay in prison for the rest of his life. I noted that he didn't wear shoes and I apologized for wearing shoes myself and asked if I should take them off. He said no. I felt a bit lost and uncertain facing this empty cell: no cooking utensils, no pictures, no decoration at all, except the flag of his home canton above his bed, which he had mentioned several times during our collaboration. He remained silent, kept looking at me, and I felt the need to start a conversation. I started to comment on what I saw. First the flag: I said that I had imagined it to be on the ceiling. He explained to me that he would love that, but it was not allowed by the management. I then went to the window and asked: 'What kind of view do you have?' and he replied: 'None, there's just the courtyard'. I then mentioned that he had hardly any private materials, like pictures. He then took a photo album out of the cupboard and showed me some pictures of his family. I wanted to know if he didn't request a bigger cell [long-term prisoners do have this option] to which he replied: 'No, I am anyway hardly inside. Just for sleeping. And besides that, with a bigger cell one has much more to do [a reference to cleaning]'. We then had a chat about my project and soon after we said good-bye by shaking hands. I thanked him for showing me his cell and stepped outside. At his workplace the following day, Lars explained to me that he doesn't intend to furnish the cell in a 'too cosy way'. Also, he doesn't want to put photos of his family on the wall because he wants to 'protect them'. To him, to settle in means 'to accept' his situation and this would mean 'giving up on himself'. (Fieldnotes, 17.2.2016)

Facing a 'cell' and not a 'home', as in the case of Clément discussed in the previous section, was a confusing experience for me, and I felt irritated standing inside the empty cell. In reaction, however, I tried to behave according to commonly accepted social rules or norms for guests (e.g. asking about taking off my shoes, enquiring about the view) in order to establish 'normality' (see Garfinkel, 1973). Through his reaction (and later his explanations), Lars made it clear to me that the cell is a place where he does not want to belong. He did not decorate the cell in a personal way (with the exception of the flag), and he described it simply as a place he uses for sleeping, a place without any view. At first glance, he also did not act like a typical 'host' (he did not care whether or not I took off my shoes and did not start a conversation), until he showed me pictures of his family members.

Like many other, Lars uses the narrative of the cell as *a place to be, but not to live* (see also Leder, 2004, p. 58). These prisoners' ways of inhabiting a cell are based on their refusal to create a home for themselves in prison, which for them would basically mean to create a 'cosy' ambiance. For them, to feel comfortable in prison is equivalent to accepting their incarceration and giving up hope (see also Crewe 2009, p. 442; Milhaud, 2009, p. 291). In this regard, Rolf mentioned that '[i]t's important for me that I never get used to my cell, and never to incarceration. I don't want that. I must avoid it. Otherwise, I will perish. It would mean abandoning freedom' (Rolf, 6.5.2016). Anton told me that 'it makes my hair stand on end when someone starts to talk about his cell by calling it 'my room' [...] for me it's just a cell. [...] It's a place to be, but not to live' (Anton, 24.3.2016). In contrast to Leder (2004, p. 58), who labels this attitude a 'strategy of escape', emphasizing that prisoners who do not want to feel at home in prison consider their 'true home' to be in the outside world, 'albeit one from which they are temporarily exiled', most of the prisoners I met who shared this attitude did not mention a home outside. Perhaps this is because most of them have lost contact with their families and friends, and many of the places they used to know have disappeared. Everything has changed outside over the years. However, some prisoners talked about their dreams of establishing a new life abroad, of creating a new home. This is in line with Cohen and Taylor (1972, p. 93), who state that for long-term prisoners 'the future in prison is unthinkable', and thus they rely upon 'ideas about a future life outside to sustain themselves through their temporally undifferentiated days'. However, for the prisoners I spoke to, the future is nearly unthinkable in the outside world, too. They fear that (in the case of their release) they will be too old to be integrated into the job market in Switzerland, and that the pension they would be granted would not be sufficient to live a decent life. Their ideas about the future consist, therefore, less of concrete plans and more of dreams and visions:

> A mate of mine whom I met here and who is now in another prison [...] we still stay in touch, we call each other, once or twice a month, when he is on holiday [temporary release]. And once he is outside, he will go to Brazil: he has a house there. And should I ever get the chance to get out again, I could go to Brazil too, that's already fixed. Here in Switzerland, I will anyway no longer have any chance. (Hugo, 25.6.2013)

> I met Marco in front of the prison officers' office; he asked me if I had time for a conversation. I agreed and we went outside to sit in the sun, at the table at the back of the garden. He told me about his prospects. If he is able to get Art. 59 or 63,[6] then he would be out even faster. For him, an 'intermediate step' would be quite ok. He also told me that he had been doing therapy again for some time now. I asked about his future plans. He wants to work in the IT business, to support customers independently, to repair PCs, about which he understands something. He would like to travel, perhaps emigrate to Belize. He gets a disability pension, on which he thinks he could live quite well. He would like to open an Internet cafe that would eventually operate without him. (Fieldnotes, 4.4.2016)

Even though the future is difficult to imagine, the majority of the prisoners who share the attitude that the prison will never be a home for them are still 'fighting' against their situation and hoping for their release. They say that fighting is something that keeps them alive; it is a way to resist. Therefore, they concentrate heavily on the future (although primarily on the near future) and, as seen in Sect. 2.3.1, are constantly waiting for something that may happen—a letter or visit from their lawyer or competent authority, an appointment at the court or a transfer to a more open prison. However, because of their strong desire

[6] Art. 63 SCC is an out-patient measure that may be ordered if the offender is suffering from a serious mental disorder or if he is dependent on addictive substances.

for change and their intense orientation towards the (uncertain) future, these prisoners are constantly suffering from 'pains of uncertainty and indeterminacy' (Crewe, 2011a) and have difficulty giving meaning to their present lives in prison.

In contrast to prisoners who want to transform their cell into a home, these prisoners do not *call* their cell a home, as they do not want to *feel* at home. In material terms, they also do not want to *arrange* their cells in a homelike fashion: they want the cell to remain a cell.[7] Most of these prisoners' cells therefore contain few objects and personal items. This echoes Leder's argument that prisoners do not want to create a home for themselves in prison; rather, they want to 'refuse to become complicit with it' and 'orient to the outside world' (2004, p. 58):

> My cell is functionally furnished. *I have everything I need … and it's clean. But I didn't put posters on the wall or things like that; I don't want to furnish it like an apartment that suits my personal taste. I keep telling myself: this is not mine.* (Heinz, 3.5.2016)

Just like Heinz, Anton emphasized that he had arranged his cell in a purely functionally manner: 'It [the cell] is expediently [*zweckdienlich*] furnished: a computer, a printer, books, envelopes, paper, CDs, a stereo system. But otherwise, nothing else' (Anton, 24.3.2016). However, there are also prisoners who want to create a home while keeping it 'functionally furnished'. In this case, it is more a matter of personal taste—'I don't have any plants. I'm not that much of a plant person' (Marco, 4.5.2016)—or because it is thought that too many objects make the room feel smaller.

Nevertheless, those prisoners who disassociate themselves from the prison through their narratives and ways of arranging their cells also

[7] Here it is important to note that the significance the individual prisoner attributes to the cell (such as calling it a 'home' or, in contrast, just 'a place where they have to be') can change over time and according to the situation see also Lussault and Stock (2010, p. 17). For instance, during our first meeting that took place within the scope of a formal interview in March 2016, Markus vehemently expressed the position that he would never call his cell a home. In August 2017, after we had had several more meetings and informal discussions, during the walking interview I conducted with him, he first showed me his cell, which he explicitly called 'my home' (Markus, 28.8.2017).

express feelings of belonging and attachment. This became apparent, for instance, when they were describing to me their feelings after they realized that their cells had just been searched—'like after a burglary' (Anton, 24.3.2016).

> I always think: They have been here again. I realize that they have searched the cell and think: They have been here again. Wednesday and Friday I clean the cell, the floor and everything, and then I can see footprints on the floor. That's how I notice that they have been in my cell. (Jonathan, 2.5.2016)

Ugelvik (2014) claims that the feeling of 'space belonging to me is [a] practical question [...] a room becomes *my* room by me taking residence in it' (Ugelvik, 2014, p. 117). Taking up residence in a room or a house is connected to the arrangement of things based on personal needs (and tastes). Therefore, it also always 'reflects those who live there, their perceptions, habits and practices' (Ugelvik, 2014, p. 117). Indeed, even though some prisoners may decide not to arrange their cells in a cosy way and do not want to feel a sense of belonging, they do store and arrange the personal objects that they keep in their cells in a way that suits them best. Perhaps they only have the basic items handed out by the prison, such as plates, cutlery and cups, a toothbrush, toothpaste, soap, a towel, clothes and shoes. But they might also have some more 'private' ones: a postcard from a friend, photographs of family members (though kept hidden from others) or a note that confirms their next visit.

I argue that the feeling of attachment may also be a result of the fact that the cell is the place where they can be alone and pass unobserved time, where they sleep, have sex, get dressed, use the toilet (see also Ugelvik, 2014, p. 121)—all activities that are (at least in so-called Western societies) considered 'intimate' and 'private' and not performed in public (Hall 1982). The cell is also the place in prison where they are 'not on show' (Ugelvik ,2014, p. 123): where they can freely express the emotions they usually try to control or hide from staff or fellow prisoners. Hence, independently of whether or not the prisoners intend to transform the cell into a home, the cell constitutes (to some degree) a personal and private territory, which, in one way or another, prisoners try to defend.

4.4 Personal Spaces, Privacy and Intimacy

The lack of privacy can be considered a central aspect of the 'pains of imprisonment' (Sykes, 1971 [1958]). However, the cell is nevertheless a place (if not the only one) where prisoners find (at least some degree of) privacy (see e.g. Cohen & Taylor, 1972; Goffman, 1961; Milhaud, 2009; Toch, 1996 [1977]).

Ugelvik (2014) explores the notion of privacy in prison with a special focus on activities and within the frame of the public/private dichotomy. As he notes, the cell is the place where prisoners 'eat, work on homework or studies, sleep, watch TV, lie and think, receive guests, go to the toilet and have sex (with themselves)' (Ugelvik, 2014, p. 121). It therefore functions as a kitchen, a dining room, a living room, a bedroom, a toilet and a home office. Thus, in contrast to common areas such as the wing, the courtyard or the workplace, the cell can be considered a 'private' and 'intimate sphere' (Ugelvik, 2014, p. 121), which is commonly—as I argue, at least in Western societies (see also Mallett, 2004)—associated with the notion of 'home'. However, Ugelvik emphasizes that while in the outside world the home consists of more or less private places—with the bedroom considered to be the most private, the dining room the most public—in prison, 'prisoners simultaneously invite guests into the bathroom, living room and bedroom' (Ugelvik, 2014, p. 121). And, in contrast to the outside world, prisoners do not have the ability to entirely control the entry of others. While it is possible to refuse or grant access to fellow prisoners, prison staff have the right to enter at any time without warning. The common order of 'public' and 'private' is therefore challenged in the prison context. The author nevertheless concludes that behind their closed cell doors, the prisoners can, at least to some extent, relax and experience private life (Ugelvik, 2014, p. 123).

For Moran (2013), a sociological conceptualization of privacy associated with the familial and domestic space is problematic in prison, because prisoners are by definition detached from home and family.

Also, there might be institutions where prisoners are accommodated in dormitories (Moran et al., 2013) or share a cell (Jewkes, 2005). Following Bailey (2000), Moran et al. (2013) suggest conceptualizing 'privacy' as mainly composed of two interrelated dimensions: 'intimacy', which locates privacy in emotional closeness between individuals (e.g. close friends), and 'the self' (i.e. the conscious, reflective and reflexive self), combined with Goffman's (1959) notions of 'frontstage' (where individuals present themselves in front of an audience) and 'backstage' (where the performer can relax, free from the expectations and norms that shape frontstage behaviour). The authors thus propose a notion of privacy that is not explicitly related to any particular space (Moran et al., 2013, p. 140). Based on their study of a women's prison in Russia, they demonstrate that while there is no objective space for privacy, prisoners construct it through a wide range of tactics—for instance, in the form of close and intimate relations with fellow prisoners, which allow them to express their 'backstage' self (Moran et al., 2013, p. 143).[8] Privacy can also be established through 'the self' in moments of spatial isolation, for instance by finding and temporarily seeking quiet places with fewer people (such as the TV room where 'no one will bother you'), by demonstrating compliance that is rewarded with privileges (e.g. a job, such as housekeeping, that grants prisoners more responsibilities and moments to be alone) or by offending in order to temporarily be transferred to solitary confinement (Moran et al., 2013, pp. 143–144). Prisoners they talked to also mentioned tactics they employ to disengage mentally as well as physically from the crowds around them, for example by working, preferably in a noisy place where there is 'time to be alone, alone with your thoughts' (Moran et al., 2013, p. 144).

Like Moran, Pallot and Piacentini's study, Cohen and Taylor's (1972) exploration of privacy in a maximum-security wing at a British prison is based on a typology that delineates different dimensions of privacy. Following Westin's (1970) definition, the authors conceptualize privacy as consisting of four basic states: 'solitude', 'intimacy', 'anonymity' and

[8] Yet, from their point of view, in the low-trust environment of the prison, such relations are rather exceptional, and relations between prisoners are more often of an 'instrumental' nature. However, according to Moran et al. (2013, p. 143), the lack of evidence also results from the study's limitations in carrying out research on these issues.

'reserve' (Cohen & Taylor, 1972, pp. 78–85). Their results generally show a 'complete lack of privacy' (Cohen & Taylor 1972, p. 78). First, due to the so-called 'Judas holes' in the cell doors and wide ranging electronic surveillance (electronic devices under the floors of the cells that allow for the monitoring of movement and CCTV in all areas of the wing), it is never possible to experience 'solitude' (i.e. 'being alone and unobserved by others') or 'free places' in the sense of Goffman (1961), in the prison wing where they conducted research. Furthermore, according to Westin's definition, experiencing 'intimacy' between two or more people in order to achieve 'maximum personal affinity' requires not only freedom from the presence of others but also from distracting noises. Again, this is 'never' possible for the prisoners in the particular wing studied by Cohen and Taylor. Third, while 'anonymity' (i.e. 'freedom from identification and observation in public spaces' [Cohen & Taylor, 1972]), which allows individuals to relax, might be available to some degree in large prisons, it is not possible to achieve in this particular wing. Cohen and Taylor (1972, p. 181) even point out a dual lack of anonymity: 'they are open to being approached and addressed by anyone in the wing, [and] their identities are public knowledge and therefore anything they do and say can be transformed into a story'. Finally, to 'reserve' means not to reveal certain personal or shameful aspects of oneself (see also Toch, 1996 [1977], p. 35). In this wing, however, the officers know the lives of the prisoners in detail, their mail is read and their conversations with visitors are overheard. Although the authors argue that the only place that provides prisoners with 'some private territory' is the cell (Cohen & Taylor, 1972, p. 80), they identified a 'lack of privacy of all kinds', which they concluded has 'serious consequences for the men' (Cohen & Taylor, 1972, p. 82).

I agree with Moran (2013) that the experience of privacy is not limited to the cell *per se* but can be created and experienced in various time–space constellations. In this section, I nevertheless propose to locate privacy in the cell. In contrast to the Russian example, in the prisons in which I undertook research, the prisoners are all held in single cells. As in Ugelvik's (2014) study, in contrast to common or 'public' areas such as the workplace or the courtyard, the cell is the place where prisoners can withdraw, where they can relax and spend some unobserved time ('solitude'). Unlike the conditions described by Cohen and Taylor (1972), none of the three prisons studied have cells equipped with electronic surveillance devices. In the *AGE*, there are also no cameras on the two floors where the cells are located. Although there is a door viewer in every cell door of the *Strafanstalt* and the *60plus*, as I observed, it is never or only rarely used, and as I was told by officers, the reason for this is precisely to grant the inmates more privacy. Also, as I describe in the following sections, the cell is the place where prisoners experience moments of closeness with fellow prisoners ('intimacy'). However, as in every prison, the prisoners cannot lock their cells from the inside, and prison staff are allowed to step in at any time of the day without warning.

While the prisoners I talked to generally agreed that 'real privacy' does not exist in prison, they nevertheless did not experience a 'complete lack of privacy' (Cohen & Taylor, 1972, p. 78), but could transform the cell into a 'private refuge' (Hugo, 7.9.2017) and experience 'peace and quiet' (Jonathan, 2.5.2016). While the above-mentioned studies argue that the degree of privacy in prison (or rather the lack of it) is mainly the result of structural factors, of 'the technique of regimentation and imperative of custody' (Moran et al., 2013, p. 139), I show in the following section that it is also greatly shaped by mundane staff behaviour, for instance when opening and entering a prisoner's cell. I then show that privacy—as a social construct (Hall, 1982)—does not mean the same thing for every prisoner, and that prisoners develop a wide range of techniques in order to create what they consider to be private and intimate spaces.

4.4.1 The Role of Prison Staff

As mentioned by all the prisoners, prison and security officers' behaviour has a major impact on the prisoners' experiences of the cell as a private place. For instance, as shown above in Sect. 4.2.2, officers can perform the ordinary practice of opening (and closing) cell doors in many different ways: they can simply open it (without any warning), or they can knock before doing so (see also Ugelvik, 2014, p. 122). In one of the prisons where I did not carry keys, I was once asked by a security officer to accompany him during his task of opening the cell doors in order to let the prisoners out for work. Even though I hesitated, he insisted that I open the doors myself because, as he said, 'locking and unlocking cell doors has an effect on you'. He explained further that in contrast to those officers who 'intentionally slam' the doors, he tries to do it in a 'gentle' way (Fieldnotes, 11.2.2016). Many of the staff members I met usually knocked, which was very much appreciated by prisoners. However, there are also different types of knocking: some use their hand, others their keys—which, of course, provoke different, more or less prison-like, sounds. Also, staff members can decide whether to acquiesce to the wishes of the prisoner in case he asks the officer to wait some minutes before opening the door, for instance because he is using the toilet or is about to get dressed.

When prison or security officers enter the cell in order to carry out a search—which usually takes place while the prisoners are at work—they can again be more or less careful, and more or less aware of the traces they may leave behind (in addition to the official report that has to be handed to the prisoner to inform him that his cell has been searched) and to the arrangement of objects and materials in general:

> I realize when it [his cell] was searched; I notice that things are put back differently. I have a specific order and now someone comes in who doesn't know that and disarranges everything. That's how I notice that they have searched, that they were searching for something. (Jonathan, 2.5.2016)

Furthermore, I was told by prisoners that during cell searches staff sometimes remove or destroy objects with or without informing the prisoner; however, this seems to happen rarely. The majority of the prisoners I talked to think that most officers search their cells in a decent way, respecting the prisoner's privacy:

> *Louis*: Sure, they do have the duty, when they control the cell then everything has to be searched. But here, it is actually humane. They try to, how can I say, that your privacy is …
>
> *Irene*: Respected?

> *L*: Respected. So yes, they do inspect it, but simply, yeah, with a certain respect. (Louis, 22.3.2016)

4.4.2 Controlling Access to Personal Territories

The nature and frequency of prison and security officers entering and searching the prisoners' cells can also be shaped by each prisoner's behaviour. By following the prison rules and through compliance with the regime, they may become 'inconspicuous', which, in their experience, can influence the intensity and frequency of cell searches or inspections and thereby strengthen the borders of their personal territory.

> The officers who search the cells, they don't know exactly what is granted or not, *one* small lamp more or less, they don't know that. But for some prisoners one more can already be enough [to be sanctioned]. But if you avoid making trouble all the time and shouting without any reason, this can have an influence on how the cell search is conducted. If you are a constant complainer and screamer … then a pair of scissors that is two millimetres too long, can be enough [to be sanctioned]. (Juris, 22.3.2016)

> As long as you have good conversations with the officers you can be a bit … they may not see certain things. (Kurt, 3.5.2016)

As already mentioned several times, during the day, and especially when the cells are unlocked, officers as well as prisoners can enter the cell at any moment. However, prisoners can gain a certain degree of control over who enters their cell and when. In order to control access for fellow prisoners, some prisoners have established codes among themselves, such as special knocks, and other informal rules, as Theo stated:

> You know when the cells are open, anyone can come in if he wants to. But I just tell myself: the cell is my private area. I let in whoever I want. […] This is structured. […] You know, they [the fellow inmates] know exactly that after dinner, from half past six to seven o'clock the door is closed. No one may knock. At seven the hole opens and then they may come in. I had to set up a regulation for myself so that I am comfortable. That I have a retreat. (Theo, 3.5.2016)

Another technique to increase the experience of privacy is the installation of an additional curtain. Even though it is prohibited (see Sect. 4.3.1), Clément and two fellow prisoners installed curtains, which they, as he explained, pull closed whenever they are using the toilet. I was at his place, in his cell, when the head of security noticed the curtain. He immediately reminded the prisoner of the rules and that an unobstructed view into the cell must be ensured at all times. Clément responded mischievously that he 'fully respect[s] the house rules except when [he is] sitting on the toilet'. The head of security did not agree; however, at that point, he did not tell him to remove it (Fieldnotes, 22.2.2016).

Private space is also linked to personal objects. These objects are usually protected from the view of others. Many prisoners told me that they avoid exposing personal objects, which for them are most often photos of family members, because they want to 'keep them out [of prison]' (Fieldnotes, 11.2.2016). Others mentioned that in order to protect their privacy, they have no personal objects at all in their cells:

> *Hugo*: Privacy is not given in here. You always have to expect that there are officers who think: I'm going to snoop around here [in the cell].
>
> *Irene*: And how do you deal with this?
>
> *H*: I don't have any very private things. Because I think this is my thing, that's no one else's business. (Hugo, 23.3.2016)

While I accompanied a security officer during a cell search, I realized that prisoners may also keep objects that do not fall into any of the above-mentioned categories (see Sect. 4.3.1), objects that, from the point of view of an outsider, are 'non-identifiable' and whose meaning and importance are only significant for the possessor:

> In the morning, I accompanied [one of the security officers] during cell searches. On our way he explained to me that years ago syringes were a big problem, later mobile phones. Today it's mainly about drugs. We stepped into one of the cells. He told me that he mistrusts the prisoner who stays in this cell because 'he always makes a friendly face … very strange'. He said that he would like to find some drugs and started to search. What he found were some empty cigarette and tobacco boxes, wondering

> why he [the prisoner] would keep them. In addition, there was a small glass full of screws, electrical parts, and many other similar items. [The security officer] frowned while examining it carefully. He then said that [the prisoner] probably 'found' this somewhere on the floor, considering the construction that goes on [in one of the wings], there is currently a lot around, and he probably 'collected' these things from the construction site. He added that if [the prisoner] had collected ten pieces of the same sort, then this would have been a 'theft', but not this way. (Fieldnotes, 3.2.2016)

4.4.3 Catching the Right Moment

Privacy is also about timing. As I was told by prisoners, at a certain point they more or less know the officers' routes and routines and at what times they are more likely to pass (or enter) their cells. Prisoners hence try to organize their intimate activities, such as using the toilet, according to their sense of the staff members' individual rhythms. However, the routines may vary from officer to officer (e.g. the route they choose for lock-up), so, as I was told by Leo (6.9.2017), it is also helpful to listen carefully at the door, in order to hear the key that helps them to locate the officer and understand the route he or she has chosen. Some prisoners said that they get up as early as 5 am to engage in personal rituals such as praying or meditating. At this particular time of the day, the workday of the prison staff has not yet begun, and prisoners can therefore be sure not to be disturbed. In one prison, prisoners told me of a staff meeting that takes place once a week. While one staff member has to remain in the office in order to answer the phone, all the others are attending the meeting. The prisoners estimate the probability that an officer will come to check to be 'very low' during these two hours (Fieldnotes, 14.4.2016). They therefore have some unobserved time, particularly because there is no camera installed on the two floors where their cells are located. This moment of the week can therefore potentially be used to engage in illicit activities, such as using and sharing a mobile phone (Fieldnotes, 14.4.2016) or spending unobserved moments of (sexual) intimacy between themselves. However, being unobserved by staff can also mean being unprotected from fellow prisoners, for example in terms of (sexual) abuse or violence. One, although extreme (and as far as I know unique), example of this is the murder of a young prisoner by a fellow prisoner in 2012, in the *AGE* at *JVA Pöschwies* (Tages-Anzeiger, 2010).

Prisoners usually said that 'there is real privacy after 8 pm', which corresponds to the time the prisoners are locked up and most of the prison staff leave the prison. For the following 11 hours, the prisoners can relax, because they generally do not need to fear any unexpected guest. This kind of privacy is therefore what Cohen and Taylor (1972) would call solitude. However, solitude in the sense of being alone (and unobserved) is often also experienced as painful loneliness (see also Crewe, 2009, p. 440), as I further explore in Sect. 4.5 below.

4.4.4 Protecting the Boundaries of the Self

Finally, privacy can also be established through the embodied self, for example by 'bolstering' (Leder, 2004, p. 62) it against possible assaults from prison staff or fellow prisoners by developing the body's energy and skills through weightlifting or yoga. Indeed, there are many prisoners who engage in physical activities while they are in the cells. Jonathan mentioned that whenever he is locked up in the cell, he walks around for several hours, or keeps busy with 'swimming' and 'shadow boxing', which makes him feel 'good and relaxed' (Jonathan, 2.5.2016). Leo commented that he sometimes practices yoga right after the locking-up, in order to 'calm down' and to 'relax' (Leo, 6.9.2017). Engaging in physical activity while in the cell is thus also a way to deal with the feeling of being trapped, which is usually most strongly felt immediately after the nightly lock-up, and to make the transition easier.

A technique with a similar purpose is 'to be awake' and 'ready' (Marco, 10.9.2013) when the officers unlock the cells early in the morning. Following Tuan (2001 [1977], pp. 35–36), the structure and posture of the human body as well as relations between human beings (close or distant) are fundamental principles of human spatial organization: 'In deep sleep man continues to be influenced by his environment. [...] Awake and upright he regains his world'. The upright position is generally associated with being assertive, solemn and aloof, while remaining prone is associated with submission and the acceptance of our biological condition (Tuan, 2001 [1977], p. 37). Hence, by facing the officer early in the morning, awake, and in an upright position (sitting or standing), the prisoners avoid exposing themselves in a 'vulnerable' condition and signify that they are 'in command of space' (Tuan, 2001 [1977], p. 36).

Some prisoners mentioned that they had started to pray and meditate after they were sent to prison. In the literature, these activities are also described as 'disembodiment', because they allow one to reach a stage of 'pure mind and spirit' (Leder, 2004, p. 63). In a similar sense, Moran (2013, p. 143) describe the tactic of 'retreat into [one's] inner self'. As expressed by Marco, being able to retreat into one's inner self allows one to regain 'mental free spaces':

> The more you accept being in prison, the easier you will find retreats. But these are to be found in yourself and not somewhere locally in the prison, in the sense of 'the thoughts are free'. And, you know, someone who has only recently come to prison, his thoughts are all about being in prison, and that he hates being in prison. Someone who has been in prison for a very long time and has accepted that he is now in prison and conceives of it as his normal life, he regains his mental free spaces, and that is his privacy, to which no one actually has access, especially not unannounced (laughs). (Marco, 4.5.2016)

4.4.5 Experiencing Closeness and Intimacy

In contrast to the prisoners studied by Cohen and Taylor (1972), the prisoners to whom I spoke mentioned the possibility of experiencing close and intimate relations with fellow prisoners, which can be defined as another form of privacy (see also Moran et al., 2013). In the prisons in which I did research, intimate or private encounters among prisoners are theoretically possible when the cells are open in the evening, and, in the units reserved for elderly inmates, also during the afternoon and on weekends. In one of the prisons, prisoners can benefit during the weekends from official 'cell visits' when they may visit each other. For a period of two and a half hours, a prisoner can host up to three fellow prisoners in his cell. Prisoners have to obtain permission in advance for these visits. Encounters between prisoners may therefore happen more or less spontaneously and more or less controlled by prison staff.

However, intimate relations and close friendships among prisoners are generally hard to establish and even more difficult to maintain, which is primarily the result of the particular institutional environment of the prison. As pointed out by Crewe, the prison is basically an environment that is 'low in trust and emotionally alienating' (2009, p. 301). Prisoners are all aware of the fact that each one of them committed a (more or less) serious crime, which leads to suspicion and defensiveness. Moreover, prisons are at the same time 'homosocial institutions' (Crewe, 2014, p. 431), which means that social bonds have to be established between individuals of the same sex. Finally, as shown by Britton (1997), as in almost all bureaucratic organizations, prisons—where the great majority of the employees are male (see Isenhardt et al., 2014, pp. 10–11)—have a deeply masculinized (workplace) culture.

This particular environment leads prisoners to 'mask' emotional expressions and put on 'fronts' of bravado and aggression, as signs of 'weakness and femininity' are usually impugned (Crewe, 2014, p. 430). Prisoners I talked to agreed that in prison it is important 'to show that one is strong' and 'to hide emotions, otherwise one becomes vulnerable' and easily 'exploited' (fieldnotes, 11.2.2016). But prisoners also think that the suppression of emotions is the result of the prison's goal to establish and maintain order and security. As they are asked to control their emotions, they are somehow forced to perform, as Marco termed it, 'superficial friendliness' among themselves (Marco, 4.5.2016), which in actuality can cause a lot of pain:

> I got used to monotony in here. It's much more the human [*das Menschliche*] that I miss. Everything is so rigid and formal. Though friendly and polite, I sometimes don't feel myself. My body yes, but not my soul. Everyone is hypocritical, saying how nice and good we have it here. Superficial behaviour, day-in and day-out. Where is the human being? Where is the real interest? There is no room for such intimacies. (Letter, 21.11.2016)

Against this background, however, as Marco told me, friendship may happen, and if it does, it can be experienced as much more intense than in the outside world:

> Friendship is rather rare. But if you meet someone with whom you get along really well and talk about everything and also like to spend a lot of time together and so on, then it can be almost more intense than outside. [...] Because, in here, how should I say, in here we have to follow like rules of behaviour. We have to be nice and friendly to each other, so that there are no fights and so on. So it all seems a bit artificial, the interpersonal. And then the contrast is even stronger if one can really make friends with someone. (Marco, 4.5.2016)

Everyday life in prison is characterized by monotony and a lack of experiences, which also shapes the prisoners' relations as they may run out of topics to discuss: 'Sometimes we sit together in silence because there are no themes to talk about, everything has been said, discussed, from our past ... our youth, sports, holidays, family ...' (Jonathan, 24.9.2013).

Another element that limits 'the chance to find someone' (Leo, 23.3.2016) involves internal rules and practices, such as the separation of prisoners into two groups, or, in the units for the elderly, the small number of prisoners. Finally, at some point, most of the prisoners get transferred—or are eventually released. While some keep in mind that their fellow prisoners will be released one day and hesitate to get too closely involved, others said that they adjust to it and try to make the best out of the time they have. Usually, the connection gets lost after release (see also Crewe, 2009, p. 309). However, I noted that several prisoners still maintain relations with those who are now in another prison, especially through letters but sometimes by phone, and very rarely also with those who have been released.

In addition to the low-trust environment of the prison that is characterized by machismo, its internal rules that aim to maintain control and security, and the possibility of transfer (or release)—which all create a certain (physical and emotional) distance between prisoners – relations among them are also structured by the prisoners themselves. That is, they draw symbolic boundaries among themselves by mobilizing various categories, such as the type of sentence (or measure), the offence, sexual orientation, nationality or personal characteristics (e.g. attributed intelligence or age). These boundaries further complicate the establishment of relations among them.

In general, prisoners serving indefinite incarceration tend to maintain relationships with prisoners 'in the same situation' (i.e. who have committed a similar crime and/or are also serving indefinite incarceration). Even though short-term prisoners bring in welcomed 'inputs from the outside world', such as what an iPhone is (Anton, 24.3.2016), and are 'still fresh in mind and capable of establishing relations' (Marco, 4.5.2016), those serving shorter, finite sentences are generally attributed different interests and bad habits: 'All they think and talk about is life after prison' (Markus, 29.3.2016) and they 'constantly complain' about prison life (Theo, 3.5.2016). They are described as being uninterested, unable or unwilling to understand 'how it feels to be [a certain] offender' (Paul, 29.3.2016) or 'what an indeterminate measure is' (Louis, 22.3.2016). Short-term prisoners sometimes 'plan new offenses after imprisonment' (Hugo, 25.6.2013), and, as they have little to lose, often participate in illicit activities, such as drug trafficking or gaining access to the Internet, and thereby endanger the stability of the environment and especially 'certain privileges [that apply to everyone]', such as having a personal computer (Hugo, 25.6.2013). Finally, short-term prisoners all will certainly 'leave the prison one day' (Leo, 23.3.2016), which is usually a painful experience for those who must remain inside. However, even though long-term prisoners are all to some extent in the 'same boat', the younger men (both in terms of age and years in prison) in particular perceive the elderly men with suspicion. From their point of view, long-term imprisonment, often combined with extensive medication use, has 'deadened' (Markus, 29.3.2016) many of the prisoners and made them look like 'zombies' (Anton, 24.3.2016), having lost all ability for or interest in interpersonal exchanges:

> Many of the *Verwahrten* [prisoners held in indefinite incarceration] in here, they are just sitting stubbornly in their cell, they don't come out, have isolated themselves, encapsulated. They are no longer interested in

people, emotions, in having conversations as we have now. Many of them are like that. (Leo, 23.3.2016)

Nevertheless, almost two-thirds of the prisoners I spoke to mentioned at least one fellow prisoner to whom they feel close. However, when I asked them if they would call it 'friendship', most hesitated. They felt that 'real friendship' in prison is rare (or even non-existent) and usually prefer to use the terms 'comradeship', 'colleagues', 'involuntary community' or 'community of fate'.

As Crewe (2014, p. 432) has demonstrated, closeness can be developed within the routine of mundane everyday activities, such as drinking coffee, watching TV or smoking a cigarette together, shared moments that allow prisoners to express 'forms of concern and sensitivity' towards each other. Prisoners I talked to mentioned that with those they feel close to, they like to play games together, cook and eat together, celebrate festivities such as Christmas or Easter, share experiences, discuss ideas, laugh, argue, sit together in silence and 'simply be together' (Louis, 22.3.2016).

Jonathan: David comes ten times a day [to my cell], or I go to him. [One of his mates] has left recently; he visited him five or six times a day to drink coffee together. And now he is a bit alone. That's why I go to him more often. Because I noticed when [David's mate] left, he came to me 20, 30 times a day (laughs). He always wanted to tell or ask me something, that's why I now go to him more often too.

Irene: Is David a friend?

J: One can say so, yes, one can say so. [...] Friendship does not happen that often, but it does exist. There was a time I used to be inseparable with someone. I spent more time in his cell than in mine. We sat together, were listening to music ... sometimes we had nothing to talk about and then we kept silent, just for hours we were silent. But I remember, after work, I went to him in his cell, not at all in my cell. Then having dinner in his cell [...] or vice versa, he came to my place. It was like that all the time. (Jonathan, 2.5.2016)

During fieldwork, I directly observed (or was told about) several practices that I interpret as expressions of concern and sensitivity: cooking someone's favourite dish, letting someone lie on one's bed during a visit, helping to write a letter, lending money or assisting with everyday activities in the case of an illness (bringing food, cleaning the cell). Sympathy for the other is also expressed through gestures and making jokes:

> Jonathan for me, he is … how can I put it, a good buddy. We have fun together, he always has a funny line in store, sometimes he teases me by caressing me with his hand on my head, asking me whether my bald head keeps me warm (laughs) […] He notices if I'm not feeling well. He then leaves me alone or drinks his coffee quietly but then leaves again. (David, 2.5.2016)

In addition to the provision of emotional and practical support, close prison friends also help each other to spend time, to experience moments of 'normality' (Markus, 29.3.2016) and sometimes even 'to forget where one is' (François, 23.11.2013). As Marco explained to me, 'the structures [in prison] create monotony, but people create life because everyone has different thoughts every day' (Marco, 4.5.2016).

However, as mentioned above, prisoners have to establish close relations within the 'homo-social environment' (Crewe, 2014) of the prison. As I was told by one prisoner who sent me a letter, he had trouble 'to open [himself] and discuss [his] feelings and most intimate experiences with men' and preferred talking to women (Letter from a prisoner, 27.6.2016). This is also an issue when it comes to sexual desire. Sexuality is a sensitive topic in general and maybe even more so in prison, where heterosexual deprivation is considered to be one of the major 'pains of imprisonment' (Sykes, 1971 [1958]). It was therefore difficult for me (as a female researcher) to address this topic; however, it twice became an issue during discussions I had with prisoners. I tried to introduce it by posing the rather general question of how it feels for them to be among men all the time. One prisoner replied after some seconds of reflection: 'The [sexual] desire is there, it is strong. But you have to suppress it, as long as you are not gay' (Fieldnotes, 9.2.2016). Sexual encounters between prisoners are not legally prohibited but generally are not allowed by the prisons in order to prevent abuse and dependencies.[9] It is known from the literature, however, that some prisoners, including those who consider themselves to be heterosexual, nevertheless engage in homosexual encounters. This behaviour is also labelled 'situational homosexuality' (Marcum, 2014, p. 8; Sykes, 1971 [1958], pp. 95–99). Issues regarding heterosexual deprivation, intimate relations and homosexual encounters in prison also emerged during an informal discussion I had with three prisoners at their workplace. Only one of them, Leo, was at that time held in indefinite incarceration:

> We were talking about trust, and I asked if they think that one can trust people in prison. Leo said that 'this is difficult, one is really alone here'. But he has one person, for two years now. He will also stay in prison for a while. Also, Leo said that he finds it difficult to talk with men about feelings. I picked up the subject and asked how it is to be among men all the time. The two others joined the discussion. The elderly one said that he was glad to be a little bit older, so he 'no longer needs it so strongly' as the younger ones. I asked about the so-called family room, which is provided by some prisons, but not by this prison. They told me that some prisoners use the toilet in the external visitor's area for having sex with their girlfriend or wife [Note: not every prisoner is allowed to receive guests in the outside visitor's area. Leo for instance, due to his offense and his psychiatric diagnosis, is not allowed]. The elderly prisoner disagreed with this practice; he said that he would surely never want to have sex with his wife in this toilet, maybe with another woman, but certainly not with his wife. Leo replied, half-jokingly, 'Aha, not with your wife, but with any other one. Why this difference?' The elderly prisoner then said: 'Yeah, you're right', and Leo pointed out that this, the public toilet, is actually the only option in prison. They started a discussion on gay prisoners and how 'good' they have it in here, such a 'big choice'! Everyone laughed. Especially one prisoner 'tries it' with everyone, they told me. Apparently, he has tried again and again, and even already twice

[9] I once attended an informal discussion among prison officers where the manager of the unit said that he does not support the internal rule that prohibits sexual encounters among prisoners. He thinks that if sexual contact is desired by both parties, they should be able to engage in it. He added that he provides his full support to officers in case they witness such an event but decide not to report it (Fieldnotes, 18.2.2016). I also noticed that condoms are made available to prisoners.

> with Leo. He said, he once tried while they were together in the cell, alone; he (Leo) then had to press the alarm button. He also tried with an older man, apparently several times, who then threatened him and told him to 'not even greet him anymore'. 'To become gay in prison' is something none of the three can imagine happening to them. (Fieldnotes, 16.2.2016)

Similarly, another prisoner said that for homosexuals, prison is 'like paradise' and that he is 'sometimes mad at them, because they have something [he] [hasn't]'. However, the same prisoner thought that this is also one of the reasons why they often are discriminated against and therefore 'don't have an easy life either' (Fieldnotes, 9.2.2016). During fieldwork, prison staff told me a few stories about sexual encounters among (assumed) heterosexual prisoners. Prisoners themselves never mentioned such issues in my presence. Two prisoners explicitly told me about their homosexual orientation and that they had already had (sexual) relationships with fellow prisoners.

Masturbation is another topic that prisoners very rarely mentioned in my presence. Again, the little information I obtained derives mainly from prison staff and some interactions that I witnessed. It seems that the problem for prisoners is gaining access to 'tools' to stimulate their imagination, as pornography is prohibited. I once witnessed a conversation between two prisoners who were playing ping pong together. One joyfully told the other one that he had managed to buy a 'Manga' book of an erotic nature. He expressed surprise that this was allowed by the management and assumed that the reason for this is that it includes drawings but not photographs. He mentioned that he 'immediately ordered more of them' (Fieldnotes, 3.2.2016). Prison officers as well as security officers also told me that, from time to time, for example during cell searches, they find pornographic material that prisoners managed to acquire illicitly, for example on a USB stick that they received from an external visitor.

As this section has shown, the cell is a place that enables prisoners to create and negotiate privacy, and, when the cell doors are unlocked, experience closeness and intimacy with fellow prisoners. In the following section, I explore their experiences of being in the cell after lock-up, the period of the day prisoners spend (at least physically) completely alone in their cells.

4.5 Being with Time

According to the regime, during the time prisoners are locked up, which is between 14 hours (on weekdays) and 17 hours (on weekends), they generally have no possibility of (direct) interpersonal communication.[10] When the cell is locked, prisoners have to be and do time *alone* with *themselves*, with only a few options for activities and restricted options for movement.

The majority of the prisoners I talked to told me that they have adjusted to it; they have learned to feel good while in the cell. Also, as mentioned in the previous sections, in contrast to other places, the cell is the one place in prison that prisoners (can) arrange in a personal way and that provides them with privacy. However, a small number of prisoners mentioned that dealing with the daily lock-up is still a challenge, especially the moment right after it happens. Some said that they still (after all these years in custody) suffer both physically and mentally after the nightly lock-up: that they experience 'claustrophobia' (Rolf, 11.9.2013) and the feeling of 'not getting enough air' (Leo, 23.3.2016).[11] Leo mentioned that lock-up often represents an 'artificial cut' (Leo, 6.9.2017) that forces prisoners to involuntarily end a good conversation or to put on hold their desire to remain outside in the courtyard. Immediately

[10] All prison cells are equipped with an intercom system that allows prisoners to get in contact with prison staff in case of emergency. Contrary to other studies (see e.g. Ugelvik, 2014), communication between prisoners through the wall or the windows was not mentioned during my research.

[11] The impossibility of leaving this place thus immediately transforms the (bodily) experience of it. I once had a similar experience in one of the units for ill and elderly prisoners. While I was usually equipped with a key and a phone (including an alarm function), one day, during a very short visit, I entered the unit without these items. Upon my arrival, I immediately entered into conversation with some of the prisoners and it happened, unexpectedly, that all the staff members present simultaneously (although for different reasons) left the unit for some minutes. When they were all gone, I realized the lack of my usual equipment and immediately felt tense: I was stuck among dangerous criminals! Moreover, I started to feel the narrowness of the place, which I did not perceive in the same way when I was carrying a key and thus technically able to leave whenever I wanted.

after lock-up, there is a transitional phase during which one needs to 'calm down' (Leo, 6.9.2017). Leo said that he does yoga exercises for this purpose. He used to take drugs, which he has since stopped. In addition to feelings of unease and restlessness, prisoners also experience loneliness and isolation while they are locked up in their cells. For these prisoners, the time that has to pass before the cells are unlocked again seems endless. Jonathan experienced this at the beginning, but has learned to deal with it:

> I used to be stressed: I looked at the clock every minute, used to behave very differently from today. I wasn't able to bear it [staying in the cell], was just waiting to go for a walk or go to work … just out of the cell. I couldn't bear it at all. Today, when I'm in the cell, I feel good. (Jonathan, 2.5.2016)

As I show in the following, there are various overlapping temporalities or rhythms that exist within this particular *carceral context*. One rhythm is imposed by the prison regime. As mentioned, prisoners spend most of their time in their cells. This is basically the place where they are supposed to rest, but also to take care of their personal hygiene and do some domestic work (e.g. cleaning the cell, changing the bed linen once a week). Yet, this imposed (institutional) rhythm may not necessarily be in accordance with the bio-rhythm of the prisoner, who is maybe not hungry at 5 pm, or who does not yet wish to take sleeping pills (if he needs them) at 8 pm—the time they are distributed by staff. Furthermore, while this protocol provides prisoners with a minimal structure while doing time in their cell, it certainly does not 'fill' the prisoners' time in the cell. I will show in this section that although prisoners are not in a position to determine the duration they have to spend in the cell every day, they do have 'scope to influence how this feels' (O'Donnell, 2014, p. 195).

4.5.1 Killing Time

For prisoners who struggle after they are locked up in the cell, 8 pm begins a period they wish would soon be over. For those who 'look at the clock every minute' (see quotation above), the cell is experienced as a very narrow and lonely space, where time seems to pass very slowly. Consequently, time becomes their enemy, and they work to find ways to 'kill it'—or, in the words of a prisoner: 'to occupy it' (Jonathan, 2.5.2016). In the following, I explore prisoners' ways of killing time in two respects: as a 'reduction of time' and 'speeding the passage of time' (O'Donnell, 2014, p. 226).

According to O'Donnell (2014, p. 226), the reduction of time refers to activities that aim to make sure that there is 'less time' to deal with, for instance by using drugs that have a soporific effect (see also Cope, 2003) or, as I was told, by 'oversleeping time' (Fieldnotes, 4.2.2016), which is especially practised during the weekends when they remain locked in their cells for much longer periods. Killing time is also about speeding the passage of time, by finding 'removal activities' (see also Crewe et al., 2020, p. 299) in order to keep busy and absorbed or even to 'lose all sense of time' (Hall, 1989 [1983], p. 137). 'Removal activities' are thus basically about distraction (see also Goffman, 1961, p. 68). As Goffman (1961, p. 189) has demonstrated, it is partially also in the interest of the prison to provide means for distraction, as this fosters compliance ('primary adjustment'). In the prisons in which I conducted research, the prisoners have the option to buy a radio, rent a TV or computer or borrow books from the prison library. However, the use of media is highly controlled by the prison. The computer and the TV can be removed by prison management as a disciplinary measure, and in one of the prisons, there is no access to TV or radio during the day. Hence, prisoners who are ill or unwilling to work and therefore spend the whole day in the cell cannot use these media devices. Furthermore, the selection of TV channels, computer games and DVDs is restricted. Finally, the prisoners' computers cannot be protected with a personal password and may be searched at any time by prison staff. I was told by prisoners that the TV and the computer are the most important means of distraction in prison (see also Jewkes, 2002). Furthermore, as already mentioned, the TV is also used to drown out silence and chase away the feeling of loneliness. Other functions that the TV and the computer fulfil will be discussed below.

Besides watching TV and using the computer (illustrated in Fig. 4.7), the prisoners mentioned other, individual activities for passing or killing time while in the cell: smoking, drinking coffee, laying on the bed, walking around, listening to or making music (the instruments I came across include the guitar, the flute and the keyboard), doing physical exercise and finally waiting (e.g. to go to work or to have lunch or dinner). These activities usually become personal habits and rituals that help prisoners structure the imposed amount of time they are forced to spend in the cell. In the following passage, Jonathan, who lives in a unit for ill and elderly prisoners, explains his personal routine while locked up in the cell:

> Me, I get up at five o'clock. Then I drink coffee, then I sit for two hours until seven, then they open the door […] then I go to work. […]. After work, it's lunchtime. We finish work at eleven and then go upstairs to our floor to wait for lunch. Usually, I watch TV and read the newspaper. After lunch, I always sleep half an hour to forty-five minutes. I don't know why, but I have learned here to sleep. […] On Friday afternoon, we have to clean our cells […] time goes very quickly during that part of the day. In the evening, we have free time. After dinner and a little TV, I read a book and listen to music. From 5.30 pm to 6.30 pm, I go for a walk. […] Sometimes I also walk in the cell, not every day but every now and then if I cannot sleep – especially during the weekend when the days are very long. When I go to bed at five o'clock [after lock-up], then I usually get up at nine and walk until ten o'clock, and as I walk I am partially listening and watching television. […] When the cell is locked, I'm usually on the bed, except when I'm walking around. Otherwise, I drink coffee, use the toilet, and then I'm walking around again. That's it, all in all. (Jonathan, 24.9.2013)

As pointed out by O'Donnell (2014, p. 183), temporal compression is actually greatest when activities are habitual, which is expressed in the following quote, again by Jonathan:

> When I was not organized, I did not work for nine years, I was bored. I was alone all day, in the cell or in the corridor or in the common room. Then I thought: In the evening I'll watch TV until midnight,

and then I'll sleep until about 10 am. Then I'll get up, go for a shower, read newspapers, drink coffee, then after lunch I used to cook, then two hours walking. And I noticed that my time was somehow busy. So, I've organized myself and time goes twice as fast as it did when I didn't do anything. Do you understand what I mean? (Jonathan, 2.5.2016)

Creating personal routines, habits and rituals not only enables prisoners to kill time and structure their day but provides them simultaneously with 'satisfaction' and a feeling of 'security' (Leo, 23.3.2016). It helps them 'to navigate their sentence' (O'Donnell, 2014, p. 199) and to control and experience a sense of personal ownership of time (see also Toch, 1996 [1977], p. 225) and feelings of self-determination, autonomy and freedom of action that are important in order to maintain their sense of self (see also Goffman 1961; Wahidin & Moss, 2004).

[B]eing alone in the cell, or dealing with myself, that's actually the hardest thing sometimes. I just don't know then … sometimes, what I should do. I cannot always write, I cannot always read, I cannot always play games. At some point you are tired of it. And then you have to be really creative, do something new, attending a course or something. Working a bit with glass or, yes, that simple stuff. Or I developed a mania for cleaning [the cell]; this is actually very common among prisoners (laughs). And yes, I have a lot of rituals that I practice. Always the same things every day. […] This also gives you a good feeling, security and a good feeling. (Leo, 23.3.2016)

In order to create a personal routine, prisoners must know the official prison schedule (including the staff's more or less formal routine) and rules. These serve as a frame of reference, and it is therefore important that they remain 'stable' and thus predictable (Marco, 4.5.2016). However, as highlighted by O'Donnell (2014, p. 199), 'habits are comfortable, but when they fossilize the humanity is gradually drained out of human beings'. Prisoners indeed mentioned the need to bring some change into their personal routine:

Whenever I meet a newcomer, I tell him that it is very important to organize oneself. […] But you should always have variety. Because always

> the same is monotonous. So this means, you start one week like this, the next, another way. Then … It is important, always something as new as possible, not new, because there is nothing new, but maybe a new book, a new newspaper, new information, that is all that is new. (Jonathan, 2.5.2016)

However, the same daily structure in prison combined with personal routines (with the primary aim of killing time) may lead to the experience of what I propose calling the *hyper-ordinary*, which increases the possibility that prisoners completely lose their feel for the passage of time, as explained by a prisoner who sent me a letter:

> I don't feel time anymore. It comes and goes, day by day. I live according to a strict daily schedule […] I see some situations in advance because they are repeated every day […] To always live the same things, always according to the same rhythm makes me tired. It's very demoralizing. (Letter from a prisoner, 27.6.2016)

Living a 'prescribed life' (Clément, 24.3.2016), perceived as being 'always the same' (Darko, 6.5.2016), has a strong impact on prisoners' sense of self and their relationship to the world. For prisoners, especially long-term ones, in addition to the need to kill or control time, it is also important to experience the passage of time, which is related to the experience of change that allows them not only to feel time but also themselves.

4.5.2 Marking Time

Challenging hyper-ordinariness and creating chronology and change can be achieved by 'marking time' (Calkins, 1970; Cohen & Taylor, 1972), which literally means 'setting off specific points as the beginning and the end of the duration of a period of time' (Calkins, 1970, p. 490). Marking time is about differentiating and dividing time and putting a personal stamp on one's temporal life (O'Donnell, 2014, p. 195). However, it requires awareness of 'events' that can be used as time markers. In a scene that is perceived as unchanging, there are fewer points to mark

(Calkins, 1970, p. 491). Prisoners who are mainly concerned with their sentence and hoping for release (i.e. those whose mode of being with time is focused on the future) may use the annual evaluations as temporal benchmarks (see also Cohen & Taylor, 1972). Others use personal events for time marking, such as visits from their relatives or friends. Prisoners can also mark time by focusing more on the present instead of the future by organizing their daily lives into tiny, 'digestible' segments or events, which is closely connected to the creation of personal habits and rituals (see also Crewe et al., 2020, p. 305).

As I observed, another practice of marking time that takes place during cell time is the collection of information and data of all sorts. Prisoners mentioned and also showed me diverse lists they had created, for instance of their correspondence with the outside world (information concerning all the letters they had written and received), statistics related to sports results or their financial transactions. Another prisoner even showed me several lists he used to create, including one of films he has watched, one of the actors and actresses he knows, another of food prices that he copied from a magazine and finally one of a number of weapons (Fieldnotes, 12.2.2016). I argue that creating a list can be done for the purpose of performing the action itself; it can therefore be a habit and a way to 'kill time'. However, it can also be an 'event' and therefore serve as a time marker (for example, to fill in the result every Sunday evening after a football match). Finally, making lists is also about creating awareness of the passage of time and the experience of changing times through the distinction between and comparison of events (for example, sports results, prices of foodstuffs or personal knowledge). Similar to the activity of writing lists is writing in a diary. As with lists, keeping a diary helps prisoners to sharpen their awareness of what is going on around them or inside themselves, to note their observations, to distinguish between and compare events, and therefore to experience change. However, it is commonly considered a tool for personal reflection and therefore strongly connected to the experience of personal development, which is discussed further in the following section.

4.5.3 Using Time

In contrast to short-term prisoners, who basically wait for their release to go on with their 'normal' lives, for prisoners who will probably stay behind bars until the end of their lives, the meaning of prison time may be different. In particular, the common strategies for *doing time* become pointless. In other words, not everyone simply wants to kill or pass time because life in prison most likely constitutes their remaining lifetime. Therefore, prisoners also seek to 'use time' (see also Flanagan, 1981, p. 218) by 'not wasting one's time, but benefiting from it' (Leo, 23.3.2016). However, as argued by several authors, being able to use time is connected to the recognition that 'one's life is that existence which takes place within the prison' (Cohen & Taylor, 1972, p. 93). As claimed by Crewe (2016), in contrast to prisoners at an early stage, long-term prisoners at a later stage in their sentence are less overwhelmed by the present and instead accept the flow of time and even perceive it as something that can be used constructively.

From the perspective of prisoners I talked to, activities involving simple distraction, such as watching TV, are therefore perceived critically. Although for many long-term prisoners television constitutes one of their only connections to the outside world, providing them with information and the possibility of mentally escaping the prison for a while (see also Milhaud, 2009, p. 303), watching TV is also defined by some prisoners as a way of 'wasting time'; it is basically regarded as passive consumption that 'takes your time away' (Anton, 24.3.2016) or even as a 'force, disruption and manipulation' (Jonathan, 24.9.2013). For this reason, there are prisoners who do not have a TV in their cells (anymore). Prisoners who are particularly concerned about mental deterioration and the maintenance of their sense of self mentioned the need to engage in mental work, such as reading and studying, in order 'to keep mentally fit', instead of watching TV and running the risk of becoming 'dulled and stupid' (Fieldnotes, 7.7.2016). In the words of one prisoner, he sought 'to develop further' (Leo, 23.3.2016) as a human being.

> I read a lot [...]. And I try to watch the news more often, to be more interested, gain more knowledge, study more, contact more people, do

> more with people, and know more about this world and get away from my own problems, this helps. You have to have a structure in your life, or you will get lost here [in prison]. The character gets lost, the psyche gets lost, one is hopeless one day, gets drug dependent … it's because of the extension of custody. (Kurt, 3.5.2016)

In contrast to prisoners who feel restless in the cell and count the hours until they can go out again, these prisoners use this particular period of the day for the creation of space and time to concentrate, to think and to reflect—about themselves and life in general. For them, being in the cell is not primarily about killing time, but about using time—that is, spending qualitative, creative and productive time. Some prisoners use this moment of the day to deal with their past and work on their autobiography; others keep a diary. As one prisoner explained to me, he wants 'to capture the experiences that move him', which helps him 'to keep the human side' of himself (Fieldnotes, 7.7.2016). Reflecting and writing about themselves also helps them to keep their memories alive, to (re)construct identities and to capture personal change over time. Finally, using time can also involve the development and implementation of personal projects (see also Crewe et al., 2016, p. 18), such as preparing (and later delivering) a lecture for a school lesson, developing a computer programme or learning a foreign language.

Using or spending time in general is strongly connected to the wish to achieve goals and experience (personal) change and development. In reference to Tuan's (2001 [1977]) argument that 'living is stepping forward', I argue that prisoners thereby express a fundamental human need: the need *to feel alive*. However, the intention to make the best out of their situation and the wish to develop further as a human being are highly constrained by the institution. For example, requests to register for distance learning can be blocked by prison management, sometimes for security reasons, as I was told by Lorenzo, who wanted to enrol in a degree programme in psychology. According to him, the institution feared that this would make him 'even more dangerous' (Lorenzo, 23.11.2013). Furthermore, because they are classified as 'dangerous' and 'untreatable', these prisoners usually do not receive any future-oriented support, such as (temporary) prison leave or psychotherapy in order to achieve personal change. Finally, prisoners seeking change and personal development constantly battle against the power of monotony. One prisoner told me that after nine years of writing in a diary, he had given up. He did not know anymore what to write down, because 'in prison, every day is the same, not much happens here, it doesn't create many memories' (Fieldnotes, 15.2.2016).

4.5.4 Transcending the Here and Now

Cell time is also a period of the day that is used to transcend the here and now and to connect to other contexts—with particular tools or through the imagination (see Lussault & Stock, 2010, p. 17). It is used to create and live imagined time–space constellations and gain personal experiences far from the carceral context—passively as well as actively.

A closer examination of the prisoners' narratives about TV suggests that although watching television is critically perceived as a simple means of distraction, it is also a connection to other worlds, which allows them to have a 'pause' (Rolf, 6.5.2016) and mentally 'escape' the prison context for a while (see also Jewkes, 2002). Through the TV, prisoners can follow 'world affairs' (Heinz, 3.5.2016), politics and sport events (Darko, 6.5.2016). They can gather scientific knowledge (Heinz, 3.5.2016) and participate in the outside world—'at least indirectly' (Rolf, 6.5.2016)—or simply 'encounter daily life' and 'be informed about trends' (Jonathan, 2.5.2016).

In addition, numerous prisoners I met subscribed to a daily newspaper, often one from their region of origin. One case that stands out in terms of the duration of this form of connectedness involves Hans, who has been in prison for several decades and who has subscribed to a local newspaper from his home region since 1958. Through this particular newspaper, he keeps informed and connected to his original community:

> If there is something in the newspaper … I know every corner of the houses there, from childhood on, when [I read that] someone died, I jerk immediately. Every now and then I call someone from there and they greet the other people, and then a greeting comes back sometimes. (Hans, 4.6.2013)

However, it was also through this newspaper that he had to learn about the death of his own grandmother—which at the same time exemplifies his disconnectedness or social exclusion from the community.

More generally, the connection to the outside world through media is furthermore a corporal experience that provokes emotions and reflection. During fieldwork, several prisoners mentioned reports they had seen on issues related to wars, refugees or climate change and described being moved by these events and topics. Through audio-visual media, prisoners are also reminded of their pre-prison lives and lost futures (see also Jewkes, 2002, p. 91). Some reported sadness and a sense of nostalgia when they watch documentaries of places with which they are familiar or see people doing activities they cannot do anymore. Others mentioned events that they will never be able to experience at all, such as starting a family. Watching a particular TV show or a documentary film can also bring back memories of happier times and thus evoke good feelings. Finally, the TV can be used as a tool to immerse oneself into another person's reality and fantasy worlds.

> Whenever I see beautiful landscapes [on TV] from Switzerland, or other places where I've been to in my life – I've been to many places around the world – then it's always double-edged: it makes me sad, you know, there are only pixels (laughs), and these are just spots of colours on the posters, you cannot jump into this lake, or walk through the forest, or across the meadow. Sure, the TV helps to distract, but I always have to be careful that I don't watch things that remind me too much … of what I miss (laughs). These are illusionary worlds, with which you can completely get involved, being aware that this is now an illusionary world, then I also temporarily do live in this illusory world. (Rolf, 6.5.2016)

> The only thing I always like to watch are fairy tale films. […] I've been watching them since childhood, until today. Every Sunday there are fairy tales at KiKa [*Kinderkanal*]. I like to watch these. I don't know why, it is unconscious, or I don't know, or because there is always a happy ending, and everything is wonderful. (Jonathan, 2.5.2016)

Transcending the prison context can also be realized more actively, for instance by playing (offline) computer games, especially those involving role-play, which allows prisoners to slip into another personality in another time–space constellation. One game that is highly appreciated is called 'The Sims', which, according to its official website, is a 'life simulation game' that allows users 'to play with life' by giving them the 'power to create and control people' (Electronic Arts, 2018). In the following extract of an interview, David talks about the characters and the everyday lives he has created through 'The Sims':

> His name is Albert, and she is called Sumi. She is his wife, and she's a little bit smarter than him. He's a bit of a phlegmatic guy. She enjoys reading; most of the time she sits in the living room in a corner somewhere while reading a book. He then usually sits in the garden [...] or he is playing with the children instead of studying, reading books and stuff. Well, I was thinking, no, now it's your turn to make a career. And now I will try to place him at the Science Centre, so that he gets a job there. But he is not trained enough yet. I just found out that he has no higher degree. Now he has to catch up, so we'll go to the public library, which is the next task, where we must find specific books together. Let's see if he finds them. (David, 2.5.2016)

Another example comes from using the PlayStation:

> I always feel tempted to escape into a virtual world (laughs) because the real world is just shit. And then I'm just much more interested in testing an exotic sports car in Hawaii, or playing a round of golf with Tiger Woods, or tennis with Federer (laughs). (Marco, 10.9.2013)

Related to this is daydreaming. While daydreaming can be described as a means of distraction (killing time) that allows prisoners to 'temporarily [blot] out all sense of the environment' (Goffman, 1961, p. 309), the prisoners I met depicted daydreaming not only as a means of escape but also as a lived experience outside of the institutional context. They often 'do' (active and specific) daydreaming about their previous lives. They recall nice memories and relive them. Thus, while in the cell, through their imagination, they are strongly connected to other time–spaces (see also Lussault & Stock, 2010, p. 17). This helps them not only to relax but also to keep alive their most precious memories and to retain a part of their former selves. However, this also provokes fears: one prisoner mentioned being scared of 'not finding his way back' or that memories of the past will fade over time (Fieldnotes, 17.2.2016).

> Today, I helped Lars with his job in the workshop. We were talking about his experience of being in prison; he talked a lot, and I asked questions from time to time. [...] He told me that he can 'lose himself' very easily in his thoughts, especially when something stresses him out, when he is plagued by fears. But he said that he was afraid to 'get stuck', to get 'lost and not find his way back'. He has also experienced this with others, who according to him have completely lost 'their relation to reality'. He doesn't want that. For him, the prison is like 'Twilight': a 'world of its own'. (Fieldnotes, 17.2.2016)

Others, such as Paul, explore unknown places in their imaginations and thereby envision particular situations while daydreaming:

> *Irene*: Are there places in the outside world of which you are sometimes thinking?
> *Paul*: I think a lot of the apartment of my girlfriend.
> *I*: Of her apartment?
> *P*: Yes, but I've never been there. She now lives in a new one, in the same village, but in a new apartment. [...]
> *I*: Did she describe this apartment to you, or did you see a picture of it?
> *P*: No, I have no idea how this apartment looks. I just imagine me being there with her. How the apartment looks, I don't know. I just imagine us being there, sitting together, eating, and lying in bed together, things like that. Being together with her. What I cannot do here. (Paul, 29.3.2016)

Paul also mentioned that he often thinks of the places where he committed his crimes, implicitly letting me know that he thereby also fantasizes about doing it again.

By transcending the here and now of the prison context—both passively and actively—while locked up in their cells, prisoners create time–spaces that let them gain experiences and emotions far from the prison context. The small prison cell then turns into a place that enables prisoners to gain freedom of movement through their wandering minds. This echoes Tuan, who argues that:

> Freedom implies space; it means having the power and enough room in which to act. Being free has several levels of meaning. Fundamental is the ability to transcend the present condition, and this transcendence is most simply manifest as the elementary power to move. In the act of moving, space and its attributions are directly experienced. (Tuan, 2001 [1977], p. 52)

4.6 Conclusion

The focus of this chapter was the prison cell and the prisoners' experiences of and within these 12m^2 (or even less) where they have to spend most of their time alone. The cell constitutes the place in prison where the prisoners' personal attitudes towards their indeterminate confinement and self-perceptions as prisoners (or rather incarcerated human beings) are both fostered and expressed.

The prisoners' assessments of the cell—in particular its materiality, namely its architecture, design and furnishings—are embedded in their self-perception as prisoners who have already served their sentences. As their narratives reveal, they wish for their status to be recognized through the provision of cells that are 'less prison-like', with more opportunities to personalize the space in order to feel less like a prisoner and more like a person living in this place. Interestingly, however, the way prisoners perceive the ambiance of the prison cell is not only linked to its materiality, but also to the prison environment (inside)—in particular its sound (often described as either too loud or too quiet) and the way they are treated by prison staff—as well as the prison's surroundings (outside). All of this together influences prisoners' sense of self and experience of their exclusion from the outside community.

Being in the cell, and more concretely the ability to furnish it, is further determined by the prison's internal accommodation regime. Despite all the restrictions, the prisoners use, appropriate and (re)arrange the institutional spatio-temporal order that defines the prison cell through individual practices, and thereby ascribe new meanings to this place and create personal space. The prisoners' ways of arranging the cell are shaped by their personal attitudes towards their uncertain future, or in other words, their modes of *being with time*: while those who try to accept imprisonment and concentrate on the present often transform it into a home, those who continue to hope and fight for their release generally want it to remain a simple place where they currently have to be, not a place where they want to make themselves comfortable. Yet, all the prisoners show attachment to this place as it is also a space of privacy and intimacy, which they, in one way or another, try to defend through a wide range of techniques.

Moreover, by creating their own rhythms during the many hours they are locked up in their cells alone, prisoners shape the experience of doing time according to their personal needs. As I have shown, the time span in the cell has many different meanings for the prisoners: some want it to be over as soon as possible and to notice as little of it as possible; others want to use their hours in the cell in a productive and self-reflective way. Still others use it as a gateway to gain experience in other, imaginary worlds—far from the prison context.

* * *

When the officers set out to unlock the cell doors at around 7 am, most of the prisoners have been awake for some time already. Some have used the early hours of the morning for praying, meditating, drinking coffee, smoking a cigarette, doing exercises or following their morning hygiene routine. Others have slept until they heard the sound of the approaching officers or, in one prison, the prison bell at 6.45 am. What happens after the doors are unlocked is the subject of the next chapter.

References

Adey, P., Brayer, L., Masson, D., Murphy, P., Simpson, P., & Tixier, N. (2013). 'Pour votre tranquillité': Ambiance, atmosphere, and surveillance. *Geoforum, 49*, 299–309. https://doi.org/10.1016/j.geoforum.2013.04.028

Baechtold, A., Weber, J., & Hostettler, U. (2016). *Strafvollzug: Straf- und Massnahmenvollzug an Erwachsenen in der Schweiz* (3rd ed., Kriminalität, Justiz und Sanktionen KJS: Vol. 17). Stämpfli Verlag.

Baer, L., & Ravneberg, B. (2008). The outside and inside in Norwegian and English prisons. *Geografiska Annaler: Series B, Human Geography, 90*, 205–216. https://doi.org/10.1111/j.1468-0467.2008.00287.x

Baer, L. D. (2005). Visual imprints on the prison landscape: A study on the decorations in prison cells. *Tijdschrift Voor Economische En Sociale Geografie, 96*, 209–217. https://doi.org/10.1111/j.1467-9663.2005.00451.x

Bailey, J. (2000). Some meanings of 'the private' in sociological thought. *Sociology, 34*, 381–401. https://doi.org/10.1177/S0038038500000250

Bennett, J., Crewe, B., & Wahidin, A. (Eds.). (2008). *Understanding prison staff*. Willan Publishing.

Britton, D. M. (1997). Gendered organizational logic: Policy and practice in men's and women's prisons. *Gender & Society, 11*, 796–818. https://doi.org/10.1177/089124397011006005

Bundesamt für Justiz BJ. (2016). *Handbuch für Bauten des Straf- und Massnahmenvollzugs: Einrichtungen Erwachsene*. https://www.bj.admin.ch/dam/data/bj/sicherheit/smv/baubeitraege/hb-erwachsene-d.pdf. Accessed 10 December 2019.

Calkins, K. (1970). Time: Perspectives, marking and styles of usage. *Social Problems, 17*(4), 487–501.

Cohen, S., & Taylor, L. (1972). *Psychological survival: The experience of long-term imprisonment*. Penguin Books.

Cope, N. (2003). 'It's no time or high time': Young offenders' experiences of time and drug use in prison. *The Howard Journal of Criminal Justice, 42*, 158–175. https://doi.org/10.1111/1468-2311.t01-1-00273

Coyle, A. (2005). *Understanding prisons: Key issues in policy and practice*. Open University Press.

Crewe, B. (2009). *The prisoner society: Power, adaptation and social life in an English prison.* Oxford University Press.

Crewe, B. (2011a). Depth, weight, tightness: Revisiting the pains of imprisonment. *Punishment & Society, 13*, 509–529.

Crewe, B. (2011b). Soft power in prison: Implications for staff–prisoner relationships, liberty and legitimacy. *European Journal of Criminology, 8*, 455–468. https://doi.org/10.1177/1477370811413805

Crewe, B. (2014). Not looking hard enough: Masculinity, emotion, and prison research. *Qualitative Inquiry, 20*(4), 426–437.

Crewe, B., Hulley, S., & Wright, S. (2016). Swimming with the tide: Adapting to long-term imprisonment. *Justice Quarterly, 34*, 1–25. https://doi.org/10.1080/07418825.2016.1190394
Crewe, B., Hulley, S., & Wright, S. (2020). *Life imprisonment from young adulthood*. Palgrave Macmillan.
Curtis, V., & Biran, A. (2001). Dirt, disgust, and disease: Is hygiene in our genes? *Perspectives in Biology and Medicine, 44*(1), 17–31.
Douglas, M. (1966). *Purity and danger: An analysis of the concepts of pollution and taboo.* Routledge and Kegan Paul.
Electronic Arts. (2018). *The Sims.* http://www2.ea.com/sims. Accessed 29 June 2018.
Flanagan, T. J. (1981). Dealing with long-term confinement: Adaptive strategies and perspectives among long-term prisoners. *Criminal Justice and Behavior, 8*(2), 201–222.
Foucault, M. (1975). *Surveiller et punir, naissance de la prison.* Gallimard.
Garfinkel, H. (1973). Studien über die Routinegrundlagen von Alltagshandeln. In H. Steinert (Ed.), *Symbolische Interaktion. Arbeiten zu einer reflexiven Soziologie* (pp. 280–293). Klett.
Goffman, E. (1959). *The presentation of self in everyday life.* Doubleday.
Goffman, E. (1961). *Asylums: Essays on the condition of the social situation of mental patients and other inmates.* Anchor Books, Doubleday & Co.
Hall, E. T. (1982). *The hidden dimension.* Doubleday.
Hall, E. T. (1989 [1983]). *The dance of life: the other dimension of time*. Anchor Press/Doubleday.
Herrity, K. (2020). Hearing behind the door: The cell as a portal to prison life. In J. Turner & V. Knight (Eds.), *The prison cell: Embodied and everyday spaces of incarceration* (pp. 239–259). Springer International Publishing.
Isenhardt, A., Hostettler, U., & Young, C. (2014). *Arbeiten im schweizerischen Justizvollzug: Ergebnisse einer Befragung zur Situation des Personals* (Reihe KJS-CJS, Vol. 15). Stämpfli Verlag.
Jacobs, B. (1977). *Stateville: The penitentiary in mass society.* The University of Chicago Press.
Jewkes, Y. (2002). *Captive audience: Media, masculinity and power in prisons.* Willan Publishing.
Jewkes, Y. (2005). Loss, liminality and the life sentence: Managing identity through disrupted lifecourse. In A. Liebling & S. Maruna (Eds.), *The effects of imprisonment* (pp. 366–388). Routledge.

Jewkes, Y. (2018). Just design: Healthy prisons and the architecture of hope. *Australian & New Zealand Journal of Criminology, 51*, 319–338. https://doi.org/10.1177/0004865818766768

Jones, P., & Jam, C. (2016). Creating ambiances, co-constructing place: A poetic transect across the city. *Area* (48), 317–324.

JVA Lenzburg. (2011). *Hausordnung: Justizvollzugsanstalt Lenzburg* .

JVA Lenzburg. (2012). *Justizvollzugsanstalt Lenzburg. Jahrbuch 2010/2011* .

JVA Pöschwies. (2016). *AGE-Info. Kanton Zürich* .

JVA Pöschwies. (2017). *Hausordnung: Justizvollzugsanstalt Pöschwies (HO PöW)* .

Kusenbach, M. (2003). Street phenomenology: The go-along as ethnographic research tool. *Ethnography, 4*, 455–485. https://doi.org/10.1177/146613810343007

Largey, G., & Watson, R. (2006 [1972]). The sociology of odors. In J. Drobnick (Ed.), *The smell culture reader* (pp. 29–40). Berg.

Leder, D. (2004). Imprisoned bodies: The life-world of the incarcerated. *Social Justice, 31*(1–2), 51–66.

Liebling, A. (2000). Prison officers, policing and the use of discretion. *Theoretical Criminology, 4*(3), 333–357.

Lussault, M., & Stock, M. (2010). 'Doing with space': Towards a pragmatics of space. *Social Geography, 5*, 11–19. https://doi.org/10.5194/sg-5-11-2010

Lüthi, H. (2013, August 4). Grössere Fenster für Fünfstern-Gäste des Lenzburger Gefängnisses. *Aargauer Zeitung.* https://www.aargauerzeitung.ch/aargau/kanton-aargau/groessere-fenster-fuer-fuenfstern-gaeste-des-lenzburger-gefaengnisses-126991323. Accessed 10 December 2019.

Mallett, S. (2004). Understanding home: A critical review of the literature. *The Sociological Review, 52*, 62–89. https://doi.org/10.1111/j.1467-954X.2004.00442.x

Marcum, C. D. (2014). Examining prison sex culture. In C. D. Marcum & T. L. Castle (Eds.), *Sex in prison: Myths and realities* (pp. 1–12). Lynne Rienner Publishers.

Martel, J. (2006). TO BE, ONE HAS TO BE SOMEWHERE: Spatio—Temporality in Prison Segregation. *The British Journal of Criminology, 46*(4), 587–612.

Marti, I. (2020). A 'home' or 'a place to be, but not to live': Arranging the prison cell. In J. Turner & V. Knight (Eds.), *The prison cell: Embodied and everyday spaces of incarceration* (pp. 121–142). Palgrave Macmillan.

Milhaud, O. (2009). *Séparer et punir. Les prisons françaises: mise à distance et punition par l'espace* (PhD thesis). Université Michel de Montaigne - Bordeaux III, Bordeaux. https://tel.archives-ouvertes.fr/tel-00441473

Moran, D. (2012). "Doing time" in carceral space: TimeSpace and carceral geography. *Geografiska Annaler: Series B, Human Geography, 94*, 305–316. https://doi.org/10.1111/geob.12000

Moran, D. (2013). Between outside and inside? Prison visiting rooms as liminal carceral spaces. *GeoJournal, 78*(2), 339–351.

Moran, D. (2019). Back to nature? Attention restoration theory and the restorative effects of nature contact in prison. *Health & Place, 57*, 35–43. https://doi.org/10.1016/j.healthplace.2019.03.005

Moran, D., Pallot, J., & Piacentini, L. (2013). Privacy in penal space: Women's imprisonment in Russia. *Geoforum*. https://doi.org/10.1016/j.geoforum.2013.01.002

O'Donnell, I. (2014). *Prisoners, solitude, and time*. Oxford University Press.

Oxford Dictionaries. (2018a). *dirt*. https://en.oxforddictionaries.com/definition/dirt. Accessed 29 June 2018a.

Oxford Dictionaries. (2018b). *rest*. https://en.oxforddictionaries.com/definition/rest. Accessed 29 June 2018b.

Oxford Dictionaries. (2018c). *tidiness*. https://en.oxforddictionaries.com/definition/tidiness. Accessed 29 June 2018c.

Pink, S. (2009). *Doing sensory ethnography*. Sage.

Rice, T. (2016). Sounds inside: Prison, prisoners and acoustical agency. *Sound Studies, 2*, 6–20. https://doi.org/10.1080/20551940.2016.1214455

Scott, J. C. (1986). Everyday forms of peasant resistance. *The Journal of Peasant Studies, 13*, 5–35. https://doi.org/10.1080/03066158608438289

Sykes, G. M. (1971 [1958]). *The society of captives: A study of a maximum security prison*. Princeton University Press.

Tages-Anzeiger. (2010, July 8). Wegen Pöschwies-Mord: Jetzt wird Einnahme von Medikamenten überwacht. https://www.tagesanzeiger.ch/zuerich/region/Wegen-Poeschwies-Mord-Jetzt-wird-Einnahme-von-Medikamenten-ueberwacht/story/14678870. Accessed 10 December 2019.

Thibaud, J.-P. (2002). L'horizon des ambiances urbaines. *Communication* (73), 185–201.

Thibaud, J.-P. (2011). The sensory fabric of urban ambiances. *Senses and Society, 6*(2), 203–215.

Toch, H. (1996 [1977]). *Living in prison: The ecology of survival*. Princeton University Press.

Tuan, Y. F. (2001 [1977]). *Space and place: The perspective of experience.* University of Minnesota Press.
Turner, J. (2016). *The prison boundary: Between society and carceral space.* Palgrave Studies in Prisons and Penology. Palgrave Macmillan.
Turner, J., Moran, D., & Jewkes, Y. (2020). Serving time with a sea view: The prison cell and healthy blue space. In J. Turner & V. Knight (Eds.), *The prison cell: Embodied and everyday spaces of incarceration* (pp. 215–238). Palgrave Macmillan.
Ugelvik, T. (2014). *Power and resistance in prison: Doing time, doing freedom.* Palgrave Macmillan.
Vigh, H. (2008). Crisis and chronicity: Anthropological perspectives on continuous conflict and decline. *Ethnos: Journal of Anthropology, 73*(1), 5–24.
Wacquant, L. (2002). The curious eclipse of prison ethnography in the age of mass incarceration. *Ethnography, 3*, 371–398.
Wahidin, A., & Moss, D. (2004). Women doing and making time: Reclaiming time. *International Journal of Sociology and Social Policy, 24*(6), 76–111.
Westin, A. (1970). *Privacy and freedom.* Bodley Head.

5
At Work

After breakfast—which prisoners eat either in the cell (as in the *Strafanstalt* at *JVA Lenzburg* and *JVA Pöschwies*) or in the common kitchen (in the *60plus* unit)—at around 7.30 am, prisoners who are physically able have to go to work. When I asked Clément what an ordinary day looks like for him, he morosely responded: 'cell, working, cell, working, cell' (Clément, 24.3.2016). Of course (and he would certainly agree), there is in fact much more going on between these two phases of the prison day. However, it is true that besides the cell, prisoners spend most of their time at the workplace, which is the focus of this chapter.

As demonstrated by Méda and Vendramin (2017, p. 7), since antiquity work has gradually increased in importance, and today it occupies a central place in contemporary 'Western societies', which can be defined as 'work-based'. The authors identify three different layers of contradicting and co-existing meanings on which our 'modern' concept of work is based (Méda & Vendramin, 2017, pp. 16–22): (1) work as a *factor for production*, producing a nation's wealth and allowing individuals a means to earn a living; (2) work as the *essence of the human*, a creative activity that allows individuals to find meaning, self-fulfilment and self-realization by transforming the world; and (3) work as a *system*

I. Marti, *Doing Indefinite Time*, Palgrave Studies in Prisons and Penology,
https://doi.org/10.1007/978-3-031-12590-4_5

for the distribution of income, rights and welfare and hence a key factor in social integration. In sum, work has gradually become 'our essence at the same time as our condition' (Méda, 1995, p. 18, my translation). It can therefore be defined as an anthropological category, or, in Mauss' (1966) terms, 'a total social fact'. Today, as further pointed out by Méda and Vendramin (2017, p. 223)—despite changes in the labour market and working conditions (which can also be damaging), as well as the emergence of 'new personal values', such as self-expression, which are all linked to the spread of the neoliberal paradigm since the end of the twentieth century—these meanings continue to co-exist and shape individuals' understandings and expectations of work.

Against this background, it is not surprising that work has historically been 'a core feature of imprisonment', oscillating between productive and commercialized forms of industry and rehabilitative strategies (Matthews, 2009, p. 41).[1] More concretely, on the one hand, within the prison, work provides goods and is a source of revenue. It is also a means to structure and control daily life in prison and to keep prisoners busy. On the other hand, it also institutes work discipline among prisoners, especially those who 'failed' in the labour market in the outside world, and provides training to prepare them for release and successful reintegration into society.

Generally, however, due to a prison's organizational and architectural structures, which are not designed for large-scale production, as well as

[1] In the 'pre-modern' era, driven by economic as well as Christian (i.e. Calvinist) ideology, work in prison basically constituted forced labour (Baechtold et al., 2016, pp. 15–25). This changed with the prison reform movements in the eighteenth and nineteenth centuries in the US and Europe and the emerging idea that the deprivation of liberty (as well as its related consequences) constitutes punishment and thus no further punishment is needed inside prison. Subsequently, work was increasingly conceived as contributing to the prisoners' education and rehabilitation (Baechtold et al., 2016, p. 25). This shift regarding the meaning and function of work in prison was also provoked by critical voices who put forward the argument that forced labour has no justification in a capitalist system of production (Matthews, 2009, p. 42). Moreover, the early (modern) prisons, which were often run as profit-making institutions, also faced growing resistance from entrepreneurs who feared that prison-made goods could undercut the price of commercially produced goods. During periods of high unemployment, it was also argued that the employment of prisoners restricts available employment and pushes down salaries. Finally, there was a concern that prisoners earning more than the poorest workers outside would undermine the 'deterrent effect of imprisonment' (Matthews, 2009, p. 42). However, in the era of neoliberalism and privatization of prisons or joint venture programmes, profiting from prison labour has again become an issue, in particular in the US (see e.g. LeBaron, 2008).

prisoners' generally low skill and education levels and their continuous turnover, the prison's productive capacity has always been limited—regarding both the quantity and quality of goods (Matthews, 2009, p. 43). Given this situation, Matthews (2009, p. 43) describes the prison's production and manufacturing as 'likely to be inefficient and in many respects [...] "primitive" and "pre-capitalist"'. Therefore, prison scholars generally agree that 'working in prison involves experiencing work in a way that is not found outside prison walls' (Guilbaud, 2010, p. 64). Given the working conditions—usually characterized by monotony and repetition (Matthews, 2009, p. 43), where there is either 'too much work or too little' (Goffman, 1961, p. 11), a lack of financial incentive (Matthews, 2009, p. 43) and a lack of control over and impact on the way (prisoners') labour power is used (Guilbaud, 2010, p. 64)—it seems that work provides few 'intrinsic interests' for the prisoners, and the concept of 'job satisfaction' as used in the outside world is fairly alien in this particular context (see also Matthews, 2009, p. 43).

Yet, there are numerous ethnographic studies that reveal that work nonetheless holds some important meanings in prisoners' lives. For example, several authors have illustrated how work helps prisoners ease the 'pains of imprisonment', especially the 'deprivation of liberty' (Sykes, 1971 [1958]), as work enables them to be out of the narrow (and in many countries and facilities overcrowded) space of the prison cell, to vanquish boredom and to pass time more easily (see e.g. Guilbaud, 2010; Milhaud, 2009). Furthermore, it has also been argued that work allows prisoners to reconnect with the outside, 'normal' world. First, through work, prisoners can create the common split between 'private life' and'work life'—spatially as well as temporally—and 'to enjoy' some 'free time', which is only possible when having 'the (opposite) experience of time constraint' that is typically associated with work (Guilbaud, 2010, p. 57). Second, as pointed out for instance by Chassagne (2017), work provides prisoners with a framework for expressing and being perceived according to an 'identity' other than the one related to their crime. For some prisoners, this particular activity—work—is crucial for the maintenance of their 'individual identity' (Chassagne, 2017, p. 9) as it enables them to reconnect with their past lives by mobilizing their previous (work) experiences and the values they attribute to work, such as the feeling of being 'useful' (Chassagne, 2017, p. 9). In a similar way, Guilbaud (2010, p. 59) outlines how through work, prisoners may 'recover a status they have been deprived of'. Hence, work in prison ensures continuity between the inside and the outside world and weakens the discrepancy between the prisoners' present and past lives. Therefore, despite all the 'demoralizing' (Goffman, 1961, p. 11) effects prison work may have on prisoners, it is nevertheless 'undeniably a resource that inmates use to cope with the depersonalization and dependence engendered by confinement' (Guilbaud, 2010, p. 59).

While these ethnographic studies have analysed the meaning of work in prison by highlighting the related functions and values work provides for the prisoners in dealing with the deprivations they face, I propose in this chapter to use a slightly different analytical lens. Here, I explore work in prison by more closely examining prisoners' lived experience during this particular part of the day, and how the experience of work shapes their general experience of imprisonment as well as their sense of self.

The chapter begins with a description of the legal and institutional framework regarding the function and conditions of work in Swiss prisons and provides an overview of the working possibilities and conditions in the prisons where I conducted fieldwork in order to offer some context. Then, I explore the prisoners' spatial, temporal and embodied experiences *of* and *during* this portion of the day. I first show *how* being at the workplace and therefore being (physically) out of the cell *concretely* looks, and how this shapes the prisoners' corporal and spatial experiences of imprisonment. After that, I outline the prisoners' experience of work in terms of time. While the literature describes work above all as a preferred means to pass time, it also notes that prison work is generally monotonous and repetitive (see e.g. Matthews, 2009). However, the ways in which prisoners experience and deal with this latter aspect are less researched. By exploring the prisoners' various temporal experiences at work, I show that repetition and monotony is not *per se* a burden and may even be of value for certain prisoners. Those who suffer through it also find ways to rearrange the institutionally established work rhythms according to their individual needs. The last section is devoted to the prisoners' experiences as 'workers'. As I show, work signifies above all an important potential social space where prisoners seek and may also receive recognition, which is of particular existential importance for these prisoners, constructed as 'absolute others' (Greer & Jewkes, 2005) and most probably permanently excluded from society—physically, socially and morally.

5.1 Work in Swiss Prisons

As with any part of the prison day that is formally organized by the prison, work is shaped by the penal system's institutional logics of punishment (including safety and security) and rehabilitation (including care and the 'normalisation' of living conditions) (see Sect. 3.1.1).

As stated by the Federal Department of Justice and Police, '[i]n view of the basic importance of having a job to any citizen's social integration, work is one of the mainstays of the penal system' (Federal Department of Justice & Police FDJP, 2010, p. 11). Therefore, according to Art. 81 para 1 SCC, '[t]he prison inmate is obliged to work'. While until the mid-twentieth century, prison work in Switzerland was basically characterized by forced labour and driven by economic interests, today it is mainly considered to fulfil 'special preventive objectives' (Baechtold et al., 2016, p. 162). This refers not only to prisoners' rehabilitation, but also to the maintenance of order and discipline inside the prison and the prevention of mental and physical disorders that can be caused by imprisonment. Given these objectives, according to the law, 'wherever possible, the work should be appropriate to [the prisoner's] skills, education and training, and his interests' (Art. 81 para. 1 SCC). If possible, prisoners shall also be given the opportunity to complete basic and advanced training, again appropriate to their skills (Art. 82 SCC). The idea of work as both a key factor for social integration and an activity that enables the expression of individuality (see introductory part of this chapter)—although the preservation of individual integrity is in the foreground—is therefore also embedded in the Swiss penal system, linked to the principle of rehabilitation. Yet, this principle is overlapped by the principle of punishment, as work is also a means of installing discipline, order and security within the prison.

Furthermore, as in the outside world, work in prison constitutes a means of earning money, as every working prisoner obtains a wage for his or her work. However, their wage level does 'not correspond to the market rate' (Federal Department of Justice & Police FDJP, 2010, pp. 11–12). Following Art. 380 SCC, every prisoner has to contribute to the costs of their imprisonment, and he or she does so through the 'unpaid part' of the wage for the work carried out in prison. Moreover, the prisoners may dispose of only part of their paid wages during imprisonment. The remaining portion is withheld for the time after release (Art. 83 para. 2 SCC). As stated by Baechtoldet al. (2016, pp. 168–169), since the introduction of the SCC in 1942, prison wages have mainly served preventive-rehabilitative objectives. In the beginning, the wage was calculated by considering the prisoners' productivity as well as their general behaviour in prison. Since the revision of the SCC in 2007, the prisoners' general behaviour, such as the tidiness of their cells, is no longer decisive. Today, wage calculations must consider a prisoner's performance *and* circumstances (Art. 83 para 1. SCC)—that is, the equipment of the individual workplaces, but also a prisoner's real performance capacity (Baechtold et al., 2016, p. 169). According to cantonal guidelines, the average wage in Swiss prisons has been determined as 26 Swiss francs per day, with 35 Swiss francs as the maximum (Baechtold et al., 2016, p. 170). These norms and guidelines also apply to prisoners held in indefinite incarceration. For prisoners spending the rest of their lives in prison as well as those serving regular sentences it is therefore impossible to make a 'career' in a conventional sense: they are not able (or only on a very limited basis) to make a fortune, nor to be promoted. Although they accumulate a certain amount over the years, prisoners are not allowed to spend it, because it is reserved for an unforeseeable 'later'. Yet, as I show further below, earning money is only one—and, as I argue, for most of the prisoners I met certainly not the most important—advantage they gain through work.

The work opportunities for prisoners in the *Strafanstalt* at *JVA Lenzburg* include jobs in workshops in which they produce items for external customers (bindery/cardboard packaging, printing, basketry/braiding, painting, industrial assembly, locksmithing and carpentry) as well as jobs related to the prison's internal operation. These include jobs related to the upkeep (cleaning, laundry service, ironing and sewing services) and maintenance (technical and construction services) of the prison, the food service (kitchen, bakery, yoghurt production, vegetable gardening) and the prison library. In the two units for ill and elderly prisoners, the offer of work is supposed to serve primarily as an 'occupation' that helps prisoners structure their days. In the *60plus* unit at *JVA Lenzburg*, this includes basic assembly work for external customers. However, during fieldwork there were days without work for the prisoners (e.g. due to a lack of external orders). The prisoners in the *AGE* at *JVA Pöschwies* can engage in handicraft work, making items for sale in the prison shop, as well as in productive work for external orders. Those prisoners who are physically or mentally unable to complete any of these work tasks have to carry out domestic work (such as cleaning their cells) and take care of their personal hygiene during official working hours. Both special units offer a few jobs in upkeep and maintenance services. During fieldwork in these two units, I noticed that foremen also create special jobs for certain prisoners, such as rolling cigarettes that will be sold to prisoners or watering plants in the unit. I also came across what might be called 'fake jobs', occupations that only seem to be productive work. For instance, one prisoner, due to mental health issues, was not capable of participating in any kind of productive work but nevertheless asked for a job. He was given toothbrushes to wrap up and told that they would be distributed to the prisoners. However, each day after he finished, they were unpacked by the staff (of course without the prisoner's knowledge) and given back to him the next day to wrap again. As I show in greater detail below, depending on the specific workplace (carpentry, technical service, etc.), prisoners may either be physically bound to a workshop or allowed to move around more freely (i.e. more independently and less directly monitored by prison staff) within an area of the prison or even the whole building, which strongly shapes their corporal and spatial experience of imprisonment.

As in every prison, although it is prohibited, some informal business was conducted during my fieldwork. For example, I met a prisoner who granted credit to fellow prisoners (those who could not repay it had to settle their debt with commodities, such as sneakers or electronic devices) and another who offered support in writing formal correspondence, such as administrative appeals, and who sold self-made gift cards. As I was told, with enough money, 'in principle, you can get everything in prison that is available in the outside world' (Heinz, 3.5.2916). Examples mentioned to me include mobile phones, USB sticks, alcohol and drugs. However, as this kind of business is not the focus of this chapter, I will not go into the matter in any further detail.

Prisoners who work full-time work approximately seven hours per day. Due to health issues, many prisoners in the special units for ill and elderly prisoners work part-time only. Furthermore, because of the ascribed rehabilitative and integrative value of prison work, which has been confirmed by the Federal Supreme Court, retirement age is not a recognized category in the prison system. Instead, prisoners are formally obliged to work as long as they are capable (Baechtold et al., 2016, p. 162).

In addition to the legal and institutional norms and rules, foremen play a crucial role in framing the prisoners' experience at work. They distribute the workload, tasks and responsibilities among the prisoners, supervise and monitor their activities, and calculate their wage level. In addition, they are responsible for running the workshop and ensuring the quality of fabricated products (Isenhardt et al., 2014, p. 28). Given their obligation to contribute to the prisoners' rehabilitation and to instil and maintain order and discipline, they also have the authority and power to act in response to the prisoners' behaviour at work. For instance, they are supposed to sanction what they consider to be 'inappropriate' behaviour in the workplace by sending the prisoner back to his cell for a day or more and/or reducing the monthly remuneration amount. Furthermore, when calculating the prisoners' wage level, at *JVA Lenzburg* the foremen have to take into account not only the prisoners' productivity (quantity and quality of work), but also their behaviour at the workplace and their degree of 'reliability', 'work interest' and 'commitment' (JVA Lenzburg, 1995, my translation), by classifying the prisoners on a scale ranging from 1 to 11. A prisoner who 'attracts no attention', 'works without any discussion' and displays 'neutral behaviour' is considered to show a 'normal performance'—classified as 7 (JVA Lenzburg, 1995, my translation). Someone whose performance is outstanding (meriting an 11) 'is stimulating, motivates other prisoners to work, actively supports the orders of the foreman' and 'shows initiative, is important to the industry, for which he shows an outstanding interest' (JVA Lenzburg, 1995, my translation). Someone who receives a 1 is 'difficult to guide', 'unreliable, indifferent, [and] indolent' (JVA Lenzburg, 1995, my translation). I argue that through these instruments—that is, the sanctioning of 'inappropriate' behaviour in the workplace and the wage system—the prison, and more concretely the foremen, not only introduce a particular work discipline but also (re)produce morally charged ideas of 'normalcy' and 'deviation', and hence what defines a 'good' or 'bad' worker or prisoner, respectively.

However, the rehabilitative (and thus to some degree the disciplinary) aspect of work is practically irrelevant in the case of prisoners sentenced to indefinite incarceration. Yet, apart from the special units for ill and elderly prisoners, where the significance of work has been shifted from 'production' to 'occupation' in order to provide prisoners with a daily structure and social contacts, the foremen have no special orders to follow regarding this particular prison population.

Consequently, the way foremen manage these prisoners and frame the hours they spend in their workshop depends on each foreman's personal values and interests. For those who focus on the rehabilitative aspect of their job, handling these prisoners can be frustrating, as there is no future goal towards which they can orient them: 'Whatever I teach him, he [the prisoner sentenced to indefinite incarceration] will probably never be able to use it elsewhere' (Foreman A., 27.6.2016). The function of work is thus limited to life inside the prison. Among the foremen I talked to, a few described their role as simply 'keeping prisoners busy' (Foreman E., 21.11.2013) and providing them with 'a daily structure, linked to meaningful work' (Foreman B., 27.6.2016).

Most of the foremen, however, told me they were interested in finding different ways to deal with these prisoners, taking into consideration that they might stay in prison for the rest of their lives. This may include providing these prisoners explicitly with 'variety', the 'possibility of choice' (Foremen F., 18.11.2013), 'as much responsibility as possible', the 'feeling of success' (e.g. by reporting on customer satisfaction) (Foreman D., 22.10.2013) or the feeling of 'still being of value' as a 'human person'

(Foreman A., 27.6.2016). Therefore, although they officially have no specific mandate, the foremen find themselves informally testing and initiating new practices when dealing with these prisoners. Yet, some of them mentioned feeling constrained and frustrated by the lack of institutional support and additional resources (e.g. additional, differently trained staff) that would be necessary to handle these prisoners appropriately, not only in order to provide them with extra support, but also to manage the day-to-day business, as some of these prisoners—due to their personal skills and capacities—need extraordinary individual treatment and attention at work.

In addition, many of the foremen noted their awareness that they may become the most important (and maybe even only) reference person for long-term prisoners held in indefinite incarceration, not least because they are generally the ones who spend the most time with these prisoners (see also Baumeister & Keller, 2011). Therefore, they are often assigned to, or simply take up, various roles vis-à-vis these prisoners:

> You are actually … from the father figure to the boss to … yes, just a supervisor, sometimes also a social assistant. You have many different functions. Sometimes you are a bit of a doctor as well because you have to help them with a small wound or something. Yes, you actually have many more functions [than just that of the foreman]. (Foreman A., 27.6.2016)

In sum, the foremen play a crucial role in the lives of the prisoners, as most of them, informally and based on their own personal values and motivations, consider prisoners' specific life situations and try to grant them more individuality at work. This is crucial for these prisoners, as I explore further below.

5.2 Physical and Mental (Im)mobility

As noted earlier, prison work is generally conceived by the prisoners as a means of getting out of the cell and having more freedom of movement (Milhaud, 2009). As summarized by Guilbaud, '[m]ost of them experience time spent working as a source of spatial and temporal release; it allows them to get out of their narrow, overpopulated cells for six hours a day and to work off some physical energy' (2010, p. 55). While many prisoners would agree with this statement, the need to be outside the cell is less pronounced in the case of the long-term prisoners to whom I spoke, especially for the elderly, who are less mobile due to their health status. This may also result from the fact that in the prisons where I did fieldwork prisoners are all housed in single cells, which for many of them has become over time their favourite place in prison—the one place where they can find peace and quiet (see Chapter 4). Nevertheless, being outside the cell or at the workplace does have meaning for the prisoners and strongly shapes their experience of imprisonment.

Prisoners who work in one of the workshops, doing carpentry or industrial assembly, for example, are usually physically bound to a single place. They spend their work hours mainly sitting or standing, more or less in the same place, while operating a machine, for instance. However, only a few prisoners commented on this issue. Those who did usually complained about it: 'You sit [...] in a chair or at a desk all day long and that's it' (Hugo, 7.9.2017). In the workshops, prisoners are hence considerably physically immobile. Moreover, the workshops are surveilled by one or two foremen who usually act simultaneously as production managers and co-workers. According to internal rules, prisoners are not allowed to leave the workplace without authorization (JVA Lenzburg, 2011, p. 37). As mentioned above, based on their personal values and interests, the foremen strongly shape the working conditions and instal a particular work discipline. Serge explained the conditions in the workshop as follows: 'In the workshop, there I sit at a table, one is not allowed to talk, that is strictly forbidden actually, and then one carries out very monotonous work' (Serge, 25.9.2013). Therefore, although work allows prisoners to leave the small and narrow prison cell, some find themselves highly immobile and corporally inactive with little variety in this place. Their spatial experience at work is therefore reduced to space at its smallest scale.

In contrast, prisoners who work in housekeeping and maintenance services are highly mobile, not only physically but also mentally, as they are generally granted more autonomy and self-determination than the prisoners assigned to the workshops. They usually have to fulfil tasks throughout the prison building, including places generally only accessible to prison staff (e.g. the staff cafeteria or cloakroom). Moreover, they are less directly monitored by staff, they largely work alone and independently and can more freely define the rhythm of their workday. As argued by Milhaud (2009, p. 307, my translation), having a job that allows for circulation around the prison—and therefore greater knowledge of the different prison areas—and for building relations with other working prisoners enriches the prisoners' 'geographical experience of the prison' and, hence, compensates for the deprivations they face. Indeed, prisoners who were at the time of my interviews working in housekeeping and maintenance services emphasized that being physically mobile and less surveilled by staff provides them with a sense of being free—or at least less imprisoned. This echoes Tuan's argument that 'freedom implies space' (2001 [1977], p. 52). However, while Tuan (2001 [1977], p. 52) considers prisoners (as well as the bedridden) as intrinsically 'unfree', living in a 'constricted space' because they are unable or have lost the ability to move freely, I argue that the *sense* of being free or unfree, respectively, remains a subjective, situational and relational experience. Compared to prisoners who 'sit in a chair all day' carrying out 'very monotonous work', prisoners working in the housekeeping and maintenance services and hence circulating all around the prison feel (and indeed are) freer:

> In the [workshop], I was in the same room for three years, 120 m^2, I was doing different jobs, working with different people, and had two good foremen, but working in the construction service [today], being able to move around freely, that makes a big difference, that's a big change. And this is something that is very important to me personally, the possibility of additional freedom in captivity. (Markus, 28.9.2017)

> *Irene*: Where do you feel the least imprisoned, or when?
> *Erwin*: When I'm working, when I'm doing something, then I'm almost everywhere [within the prison building].
> *I*: So feeling less imprisoned means for you being able to move?
> *E*: Yes. (Erwin, 18.10.2017)

I argue that being allowed to circulate around the prison during work not only enriches the prisoners' 'geographical experience' of the prison but also shapes their general 'sense of space' (Tuan, 2001 [1977]) and hence their personal representation of the prison. I became particularly aware of this as the prisoners showed me their workplaces during the walking interviews. This enabled me to explore in situ their perception of the physical environment of the prison, 'filtered' (Kusenbach, 2003) through their experiences and practices as workers. For instance, while showing me his various workplaces, Markus, who worked at that time in the construction service, primarily talked about 'walls'—walls he had to 'grind', walls he had to 'smooth' or 'plaster', walls he had to 'paint'. He talked about 'scaffolds' he had to instal on walls and showed me the 'rotting masonry' (Markus, 28.9.2016), which was (at least the rotted aspect) invisible to me, and other 'weak points' regarding the building's materiality, which he was able to witness from his professional viewpoint (see Fig. 5.1).

Fig. 5.1 Scaffolds installed on the prison grounds (*Source* Photo by a prisoner)

While I was walking around with Erwin, who was working in the housekeeping (cleaning) service, I was again offered another picture of the prison. 'His' prison consists of many 'corridors' as his main task was to clean them throughout the entire building (illustrated in Fig. 5.2).

Prisoners who circulate throughout the prison during work generally also have access to *spaces of authority*—that is, places that are usually only accessible to staff, such as the staff canteen. This not only enriches their geographical experience of the prison and sense of space but greatly impacts their sense of self, as having access to these places is an explicit expression of trust by the prison management (the issue of trust will be discussed in detail in Sect. 5.5.2). Yet, although they are highly mobile during work, their workplace consists of *spaces of transit* as the prisoners are forced to be mobile, or unfree to stay in one place as long as they wish.

5.3 'Less Prison-Like' Spaces

In addition to the degree of mobility prisoners are granted, being at the workplace also means having access to places that are less obviously marked by the carceral. First, this applies to their spatial characteristics, such as the material equipment and decoration in the workshops and work areas (see also Guilbaud, 2010) (illustrated in Figs. 5.3 and 5.4). At first sight, the prison workshops look quite similar to workshops in the outside world. This was a detail mentioned by the prisoners as well. For instance, during our walking interview, Markus was eager to take a picture of the depot of the construction service, because, according to him, 'it doesn't look like prison'. It reminds him of a depot in the outside world, which, he added, fills him 'with pleasure' (Markus, 28.9.2017).

Many machines and tools in the prisoners' workplaces are the same as those in the outside world.

During our walking interview, Erwin showed me the equipment (machines, cleaning products) he must use for cleaning work, emphasizing his familiarity with it as he had his own cleaning company in the outside world (see Fig. 5.5). Hence, his experience of his particular work situation is also shaped by his memories of working in the outside world.

Fig. 5.2 Prison corridors (*Source* Photos by a prisoner)

Fig. 5.3 A prisoner's workplace or a space 'not looking like prison' (*Source* Photo by a prisoner)

Fig. 5.4 In the prison's printing plant (*Source* Photo by a prisoner)

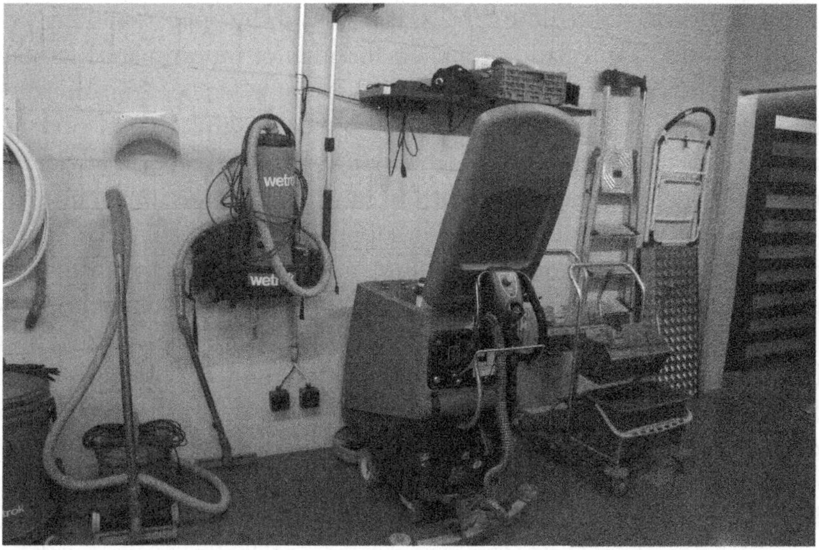

Fig. 5.5 Working with 'familiar equipment' (*Source* Photo by a prisoner)

However, some tools have been adjusted by the management to address the prison's security concerns. For instance, as emphasized by Rolf, who is supposed to work with pieces of wood, some saw blades are 'totally dull (laughs), no carpenter would work with that for a second' (11.9.2013). This, I argue, may transform a workshop clearly and immediately into a highly constrained space (see also Sect. 5.5).

In addition to the materiality of the workplaces, their less prison-like character also emerges from the fact that the workshops can generally be understood as particular social spaces where social relations are 'likely to develop on the basis of other values' (Le Caisne, 2004, p. 531, cited in Guilbaud, 2010, p. 44). Hence, the often-proclaimed antagonism between staff and prisoners (Goffman, 1961) as well as hierarchies among prisoners (Clemmer, 1958 [1940]; Sykes, 1971 [1958]) may be neutralized or temporarily drift into the background. For instance, as illustrated by Guilbaud (2010, p. 44), the workplace may be the only place in prison where prisoners (may be allowed to) shake hands. Similar to the sports context, as came out in my interviews, the crucial relationship in the work context is not that with one's fellow prisoners but that with prison staff. Although I was also told the opposite, many prisoners expressed appreciation for their foreman or forewoman. For many prisoners, he or she constitutes an important reference person whose significance often goes beyond the work relationship. Several prisoners told me that they seek out their foreman to receive practical advice and support concerning their life in prison in general. For example, one prisoner told me that he had received support (i.e. the required material) from his foreman in order to realize his desire to start painting as a hobby. Another mentioned that from time to time his foreman provides him with the latest technical literature so that he can keep up to date in the professional domain in which he has been trained. Certain prisoners also mentioned that they discuss personal issues with their foremen and seek emotional feedback. The various roles the foremen may play in prisoners' lives were also mentioned by the foremen themselves who, during the interviews, expressed their awareness of the situation and their willingness to use their authority in such a way that they are more than a 'simple boss' to these long-term prisoners (see also Sect. 5.1).

> When I feel bad I can talk to [the foreman]. I have such a relationship with him that I can also speak about private issues. […] [I feel] a sense of humanity [from his side], also an interest in the person he is talking to … One can see it very quickly when I feel bad, or if something oppresses me, I don't say anything, but somehow one can see it. And then he, [the foreman], he always looks at me and asks: 'What is it?'. And I say: 'Nothing, everything is all right', and he: 'No, something is wrong'. And I think that's great, I mean you cannot ask for it in here, because … yes. That's why I appreciate that very much. (Leo, 31.8.2017)

> In the foremen's office: Patrick passed several times to see his forewoman, he wanted to know if he was doing his job alright (he was creating gift cards out of paper). She praised him but showed him at the same time how to do it better. She emphasized several times that what was produced in this workshop was 'no *bricolage*' but 'professionally produced cards', which 'should be recognisable'. While watching how she tried to enhance the quality of the card he was working on, Patrick told her that he is about to participate again in group therapy and therefore soon will go on prison leave. The forewoman replied that this is very good news and

> that she is happy for him, but also wanted to know from him why he hadn't joined the therapy group earlier. Patrick didn't answer. He then went back to his workplace where I joined him. He prepared a space to work for me and showed me how to create cards: just 'professional, high quality cards', 'no *bricolage*' he repeated the forewoman's words. I cut out flowers for him. He wet his finger with his tongue and stuck the flowers on the cards – including his fingerprint ... (Fieldnotes, 11.4.2016)

As the extract from my fieldnotes above suggests, the foremen and forewomen are clearly also important in terms of prisoners' identities as workers, which is addressed more fully in Sect. 5.5.

Finally, for some prisoners, the workshop is also a place that allows them to come into direct contact with people from the outside world. In one case, a prisoner had the opportunity to spend some time working together with several workmen from the outside world, during renovation work in the prison. Although he was working very hard physically, he described this particular moment as 'pure recreation and holiday' (Markus, 29.3.2016) as it made him forget that he was in prison. As he further explained, for a certain period of time, they jointly carried out hard work, facing each other, above all, as professionals or co-workers. Hence, through interaction with external workers who gave him the feeling of being of equal value, Markus experienced a situation where the carceral sensation declined:

> I also enjoyed working on this construction site, [...] even if it was really very hard work [...] it was nice. [...] That has been an enormous change for me. Something the others [fellow prisoners] don't have. They have no contact with these workers. And I mean they [the workers] were electricians, plumbers – the same people I worked with in the outside world. [...] They were always very decent to me, and they have not, no one was condescending, of course there were questions like: How is life in here? or: We heard that ... and stuff. So I said: It's not as terrible as you imagine. [...] One has the feeling that people from the outside have a lot of respect. [...] And there were moments, from time to time, just when I was having a conversation with someone, while working together, that I really forgot that I'm locked up. And those moments were worth gold. This is pure recreation and holiday. When you can just forget for a

> moment where you are. Not by drifting away mentally, or daydreaming, but during work, during action, and then just forgetting it for a moment. These are moments that I really enjoy. (Markus, 29.3.2016)

Rolf told me about the time he used to work in the prison's garage, where he was directly connected to the outside world as people brought in their malfunctioning cars. As he explained, this job allowed him to experience some kind of 'normalcy':

> In the garage it was really nice [...] The garage is one of those places in here where you feel the least in prison, it's always open and ... of course it's behind a wall and all that, but cars are coming and going, you do the service and other things for the cars people bring from outside. Yes, you have a lot of normalcy there. (Rolf, 11.9.2013)

I argue that Rolf's feeling of 'normalcy' results from the permeability of the prison, which enabled him to have direct contact with people and objects (cars) from the outside world, but probably also from the fact that he was of direct 'use' to people in the outside community and therefore in some way still part of it. This echoes Guilbaud's argument that '[t]hough they have been removed from social life by a judicial decision, they are nonetheless "organically" linked to society by way of their productive labour' (2010, p. 42).

5.4 Repetition and Monotony

In the literature, work in prison is not only regarded as an opportunity for prisoners to leave the cell but also a preferred means to make doing time easier (Guilbaud, 2010; Milhaud, 2009). Indeed, many prisoners I spoke to agreed with this statement, because during work, one is 'occupied' and has 'something to do' (Jonathan, 24.9.2013). Thomas identified this as the only benefit of prison labour. As he mentioned, time 'passes better' during work (Thomas, 11.6.2013), which for him was also related to the smoking ban. While he structured his time in the cell into 15-minute segments based on his desire to smoke—which at the same time increased his awareness of the passage of time—due to the smoking ban, the rhythm at work could not be rearranged in the same way. This shaped his experience of time as it weakened his awareness of its passage:

> In here I just try to make it through the day, if possible by working, then at least time goes a bit faster. But this is the only reason, it's not because I'm an enthusiastic worker, but just because time passes better, that's all. And then you don't constantly think, every 15 minutes, that it would be time for a cigarette. Because smoking is not allowed down there [in the workshop]. (Thomas, 11.6.2013)

As mentioned by François, working and therefore being occupied 'breaks up the monotony' that prevails in his everyday life. This is especially linked to the possibility of having social interactions at work:

> Yes, work is an occupation that also brings some change in everyday life, and that is something very, very important for me to have an occupation. I cannot imagine now, these six years, a little bit more than six years that I've been in prison now, that I could have done it without working, without any occupation. [...] It's the change, that you work together with other people, this breaks up the monotony that otherwise prevails in prison. (François, 23.11.2013)

Yet, in the prison literature, prison work is also described as monotonous and thus as having demoralizing effects on the prisoners (Goffman1961; Matthews, 2009). As I show in the following, a closer look at the prisoners' lived experiences reveals their manifold ways of experiencing and dealing with repetition and monotony.

During fieldwork, I met prisoners—such as Jonathan, who was felting red hearts to be used as key rings, and Clément, whose job was to unpack candles with production faults—who did not mind the repetitive and often simple character of their work. On the one hand, for them, monotonous work was synonymous with 'easy work', providing them with a clear structure and orientation. Being occupied without being personally challenged (intellectually or physically) allowed some prisoners to concentrate and *to immerse themselves into the present* and thereby get distracted from personal worries and daily troubles (see also

Chassagne, 2017)—maybe even to 'lose all sense of time' (Hall, 1989 [1983], p. 137) and space:

> During that time, I'm thinking of the work that I'm doing, nothing else. I think the work is not bad, I think it's like work for disabled people, it's not difficult work, it's very easy work. (Jonathan, 24.9.2013)

On the other hand, carrying out repetitive work that does not require much thinking allows others 'to let [their] thoughts wander' (Clément, 26.9.2017) and therefore *to transcend the present*.

However, there are also prisoners for whom repetition and monotony have no value and who complained about the work they had been assigned by emphasizing the feeling of boredom. This was not only because of the job content—'I've been here since March, now it's September, since then it's my turn to draw little stars on a board, using a template, and then cut them out. And I've been doing this for months now'. (Serge, 25.9.2013)—but also because of a general lack of variety and change at the workplace, which adds another layer to the overall repetitive nature of prison life:

> I have a strict daily schedule [that starts] with the ring of an annoying bell that will drive me crazy one day. I've been working in the printing service for seven years now, always seeing more or less the same people. When I look outside [the window], it seems to me that freedom is hidden behind glass. I see certain situations in advance because they repeat themselves every day. (Letter from a prisoner, 27.6.2016)

In contrast to prisoners who benefit from monotonous work, which allows them to immerse themselves into or transcend the present, prisoners who suffer due to the working conditions feel, in the sense of Hall, 'stuck in endless time' (Hall, 1989 [1983], p. 132).

Hence, although work is a welcome change from being in the cell, and many prisoners named it as the most important resource for doing time, the workdays get long, and time passes slowly when the work generally provides prisoners with little variety, unforeseeable events or other personal benefits. Yet, as I show in the following section, prisoners also find individual ways to rearrange the institutionally installed working rhythms.

As I discovered, the prisoners developed various techniques or ways of 'doing with' (Lussault & Stock, 2010) time at work. They rearranged the institutionally imposed rhythm of the workday, characterized by repetition and monotony, by creating interruptions and changes during work hours and making use of their working spaces.

For instance, one technique is to try to arrange internal appointments, such as with the masseur (in one of the units for the ill and elderly), or phone calls during specific, individually defined moments during work. Another possibility is to participate in activities offered by the prison during work time, such as sports or school lessons. Other ways of creating change during work include engaging someone in a chat or stretching out the amount of time spent away from the workplace. For instance, after having received a visitor in the visitors' room, prisoners mentioned that they walked back to the workshop 'particularly slowly' (Michael, 6.5.2016) (see also Sect. 6.3.1). Also, a few prisoners mentioned their view from the workshop, saying that from time to time, they look out of the window for a while, gaining further impressions: 'Vans always drive through here, there is always something going on out there. And when I feel a bit depressed, then I stand here [at the window], for one, two minutes' (Leo, 31.8.2017) (illustrated in Fig. 5.6).

Moreover, I witnessed one prisoner's daily routine, which involved filling a bottle with water from the water dispenser located on the ground floor whereas his workplace was located in the basement. He usually did this only shortly after he had handed in his cell key to staff in the office in order to go to his workplace, passing by the water dispenser. As he told me that he was always keen for a distraction from work, I suspect that this interruption was carefully scheduled. The prospect of achieving distraction at work also became an issue when I arranged appointments for the interviews. While the prisoners preferred that I schedule the interviews during work hours, some foremen angrily identified this as a strategy to 'shirk' their responsibilities and insisted that the prisoners meet me during their leisure time (Fieldnotes, 2.5.2016). With all these techniques, along with the development of various attitudes and feelings

Fig. 5.6 A glance out of the window: Watching the vans arriving from the outside world (*Source* Photo by a prisoner)

towards the workday, prisoners can individually modify the flow of the work week:

> Monday is difficult; it comes right after the weekend. But I go to school in the afternoon, which is very good. Tuesday we have sports, so we work less. Then I have a massage, from 1 to 2 pm. On Wednesday, we enjoy a half-day [in this section, Wednesday afternoons are free]. Thursday is the worst day: it's the longest day; there's nothing to do the whole day, just work. Then on Friday we are somehow all looking forward, because on Friday the weekend starts. (Jonathan, 2.5.2016)

5.5 Seeking Individuality and Social Belonging

In addition to the various spatial and temporal experiences that prisoners have at work, what specifically happens there also affects the prisoners' sense of self. In the prison literature, working prisoners' sense of self is often discussed by pointing out the possibility of reconnecting with their previous lives and status (see the introductory part of this chapter). In short, working is described as a means of breaking down the walls that separate their experiences on the inside from those in the outside world. This was certainly also the case for the prisoners I met during my fieldwork. However, I discovered that for long-term prisoners held in indefinite incarceration, in addition to the chance to reconnect themselves with their *past (working) lives*, the meanings they attributed to work are also strongly linked to their *present (prison) lives*. This is not surprising as many of them have been imprisoned for decades, and the prison has inevitably become the centre of their lives.

As my empirical material reveals, work signifies above all an important potential social space for prisoners to experience recognition. This is again not surprising because, as demonstrated by a wide range of studies, in our society recognition is primarily sought and demanded in the context of work. For instance, as demonstrated by Osty (2003), it is at work that we seek the experience of trust, respect and responsibility, the valorization of personal competences and abilities, and a sense of togetherness. As argued by Renault (2001), following the Hegelian tradition, being recognized and appreciated by both individuals and institutions is essential for the development of our 'personal identity', through which we constitute ourselves as both 'a unique human being' *and* 'a member of the human species' (Renault, 2001, p. 184, cited in Guéguen & Mallochet, 2012, p. 38, my translation). As I show in the following, for the long-term prisoners held in indefinite incarceration, recognition is not only decisive for the development of a positive relationship to themselves and others, but also of existential importance due to their permanent physical, social and moral exclusion from society. In the following sections, I explore two expressions of recognition that were experienced by the prisoners I talked to: first, the appreciation and valorization of their individual skills and competences, and second, the attribution of trustworthiness.

5.5.1 Being 'an Expert', 'the Man for All Cases'

While it is prison management that allocates prisoners to particular workplaces (if possible by considering their personal skills and interests), as mentioned in Sect. 5.1 above, the foremen are in charge of the assignment of the specific tasks that the prisoners must carry out and the calculation of each prisoner's monthly remuneration. The official instrument of the wage system, which I described as a powerful tool for imposing certain norms and values at the workplace, is also, at least at first glance, a means to express recognition (or not) vis-à-vis the prisoners, most directly in the form of so-called premiums that can be granted on a monthly basis to prisoners for an additional workload or extraordinary performance. By means of the wage system, the foremen evaluate each prisoner's individual productivity and behaviour at the workplace and hence assign to him a certain *value* as a worker (through his performance and productive contribution) and *status* as a prisoner (in comparison to his fellow prisoners).

Interestingly, however, during the conversations I had with the prisoners, the wage level was rarely explicitly described as an indicator of recognition. It was rather discussed in terms of the living standard it allowed them to reach (or not) inside prison in relation to the comparatively high prices the prisoners had to pay for everyday products at the prison's kiosk. Moreover, the prisoners' wages, and more concretely the amount of money available to spend both inside and outside the prison (e.g. by ordering food or clothes), were also noted in comparison with short-term prisoners, who generally have more contact with the outside world and therefore more options for receiving (and spending) money. However, for most of the long-term prisoners I met, regarding the experience of recognition, far more important than the actual wage seems to be the way they are treated by their foremen. It is hence the 'area of work relationships' (Osty, 2003, my translation) that is crucial in this regard. More concretely, what provides prisoners with the feeling of recognition is not so much material but symbolic in nature.

As I was told, recognition is above all gained through the foremen's situational face-to-face expressions of appreciation and respect and their (enduring) consideration and valorization of the prisoners' individual skills, competences and work experience, which are often less related to their pre-prison lives than to the decades they have spent in prison. These experiences allow them to construct and perform their personal role as a (unique) worker inside the prison. For instance, while Marco became over time 'the man for special tasks', Darko presented himself as 'the man for all cases':

> Because when I'm in the workshop, I want to work (laughs). I don't have much attendance at the workplace [due to health reasons], but when I'm there, I work, and then I work better than most of the others there. And I'm also … just today I got a compliment again, that I was the man for special tasks. If a single-unit production is required, made of wood, then he [the foreman] just hands me the plan and the material and waits until I bring him the finished object (laughs). […] Because I haven't been working with wood since yesterday. I have many years of experience actually. And I find it very pleasant that I can work independently, that not every step is dictated to me, like to a toddler. (Marco, 4.5.2016)

> I was the man for all cases. I did everything: I worked with wood; with glass; with paper, labels, cards; then with the welding torch, I made cans, candelabras, lanterns; then I soldered, actually everything, yes (laughs). And then one [prisoner] was about to leave and they needed a successor for rug production, someone who is trustworthy, where one can say: Yes, he can do that. And then they came to me. At first I thought: No, I don't want to leave this place. […] But then I said: Wait a minute, everything is not so easy out there as well, there are also changes, and you have to make something new again. That doesn't mean that the other thing you did was bad. And I actually like it. (Darko, 6.5.2016)

Another example comes from Hans, who was from time to time asked by one of the foremen to help him weed the prison's surroundings (within the walls) as only he—as a 'plant specialist'—was able to recognize the undesired plants that had to be pulled out:

> They heard from the [prison where he had been before] that I'm a dock specialist … the thing the cows don't eat […] they have big green poles, green stems (he makes hand movement), green leaves and green seeds, and when the leaves turn black, the seeds are also black, all fall out,

> then they come back again. They have long roots like this (makes hand movement). [...] And then they [prison staff] always asked me to come out with them to cut them out, because I know what it is. [A foreman] always asked me: Is this dock? Yes. Is this dock? Yes (laughs). After that he didn't ask me anymore, he [recognized] it himself. (Hans, 4.6.2013)

As these examples suggest, experiencing the foremen's valorization of the prisoners' engagement at work and of their individual and personal competences and (work) skills is crucial for each prisoner's sense of self. It allows prisoners to construct a particular role for themselves as workers, through which they can *be* (i.e. to perform and be perceived as) something different than a criminal or, maybe even more importantly, a 'simple' prisoner, namely a specialist or expert in one particular domain.

Moreover, as a recognized and appreciated worker, they may (re)gain the feeling of having social value. The importance of feeling useful to the community was explicitly mentioned by Rolf. He first worked in the prison garage (as described above) before he moved to the unit for ill and elderly prisoners, where for a short time he carried out one of the two jobs available, namely distributing the delivered food to the prisoners and cleaning their common dining room—a job that he soon lost due to problems with some staff members. As he explained to me, he appreciated this latter job because it allowed him to make a meaningful contribution to the prisoner community: 'It's a job that has to be done, which makes a contribution and pleases people'. As he added, to carry out a job that is useful was most important for him (Fieldnotes, 5.4.2016).

As indicated, the effects of the prisoners' construction and maintenance of their roles as unique and (useful) workers goes beyond self-representations. They are also expressed and performed through particular attitudes and 'body techniques' (Mauss, 1968). For instance, when Juris told me about his previous job in the prison's technical service, he presented himself as an independent, hard-working person who imposed upon himself a lot of stress as he felt compelled to 'take work home' and sacrifice his leisure time, which finally 'forced' him to take sleeping pills. At the same time, however, he made himself indispensable for the running of the prison:

Juris: I have taken sleeping pills since last August. I have reduced that to half of it now [thanks to the new job]. And it will take one more month and I'll leave it all behind and drink my tea again so I will again be sleeping like a log.
Irene: You couldn't sleep because you couldn't switch off?
J: Yes, I couldn't stop thinking. They [the thoughts] kept on turning. Because … I was physically tired, but I didn't have the freedom anymore to do anything else.
I: Because of your job?
J: Yes. Sounds exaggerated maybe, but if I do something, then I do it with heart and soul. If I see a problem, then I cannot … like changing my uniform and going home. I keep on thinking about it. About a third of the administration, which should have been done by the bosses there, it was me who did that at night, on my computer.
I: For the technical service?
J: For the company, yes. Including registration, TV, […] [I] registered everything.
I: I see. Then you didn't have any free time anymore.
J: In my free time, I also made lists. I took along a pile of folders at the weekend. Nobody asked what I was doing with these folders. I just wanted to maintain order. And you wouldn't believe it: the day after I quit, the problems started [at the technical service]. (Juris, 22.3.2016)

Interestingly, what appears in all the extracts presented above is that the prisoners' representations of their roles as workers do not indicate (or perhaps only very vaguely as in the case of Hans' story) that the work they are talking about actually takes place in a prison—it could be anywhere. Thus, the experience of being a recognized and appreciated worker allows prisoners, first, to transcend the framework of the institutional context that assigns uniform roles and statuses to the prisoners and to experience individuality, and second, to reconnect with the (working) community beyond the prison walls.

To conclude, I argue that the feeling of being recognized as a unique and at the same time socially 'useful' individual through the experience of appreciation at work is particularly crucial for long-term prisoners held in indefinite incarceration. Indefinite incarceration is accompanied by a loss of those roles and social statuses, which to a great extent, at least in so-called Western societies, as mentioned above, prisoners had established through participation in the labour market. In the literature, this loss is often also described as 'social death' (see Goffman, 1961). This applies to prisoners in general, and in particular to prisoners who are physically, socially and morally excluded from society. Hence, for many of the prisoners I talked to, work, and more precisely the work context, constitutes an important (potential) source for developing and maintaining a positive sense of themselves, by (re)gaining self-esteem and (re)constructing an identity other than that of a 'dangerous' criminal (to the public) and a 'simple' prisoner (within the prisoner community). As I show in the following, recognition is also strongly connected to the experience of trust, which, as I argue, is another issue of existential importance for these prisoners.

5.5.2 Being Trustworthy

Prisons are generally described as environments characterized by a high degree of mutual distrust among prisoners, and also between staff and prisoners (Crewe, 2009; Goffman, 1961). Based on a recent study on trust in maximum-security prisons in England, Liebling et al. (2015) emphasize that although trust is generally rare, it does, in different forms and to various degrees, exist in this kind of institution. According to the authors, the 'best forms of trust' were used:

> as a way to connect with an individual or facilitate growth. They included getting to know prisoners, finding their talents and strengths, encouraging them to explore new avenues, and giving them (often creatively found) opportunities to demonstrate trustworthiness. (Liebling et al., 2015, p. 6)

In contrast, 'bad forms of trust' are identified when trust was used for 'self-serving ends, such as when prisoners were trusted with information about other prisoners that they should not be party to' (Liebling et al., 2015, p. 6). The authors point out that 'where trust was used intelligently, it could have life affirming and damage repairing consequences' (Liebling et al., 2015, p. 6).

The experience of trust, more precisely 'good' forms of trust, also surfaced in my interviews. Being assigned the status of trustworthiness within the work context seems to have a strong and positive impact on the prisoners' experiences at work and essential consequences for their sense of self. As I show in the following, the feeling of being trusted in prison is further linked to the following experiences: (1) being granted more autonomy and responsibility, (2) being allowed to bypass internal rules, (3) having access to exclusive and 'untouched' places and (4) being 'heard' by the prison management—all rare 'goods' in the carceral context.

The experience of trust in the prison's work context may emerge in various settings and different situations. However, it is above all an issue for prisoners who are officially deemed trustworthy by being given one of the (less available) so-called *Vertrauensjobs* (i.e. jobs that are based on trust). These usually include, as mentioned earlier, jobs in the housekeeping and maintenance services (including technical service and construction), as well as the prison's library.

5.5.2.1 Being Granted More Autonomy and Responsibility

Trust is at the core of the *Vertrauensjobs* as they generally grant the prisoners a comparably high degree of autonomy and responsibility, and often also access to places throughout the prison, including those generally only accessible to staff. Moreover, for prisoners, holding a *Vertrauensjob* means being less closely monitored during work hours and officially allowed to structure their workday more freely and define their own working rhythm—thus, being their own boss:

> For ten months now I've been [working in housekeeping]. I clean [the unit]. I'm my own boss, no one commands me, no one sets the pace for me, I organize myself. I do that, then this, then that, then I take a break, then this again, then another break, and that's how I get time done. (Jonathan, 24.9.2013)

> I worked in the medical service [doing the cleaning work]. This is a job of trust, just like in the social service, granted by the management. They

> first check how he [the prisoner] is and what he does and so on. And then I was there for ten years, in the medical service, and now I work in the social service, where you have seen me //exactly// And what's nice about it, I like to work independently. So that means I don't like it, if there is always someone behind me: Hey, it's not time for a break yet, go on working. They can forget that. I used to work independently and will do it until the end of my life. I don't like to be ordered around. Well, I did the military, but still. (Theo, 3.5.2016)

As I noted, these *Vertrauensjobs* are predominantly assigned to prisoners held in indefinite incarceration. This is not surprising as these prisoners are long-term residents and hence known by the prison management and staff. These prisoners are also certain to stay for a longer period of time, if not forever. Consequently, many of them are generally keen to have a job that provides them with some variety, a bit more responsibility and autonomy. Simultaneously, the prison management and staff are equally interested in keeping them satisfied in order to avoid unrest. In addition, these prisoners are generally known for following the rules and knowing the system (see also Sects. 2.2.1 and 2.2.2).

However, trust—in the form of being granted more autonomy and responsibility—can also be experienced in the common workshops, although this was rarely mentioned by the prisoners working there. One prisoner, Leo, completed two vocational trainings inside prison. His newly gained competences and skills were appreciated by the foremen, who, as a result, allowed Leo a bit more freedom compared to his fellow prisoners:

> I […] get well along with the bosses. They practically give me every job. And this is important, the diversity, that you have variety. Well, you have repetition everywhere, a routine, that's part of every profession … but they also notice, if I have to [do the same job for a long time] then they know exactly, the next day I get restless and start running around, still working, but then they know exactly that I feel bored, and then they just look that I can somehow do something else. Of course, I enjoy that too, that freedom, and it's a huge support […] [This makes me] happy and also proud. And that I can move a little bit more freely than others, that they allow me a bit more. (Leo, 31.8.2017)

Finally, Michael made me aware that the experience of trust can also be more subtle and less observable, though no less important for the prisoner concerned. Trust ultimately remains a relative and subjective experience:

> I'm glad that I can work, that I have my work there [in the workshop]. [The foremen] they have confidence in me. I always do the cutting of the labels, as you have already seen //yes, exactly//, this is now work that I like to do: it's also monotonous, but I like it. Now it's only me who cuts, so to speak. Before that, two, three others had to help me. (Michael, 6.5.2016)

In addition to being granted more autonomy and responsibility, holding a *Vertrauensjob* is also related to other advantages, such as 'bypassing' internal rules.

5.5.2.2 'Bypassing' Internal Rules

Among those who hold an official *Vertrauensjob*, certain prisoners emphasized that this is also connected to the ability to officially 'bypass' certain house rules. When a prisoner ignores a rule, this can often be *heard* and *seen* by others due to the immediate reactions initiated by technical security measures (e.g. alarm devices) or attentive personnel. Being allowed to 'break' rules (or, as an outsider would argue, having to follow different ones) without causing any institutional intervention was mentioned by the prisoners as a clear and important sign of trust:

> [While working in the technical service] I was a prisoner who was allowed to go everywhere. Of course not with a key, but they let me in everywhere when I rang or knocked. And I was always allowed to go through the metal arc [metal detector] during work hours, it was whistling and whistling [but no one was checking]. (Juris, 22.3.2016)

> I'm the only one in this prison who is walking around with a tool bag. And the employees, they got used to it, they know that, and when I come in from outside, of course, I have to go through the metal arc; I have to pull that off too. And in the beginning, they took everything out,

> rummaged through it, searched it, they were doing this for two years, and then they gave up. They just ran out of patience. And this is also a bit of freedom, a piece of trust. Because just like I said, it's just screwdrivers, but they can be used as weapons, they can also be misused to demolish things. But I earned trust over time. (Markus, 28.9.2017)

As these quotations illustrate, what is at stake in being allowed to bypass internal rules is less the fact that these prisoners' working conditions are less restrictive, but rather the ability to stand out clearly from the prison crowd, which again affects their sense of self in a positive way.

When I first came across Markus, I thought he was a staff member. His appearance and way of moving made me draw this conclusion. This experience leads me to suggest that the trust these prisoners are granted probably also influences the way they experience and use their (imprisoned) bodies.

5.5.2.3 Having Access to Exclusive and 'Untouched' Places

As discussed above, prisoners who are allowed to circulate more freely within the prison may gain an enriched geographical experience of the place and the feeling of being less imprisoned (see Sect. 5.2). This again applies to those prisoners with a *Vertrauensjob*. They are not only freer to circulate; they also have access to exclusive places, generally not accessible to the rest of the prisoners: *spaces of authority*. These include the staff offices, cafeteria and cloakroom. Having access to these places plays an important role in the prisoners' feelings of self-worth and experience of imprisonment.

Among other things, Hugo was at the time we met in charge of cleaning the staff canteen (illustrated in Fig. 5.7), which has to be carried out on a daily basis. As the following extract of our interview suggests, for him, the canteen (which represents for the prison staff a recreational space) clearly signifies a space where he experienced an almost family-like atmosphere and where interactions with staff made him feel respected as an (equal) human being. It is a place where staff members chat and joke with him, and would even offer him a cup of coffee from time to time:

> From time to time, someone comes in to have a cup of coffee [...] to smoke a cigarette, to chat with me a little bit, to offer me a coffee. Here I have a lot of contact with the employees. [...] Here [in this prison] it's just ... yes, a little more relaxed [...] almost a bit familiar. You know each other, you can joke with each other, you can talk to each other. (Hugo, 7.9.2017)

As he further explained, it also happens that the officers talk to each other about issues that probably should not be heard by prisoners, or that they unintentionally leave internal documents or personal items in the room. This provides him with additional opportunities to prove his trustworthiness as he remains silent about what he has heard and immediately hands over to the management documents officers accidentally left in the canteen—'without having a look' (Hugo, 7.9.2017).

Jobs in prison housekeeping may also include cleaning the staff cloakroom and the room where standby staff spends the night (see Fig. 5.8).

Fig. 5.7 Access to spaces of authority: The staff canteen (*Source* Photo by a prisoner)

Fig. 5.8 Access to spaces of authority: The place where prison staff spend the night (*Source* Photo by a prisoner)

Fig. 5.9 An 'untouched place' (*Source* Photo by a prisoner)

When standing together in the staff cloakroom, a small room without windows that is used by those officers who do sports during their break—containing some (perhaps sweaty) sports clothes and shoes belonging to prison staff—Erwin explained to me that having access to this kind of backstage area, where he must clean the toilet and the shower, gives him great 'satisfaction' and reassurance:

> *Irene*: How is it for you, to have access to [the staff cloakroom], there are personal things in here …
> *Erwin*: It's of course a great satisfaction. […] You see, this is the shower that I have to clean; [it] is the shower for the staff.
> *I*: You said it gives you satisfaction to be allowed to be in here, did I get that right? That you receive confidence //yes//
> *E*: Exactly.
> *I*: And what do you think then, you always see the staff in uniform, and here you see their shoes and the towels and the bags …
> *E*: Yes, it's actually normal for me.
> *I*: You're actually looking a little bit behind the scenes.
> *E*: Yeah, that's what reassures me, because they have confidence in me. (Erwin, 18.10.2017)

Prisoners who circulate throughout the prison also have access to what Markus labelled 'untouched' places. These areas are generally accessed neither by fellow prisoners nor employees. Such places, which are of emotional importance for the prisoners, may be rooms in the prison that are largely inaccessible (e.g. because they need to be renovated) as well as places that have simply no significance (or no concrete function) and hence do not exist for the prison (similar to the 'free places' described by Goffman, 1961, p. 230). One concrete example is the small meadow illustrated in Figure 5.9, which is located in the outdoor area of the prison.

> During our walking interview, Markus and I walked among various places along his work route. As he was at the time of the interview working in the prison's construction service, his workplace also included the area around the prison (still within the walls). At some point, he led me to this small meadow, located very close to the prison walls.

Markus: This [meadow] is my absolute favourite place in prison.
Irene: Really?
M: Yes. […] This is where I find peace. During the break in the afternoon, when I work outside, I always spend the break outside … then I lie down here, take off my t-shirt, lie down and take a sunbath. Very comfortable, I have my rest, I can switch off … I close my eyes, snooze for ten minutes, then I'm not in prison.
I: What exactly is it that makes you feel like this? //I have no idea// Because me, I basically see fences and the wall.
M: I cannot answer that question, I just don't know, maybe it has to do with the fact that we are here in front of one of our depots, so the place here is just ours, the construction service. That's a bit, I don't know, I'm territory-related like a dog, have no idea (laughs).
I: It's like your territory.
M: This is our territory, yes, mine. And that's why this is actually the place where I can say, when I take a break there in the afternoon, alone, when I have my peace, then I feel good, as amazing as it sounds.
I: Mh. Do you want to take a picture of this?
M: Yes. It's actually just a meadow, but it's not a lawn, it's a real meadow, a wild meadow. And everything that has something to do with vegetation reminds me a little bit of the outside. It's not that … they do cut the grass, but it's really wild compared to the other places, because nobody is interested in this place behind here.
I: Yes, I think I can see now what you mean.
M: Do you understand what I mean?
I: Yes.
M: It's an untouched place, so to speak. [He takes a picture with the fences and wall at his back]
I: And are you actually here every day?
M: Pretty much, yes.
[…]
I: May I take a picture from this side?
M: Of course.
I: So that I remember //the contrast//, yes and because I find it exciting that I perceived this place completely differently, because I don't have any connection to this place. (Markus, 28.9.2017)

During our walking interview, I was able to access Markus' perception of this meadow, filtered through his values and emotions, as he presented the meadow as an 'untouched place'—by fellow prisoners as well as by the management—which let it remain 'wild'. His perception was also filtered by his intention to not focus on the fences, the walls and the cameras, which are particularly obvious in that area. He instead emphasized the fact that this place, the meadow, provides him with the experience of getting in touch with 'vegetation', which allows him to feel connected to the outside world. As this extract also shows, having access to Markus' filtering of his perception *in situ*, allowed me to become aware of and de-emphasize my own perceptual presuppositions and biases (see also Kusenbach, 2003, p. 469): what I perceived, above all, were fences and the wall, all clear indications that this place is a prison. While I had a *horizontal* field of vision (see Figure 5.10), Markus' perspective was clearly *vertical*: focusing on the ground and the sky.

Furthermore, I not only gained access to Markus' perception, but also to his particular ways of engaging with the prison context through spatial

Fig. 5.10 A 'simple meadow' within the prison walls (*Source* Photo by Irene Marti)

practices. The meadow is the place where he spent his official breaks during work hours. However, as he revealed during our interaction, he tried to make the routine of having a break as rewarding as possible through particular bodily practices. By lying in the meadow, closing his eyes and having a rest, he transcended the here and now and found peace and quiet. By means of the mundane practice of taking a work break in a meadow, he created a moment of freedom.

5.5.2.4 Feeling Heard by Prison Management

As my empirical material also suggests, being considered a trustworthy worker may also lead to the experience of being taken seriously as a prisoner, and, more concretely, being heard by prison management. Juris, who, as he explained to me, is 'known as a trustworthy prisoner', successfully 'managed' to get a job in the prison's technical service by highlighting his professional qualities and mentioning that hiring him would be 'a win-win situation' for all parties:

> *Juris*: Two weeks before this job became vacant […] I heard from my predecessor that this job became vacant, that he left. Then I asked if they already had someone and he [the staff member responsible] said that there were a lot of applicants. Then I went […] wrote a letter to the head of security. Like an application on the outside. I wrote about a win-win situation, but also that both would have to take a risk.
>
> *Irene*: And what did he gain with you?
>
> *J*: Well, an absolute top professional. I can do everything. No, I cannot do everything: I have to see it once, but then I can do it. […] And then, he actually gave me this job. […] And I always said: if I leave this place, moving away from the technical service is at the same time a departure from [the place where the prison is located]. (Juris, 22.3.2016)

More recently, another job was 'offered' to him: the job of librarian. He was able to take 'time for reflection' before issuing any commitment, because, as he pointed out, he is known to be reliable and someone who can be trusted. He emphasized again that he reached his goals in a self-determinate way:

> Last summer I decided that something has to change. But I didn't want to throw everything away. […] It was a coincidence that this library opened. It [the job] was offered to me in November. At first I thought, for the sake of God, no, that's [not at all a job for me] (laughs), I don't see myself there. Then I took some time for reflection and my luck was that no one else was really interested. […] Only a reliable person is suitable for this job, someone who can be trusted and also be left alone. Because [there], you're not under supervision all day. It has to be someone … it cannot be a newcomer who said he is a trained librarian – who knows what person hides behind? (Juris, 22.3.2016)

These examples from Markus refer to the negotiation of the prisoner's wage:

> I know that I'm a good worker; otherwise I wouldn't have this job. My boss gets the most out of it regarding bonuses, what he still can, he is aware that I'm not satisfied if I don't receive the maximum possible. (Markus, 29.3.2016)

> [We had to do this job] under the blazing sun, and I really cannot bear the sun. And then, after five weeks, when we finished and got the next wage and I saw that we didn't get any bonus for that, I got pissed off. And that was the first time I said to the boss: now something has to change, otherwise I'm looking for a new job. That's slavery. So, we'll see [he refers to the next payroll]. (Markus, 28.9.2017)

In the narratives presented above, based on the knowledge that they are perceived as trustworthy and reliable, the prisoners reverse the institutionally established power relations between staff and prisoners. In a confident and assertive manner, the prisoners negotiate with the prison staff and management in order to obtain a desired job as well as particular working conditions (i.e. the wage). However, I claim that the fact that these prisoners are 'heard' by the management is also linked to the long-term nature of these prisoners' stays. As mentioned in Sect. 2.2.2, the staff are interested in having satisfied (in particular long-term) prisoners who do not cause too much trouble. Hence, they are also more willing to cooperate with them.

In sum, experiencing recognition in the prison's work context, in connection with the feeling of being appreciated as a valuable and trustworthy person, is of particular existential importance for these prisoners. Against the background that they will most likely be permanently excluded from society, socially constructed as 'absolute others' (Greer & Jewkes, 2005), work allows them to raise their self-esteem and (re)create a positive conception of themselves. Being an *imprisoned worker* rather than a *working prisoner*, which is the topic of the next section, enables them to feel like unique human beings as well as (still) members of society.

5.5.3 Being a 'Simple' Prisoner

Just as work allows prisoners to experience trust, respect, responsibility and the valorization of personal competences and abilities, it is also a context where prisoners may encounter the opposite: contempt, misrecognition or indifference. Such experiences may evoke feelings of being treated 'simply as a number' (Marco, 4.5.2016) rather than an individual with a biography, personal skills and interests. This experience was put forward, especially, by prisoners with a high work morale, who consider the professional context an important arena for finding meaning and self-fulfilment.

For certain prisoners, the workplace constitutes a social space where they experience frustration or even humiliation due to a lack of recognition of their skills and expertise, and also their personal potential. Such an experience can emerge in situations where the foreman does not acknowledge or consider the prisoner's work experience. This is reinforced in cases when the prisoner feels superior to the foreman regarding his or her professional expertise, as the following quotes indicate:

> The [foreman] doesn't know much about woodworking tools, me I've learned that. And then he gives [...] someone [a prisoner] a saw to work

with but cannot show him how to use it properly. [...] And then I cannot stay idle, I cannot, but I have to, it's not allowed to show anyone how to do something. (Rolf, 11.9.2013)

At work you can ... Me, I'm a trained carpenter, but I cannot say anything to a younger [fellow prisoner] or show him how I learned and used to do it [a particular step], the boss doesn't want that. The last time he scolded me. I don't like that. [...] I'm not allowed to work according to my own approach: I have to do it the way the boss wants it. Well, I'll do it that way, but as a specialist I'm not allowed to help someone else or tell him how to do it. [...] That's a bit of a disadvantage in here. (Franz, 10.9.2013)

A similar experience was reported by Lars, who was at the time of my fieldwork engaged in a job that was very frustrating for him as, according to him, his foreman did not acknowledge his skills and interests, and also would not allow him to further develop his personal potential. He used to tell me again and again how much he disliked it because it was a job that, according to him, 'anyone could do' and 'you don't need to think' while performing it. He, in contrast, needed to be 'challenged mentally' in the workplace and to experience 'independence and personal responsibility' (Fieldnotes, 11.2.2016).

The lack of recognition of prisoners' skills, expertise and personal potential may not only cause frustration but also have a strong negative impact on their sense of self, thereby reinforcing their experience of social exclusion. When I talked to Rolf in 2013 and again in 2016, he was staying in one of the units for ill and elderly prisoners, where work is to a great extent not supposed to be productive in an economic sense but instead aims to occupy and structure the prisoners' daily lives. The products the prisoners produce are usually sold at the prison shop. What Rolf was at that time experiencing in this unit was in great contrast to his previous experience in the prison's garage, which I presented above in Sect. 5.3:

I have achieved so much in my life that I can be proud of, and now I'm supposed to glue together the filthy bits of driftwood, sometimes so porous that they collapse after a week, to stick them together with hot

> glue. I create characters, that's all well and good, you see, they are partly, yes, still pretty. But people buy them just because they are cheap. And I think that's a humiliation of old prisoners who have spent a lifetime struggling to acquire skills to make a good contribution to society. I think that's bad, an unnecessary humiliation. (Rolf, 11.9.2013)

> I think it's really bad for the prisoner when he's forced to do work which he doesn't believe in, which he doesn't enjoy, and, above all, he is aware, or at least has the impression that if somebody buys it, at best he buys it out of pity. I think that's bad. [...] A so-called Christmas tree, with a terrible wooden frame, with a huge wooden block underneath, as a foot [...]. And then all sorts of driftwood, worm-eaten, rotten, [which is] glued to it, that's supposed to be a Christmas tree. You work on it for three weeks, four weeks, five weeks, one month because it's so cumbersome, laborious to make it, to make it last. And then it's sold for maybe 60 [Swiss] francs. Well, that's just not normal. (Rolf, 6.5.2016)

From Rolf's perspective, the work he has to carry out in the special unit is anything but 'normal'. This is related to the material he is supposed to work with ('worm-eaten', 'rotten driftwood'), the tools he has to use (not adequate), the price his work is sold for (too low) and the reason it is bought (pity). I argue that due to his high work morale and identification with what he is creating, being forced to do an 'abnormal' job (both regarding the mode of production and the value and usefulness of the product) makes him feel worthless (i.e. not 'normal') as a person and thereby even more excluded from a society to which he can only connect (i.e. contribute), if at all, through pity.

In sum, while some prisoners experience recognition and feel respected as individuals and, in a way, as 'equal' human beings by their foremen, others encounter foremen who exercise their authority in a way that makes the prisoners feel incompetent or like a simple and exchangeable worker. From the prisoners' perspective, these foremen neither respect nor acknowledge the prisoners' individual interests, skills and previous work experience. Additionally, this kind of work relationship does not allow these prisoners to flourish. Therefore, they are not only missing individuality and autonomy in this particular carceral context, but also the fact that neither their *past* nor their *future* is considered—they are held in the present, specifically a (repetitive) present determined by the prison. Finally, being forced to carry out work in which they do not believe (e.g. non-productive work with no value for the community) can damage prisoners' relationship to themselves as they may come to feel not only useless, but worthless. In their narratives, these prisoners made clear that in this institution, they cannot be the person they 'normally' are (or could become), but just a (working) prisoner.

5.6 Conclusion

This chapter has explored work in prison by more closely examining prisoners' lived experience during this particular part of the day, and how the experience of work shapes their general experience of indefinite incarceration as well as their sense of self.

Depending on their concrete job and tasks, the prisoners are granted various degrees of mobility and freedom of movement. This is crucial as it shapes not only their geographical experience of the prison but also their 'sense of space' and hence their personal perception of 'the prison'. Moreover, through work they may also access places less marked by the carceral. This is related to both the physical configuration of the workplaces and the way they are treated by the foremen, who are often more than 'a simple boss', but an important reference person for these long-term prisoners.

However, as in the outside world, work signifies above all a potential and important social space where prisoners search for recognition, which they may experience through the valorization of their individual skills and competences as well as the attribution of trustworthiness. As a recognized and appreciated worker they may (re)gain the feeling of being a unique individual as well as (still) a member of society. This is of existential importance for these prisoners, all labelled 'dangerous' and hence not only physically but also morally and socially excluded from society, to which, however, they theoretically may return one day. The opposite experiences of contempt, misrecognition and indifference not only cause a high degree of frustration but also reinforce their experience of social exclusion.

* * *

The prisoners' workday ends at around 4.30 pm. After dinner, the official leisure time begins, which is the topic of the next chapter.

References

Baechtold, A., Weber, J., & Hostettler, U. (2016). *Strafvollzug: Straf- und Massnahmenvollzug an Erwachsenen in der Schweiz* (3rd ed., Kriminalität, Justiz und Sanktionen KJS: Vol. 17). Stämpfli Verlag.

Baumeister, B., & Keller, S. (2011). *Alt werden im Straf- und Massnahmenvollzug*. ZHAW Departement Soziale Arbeit, Dübendorf.

Chassagne, A. (2017). Les temporalités de la vieillesse en prison. Le temps oublié des « vieux » détenus. *ethnographiques.org*(35), [en ligne].

Clemmer, D. (1958 [1940]). *The prison community*. Holt, Rinehart & Wilson.

Crewe, B. (2009). *The prisoner society: Power, adaptation and social life in an English prison*. Oxford University Press.

Federal Department of Justice and Police FDJP. (2010). *The execution of sentences and measures in Switzerland: An overview of the system and execution of sentences and measures in Switzerland for adults and juveniles*.

Goffman, E. (1961). *Asylums: Essays on the condition of the social situation of mental patients and other inmates*. Anchor Books, Doubleday & Co.

Greer, C., & Jewkes, Y. (2005). Extremes of otherness: Media images of social exclusion. *Social Justice, 32*(1), 20–31.

Guéguen, H., & Mallochet, G. (2012). *Les théories de la reconnaissance*. La Découverte.

Guilbaud, F. (2010). Working in prison: Time as experienced by inmate-workers. *Revue Française De Sociologie, 51*, 41–68. https://doi.org/10.3917/rfs.515.0041

Hall, E. T. (1989 [1983]). *The dance of life: The other dimension of time*. Anchor Press/Doubleday.

Isenhardt, A., Hostettler, U., & Young, C. (2014). *Arbeiten im schweizerischen Justizvollzug: Ergebnisse einer Befragung zur Situation des Personals* (Reihe KJS-CJS, Vol. 15). Stämpfli Verlag.

JVA Lenzburg. (1995). *Kantonale Strafanstalt Lenzburg. Beurteilung und Verdienst.*

JVA Lenzburg. (2011). *Hausordnung: Justizvollzugsanstalt Lenzburg* .

Kusenbach, M. (2003). Street phenomenology: The go-along as ethnographic research tool. *Ethnography, 4*, 455–485. https://doi.org/10.1177/146613810343007

LeBaron, G. (2008). Captive labour and the free market: Prisoners and production in the USA. *Capital & Class, 32*, 59–81. https://doi.org/10.1177/030981680809500103

Liebling, A., Bramwell, R., & Williams, R. (2015). *ESRC Transforming Social Science Scheme: Locating trust in a climate of fear: Religion, moral status, prisoner leadership, and risk in maximum security prisons.*

Lussault, M., & Stock, M. (2010). 'Doing with space': Towards a pragmatics of space. *Social Geography, 5*, 11–19. https://doi.org/10.5194/sg-5-11-2010

Matthews, R. (2009). *Doing time: An introduction to the sociology of imprisonment*. Palgrave Macmillan.

Mauss, M. (1966). *The gift. Forms and functions of exchange in archaic societies.* Cohen & West.

Mauss, M. (1968). Techniques of the body. In M. Mauss (Ed.), *Sociologie et anthropologie* (4th ed., pp. 346–386). Presses Universitaires de France.

Méda, D. (1995). *Le travail: une valeur en voie de disparition* (Alto). Aubier.

Méda, D., & Vendramin, P. (2017). *Reinventing work in Europe. Value, generations and labour*. Palgrave Macmillan.

Milhaud, O. (2009). *Séparer et punir. Les prisons françaises: mise à distance et punition par l'espace* (PhD thesis). Université Michel de Montaigne - Bordeaux III, Bordeaux. https://tel.archives-ouvertes.fr/tel-00441473

Osty, F. (2003). *Le désir de métier. Engagement, identité et reconnaissance au travail*. Presses universitaires de Rennes.

Renault, E. (2001). Identité et reconnaissance chez Hegel. *Kairos, 17*, 173–197.

Sykes, G. M. (1971 [1958]). *The society of captives: A study of a maximum security prison.* Princeton University Press.

Tuan, Y. F. (2001 [1977]). *Space and place: The perspective of experience.* University of Minnesota Press.

6

During Leisure Time

After a snack in the prison staff canteen, I was ready to join the security officers for the evening shift. At around 5.30 pm, I accompanied one of them, who had to unlock the cells of those prisoners who had registered for a leisure program, such as sports or education. The prisoners immediately started chatting and joking with each other. The mood among them was noticeably more relaxed than in the morning or afternoon when the prisoners gather (at the same place) before going to work. […] At 6 pm, all the other cells were unlocked, but the wings were closed as prisoners must remain in 'their' wing during the evening. From time to time, officers walked through the wings in order to check that everything was 'quiet and orderly'. […] I decided to join one of them and walked with him through the corridors, occasionally catching a glimpse into one of the prisoners' cells. Many doors were open, the air in the wing was filled with the sound of music and the smell of food; in many cells, I could see them sitting in twos or threes, eating, discussing or playing games together. Some were alone. One was busy cleaning his cell. Others were standing outside in the corridor, having a chat with their neighbours or a fellow prisoner standing on the upper or ground floor. Yet others were in the wing's common room, playing billiards together. The mood was lively and pleasant. At around 8 pm the prisoners were again locked in their cells – immediately silence returned. (Fieldnotes, 22.2.2016)

I. Marti, *Doing Indefinite Time*, Palgrave Studies in Prisons and Penology,
https://doi.org/10.1007/978-3-031-12590-4_6

As illustrated in this extract from my fieldnotes, in addition to resting and work time, 'leisure time' is another specific part of the prisoners' day. As this first impression suggests, it seems to be a moment where prisoners are generally relaxed and in a good mood.

This first impression corresponds quite well to the common definition of leisure time. According to the Oxford Dictionaries, it can be defined as (1) 'time when one is not working or occupied, free time'; (2) 'use of free time for enjoyment'; (3) 'leisure for/to do something' (Oxford Dictionaries, 2018). Apparently, there is a dialectical relationship between work and leisure. As emphasized by Matthews (2009), in reference to Thompson (1967), leisure time only became an issue with the rise of industrial capitalism and the commodification of time. From then on, time was no longer 'passed' but 'spent'. As Matthews argues:

> [t]he changes in manufacturing technique demanded a greater synchronisation of labour as well as a greater degree of punctuality and exactitude in the routine of work. The twin processes of the social dislocation of time and its technical calibration provided the basis on which labour time could more easily be calculated, while non-work time became seen as 'spare' or 'free' time. (Matthews, 2009, p. 37)

However, in the academic literature, 'leisure time' is often described as something that cannot exist in prison. Various arguments have been put forward. For instance, according to Matthews (2009), as prisoners are 'removed' from the workplace and labour market as well as from their communities and families, they are no longer able to experience 'free' time (Matthews, 2009, p. 38). Moreover, he argues that time inside prison is fundamentally different from the outside world. Due to the institutional context of confinement, 'time served in prison is not so much "spent" as "wasted"' (Matthews, 2009, p. 38).

Clemmer's (1958 [1940]) argument points to the lived experience of time in prison as well. According to the author, 'the distinction between leisure-time and non-leisure time, which is clear in the normal community is less evident in the penitentiary where every hour, whether designated leisure or not, is "time" in a very real sense' (Clemmer, 1958

[1940], p. 206). More concretely, from his point of view, the impossibility of experiencing 'real' leisure time in prison results above all from the fact that leisure activities are commonly associated with the experience of a 'pleasurable state of mind' (Clemmer, 1958 [1940], p. 206), which is not possible in prison as the 'prison environment prohibits the development of basically pleasant feeling states' (Clemmer, 1958 [1940], p. 206): '[T]hat deadening sense of confinement' is constantly present and 'prohibits the complete release of the personality to the activity at hand' (Clemmer, 1958 [1940], p. 248). Nevertheless, despite all the constraints, in contrast to work hours, leisure time in prison is a moment of the day where prisoners are less directly monitored and managed. Clemmer therefore suggests adapting the notion of leisure time to the prison context, defining it as 'that time when the prisoner is not engaged in the more formal and obvious duties which his status as an inmate demands [...] and when custody is less strict' (Clemmer, 1958 [1940], pp. 206–207). He divided leisure time into two general categories: 'officially regulated leisure time', such as sport, movies, religious activities, football games or reading and studying; and 'unregulated leisure time', such as gambling, drinking and reverie (Clemmer, 1958 [1940], pp. 211–248).

Similarly, Goffman (1961) pointed to the lack of any spatial separation of work and leisure in prison. While '[a] basic social arrangement in modern society is that the individual tends to sleep, play and work in different places, with different co-participants, under different authorities and without an overall rational-plan [...]' (Goffman, 1961, pp. 5–6), in prison, as in any total institution, the three spheres of life (sleep, play, work) are experienced 'in the same place under the same single authority' (Goffman, 1961, p. 6). In his analysis, Goffman was interested in so-called 'removal activities' and their function for the institution as well as for the inmates. According to Goffman (1961, p. 69), prisoners can participate, on the one hand, in collective and 'official' removal activities provided by the institution. Such activities aim to provide inmates with the means to 'kill time' and thus to reduce stress and boredom. However, they are also part of the institution's strategies to transform the prisoners into 'co-operators' and to undergo 'primary adjustment' (Goffman, 1961, p. 189). Such activities include, for instance, formal education and the possibility of receiving external visits. On the other hand, inmates themselves develop individual techniques for distraction (Goffman, 1961, p. 69). Such distractions may make use of material provided by the prison, such as a TV, books or newspapers, or involve activities that are unauthorized and more or less hidden from prison staff (e.g. gambling or homosexual activity). The latter constitute what Goffman labelled as 'secondary adjustment', which enables inmates to maintain a sense of self and autonomy (Goffman, 1961, p. 189). All these practices, taken together, represent what Goffman called the 'underlife' of an institution (Goffman, 1961, p. 199).

In this chapter, I explore what Clemmer (1958 [1940]) designated as 'regulated leisure time'. This means that I first approach leisure time from the angle of the prison system. From an analytical perspective, however, I propose to look at the concept of leisure less in direct comparison with the outside world (linked to the question of whether leisure or 'free' time can even exist in prison) and without focusing primarily on its concrete function from the point of view of the prison (e.g. to exercise social control) or the prisoners (e.g. secondary adjustment). Instead, I look at the prisoners' spatial, temporal and embodied experiences *of* and *during* this particular part of every day that is labelled and organized by the prison as 'leisure time' and takes place in a wide range of contexts.

I include in this chapter additional time–spaces that provide prisoners in one way or another a break from the prison (working) routine, such as the daily walk in the courtyard, encountering people from the outside world or going on temporary prison leave. Generally, during leisure time, prisoners are most directly confronted with the outside world—physically, intellectually and emotionally—which not only provides them with a break from the routine, but also evokes ambivalent feelings. Simply put, these moments generally intensify their lives and allow them to feel free, or less imprisoned, while at the same time making them intensely aware of their imprisonment, of what they have lost, miss and will probably never experience again.

The prisons in which I undertook research provide different opportunities for prisoners to pass or spend time outside of work hours. While prisoners spend a large part of their leisure time in the cell (see

Chapter 4), this chapter focuses primarily (but not exclusively) on scheduled leisure situations that take place outside the prison cell. In the following section, I provide a brief description of the legal and institutional norms regarding leisure time in Swiss prisons to provide first an idea of what leisure time means from the institution's point of view. It includes a description of the different internal rules and offers regarding leisure time activities—that is, a glimpse of the prison's *spatio-temporal regime* regarding leisure time—in the three prisons where I conducted fieldwork. The following six sections are dedicated to the prisoners' multiple ways of *doing* leisure time.

6.1 Leisure Time in Swiss Prisons

At the national level, no explicit norms exist regarding leisure time activities in Swiss prisons; however, every institution offers such activities. According to the Swiss Competence Centre for Law Enforcement, leisure programmes offered in prison shall aim, on the one hand, to foster 'the meaningful organization of free time', thus in the broadest sense ensuring security during and after imprisonment and, on the other hand, to allow prisoners 'on a voluntary basis to increase their level of education, to acquire social skills, as well as to engage in sports' (Schweizerisches Kompetenzzentrum für den Justizvollzug, 2019, my translation). While training and education is often part of the leisure programme, following Art. 83 para. 3 SCC, it can also constitute an alternative to work and must therefore be adequately remunerated (Baechtold et al., 2016, p. 262). As stipulated in Art. 82 SCC, prisoners shall be given the opportunity for training and (basic and advanced) education appropriate to their skill level. Activities that are not explicitly labelled leisure time but nevertheless (in general) take place during prisoners' leisure time include walks in the courtyard—according to the Federal Supreme Court, one daily walk of one full hour is a prisoner's fundamental right (Baechtold et al., 2016, p. 209)—and receiving visitors and cultivating contact with people from the outside world (according to Art. 84 SCC). Finally, leisure time activities are commonly associated with the use of entertainment media. As the prisoners' access to media is not explicitly regulated on a national or cantonal level, through its jurisprudence the Federal Supreme Court has formulated extensive rules regarding access to TV, radio, books, magazines and newspapers (Baechtold et al., 2016, pp. 190–192).

Access to leisure activities (as well as contact with the outside world) may be used by management both as a disciplinary sanction (by denying access) (Art. 91 SCC) and a privilege (by providing additional access) (Fieldnotes, 22.2.2016). Thus, as Norman (2017) argues, leisure programmes offered in prisons constitute tools to provide prisoners with the means to cope with imprisonment as well as to exercise control over their behaviour and the general social environment of the prison, for instance, by reducing tensions among prisoners.

To find out what leisure time concretely looks like in prison, a closer look at each prison's individual house rules is needed. In the *Strafanstalt* at *JVA Lenzburg*, leisure activities basically include sports, education and training (JVA Lenzburg, 2011, p. 27). A so-called 'guided leisure time' takes place Monday through Friday, from 5.45 pm to 7.30 pm (JVA Lenzburg, 2010). All prisoners have the right to register for courses and other activities, such as going to the gym, yoga classes, political education and language or music lessons.[1] All of these take place in rooms designed specifically for this purpose. Prisoners who do not participate in one of the prison's official leisure programmes can spend this period of the day outside their cell. From 6.05 pm to 8.20 pm, all the cells are unlocked and prisoners are granted some so-called 'unguided leisure time' (JVA Lenzburg, 2010, my translation). This means that they can meet each other in the wing or spend time in one of the common rooms or in someone's cell. During their spare time, prisoners are also allowed to do handicrafts in their cells. However, tools and materials need to be authorized by the head of security (JVA Lenzburg, 2011, pp. 29–30). The prison further has its own library, and prisoners also have access to the Cantonal Library. Moreover, they have the opportunity to buy books, magazines, newspapers, DVDs and CDs from shops outside the prison,

[1] As I noticed during my stay in the *Strafanstalt*, the prison's leisure programme is offered on a semester-by-semester basis. While some programmes are consistently offered (e.g. the gym), others, such as music workshops, may take place at irregular intervals and be replaced by another offer.

in accordance with the house rules (JVA Lenzburg, 2011, pp. 30–31). Finally, prisoners can buy certain electronic devices, such as a computer, a stereo system or a gaming console, as well as musical instruments, and they have the ability to rent a TV from the prison (JVA Lenzburg, 2011, p. 32) (see also Sect. 4.5). For crime preventive reasons, the prison permits only computer and video games that are released with the age rating 'under 18 year olds' (JVA Lenzburg, 2011, p. 35). Mobile devices, such as laptops and those permitting mobile telecommunication (mobile phones, modems), are prohibited (JVA Lenzburg, 2011, p. 34).

In the two units for ill and elderly prisoners, the days are characterized by longer cell opening times and a reduced workload. According to the internal house rules, in the *60plus* unit at *JVA Lenzburg*, on weekdays the cells are open from 7.30 am to 11.30 am and from 1.15 pm to 8 pm (Fieldnotes, 30.4.2013). Compared to the regular prison population in the *Strafanstalt* at *JVA Lenzburg*, the prisoners can spend more hours outside the cell, for instance in the common rooms of the unit or in one of the two courtyards. According to the house rules, in addition to health-related offers (including gymnastics for the elderly), a special focus is put on creative or handicraft activities, which, however, take place in the common rooms of the unit (Fieldnotes, 2.5.2013). During my stay in this unit, there was a cooking class going on in the unit's kitchen (led by an external person). Moreover, prison officers generally would spend a lot of time playing cards or society games with the prisoners. I also came across personal initiatives: for example, there was one prison officer who, from time to time, spent the afternoon baking cookies with one of the prisoners, while another initiated crafting afternoons. In the *AGE* at *JVA Pöschwies*, the rules are similar to those of the *60plus* unit. In this unit, sport is mandatory for everyone who is physically capable. Sports lessons take place during work hours (twice a week for one and a half hours) and are thus also credited as work time. Those who are physically able but refuse to actively participate are sanctioned, which means in this prison that they are locked in their cells for the whole day (JVA Pöschwies, 2016a). The prisoners in this special unit do not have access to the prison's official evening leisure programmes offered for the regular prison population accommodated in the same prison. Nevertheless, they can register for basic education programmes, buy entertainment electronics (radio, stereo system) and rent a TV or a PlayStation (see also Sect. 4.5). During my stay in this unit, some activities were offered based on personal initiatives by staff, such as a music lesson over lunch time and gymnastics for elderly people in one of the unit's workshops.

In general, in all the prisons where I undertook fieldwork, leisure time activities are supervised by an external person. Furthermore, as mentioned, there are specially designed places for leisure time activities, such as the gym, the classroom and the courtyard. Moreover, during leisure time, prisoners can wear clothes other than those worn during work hours. They are allowed to wear training pants or their 'private' trousers, such as shorts (JVA Lenzburg 2011, p. 51). Hence, although leisure and working activities all take place in the same building, they are still spatially segregated and very often do not, in a strict sense, take place under the same authority (in contrast to Goffman's argument), which is crucial to the prisoners' experience.

In the following, I explore the lived experiences and various meanings prisoners ascribe to leisure time situations by looking more closely at their concrete ways of *doing* leisure time. As mentioned, I thereby take into consideration official leisure programmes as well as walks in the courtyard and prisoners' various approaches to having contact with the outside world, because all these moments, or 'fragments', to put it in Leo's words, provide prisoners with a break from the (work) routine and sometimes even with the feeling of being imprisoned. When I asked him if there are any places in prison where he likes to go, he replied:

> Of course [in the gym], during sport, when you can let off steam. [During] badminton, for example, where you can just forget the whole thing for one and a half, two hours. Where else do I like to be? Outside [in the courtyard] of course, while walking. The fresh air, the sun shines. Receiving visitors outside [in the special open-air area for visitors]. Yes, these are always like fragments, like moments. It's not always good, visits are not always good. Sometimes you talk about more serious issues, the uncertain future, or what if this or that happens, or the parents die. But basically, it's always nice when I'm outside, when I see the sky. (Leo, 23.3.2016)

6.2 In the Courtyard: Sensing the Outside World[2]

The walk in the courtyard was the first thing I imagined to be part of the prisoners' leisure time activities. As mentioned above, the one-hour walk per day is one of a prisoner's fundamental rights (Baechtold et al., 2016, p. 209). Therefore, it is often not listed in the category 'leisure time', but 'daily routine', such as at JVA Lenzburg (JVA Lenzburg, 2011, p. 19).

In the *Strafanstalt* at *JVA Lenzburg*, there are two courtyards (see Fig. 6.1), and prisoners spent time there (divided into groups) either in the morning or in the afternoon. During summertime, they have the chance to spend some additional time there in the evening. Once they have decided to go outside, however, they have to stay there for the whole hour; they cannot independently go in and out. During this particular moment of the day, prisoners have the opportunity to spend time out in the open air: they can walk on the grass, or sit under a tree, meet fellow prisoners, play games or do exercises. Prisoners can also experience some degree of privacy among themselves as the courtyard is one of the places that is less directly observed by staff, and officers who are in charge of monitoring generally keep a certain distance. Thus, as I was told by prisoners, this hour of the day can also be used for talking about or engaging in more or less illicit activities (so-called 'deals'). From the prisoners' perspective, the courtyard is generally a 'public' area and thus also a social space where boundaries among them are redrawn and defended, and where prisoners can experience both inclusion and exclusion.

In the *60plus* unit in the *Zentralgefängnis* at *JVA Lenzburg*, prisoners also have access to two courtyards (see Fig. 6.2). One is located on the same floor as the unit; the other, larger one is on the ground floor. While the one on the same floor as the unit is open the whole day (except during lunch) and prisoners are allowed to go in and out as they wish, the one on the ground floor is only accessible during two periods of the day (one in the morning, one in the afternoon), and prisoners must be

---

[2] Parts of this section have been published as Marti (2021): 'Sensing freedom: Insights into long-term prisoners' perceptions of the outside world', Incarceration SAGE, Vol. 2(2): 1–20.

Fig. 6.1 The courtyards in the Strafanstalt at JVA Lenzburg (*Source* Google Maps)

escorted there by a prison officer who has to unlock the many doors on the way. Like in the *Strafanstalt*, once the prisoner is out, he has to remain there until the official time is up. While the courtyard next to the unit is entirely constructed of concrete, equipped with a table tennis game in the middle of it and covered with steel grate (as it was initially designed for prisoners on remand), in the one downstairs, prisoners have an unrestricted view of the sky. Moreover, they have access to diverse plants in the raised bed (and can help plant them), including herbs they can gather for cooking. They can walk around or sit at the pond. The ground, however, is made of concrete.

During my stay in this prison, I noticed that this second courtyard was very rarely used. While one prisoner went there every day—no matter how 'bad' (from my perspective) the weather was—the others usually said that it was too complicated for them to go there (a lot of stairs, no

Fig. 6.2 The courtyards for ill and elderly prisoners in the Zentralgefängnis at JVA Lenzburg (*Source* Google Maps)

flexibility in terms of the duration one stays there). The courtyard on the same floor as the unit, however, was frequently, if only briefly, used. As I observed, the prisoners often went there during their leisure time to have a cigarette or a chat with fellow prisoners. Sometimes, they played a round of table tennis or darts, sometimes with a prison officer.

In the *AGE* at *JVA Pöschwies*, the courtyard (see Fig. 6.3) is open the whole day, from 7.30 am until 7 pm (4 pm on weekends) (JVA Pöschwies, 2016c). As I observed, the courtyard fulfils several functions, and the majority of the prisoners spend most of their non-working hours there. It is also the place where they would go during their short work breaks: to smoke a cigarette, drink a coffee, have a chat with a fellow prisoner, walk a few steps or read some lines in the newspaper. According to my observations, prisoners often also went there to simply pass time or wait for lunch or dinner. On Wednesday, the prisoners have the afternoon off, and, depending on the weather, many of them spend this time in the courtyard: reading, playing games, doing exercises, smoking, chatting, sunbathing, sitting in the grass, feeding the ducks if they are around (in the pond) and interacting with fellow prisoners. The same applies to the weekends.

The courtyard in the *AGE* was also frequently used by prison officers during their breaks. It is thus not only a place where prisoners meet, but also a social space for interactions among prison officers and between officers and prisoners. As I could observe, during these particular moments, institutionally ascribed (opposed) roles and individual

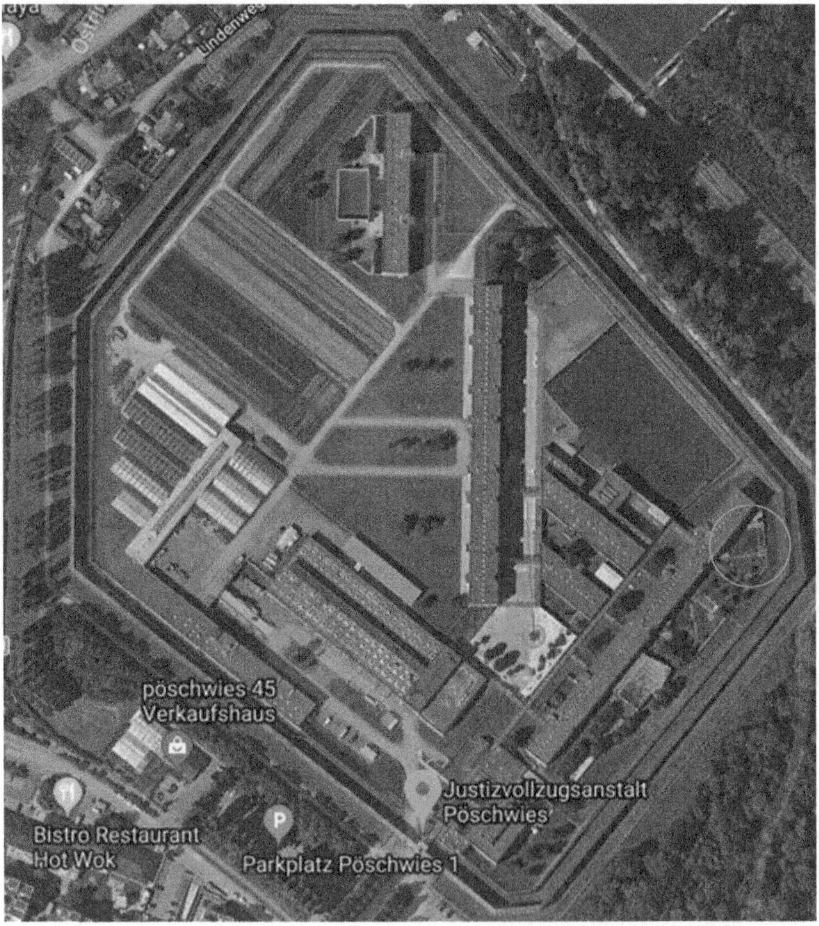

Fig. 6.3 The courtyard in the AGE at JVA Pöschwies (*Source* Google Maps)

status were both accentuated and blurred. For example, while the staff uses the whole courtyard, including its equipment (such as the billiards table, chairs or ashtrays), and also participates in some of the prisoners' activities (e.g. smoking, playing a round of billiards), there is some territory that staff members have seized for themselves: a table and a chair in the rear area of the courtyard where they spend their breaks when the weather allows it and from which they have a perfect view of the activities 'on the other side'.

6.2.1 Having Access to 'Nature'

Generally, being in the courtyard means being outside—in the 'open air' (Markus, 28.9.2017). Even though long-term prisoners get to know 'each spot' of the courtyard (Theo, 3.5.2016), they can experience change and variety in terms of the courtyard's 'ambiance' (Thibaud, 2011). While the ambiance inside the prison is described with reference to the prison's materiality, social environment and surroundings (see Sect. 4.2), the courtyard is the place where prisoners have the most direct access to 'nature', mainly in the form of the weather and the changing seasons.

Indeed, prisoners referred to their sensory experience and mentioned that in the courtyard, they can smell and feel the 'fresh' (Darko, 6.5.2016) or 'warm' air (Paul, 29.3.2016), the sunlight—or the lack of it (because of the fixed time they are allowed to spend in the courtyard)—and the rain or snow on their skin. As mentioned above, during the warm seasons in the *Strafanstalt* and in the *AGE*, prisoners can lie on the grass—on 'a real lawn' (Anton, 24.3.2016), which is not possible in every prison as the lots are often made of gravel or concrete, and which is thus for certain prisoners 'already quite a particular feeling' (Leo, 31.8.2017) (see also Moran et al., 2018). They can see (and touch) trees and plants growing and blooming; they can hear, observe and maybe even feed animals (mostly birds, but also fish or ducks in the units for ill and elderly prisoners).

Leo: There are quite a lot of birds in these trees. We already saved two. Two young ones, but they were then eaten by the dogs that patrol at night. We tried to feed them up a bit, but we knew they would not survive. […] Up there [at the roof] it often has swallows. Two also fell down once, two young ones. They fell out of the hole, there on the floor. Then we supplied them with water. Yes, but they didn't have a chance.

Irene: Yes, and I think once they got touched by a human being …

L: Yes, then they are no longer accepted by the mother. The mother probably had too many young ones and then she had to throw some out. Because they don't just throw them out like that, they do not. Maybe she didn't have food, or not enough. (Leo, 31.8.2017)

Finally, it is also a place where prisoners can gain sensory impressions of the outside community, especially its sounds (airplanes, cars and people). In sum, it is a place that potentially stimulates the prisoners' senses in various yet particular ways, which is crucial as prisoners are generally suffering from sensory deprivation (see also Cohen & Taylor, 1972; Moran & Turner, 2018). Moreover, in contrast to the institutionally established 'ever-same present' (see Sect. 2.3.2), the experience of the changing seasons and rhythms of 'normal' life gives prisoners a sense of the passage of time (see also Turner et al., 2020).

Due to this access to 'nature', which is assumed to have positive effects on the prisoners' well-being (Moran & Turner 2018; Wener, 2012), I used to associate the courtyard with a feeling of freedom. I always assumed that the courtyard *must* be the best place in prison and was astonished to find out that many prisoners actually avoided this place. In the beginning, it was not easy to uncover the reasons for this attitude. One prisoner told me that he avoided going out because of the social exclusion he had experienced in the past. He told me that he had been subjected to psychological harassment by fellow prisoners because of rumours that have been circulating about him for several years now. As noted in the literature, within the prisoner hierarchy, prisoners who were sentenced for sexual violence, especially child abuse, are generally at the very bottom of the social order (see e.g. Crewe, 2009, p. 272). As there were many sex offenders among the prisoners I talked to, I assume that their stigmatization could indeed be a reason for their avoidance of the courtyard, although they never mentioned it explicitly. There are, however, additional reasons. After I found out that Lars had not been outside for the past five years and asked him for his reasons, he explained: 'It's always the same, the same people, going around in circles, I'm not interested'. I countered by saying 'but the weather is different each time!' He ended the conversation by saying that he preferred to remain in his cell in order to use this time 'constructively' for studying (Fieldnotes, 3.2.2016). As I later came to understand, the courtyard may indeed provide prisoners with a 'little piece of freedom' (Fieldnotes, 7.7.2016)—however, not everyone can deal with it.

6.2.2 Encountering 'a Little Piece of Freedom'

Many of the prisoners mentioned that the courtyard is a place where they like to spend time. Often, together with the cell, prisoners declared the courtyard their 'favourite place' in prison. The well-being certain prisoners experience in the courtyard is, on the one hand, the result of the fact that it is an open-air place with trees and other plants. Due to this connection to 'nature', it is for these prisoners a place where they may find 'peace of mind' (Leo, 23.3.2016) and even forget for a while that they are in prison. On the other hand, the courtyard is also a particular social space 'out of the prison routine' (Leo, 23.3.2016), which also lets prisoners forget that they are actually behind the walls. As explained by Anton:

> There [in the courtyard], most inmates feel free. And there it is the most … where I forget the walls all around, the fences; I forget that it's a prison. Because what counts in that moment is that you're together [with fellow prisoners] and that you have fun with each other and that's good. (Anton, 24.3.2016)

However, as revealed in most of these interviews, the courtyard is not a priori a nice place, but has to be actively transformed or arranged into one. This transformation becomes visible by looking more closely at the prisoners' individual perceptions and their corporal and practical engagement with the courtyard, mobilizing their 'spatial competences' (Lussault & Stock, 2010, p. 13).

Anton, for instance, mentioned that he intentionally 'filters' out everything that reminds him of being in prison and instead focuses on all the elements from which he gains the feeling of being free:

> I just see what I want to see, and I don't want to see the fence in the courtyard. I see the trees, I see the birds, hear them chirping. Another inmate, too, is like this, he said: Do you see this bird? It's a Milan! [...] And these are moments when I say: This is it. I don't want to see that I'm imprisoned; I don't want to feel as if I were imprisoned. (Anton, 24.3.2016)

The importance of focusing on elements that do not relate to the prison also surfaced during the walking interview I conducted with Leo. Following this encounter, I became aware of his perception of this particular place in situ, filtered through his values and emotions, and in particular his intention not to focus on the fences and the walls, which are particularly close in that area, but instead to emphasize the elements that allow him to feel free, or less imprisoned (see Fig. 6.4).

His attitude was also expressed while he was taking pictures of the courtyard. For instance, Leo took a picture of a flower arrangement in order to point out that 'the prison is not only about walls' (Leo, 31.8.2017) (illustrated in Fig. 6.5).

Our conversation continued as follows:

> *Leo*: You can see what you want to see.
> *Irene*: This means you can also decide to stand like this [having the wall in the back] and to look in this particular direction?
> *L*: Exactly, and the longer I'm here, I just do it. If I keep looking at the wall, I'm not feeling any better, of course. And this became automatic: I simply ignore certain things, look through them, yes. But at the beginning, of course, that [the wall] was overwhelming. (Leo, 31.8.2017)

To transform the courtyard into a space where one feels free (or less imprisoned) can also be reached through particular bodily practices and by making use of spatial elements in a way that allows them to create personal and intimate spaces. This again became apparent to me during

Fig. 6.4 The wall or the chapel: 'you can see what you want to see' (*Source* Photo taken by a prisoner)

Fig. 6.5 Plants in the courtyard: 'the prison is not only about walls' (*Source* Photo by a prisoner)

the conversations I had with Leo. During our first interview, he told me about a particular tree in the courtyard, under which he likes to lie down, read a book, take a nap or spend some time sunbathing. By doing this, he again filters out everything that reminds him of being in prison and focuses on things he can perceive that remind him of the outside world (e.g. the sound of birds, the smell of the summer air). But there is more at stake than simply relaxation and blocking out the prison environment. It is a moment when Leo recalls nice memories and relives them:

> I push myself to recall the memories that are still present and to put myself back into them. I then concentrate on the odours, the sounds. When I'm lying under this tree, I try to listen carefully and also to smell this summer air, or that I'm outside. Then I maybe hear a bird somewhere, and all the people [fellow prisoners] who walk around, and all these different languages, this I filter out so that I won't hear it anymore, only the birds, so that [it feels as if] I am lying in a meadow outside somewhere or recall nice memories from the past, my childhood, holidays, nice experiences. [...] And sometimes I succeed and sometimes I don't. And if it goes well, then I feel like totally reenergized, like a newborn, as if I had been outside (laughs). (Leo, 23.3.2016)

We visited the tree—'his' tree (illustrated in Fig. 6.6)—during our walking interview, which Leo presented in the following way:

> This is my tree. That's just the one I told you about //yes, you told me about it//, and so when I'm outside, during the summer, I'm mostly under that tree, on the towel, next to the shower, because I quite like that, when people take a shower, then there's a fog, a wet fog, and just the sound, lido-like noises, and when I'm lying there with the book, yes, it's comfortable, it's really comfortable. (Leo, 31.8.2017)

While daydreaming can be described as a simple distraction that allows prisoners to 'temporarily [blot] out all sense of the environment' (Goffman, 1961, p. 309), for prisoners like Leo, daydreaming is not only a means of escape but a way to *transcend* the here and now and gain personal experiences far from the prison context. As explained in the

Fig. 6.6 A prisoner's tree in the courtyard (*Source* Photo by a prisoner)

quotes above, daydreaming is something Leo is consciously *practising*—he actively and specifically recalls his pre-prison memories and relives them. This helps him not only to relax but also to keep his most precious memories alive, to feel connected to the outside world and maybe also to retain a part of his pre-prison identity. Thus, Leo tries to make the routine of going for the one-hour walk in the courtyard as rewarding as possible. However, as he told me later, this practice does not always work. Whenever he is stressed or in a bad mood, this stage of feeling free is difficult or even impossible to reach:

> It depends on my mood. If I feel like it, then I want to enjoy it, then I want to feel the freedom, then I can do it ... I cannot do it every day, when I'm in a bad mood or stressed out, or don't feel like, then I just cannot do it that way ... cannot reach this stage. [...] I have to really concentrate. (Leo, 31.8.2017)

Being in the courtyard also means being physically closest to the walls and therefore also to the outside community (see Fig. 6.7), which evokes mixed feelings among the prisoners with whom I spoke. Certain prisoners mentioned that they like the possibility of sensing the outside world and realizing that 'normal life' goes on as it makes them feel less isolated and (still) connected to it.

There are others, in contrast, who told me that by standing so close to the outside world, they above all are reminded of what they miss—what they have lost and will probably never experience (again). In other words, the courtyard may also be the place where prisoners have sensory experiences (especially through hearing and smelling) that remind them

Fig. 6.7 In the courtyard: being close to the outside community (*Source* Photo by a prisoner)

not only of their physical but also their social exclusion from society (see also Turner et al., 2020, p. 231)—their former lives, rhythms and routines. Hugo described this (once during our formal interview, and again during our walking interview, one year later) as follows:

> I get reminded of the outside. When the weather is nice, then you go out, the sun is shining, and you realize that all your friends out there are sitting somewhere in the garden or somewhere by the lake and enjoying the nice day and you are actually sitting in here and at half past seven you are again locked up in the cell. This makes you think a lot, and during a period you don't feel well it can be too much. (Hugo, 23.3.2016)

> *Hugo*: Yeah, sometimes you can hear the highway, sometimes you can hear when the ambulance or police are on the move again, when there was a crash somewhere and so on. If it is very quiet then you […] hear the train down there from time to time, and the people around here, when they are having a party in the garden outside or something, then you can sometimes hear children screaming. […] And then, when they are having a barbecue during summer, over there (laughs).
>
> *Irene*: Can you smell that?
>
> *H*: You can smell it, yes; the smell comes from there (laughs). And that's actually what annoys you a little bit, you know. (Hugo, 7.9.2017)

As I noticed, being outside in the courtyard and thus physically (and sensorially) closest to the outside world, from which they are separated by a wall, evokes bittersweet feelings for many prisoners. The wall, fences and cameras (see Fig. 6.8) cannot easily be filtered out by everyone. Lars, for instance, agreed that the courtyard provides prisoners with 'a little piece of freedom'; however, whenever he stands outside, 'in front of the wall', he 'start[s] to cry like a baby' and gets terribly 'homesick'. After his prison friend made him aware that he returned in an 'edgy' mood whenever he had been to the courtyard, Lars finally decided to go there no longer. As long as he stays inside and keeps himself busy, he is not constantly reminded of where he is (Fieldnotes, 7.7.2016).

It is similar for Erwin, who lives in the unit for ill and elderly prisoners, as the courtyard (see Fig. 6.9) is the place where he is reminded most strongly of being in prison:

Fig. 6.8 The courtyard: a 'little piece of freedom' (*Source* Photo by a prisoner)

Irene: Do you often come here [to the courtyard]?
Erwin: I don't like to be here, because I feel like in a dog kennel, wall and fences, which is not needed, because nobody will go over this wall.
I: So here you actually feel quite locked up?
E: Down here? Yes. [...]
I: But it's actually the only place where you can see the sky, right?
E: Yes, yes. This is the advantage, yes. But here I really realize, because of these bars and so on, that I'm in prison. That's the only place [in prison] I don't like that much. (Erwin, 18.10.2017)

Thus, due to the experienced closeness to 'nature' and the 'free world', the courtyard signifies for some prisoners the time–space in which they feel the least imprisoned and thus physically (and mentally) the freest, while for others, in contrast, it is a context where they feel the most captured, or most unfree—depending on how they manage to deal with the walls. This experience is therefore similar to that of sensing the outside world through the window of the cell (see Sect. 4.2.3). This potential (sensory) connection to the outside world therefore constitutes

Fig. 6.9 In the courtyard: 'like in a dog kennel' (*Source* Photo by a prisoner)

a source of both well-being and discomfort, as it can intensify as well as ease the 'pains of imprisonment', in particular the 'deprivation of liberty' (Sykes, 1971 [1958], pp. 65–67).

This ambivalent experience of the courtyard is also strongly shaped by the prisoners' particular legal status—that is, the indeterminate and preventive nature of their incarceration. As Hugo explained, this little piece of freedom he gains in the courtyard would be more bearable if he had a clear perspective, a concrete date of release. Thus, their experience of time and ways of dealing with the indeterminate nature of their imprisonment strongly shape their experience of and ways of dealing with this particular place:

Hugo: I think if you somehow knew that you would get out again and when, then it would be something else. Then you know, then and then I come out, then it's a different feeling too.

Irene: It would be a different feeling to go out, to the courtyard?

H: Yes. Because then, then you have a perspective, you know exactly when you will be out again and have the experience [of really being outside] again. But if you just have to expect that you spend the rest of your life here inside … it's hard. (Hugo, 7.9.2017)

Serge, too, evaluates the experience of being in the courtyard against the background of his situation of being held in indefinite incarceration. He defines the garden of the *AGE*, which he describes as 'beautiful', as a 'deception' that aims to 'lull' the prisoners so that they do not really realize (and complain about) where they actually are and probably will have to be for the rest of their lives. He drew parallels to sedatives, which make it impossible for consumers to feel 'real' life. Thus, for him, the nice courtyard is in fact a tool to manipulate prisoners and transform them into 'co-operators', as described by Goffman (1961):

Here where I am, I feel very much … the garden, the beautiful garden, the two floors [where the cells are located], that doesn't suit me, it's kind of a fraud (laughs), it's kind of a deception, it's like drugs that people receive to be sedated, and then they sit in this crap and if you ask someone: how long have you been here now, [he replies:] yes, for 19 years. And then they enjoy the garden and … that's just not right. Then I [prefer to] really feel what is, I mean I'm still alive, I'm not dead, I want to feel […] I cannot stay here, that's a fraud what they do, a fraud. I cannot go up and down the two floors, go to work, say nothing, and then sit in the garden, that's not possible. (Serge, 25.9.2013)

Not going outside makes some prisoners who suffer from being incarcerated feel better, but at the same time it has negative consequences for their health as they may develop a vitamin D deficiency, which was quite common among the prisoners I met. That the human body needs some fresh air and sunlight, however, is something that was nevertheless mentioned. Among those who try to avoid this place, there were prisoners who agreed that being outside from time to time 'is doing you some good' (Hugo, 7.9.2017). Certain prisoners also spoke about 'the urge to go outside' (Markus, 28.9.2017).

Irene: There are also certain people who don't go out because they cannot bear this anymore, right?

Leo: Yes, I also know these statements, yes. But it doesn't get better staying inside. Especially if I haven't been outside for a really long time, then I feel the urge to go outside. Then I go out because I have to go out.
I: What is a long time?
L: Two and a half months, three months.
I: Ah yes, this is … //yes//
L: Especially in winter I'm rarely outside. And then I really, I realize that I need some fresh air again or just once again, yes, to have this feeling. (Leo, 31.8.2017)

However, I nevertheless met prisoners who categorically rejected the idea of stepping even one foot into the courtyard and who prefer to stay in their cells, often behind closed curtains, immersed in their own world:

I followed [a prisoner] to his cell as he wanted to show me some of his drawings. It strongly smelled of cigarette smoke, both curtains were drawn, and he hung a bath towel in the middle of the window; one could no longer look outside. I asked him if he sometimes goes to the courtyard; he demurred and explained that he got used to being in his 'room'. Preferably, he plays computer games where 'you just have to shoot without thinking'. (Fieldnotes, 12.2.2016)

The courtyard is hence a highly ambiguous place, which causes multiple, contradictory and sometimes even overlapping bodily responses and thus shapes the prisoners' sense of self and experience of their indefinite incarceration in particular ways. At the same time, prisoners deal with it individually. Some completely avoid it, others use, appropriate and (re)arrange this place according to their needs and interests—for example, to create and experience personal and intimate space—and gain the feeling of freedom and of being less isolated from the outside world.

6.3 Connecting with People from the Outside World

Until the mid-twentieth century, prison regulations in Switzerland regarding direct contact with the outside world were highly restrictive. For instance, prisoners were allowed to send only one letter per week, strictly censored by the management. Phone calls were authorized only in exceptional circumstances and were monitored acoustically. Finally, only close relatives were allowed to visit prisoners, and only twice per month (Baechtold et al., 2016, p. 172). Beginning in the mid-twentieth century, initiated by critical prison governors, the jurisdiction of the Federal Supreme Court regarding prisoners' basic rights (in particular regarding personal liberty and freedom of information), technical innovations (e.g. portable radios), and changes in the prison population (i.e. more and more foreign prisoners, which made the rigorous censorship of letters and acoustic monitoring of phone calls and visits impossible), the thorough isolation of prisoners from the outside world has been abolished (Baechtold et al., 2016, pp. 172–173). Thus, today's 'total institution' is much more permeable than that outlined by Goffman (1961) some decades ago as prisoners today have 'the right to receive visitors and to cultivate contacts with persons outside the institution', and the prison is supposed to facilitate 'contact with close relatives and friends' (Art. 84 SCC).

These moments are also of particular importance for prisoners who suffer from a lack of physical contact. In prison, as I explored in Sect. 2.2.3, for security reasons prison staff and prisoners must maintain physical distance and not touch each other (which, of course, does not apply to emergency situations or body searches).

However, contact with the outside remains highly controlled by the prison system (including the enforcement authorities), for example regarding who and how many people a prisoner is allowed to receive as visitors as well as how many (and who) may visit at the same time. Moreover, the frequency, time, location and duration of visits are determined by the prison management, and they all have to be registered and approved in advance (JVA Lenzburg, 2011, pp. 55–57). Thus, prisoners cannot meet people from the outside world *spontaneously*. Moreover, as I show in this section, the permeability of the institution, in other words, the bridge that the prison builds between the inside and the outside world through direct contact (including letters and phone calls), is experienced by prisoners, and especially long-term prisoners, as something dynamic and highly fragile.

6.3.1 Receiving Visitors: When the Inside and the Outside Worlds Blur and Collide

In the literature, the visiting room is described as the location in prison where the 'inside and the outside worlds blur and collide' (Crewe et al., 2014, p. 60). It is the place where 'visitors gain an experience of prison, of the *inside*, and where the detainees are closest to freedom, to the *outside*' (Ricordeau, 2012, p. V).

Generally, in this place, it is all about emotions. This is not surprising, as the separation from their loved ones constitutes a major stressor for prisoners (Flanagan, 1980; Leigey & Ryder, 2015; Richards, 1978). In the visiting room, prisoners have the chance to meet them (again) for a limited amount of time. Toch has argued that whenever we are emotionally tied to someone, we strongly depend on his or her 'emotional support' and 'emotional feedback'—in the shape of 'positive affect or through recognition of, and response to, our feelings'—in order '[t]o live our emotional lives' (1996 [1977], pp. 69–70). For those prisoners who are particularly concerned with emotional feedback, visits (as well as letters and phone calls) from their loved ones therefore constitute an important source for improving their mental well-being. Indeed, as described by Crewe et al. (2014), who explored these rooms from an emotional geography perspective, visiting rooms are one of the 'emotional zones' in prison, which they define as 'marginal spaces or intermediate zones where many of the normal rules of the prisoner community were partially or temporarily suspended, permitting a broader emotional register than was possible in its main residential and most public areas' (Crewe et al., 2014, p. 67). The authors observed that in the visiting room, prisoners showed 'forms of warmth and tenderness that were taboo on the landings'; thus, for some prisoners, visits may be 'the only opportunity to display authentic feelings and show warmth' (Crewe et al., 2014, p. 67). This is in line with Ricordeau's argument that for both prisoners and external visitors, 'visits are generally retained among the most emotionally powerful moments of their affective and family relationships because of the meaning attached to the shared time' (2012, p. XXII). However, with all its rules and regulations, the prison acts both as a mediator of and barrier to (emotional) feedback from the outside world.

In the following, I shed light on the prisoners' experience of getting in touch with external visitors by looking more closely at the experience of their sense of self before, during and after the visit. I thereby also explore how they address temporariness, and the fact that these kinds of visits can never take place on a spontaneous basis, and present the multiple (and ambivalent) meanings visits have for those prisoners who do not know if they will ever be released. I further describe how the visiting room signifies not only the place that allows for the maintenance of contact, but that for some prisoners it is also the place where their bonds to the outside world get broken—perhaps forever. Finally, I also highlight the extent to which the particularities of the visiting spaces matter.

6.3.1.1 Expecting Visitors: 'Highlights' to Look Forward To

Of all the prisoners (32) with whom I spoke, eight did not receive any visitors (anymore) at the time of my fieldwork. The other 24 received visits mainly from family members or friends, but also from voluntary visitors.

Generally, prisoners described visits as 'highlights' (David, 2.5.2016) and as a break or 'change' from the daily prison routine (Clément, 24.3.2016). Visits thus have, first of all, a particular influence on prisoners' experience of time. As 'events', they are often used as time markers (Calkins, 1970), which allows prisoners to challenge the prison's (hyper-) ordinariness and create and experience some chronology. Visits are something prisoners look forward to, something they can target as realistic, in the sense of achievable 'goals', and something for which they can 'plan' and 'prepare' (see also Cunha, 1997):

> I set for myself small goals, again and again, which I can work towards, for example visits that you receive, visits for which you know the date, when you know, then and then I'm visited, and using this as a small sub-goal. It's important to not set goals that are too far away. (François, 23.11.2013)

> I take every day as it comes, I set no further goals. I gave up hope [for release]. I take every day as it comes and make the best of it. I feel better that way. What I might plan ahead are perhaps the visits. Because I always paint little pictures [for the visitor], or send a card, and then I paint something, something new, for this card. [...] But otherwise I don't plan ahead. (Franz, 10.9.2013)

Furthermore, expecting visitors is usually connected to the experience of particular emotions. Some prisoners mentioned feeling 'impatient' (Michael, 6.5.2016), 'nervous' and 'euphoric' (Leo, 23.3.2016) before the visits. Others said that, over time, they 'got used to it' and visits became something 'normal' (Clément, 24.3.2016), so that they were 'fully relaxed, not tense or nervous, nothing' before the visits (Darko, 6.5.2016). However, maybe this explicit denial of the feeling of any emotions before the visit—to mention that one feels 'nothing'—still references the fact that visits from the outside are something special in a prisoner's life. While some prisoners said that knowing that one will have a visit and thus 'two hours of a change in prospect' makes 'the week pass more quickly' (Clément, 24.3.2016); for others, those who 'can't wait' (Louis, 22.3.2016) for it, time does not pass quickly enough.

Almost all the prisoners expecting visitors mentioned paying attention to the impressions they create when interacting with their guests. Thus, they put a lot of effort into the construction and presentation of a particular self, in Goffman's (1959) sense. However, as demonstrated by the same author, the opportunities in prison are greatly limited because prisoners are to a great extent stripped of their 'identity kit', which is necessary for the management of the 'personal front' and the exertion of control over the personal appearance one shows to others. As Goffman argued, '[c]lothing, combs, needle and thread, cosmetics, towels, soap, shaving sets, bathing facilities – all these may be taken away or denied him, although some may be kept in inaccessible storage, to be returned if and when he leaves' (1961, p. 20). Moreover, the substitutes provided by the prison are generally of a '"coarse" variety, ill-suited, often old, and the same for large categories of inmates' (Goffman, 1961, p. 20). Goffman concluded that by losing control over one's identity kit, one suffers 'personal defacement' (Goffman, 1961, p. 21). Even though the mechanisms outlined by Goffman (many decades ago) are (still) also at work in the prisons where I did my research, the prisoners are clearly granted more opportunities to manage their 'personal front'. For example, two of the three prisons allow prisoners to wear 'private clothing', namely shirts, jumpers, t-shirts and shoes. Moreover, in every prison, they have access to a (small) variety of shower gels and colognes, offered in the prison shop. Finally, they are free to choose their hairstyle and whether they want to have beards or not.[3]

The prisoners made clear in their interviews that in order to get ready for the visit, they pay particular attention to their 'olfactory identity', which is important 'to avoid moral stigmatisation', at least in our society, as Largey and Watson have noted (2006 [1972], p. 35). Washing, shaving, and using cologne were the most mentioned techniques in this regard. The prisoners also brought up other techniques. For instance, Louis, who is a smoker, mentioned that the day of visits, he abstains from smoking from the early morning on, especially when he will be meeting someone who is not a smoker. For Heinz, visits are moments for putting in his false teeth, something he finds unimportant during everyday prison life.[4] Many prisoners also make sure that they wear 'clean' and 'fresh' clothes and, if it is allowed, their own sweaters or shirts, in order to appear 'less-prison-like' (Hugo, 23.3.2016). Even where prisoners must wear a uniform and do not possess any private clothing, they distinguish

[3] However, as I came to understand, prisoners cannot freely choose when to go to the hairdresser. I was once in one of the units for ill and elderly prisoners when the hairdresser came by. The prison officers had a list of the prisoners who wanted to see him. However, due to a lack of time, the officers themselves decided for whom it was 'necessary' and who 'can wait' until next time (Fieldnotes, 22.4.2016).

[4] During fieldwork, I witnessed other situations where the prisoners' teeth—or rather their absence—became an issue. For example, there was one prisoner who categorically refused to put in his false teeth during everyday life. However, I do not know if or why he put them in when he received visitors. There was another man who had almost no teeth left but refused any dental intervention, even though it would have been paid for by the prison, stating that there is 'no need' as he was 'anyway in prison' (Fieldnotes, 2.5.2013).

between *nicer* and *less nice* items of clothing. In the *AGE*, where prisoners have a choice between a blue T-shirt and a brown shirt, the latter is clearly considered the nicer option:

> Yes, I always prepare myself [before a visit]. I always make myself a bit pretty. Upstairs in my room. Put on the nice shirt, the brown one, the pants, because with the training pants you are not allowed to go to the visiting room, put on some cologne, cologne that I otherwise don't use, comb my hair, shave myself. (Michael, 6.5.2016)

In reference to Ricordeau, I understand these practices as a 'process of purification', with the aim of 'getting rid, temporarily, of the identity of "detainee" in favour of that of "friend/family member"' (2012, p. XIV). Indeed, 'making oneself pretty' is for many prisoners something that makes no sense during ordinary prison life—not only regarding false teeth, but also in terms of clothing. As Lars explained to me when I joined him at his workplace:

> In the past, he used to put a lot of effort into his appearance, hygiene, and clothing. As he told me, he always wore black and silver, while today he wonders: 'What for'? It doesn't make any sense to him; there are no women around and anyway he is in prison now. 'Why make oneself beautiful?' he asked again. He also hardly wears private clothes. This is something that doesn't matter to him anymore. According to him, those who still wear private clothing 'can't let go'. (Fieldnotes, 23.2.2016)

However, the process of purification before visits is for some prisoners also a way to prove that one is (still) able to behave according to common or ordinary social conventions. This was made clear by Marco, who described preparation for the visit as 'self-evident', as something that 'any ordinary citizen outside' would do as well in order 'to present oneself in the best shape' (Marco, 4.5.2016). In this sense, the 'process of purification' (Ricordeau, 2012, p. XIV) is also about feeling 'normal'—and feeling excited about it. Yet, as Marco further explained, to appear 'not like the last person on earth' is for him also an obligation he has as a prisoner and a way to express respect and appreciation for a visit:

> In here you have just like an extra obligation actually ... because the person takes all the effort and time to come here and to visit you, so you have to, like give something back. [...] Yes, just, at least appearing in a reasonable manner and being awake for example (laughs). Yes, I mean, I know people they just smoke grass before they go to the visit, (laughs) then they just sit there for an hour without moving and the visitor talks and talks and talks, no, no, it shouldn't be like that (laughs). (Marco, 4.6.2016)

As this quote further highlights, the presentation of the self is also about gestures, body movements, facial expressions and so on (see also Goffman, 1959). Kurt also thinks that appreciation can best be expressed by the way one appears in front of one's visitor. However, he points to the limits of the possibilities in prison, and he worries of being 'always the same':

> I try to get something from these people. They bring us a bit, a bit of freedom. I notice that. And that's enough for me. But for these people, we are always the same: same prison clothes, same look, sometimes we maybe have the hair a bit different (laughs), but still ... (Kurt, 3.5.2016)

In sum, even though the possibilities are more or less restricted depending on the internal rules of the prison, for prisoners who will soon hit the road to the visiting room, it is most important to smell good and to look nice.

6.3.1.2 Entering the Visiting Room

In the *Strafanstalt*, the visits take place either in the cafeteria-style visiting room with tables and chairs and a snack machine (illustrated in Fig. 6.10), or, with permission, in the open-air visiting area. Prisoners in the *60plus* unit are allowed to receive their visitors in the unit's common room. In the *AGE*, the prisoners receive their visitors in a visiting room that is similar to the one in the *Strafanstalt*. *JVA Pöschwies* also offers so-called 'family rooms' that allow prisoners and their visitors to experience more privacy and intimacy over a longer period of time. However, the prison is very restrictive in providing permission. Among the prisoners to whom I spoke, no one benefited from this kind of visit.

On our way to the visiting room, Clément explained to me that since he changed prisons, he receives visitors more frequently. He claimed that the reason for this lies in the particular way visitors are treated by prison staff when entering the prison (visitors have to show their ID cards and pass through security control, similar to the protocol at the airport). While in the prison where he was held previously, staff treated his family members 'like dangerous criminals' (see also Ricordeau, 2012, p. VI), in the prison where he is now, the staff is, according to him, 'extremely friendly' (Clément, 26.9.2017). He mentioned this during our first encounter, four years earlier:

> I have visitors every week, I really have to say that I never had that much. But this is related to the fact that people like to come because they are treated decently when entering [the prison]. The visitors are treated normally by staff. […] This is something very important. […] The relatives, colleagues and friends who come, they very much appreciate how

Fig. 6.10 Inside the prison visiting room (*Source* Photo by a prisoner)

> it is [organized] here. And that's really why I receive visitors every week. And if this were not the case, I can't imagine how it would be. (Clément, 25.6.2013)

However, it is not only the visitors who enter this place, but also the prisoners. As noted above, in the visiting room, while 'visitors gain an experience of prison, of the *inside*', prisoners 'are closest to freedom, to the *outside*' (Ricordeau, 2012, p. V). The prisoners I met described the visiting room as a rather loud place, especially when there are children playing and shouting. Also, they described the arrangement of the seating areas, the chairs and tables, as narrow. As we entered the visiting room together, Leo observed the smell of it, which, he said, he always notices immediately. He described it as 'not so fresh, [...] not so welcoming'. As he said, he 'can smell' that 'there has been a lot going on in here, heated discussions, that the room has already experienced a lot, [...] nothing good actually' (Leo, 31.8.2017). Yet, despite the emotions that may remain in the room in the form of a (bad) smell, visitors provide prisoners with 'fresh air'—fresh air 'coming from the outside'—that brings the prisoners 'a little piece of freedom' (Kurt, 3.5.2016).

Once the prisoners and their visitors have installed themselves around a table, a moment is initiated for prisoners to get *in touch* with the outside world—intellectually, emotionally, as well as physically.

6.3.1.3 Managing Temporariness

For some prisoners, the visit is a moment in their everyday lives that allows them to (almost) forget for a while that they are in prison. This state is basically reached when the visit is experienced as something rewarding and enjoyable, but also through a strong and careful concentration on the visitor(s) and their conversation:

> When my wife is with me, during these two hours, I enjoy this moment, this moment when I can be with my wife, this moment when you can just a little, not to forget, but it's a moment when it's just about me and my wife. We try to stay a little bit among ourselves and to enjoy the moment. And the other thing is ... in a bigger radius, the walls are a

> little further away, but of course you still know that you are in prison. (Louis, 22.3.2016)

As the following quote suggests, this particular state, in which one almost or partially forgets that one is in prison, is also strongly linked to bodily contact, which is something prisoners rarely experience in their daily lives:

> During the visit, while embracing each other, or when you are engaging in an intense conversation, it happened, like in the outside, that I forgot [where I was], I was shocked (laughs) [to notice] that I'm in there and now it's over, and now we have to [say good-bye] again. (Leo, 23.3.2016)

In order to forget about time and space, and to let oneself be absorbed by the pleasant moment, we may assume that these prisoners do not pay attention to the passage of (clock) time. However, some of the same prisoners who said that they let themselves be absorbed also mentioned that, at the same time, they still closely monitor and manage (clock) time, so that they can make full use of every minute they spend with their loved ones, and to ensure they have enough time to bring up all the issues they intend to. It is for this reason that some prisoners bring a list into the visiting room, with all the topics they want to discuss. Louis makes a phone call before the visit, so that he can exchange some information with his wife in advance, which provides them with 'more time' during the visit, where time always passes too quickly:

> On Tuesday and Friday, I always make a phone call. […] Although we see each other on Saturday or Sunday … but there may also be things to discuss, so we will have more time [during the visit], and don't need to discuss it during the visit. (Louis, 22.3.2016)

However, although rarely mentioned by prisoners, time can also be experienced as passing slowly in the visiting room as visits are not always entirely pleasing. Sometimes one has nothing to say to each other (anymore), or it leads to a dispute.

As carceral time–space constellations, visits in prison are artificial moments in the sense that they cannot take place spontaneously: the location and duration of the meeting are fixed, and its basic content is face-to-face conversation as there is no possibility (with exception of the 'prisoners' oasis', see below) for prisoners and their guests to engage in other activities, such as going for a walk, cooking and eating together, or experiencing intimacy, as is possible in other prisons (see, for example, Comfort (2002) on so-called family or conjugal visits). During the exact two hours, the prisoners and their visitors, sitting at a table (usually) face-to-face, are supposed to talk. As I uncovered in my conversation with Leo, the pre-programmed nature of this encounter and its clear restrictions regarding time and space can evoke ambivalent feelings and differing ways of coping among prisoners and their guests. Together with different expectations, this can lead to a disturbance or disruption to the flow of the visit as the different rhythms followed by prisoners and their visitors may create what Lefebvre (2014) calls 'arrhythmia'. Such situations are often experienced as stressful, as the following explanation by Leo suggests:

> Sometimes, I'm very euphoric before the visit, feel great and can't wait, and when it's time and I sit at the table, then sometimes I feel like I just want to sit there and just enjoy the moment. Sometimes I don't feel like talking. They [the visitors] don't understand it at all. Because they, the people from outside, they are under time pressure: so, come on, talk now, tell us something! […] [They are] completely under time pressure. And then, yes, this is then like dampening the mood a little bit. Me, I always think like: Yes, don't give a shit! Let's enjoy the moment for a few minutes. Then we can talk again. Sometimes this ruins their moods. So, this kind of stress: come talk now, I notice that. Me, I'm like the opposite. I'm more relaxed and take it slowly … yes. And then, the visit goes, depending on how the pressure is from them. (Leo, 23.3.2016)

6.3.1.4 Performing and Experiencing the (Non-)Prisoner Self

The prisoners I met received visits from family members, friends and voluntary visitors. Moreover, in the visiting room they can potentially meet new people. It thus constitutes a space where (existing) social relations are maintained and maybe even (new ones) established. Furthermore, as I show below, it is also a space where relations can end. As referred to earlier, for the prisoners, visits are time–spaces where they can access the outside world. This provides them with distinctive physical and emotional experiences.

First of all, in Goffman's (1959) sense, the visiting room can be considered a 'stage' where the self can be experienced and performed in very particular ways by adopting different roles. Broadly speaking, during visits, prisoners can experience themselves as something else than a prisoner: a parent, a child, a sibling, a friend or a lover.[5] Visits allow them to feel connected to the outside world, to maintain bonds with their friends and family members and to continue to stay informed about their lives and the events of the outside world in general. Also, as mentioned, visits constitute for many prisoners situations where they obtain 'emotional feedback' (Toch 1996 [1977]), emotional support and motivation to keep going, including hope for a better future. Moreover, visiting rooms are particularly 'emotional zones' (Crewe et al., 2014) where prisoners can not only show, but also experience emotions that are taboo and unavailable elsewhere in prison, especially familiarity and intimacy. Furthermore, in the visiting room prisoners can also see and observe other people. Two prisoners mentioned that they could even make new contacts:

> It was at my birthday, I turned 51, and we were standing at the coffee machine, and I said to him [his visitor]: I'm 51 now, from now on, it will go downhill. She [a visitor of a fellow prisoner] stood next to us and when she heard that she said to me: No, no that's not true, it's only now that life really begins. Then we started a conversation and [she is] really just, a really relaxed, nice woman, really open-minded and so on. And then, after the visit, I told my fellow prisoner: I've just met a really nice woman, really funny and so on, and he wanted to know what she looks like, then I briefly described her to him, and he said: Yes, this is [name of the woman], she is a friend of mine who comes to visit me. Then I

[5] It has to be emphasized that the visiting room is also a place where prisoners meet their lawyers and representatives of the enforcement authorities—of course, in the role of the offender/prisoner.

told him that I [would like her to be my visitor too] and he said that he wouldn't mind and that he would talk to her. She agreed and then I went to my social assistant and from her side it was ok too, but then she had to make a phone call to Zürich [the prison authority], and there they first were against it, saying that this was not a request programme, but the social worker stood up for me and so they finally made an exception. That's how it took place. (Hugo, 25.6.2013)

Today at his workplace, Leo told me about a recent encounter he had in the visiting room. A fellow prisoner introduced Leo to his visitor; they 'matched right away'. She [the fellow prisoner's visitor] also expressed an interest in establishing contact with Leo. Now, they write each other letters. (Fieldnotes, 5.2.2016)

Based on these two examples, I argue that meeting new people (especially women) provides prisoners with the additional opportunity to rediscover or perform certain roles that are maybe not available during their encounters with family members or people they have known for a long time.

Moreover, visits allow prisoners to gain distinct sensual experiences. In her paper on sexuality and intimacy in a French prison, Ricordeau (2012) demonstrated that although it is prohibited, by identifying and using the places in the visiting room that are less monitored, it is not unusual that prisoners and their visitors engage in sexual activity during visiting hours. While hugging, cuddling and kissing are accepted in all the three prisons where I conducted fieldwork, sexual activity is not allowed. While *JVA Pöschwies* is one of the few prisons in Switzerland that is equipped with a so-called 'family room', prisoners in the *Strafanstalt* at *JVA Lenzburg* are—although informally—granted the option to engage in sexual activity once they are allowed to receive their visitors in the open-air visiting area, the so-called 'prisoners' oasis' (Clément, 26.9.2017), which is discussed below in greater detail.

However, receiving visitors is also experienced as challenging and stressful, which is directly linked to the prison context and the prisoners' status as *prisoners*, which, nevertheless, cannot entirely be pushed to the background by playing other roles. For instance, some prisoners mentioned the need to perform like a host as stressful, others the feeling of being in charge of creating a positive experience, so that the visitors 'don't feel obligated to come to see us' (François, 23.11.2013). It is particularly striking that many prisoners mentioned the challenging feeling of emptiness that may arise during visits. They feel that—compared to the people who live in the outside world—they do not have much to contribute, in terms of appearance ('always the same' (Kurt, 3.5.2016), see above), objects they can offer (all they can offer their guests are items from the snack machine), and the experiences they can share. As pointed out by Heinz (3.5.2016): 'in order to talk about something, you must have experienced something':

> There is not much to talk about, every day is the same. And I cannot tell [my mother] what prison means. And I don't experience anything else, I don't go skiing or to the *Schilthorn* [in the Bernese Alpes] on a Sunday, yes, you really have little to talk about. (Heinz, 3.5.2016)

Jonathan expressed similar feelings:

> Those from outside are full of topics and me I'm empty, I have nothing to say, what can I say, I saw the foreman, that I ate a sausage? That's not of interest to those outside. I notice that when I have contact with my family, they are full of stories, they can talk for hours, and me, I cannot think of anything, I'm somehow limited with experiences. And there's nothing new on my side, what shall I say, that I've read something new in the newspaper, should I quote from a book, newspaper, or television? [...] I'm somehow empty. (Jonathan, 24.9.2013)

6.3.1.5 The 'Prisoners' Oasis'

As highlighted by Moran (2013b), it is important to consider the particular nature of the visiting rooms when researching the experience within them. As already mentioned, in the *Strafanstalt* at *JVA Lenzburg*, prisoners have access to a particular visiting room, which is actually not a room but more like a small 'park' (Markus, 28.9.2017) (see Figs. 6.11, 6.12 and 6.13). During the walking interviews, this was one of the places shown to me by all the participating prisoners. It was represented as 'my most beautiful place in prison' (Leo, 31.8.2017), as a place where 'the atmosphere is different' and one 'feels freer' (Hugo, 7.9.2017). Markus (28.9.2017) described this open-air visiting area as 'our place'; for Clément (26.9.2017) it is 'the prisoners' oasis'. The prisoners pointed out several features that are relevant to the experienced particularity of this open-air visiting area. First, in terms of its spatial arrangement: it is bigger than the normal courtyards, there are grass and trees—interestingly, all the prisoners who led me to this place mentioned the small wall under the tree in the middle (see Fig. 6.12) as their favourite place to sit down with their visitors—a well, benches and tables, a playground for children and a table tennis game. Second, it is a place where prisoners come across other people from the outside, often parents with their children.

Fig. 6.11 The open-air visiting space in the Strafanstalt at JVA Lenzburg (*Source* Google Maps)

Fig. 6.12 The open-air visiting area: a 'less standardized' place (*Source* Photo by a prisoner)

Fig. 6.13 The open-air visiting area: 'the most beautiful place in prison' (*Source* Photo by a prisoner)

Third, compared to the visiting room inside, where they have to sit at a table, prisoners can move around more freely in this area. During the visit, they can decide to walk a few steps, sit on a bench or on one of the walls, walk again, play a round of table tennis, let their children (or grandchildren) use the '*Gigampfi*',[6] and so on. In sum, a visit in the outside area is, according to Leo, experienced as less 'standardized':

> I think ... those from the outside, they always think that it doesn't matter whether you can go outside or not. But me, I think it makes a difference whether you are sitting [inside] there at the table for two hours or whether you are doing a few laps out here. And also to feel that you can be outside with a person you love. Inside [in the visiting room] it's so static, so standardized. Inside there are these partitions, so you are really in this box knowing that now I will be sitting here for two hours. Sure, it's good to meet someone there as well. (Leo, 31.8.2017)

Indeed, the atmosphere is different in this open-air place, even for someone like me with no emotional relationship to it. If one strictly ignores the bars in front of the windows, the fences, and the wall, one really has the sense of being in a public park.

However, the 'prisoners' oasis' is visually obstructed by the grey high-security unit made of concrete nearby, where prisoners are locked up 23 hours a day without any access to the facilities of the main prison (see Fig. 6.14). It is a prison within the prison. Interestingly, this massive building was only spontaneously mentioned once, by Leo. As his statement suggests, it is mainly something that is noticed by external visitors (including me). It seems that the prisoners (perhaps intentionally) 'filter' (Kusenbach, 2003) it out.

> This is the SITRAK [high-security unit], you see, [the building] is clearly separated from the other, it even has another, it's even drearier, it's not even painted. That there is no place for these people with us ... I'm kind of sorry about that. [...] It's open at the top, but everything is barred. I saw it on TV, how it looks. You don't hear anything from these people, you never see these people, you don't know how many are in there. And

[6] Swiss-German word for a child's swing.

Fig. 6.14 The high-security unit next to the open-air visiting area (*Source* Photo by a prisoner)

> every visitor asks: What is this? Somehow, that's just noticeable, I realized. People coming for the first time, they want to know what it is. (Leo, 31.8.2016)

Also, in contrast to the courtyard, in the 'oasis' the prisoners did not mention the wall and the fences, or that the general (physical) closeness to the outside world might be an issue for them. When I asked Hugo for the reasons, he told me that in this place, one is 'entirely concentrated on the visitor' (Hugo, 7.9.2017). A similar statement was shared by Markus, who talked about the visits by his girlfriend, although it also reveals that a little effort has to be made in order to forget about being in prison:

> [When] we [he and his girlfriend] come outside, we don't really see the bars, we don't see them, we walk our rounds, we go to the toilet, come out again, go to the table, eat something … you try to be carefree for a while. (Markus, 28.9.2017)

Finally, the open-air visiting area is also a place where the prison system is less present: prisoners feel and actually are less supervised by staff. Furthermore, the place is to a great extent maintained by the prisoners themselves:

> Here, one is somehow on their own, and it works, it really is like that. There are always two prisoners who take care of this place and really care for it, that's something I find very nice. Me, for example, I am responsible for putting away the *Spielrössli*[7] and the *Gigampfi* in the winter, that everything is removed and so on. We care for it, because that's like our place, our space. And none of the employees have anything to do with it, that's for us. And even the guards who have to control the yards, they also have to walk through here, they usually don't do that, but walk along behind it when they see that there are visitors. (Markus, 28.9.2017)

Precisely because this open-air visiting area is less monitored compared to the common visiting room, not every prisoner has permission to go there, at least not with every visitor. For instance, as I was told by prison staff, a prisoner who is sentenced for a sex offence and who has additionally been diagnosed with a particular personality disorder, may not be allowed to go out there with female visitors (with the possible exception of their mother) (Fieldnotes, 22.2.2016). One reason for this is the unsupervised toilet that is located in this area. As mentioned, there is no official place—unlike other prisons, where there sometimes exist so-called 'family rooms'—that allows prisoners to spend intimate time with their spouse or girlfriend. In the 'prisoners' oasis', prisoners and their visitors use this toilet for sexual activity. Although the prison officially provides no so-called conjugal or 'contact room' (Bundesamt für Justiz BJ, 2011, p. 7), this practice is implicitly tolerated by the management. These intimate moments, however, have to be negotiated among prisoners. Usually, there are several couples who want to benefit from this opportunity, and time is limited:

> Of course, those who also have a free visit [a visit in the open-air area] and have a girlfriend always also want to go to the toilet … But one takes

[7] Swiss-German word for a rocking horse.

> care, so maybe half an hour, and if there are maybe more people in the yard, you have to be aware, if you go out you can see how many people there are, how many couples, in some cases you know it's just the mother or something like that. Then you know that you can certainly take more time [in the toilet]. But if you are in the toilet and you know that there are more people, or more couples, unfortunately this doesn't work in any case, but that you maybe show consideration for them, saying: Hey, we are not the only ones here. And then maybe take a bit less time. It's not pleasant to have sex on a toilet with the wife or partner. But that's the way things are. […] And otherwise, there are some who sometimes forget about time, and then you go, let's say after 20, 30 minutes, depending on how many people there are, you go knocking and then the one inside actually knows. And usually it works quite well and within the next five minutes, they really come out. (Louis, 22.3.2016)

Although I met only two prisoners who regularly have (or used to have) sex in the toilet, the prisoners have clear opinions about having sex in a toilet (see also Sect. 4.4.5). They generally describe it as 'unworthy'—both of themselves and of their partners (see also Ricordeau, 2012, p. XII, on having sex in the visiting room of the prison)—however, it is the only option they have. The fact that this toilet is there and that only a limited number of prisoners can use it to have sexual intercourse can also provoke frustration by those who have access to it but have no one with whom to engage in sexual activity. The toilet can thus be a constant reminder of the absence of (hetero)sexual intercourse in their lives.

6.3.1.6 Leaving the Visiting Room

The experience of the approaching and actual end of the visits vary widely among the prisoners. Of those who are aware that the end is near, some feel that time is speeding up during the last minutes, which causes a lot of stress:

> Towards the end, regularly, I almost break out in panic. Have I forgotten anything important, which I still wanted to, topics or questions that I absolutely wanted to ask? It's almost always like this towards the end

> (laughs), a lot of stress. And then it rings [the official reminder that time is over]: No, alas, now it's over! (Rolf, 6.5.2016)

Others try to be prepared, to anticipate the end by carefully watching the passage of time in order to have enough time to say good-bye calmly. Again others are caught by surprise and experience the ringing of the bell as an interruption in the middle of a conversation.

In any case, the moment of the good-bye is a transition where the two worlds (the inside and the outside), which have blurred and collided during the visit, are again separated from each other. Louis described the good-bye as the moment 'in which you will be caught by the prison life again and it becomes [again] more present where you are, [...] my wife is going in this direction, me I have to go in that direction' (Louis, 22.3.2016). Generally, it is a moment 'that hurts', because it is a 'good moment that ends' (Louis, 22.3.2016) and because 'one would like to go with them' (Michael, 6.5.2016).

Leaving the visitor's room means going back to the 'ordinary' (Kurt, 3.5.2016), with all its laws and rules, or back to 'reality' (Rolf, 6.5.2016). Prisoners mentioned that after a visit, they often feel exhausted and sad, but also restless, feeling the need to speak to and see those who have just left again immediately. As emphasized by Ricordeau, '[t]he "postvisit" period is, in fact, often a "still-visiting" period, a private time, where, on the outside, as on the inside, those involved try to nurture and prolong the feeling of the presence of the other' (2012, p. XV). Indeed, several prisoners told me that after the visit they walk back 'particularly slowly' (Michael, 6.5.2016) in order to continue to dwell in the feelings they have had during the visit. They carry back the memories of the two hours they spent in the visiting room like little treasures; once they are back in their cells, they 'keep on thinking about these two hours' (Leo, 31.8.2016), 'reflect' on the issues they spoke about (Rolf, 6.5.2016) and 'try to keep on enjoying this moment' (Louis, 22.3.2016). The memories are a source of energy, giving them motivation, and helping them to keep going. But then, slowly, the prison reality becomes recognizable again:

> And then, when you're in the cell again, you're still in this thing, but I'm trying, or we're actually trying to enjoy that moment a little bit longer. So,

> the memories, what we experienced //to remain a little bit in the feeling?// exactly, it's still fresh … and then at some point you realize, well, now you're really back in the cell. And then, of course, the positive thing is just that you can talk with people or fellow prisoners, or participate in a leisure time activity or whatever, where you can distract yourself a little bit. (Louis, 22.3.2016)

Prisoners try to maintain the bridge they built to the outside world through their visitors as long as possible, either through reflection or activities, such as making phone calls (only in cases where spontaneous phone calls with relatives are possible) or writing letters right after the visit. Louis, quoted above, emphasized this by using the word 'we' when talking about the post-visit phase and the (emotional) extension of the visit experience after the good-bye. The bridge to the outside world is also maintained by looking forward to the next visit: 'When I'm back, I'm always sad. I don't cry, I do not cry, but I'm just sad. But then I prepare myself already for the next visit' (Michael, 6.5.2016). However, there will not always be a 'next time', as I show below.

Moran (2013a, 2013b) examines the effect of prison visits on prisoners by conceiving of the prison visiting room as a 'liminal carceral space', where the immediate reality of incarceration is temporarily suspended. However, as she addresses, in its original conceptualization liminality is not just about betweenness, but also about transformation (Turner, 1969; van Gennep, 1960). As summarized by Moran, '[i]n the post-liminal, individuals reintegrate into their "new" life, adopting a new social status and re-entering society in accordance with this new status' (2013b, p. 183). Although the visiting room of the prison can clearly be identified as 'a liminal space in the sense of betweenness and indistinctiveness, its transformative role is less clear' (Moran, 2013a, p. 347). It is a space that can be repeatedly entered and left, and after the visits, prisoners always return to the daily routine of prison life and 'have to let them [the visitors] go again and again' (Markus, 28.9.2017). There is thus no immediate progression to another status. Yet, Moran (2013a, 2013b) identified a cumulative effect in the sense that through visits, prisoners are reminded of the outside world and are thus motivated to complete their sentence successfully in order to be able to return to it as soon as possible. From this perspective, visiting spaces are of a transformative nature.

In the case of prisoners serving very long sentences, in particular when they are held in indefinite incarceration without any date of release, the transformative nature of the visiting space is rather a potential; however, it is very fragile. Although, as seen above, visitors generally help these prisoners to stay motivated and not lose hope, as emphasized by Cohen and Tylor (1972, pp. 72–75), the maintenance of relations to the outside world is difficult and can cause great frustration in the longer term. According to the authors, the reason lies, in part, in the visiting regime of the prison, which imposes lots of restrictions. Additionally, maintaining contact to the outside world can also be very demanding emotionally, as prisoners who keep in touch with their relatives and friends live in a separate world, always worrying that the relationship may break down during this very long physical separation (see also O'Donnell, 2014, p. 223). Many long-term prisoners thus decide to cut off contact in order to reduce suffering and to concentrate on the here and now. These issues were also mentioned by the prisoners to whom I spoke. But in addition to the emotional stress caused by the connection to the outside world, I observed that through visits, prisoners serving indefinite sentences are also constantly reminded of what they are missing: a life of freedom, having family and being physically present with them, living a (unrestricted) partnership, having a love life and all the other experiences they have lost and will probably never have (again). This can also hinder them, as well as their loved ones, from going on with their lives:

> I said [to her]: I don't want to talk to you in five years, saying: we tried, but unfortunately it didn't work out. After ten years I would have to say: The girl has lost ten years with me. […] She was [at that time] the secretary of a colleague. And that's why I told him: You have to make sure she moves on. But me, I don't want that. I don't want that because I have zero perspective and no idea where I am going. (Juris, 22.3.2016)

Although the visiting room is also a place where relations end, I argue that it may still (or maybe precisely because of this) be regarded as a transformative space, as outlined by Moran (2013a, 2013b). In the experiences of some prisoners presented above, however, being confronted and reminded of the outside world constitutes for them less a motivation to keep hoping, as argued by Moran, than a reason to let go of their pre-prison identities and accept that life is now the existence that takes place in prison and, as a consequence, to cut their bonds with the outside world. This also becomes clear in the following statements:

> While we were working together at his workplace today, Lars told me that his [prisoner] friend had voluntarily broken his last contact to the outside. If he stays here forever, Lars told me, he sooner or later would do the same, before they [his family members] die or pre-empt him, which, according to him, would make the loss even worse. (Fieldnotes, 17.2.2016)

> I notice that the more I let go and just accept that I won't get out, I then find it actually easier to feel comfortable [compared to] when I am constantly worrying if I will ever get out, if there may still be possibilities, [and] put pressure on myself. [...] But this also means that I would need to give myself up. I just talked to someone, just yesterday, who is in exactly the same situation as I am. He has now resigned, has given up. He denies everything, therapy and all that, and yes, he said he felt extremely comfortable. (Leo, 23.3.2016)

However, in many cases the relationship is ended by those in the outside world. Friends, in particular, are gradually lost over time (see also Cohen & Taylor, 1972, p. 67), but so are family members and lovers. Many prisoners mentioned that relatives and friends have abandoned them, some immediately after the arrest, others over the course of time. The explanations the prisoners shared range from the emotional burden of coming to prison and not knowing how long the situation will last, to the prisoners' criminal history, as well as a lack of time, living too far away, or having become too old or sick (and thus not mobile enough) to visit them in prison:

> I haven't had any contact with [my brother] for years. [...] I understand him; I understand that he's mad at me. But he came to visit me once,

> in 2005, saying: Michael, I forgive you. I was so happy and satisfied. And then I asked him: Will you come back again? But he never did. He never came. Believe me, I wrote him eight, nine, about ten times. He never even replied. Before, he used to answer. And of course, I had his phone number, but I was afraid to talk to him. That he might hang up or something. […] Yes, I have disappointed him, I have disappointed everyone, not only him, but [my brother] is just one who takes everything very literally. That's a bit the problem with him. But he is … we used to do lots of things together when we were young. (Michael, 6.5.2016)

In the following extract from a letter that I received, a prisoner describes an additional element: the feeling from someone in the outside world that the behaviour of the one inside has changed. This observation makes this prisoner feel like he is not only stuck in prison, but also in his 'own body', which has changed its expressions without him noticing:

> It just became too much for her [after all these years]. She felt this depressing mood every time she came to visit me. It was a huge burden for her to come to the prison. We had known each other a long time before [incarceration], and she was the woman I wanted to spend my life with, but she told me a few times that I had changed, not even negatively, but that my behaviour was very limited, absent and alien to her. Then I realized that being imprisoned can be painful. It is not the fact of being incarcerated that frightens me, but the fact that you are caught in your own body. Now we have gone our own separate ways. (Letter from a prisoner, 21.11.2016)

Based on the recognition that the relationship 'will lead nowhere', as it is difficult to share a life and imagine a common future when one of the two partners is held in prison (for an undetermined but certainly long duration), some also decided together to break off contact:

> So, actually, we broke up about a year ago, she came to visit me for a few more months, for about half a year, and then we said we slowly let it come to an end, and it's ok like this. And I think it wouldn't be right, if [she would continue to visit me] … I would feel guilty about it. Why should she be visiting me in prison for the rest of my life, feeling sad and depressed every time she comes here? And for me, indefinite incarceration

> is really nothing else than a very inhumanly sustained death sentence, nothing else. And she doesn't have to watch me dying in here. I think to truly love a person means to love someone more than yourself. And then you have to be able to say: no, that will lead nowhere. We had very, very emotional, very deep conversations and it was very difficult for both of us, but I think it's better this way. And I would be happy if she would find happiness and peace in her life, because, as bad as I was, she has always been so good and she deserves nothing better than what she really is herself, a really good person. I know that there are also people who are disappointed and sad when their partner leaves them or doesn't visit them or the family members who don't maintain contact. But I just think that the reason why I'm here is my fault and that's part of my punishment. So I see this as part of my sentence. It's not nice, it's not easy, but over time it just becomes part of it. (Markus, 29.3.2016)

As shown in this section, the visits in prison are emotionally charged moments that have an impact beyond the actual event. As time markers, prisoners can look forward to a visit for a long time beforehand and draw from it for some time afterwards. During the visits, by getting in touch with the outside world, in the visiting room, prisoners can experience and perform a different self, although the prison context and their status as prisoners can never fully be masked. Moreover, these moments provide them both with motivation and frustration, as those from the outside help them to forget temporarily about their situation and to maintain their motivation, but also to be reminded of their confinement. To maintain contact beyond the prison walls within the frame of formally established carceral spaces is highly challenging, and, as I have illustrated, many relations will be broken over time. It is, however, also possible, although it seems to be rather exceptional, to establish new ones.

6.3.2 Letters and Phone Calls

According to Art. 84 para. 1 of the SCC, prisoners have the right to cultivate contact with people in the outside world, not only through visits but also through letters and phone calls (Baechtold et al., 2016, p. 188). Prisoners can send and receive as many letters as they wish;

however—with the exception of correspondence with legal actors (e.g. lawyers, supervisory authorities)—incoming as well as outgoing letters and parcels (which are restricted in number and content) are controlled by the prison (JVA Lenzburg, 2011, pp. 52–54; JVA Pöschwies, 2017, p. 19).

As pointed out by Toch (1996 [1977], p. 70), for those prisoners who are particularly 'feedback-oriented', exchanging letters with the outside world is 'not only [...] the most significant feature of their routine, but becomes the weather vane to their mood, disposition, or ability to cope'. Indeed, I came across quite a few prisoners who used to exchange letters with the outside world, especially with family members, in large part also with former fellow prisoners who had been transferred to another prison, and, finally, with the prison authorities.

Corresponding with the outside world is also an important means of dealing with time. For instance, sending a letter is usually connected to the expectation of receiving a reply. Writing letters thus allows prisoners *to wait* for something. For example, throughout the time I have known him, Clément has been intensively engaged in writing complaints and arguing with lawyers and authorities. Along with his intention to improve his situation and achieve his release, my impression was that he also understands complaining as a (playful and almost ritualized) battle as he often anticipates the response; therefore, I argue that it is also a way to 'kill time' (see Sect. 4.5.1). As he told me, the usual negative responses constantly provide him with 'material to fight back' (Clément, 26.9.2017), again and again. The following extract illustrates his knowledge of the procedure:

> I can prove that all my therapy reports are alright, since 1995. [...] But then there comes a reviewer, and then everything goes again down the stream [...]. And I even got a written notification. I'm doing therapy although I'm held in indefinite incarceration ... [but] nothing is accepted. [...] Now, [my lawyer] makes a complaint. And it will probably be rejected again, then [he will] lodge an appeal, and then he would go to the administrative court, and depending on how it will be decided we will go to the Federal Supreme Court. It may take a long time. (Clément, 24.3.2016)

As discussed in Sect. 4.5.2, some prisoners also document their correspondence (e.g. listing all the outgoing and incoming letters, dates and names) and thus transform letters (the writing and the receiving of them) into 'events', which allows them to 'mark time' and create chronology.

Furthermore, by writing letters, especially to their loved ones, they also construct spaces for living out emotions and fantasies, developing wishes and hopes. For instance, Louis, who got married when he was already in prison, uses every opportunity to communicate with his wife. Sometimes, they write each other 'intimate' or 'special' letters:

> Every week, we have the opportunity to see each other, we hear each other twice a week and we exchange letters, sometimes you might even come up with something special, an intimate letter or a special one, I always call it a special letter. (Louis, 22.3.2016)

By exchanging letters with his penfriend (or 'contact', as he specified), whom he met by chance in the prison's visiting room, Leo rediscovered the experience of getting to know a woman. As he said, he did 'not remember exactly how this is done' and was trying to be very cautious to 'not rush anything' (Fieldnotes, 5.2.2016). However, some weeks later, he told me that he was already thinking about breaking off contact, because of an imbalance that had developed, or, in Cohen and Taylor's words, a growing 'sense of the unilateralism of the relationship' (Cohen & Taylor, 1972, p. 67), as his penfriend asked a lot of questions, especially regarding the offence that put him in prison, without revealing much of herself. Another reason for his intention to end it was linked to the fantasies and wishes that these letters stimulated, but which cannot be fulfilled as long as he is in prison:

> Of course, one has desires and dreams and fantasies, especially in here. And I also have a bit a problem with that […]. I then imagine things, or wish for something, which then doesn't happen, will not come true, and me, I absolutely want it to happen […] and then this creates again disappointments. (Leo, 23.3.2016)

The prisoners' correspondence with the outside world is of course strongly influenced by the prison management's right to monitor the exchange of letters. To know that the prison can read what they have written hinders some prisoners from freely expressing their feelings and writing about their experiences in prison. They fear that what they write may not be tolerated, that it may have negative consequences for the prisoners, and that letters (outgoing as well as incoming) may be withheld by the management. Some prisoners indeed told me about serious consequences they experienced after the prison inspected letters they wrote to their relatives. In one case, the prisoner described his feelings of hopelessness, which the prison interpreted as a sign of suicidal behaviour. He told me that he was immediately transferred to a psychiatric clinic where they bound him to the bed and sedated him with drugs. As he told me during an informal conversation at his workplace, he 'never want[s] to experience this again. [He] will never write such letters again' (Fieldnotes, 5.2.2016). Another prisoner found out that in creating an assessment of his case, the competent authority, without his knowledge, included a letter he had sent to his family. He said that since then he had never written any letters at all. I also came across other ways of dealing with these controls. Jürg said that after he had discovered that 'everything is read', he decided to nevertheless continue writing letters to his son, but to reduce the content to a minimum—'just to ask from time to time whether everything is OK'. In addition, he communicates by sending him money on a regular basis. Once, the boy wrote to him that he had spent it on a new iPhone (Fieldnotes, 22.4.2016).

Communication with the outside world is not only restricted by the fact that letters are read and maybe also withheld, but, according to Rolf, also because prisoners have no access to online and social media, which makes them feel left behind, or artificially held in the past, and thus reinforces the experience of social isolation (see also Jewkes & Reisdorf, 2016):

> I don't want to imagine a future [in here], as it is now, without any change, without more freedom, especially freedom to communicate. Because you can now find everything on the Internet, you can only watch half of the news on TV because it's always mentioned: You'll find more information on www […] It's getting worse and worse, phone numbers, you no longer find them out if you don't have access to the Internet, it's

the same with postal addresses. And if you still write letters, you don't get a reply, because people want to write emails, to text, or how is it called (laughs). […] That can't be. (Rolf, 11.9.2013)

In addition to correspondence, prisoners are allowed to cultivate contact with people outside the institution through phone calls:

Jonathan: I have a very big family. […] On Sundays at three o'clock I always call them, ten minutes before three I call them, because at three they start to eat. And often they come together at the weekend at someone's home, sit together and then they talk and so on. And then I call them.

Irene: Every week?

J: Every week. Four times a month my family, and a few times my friends whom I met here or know from outside. So usually I make calls between 70 and 80 minutes.

I: Per month?

J: Per month, yes. 120 are allowed. (Jonathan, 2.5.2016)

As this extract from the interview I conducted with Jonathan reveals, interacting with the outside world by means of the telephone is, like any other means of communication, restricted by the prison. While the duration of discussions with legal representatives, such as lawyers, is unlimited, the time allowed to speak to friends and family members is restricted both in terms of each single call (between 10 and 20 minutes) and the total duration of all the phone calls per month—120 minutes per month at *JVA Pöschwies* (JVA Pöschwies, 2016a, p. 9) and 180 minutes per month at *JVA Lenzburg* (JVA Lenzburg, 2011, p. 55). Moreover, with exception of the *AGE*, where prisoners possess a telephone card and have more options to make calls during the period when the cells are unlocked, phone calls generally have to be registered and approved in advance. The possession of mobile phones is strictly forbidden (JVA Lenzburg, 2011, p. 55). Prisoners cannot receive incoming calls and, finally, although not systematically monitored, phone calls may be recorded (Baechtold et al., 2016, pp. 188–189).

The prisoners' experiences of the restrictions concerning phone calls are diverse. They not only mentioned the limited duration of the call time, but also the impossibility of calling someone spontaneously, for instance in the case of an acute crisis. The limited duration, however, is not a problem for everyone. This, as illustrated in the following extract from my fieldnotes, is directly linked to the uneventful prison context:

> Today at Leo's workplace, we were talking about his contact with the outside world. He said that it bothers him that one always has to fix the phone calls in advance. Spontaneously, when things go bad, he cannot talk on the phone. [...] Another prisoner joined in our conversation and said that 20 minutes a week were enough, because 'you don't experience much in prison anyway, so you don't have anything to talk about'. (Fieldnotes, 5.2.2016)

However, Darko felt that with the limited duration of ten minutes per call, it is impossible to really maintain contact with the outside world:

> What bothers me is the ten minutes per phone here [in this prison]. I don't like that. If you want to maintain your contacts then ten minutes is too little. And then, after these ten minutes, you can only call again after one hour. [...] Before that, I had more phone [time], could talk for up to half an hour, or up to one hour or so. (Darko, 24.9.2013)

Rolf, too, wishes to have more call time. He has a big social network in the outside world, and not being able to contact his friends and family members whenever and for how long he wishes makes him feel (corporally) even more isolated from them. As he said, this was the reason why he once illicitly gained access to the Internet:

> *Irene*: And how about outside contacts, is it easy to maintain them?
> *Rolf*: I have a lot of contacts, but I don't have enough telephone minutes [...] that was the reason why I [gained] Internet access ... when I had the opportunity, because I couldn't stand it anymore, I just suffered so much from claustrophobia. (Rolf, 11.9.2013)

As this example suggests, prisoners also find (more or less legal) techniques to evade the restrictions regarding phone calls. It is an open secret that mobile phones or USB sticks allowing Internet access circulate in the prison every now and then (e.g. 55 items were detected in 2015, 40 in

2016, as officially reported by *JVA Pöschwies*) (JVA Pöschwies, 2016b, p. 53). During an informal conversation that I had with another prisoner at his workplace, he provided me additional insight into such illicit activities:

> I joined [a prisoner] who was felting ladybugs. He immediately started chatting, told me about prison life. [...] For example, that every now and then there is a mobile phone in the house, which is used by the prisoners and their fellow prisoners. Especially when the staff meets on Wednesday. The prisoners would then queue up in front of the cell of the inmate who has a mobile phone. They use it to make phone calls and go on Facebook. As he told me, the phone must be well hidden and covered with paper so that it doesn't show up on the detector that the staff would use to search for it. But usually, sooner or later, the prisoner gets caught, he laughed. As he said, mobile phones can be bought from other inmates for 1,000 Swiss francs. He suspects that it is also the sellers who squeal on the buyers, so that they always find buyers. As he further told me, they also manage to get Internet access [from their computers] from time to time. He proudly mentioned that he had seen the new James Bond movie even before it was released in Swiss cinemas. He laughed. Staff think they have everything under control, he said, but they don't: 'One always finds a way'. (Fieldnotes, 14.4.2016)

I came across another, more legal technique of dealing with the restrictions regarding phone calls. I was once sitting in a social assistant's office when one of the prisoners came in and asked the social assistant whether he may use the phone (the social assistant had an additional phone in his office). He explained that his girlfriend had been crying on the phone the day before and as the call got interrupted they could not continue to talk and now he had no idea how she was doing. He got permission. After he left the office, I asked the social assistant about the function of this second phone. He explained to me that it was 'actually an emergency phone' allowing prisoners to 'finish an important conversation'. However, as he continued to explain, many prisoners also come to use it to order something or to clarify something that only takes a few minutes and for which they do not want to sacrifice the ten minutes of calling time they have available per week—a practice that he tolerates in most cases (Fieldnotes, 22.2.2016).

6.4 Blurring Physical and Social Boundaries During Sports

During leisure time, prisoners also have the opportunity to take part in sports. In the prison literature, as summarized by Norman (2017), sport is examined from two perspectives. On the one hand, it is considered to have positive effects, for example on prisoners' mental health and their ability to cope with incarceration (Gallant et al., 2015; Martos-García et al., 2009; Meek, 2014; Norman, 2015; Sabo, 2001), or on their rehabilitation, due to the acquisition of 'post-release skills' (Gallant et al., 2015; Meek, 2014). On the other hand, it has also been claimed that sport, especially weightlifting and competitive sports, can contribute to the development of a hierarchical and violent 'inmate culture' (Abrams et al., 2008; Ricciardelli, 2014; Sabo, 2001). Norman argues that sport can further be used by the management 'to control both the prisoners' behaviour *and* to impose a particular moral or ideological order upon prisoners' (2017, p. 600). The social values that are supposed to be transmitted through sport are, according to Norman, hard work, discipline and respect for authority. Sport is also seen as a tool that supposedly contributes to the overall safety of the prison environment by reducing tension among prisoners. At the same time, however, as again demonstrated by Norman (2017), for the prisoners, sport can constitute a vehicle for resistance and subversion and thus facilitate the development of 'secondary adjustment' that contributes to a prison's 'underlife' (Goffman, 1961). Based on a study conducted in Canada, Norman (2017) demonstrates how prisoners 'refashion sport activities, materials, and spaces to their own purpose – and, in doing so, [...] they resist, in a limited fashion, the prison's social control aims' (Norman, 2017, p. 598) and establish 'a sense of identity within the institution' (Norman, 2017, p. 609).

Against this theoretical background, I propose to put aside the analytical framework of power and resistance and instead to approach sports in prison by looking more closely at the prisoners' lived experience of their moving and interacting bodies during sports lessons, and how this shapes the experience of their sense of self and (indefinite) incarceration in general.

6.4.1 Feeling and Using One's Body

In all three of the prisons where I conducted my research, prisoners have access at least once a week to sports courses and the possibility to pursue physical activities in the courtyard (e.g. jogging, doing exercises) on a daily basis. Despite these opportunities for movement, the prison environment and its particular spatio-temporal regime have significant effects on prisoners' bodies—on their general health, physical fitness and agility.

Prisoners spend much of their time sitting (at their workplace, which they reach in a few steps, as well as in their cell) or lying down (on the bed in their cell). As a consequence, as observed by one of the gym teachers as well as staff members who used to escort prisoners on temporary prison leaves, generally prisoners 'gradually lose their balance and body tension' (Fieldnotes, 25.2.2016). According to the gym teacher, this is also due to the fact that 'the entire ground in prison is flat' (Fieldnotes, 25.2.2016). In addition, from the gym teacher's point of view, the limited access to daylight in prison, the food prisoners eat (not only the usually very nourishing prison food, but also the generally unhealthy food they buy at the prison shop) and the fact that they generally have no or only very limited access to a wide view all affect the prisoners' health. Moreover, according to one of the prison doctors, due to the fact that in prison 'every thought, every idea, every wish is regulated', the prisoners face few mental and physical challenges, which causes them to 'become dull' over time:

> All the challenges, both physically and mentally, that everyday life brings with it, that you have to go shopping, to pay, that you give a one-hundred franc bill and then you calculate, how much will I get back now? To get out in the cold air, to put on a jacket, the need to be careful when it is icy. To take stairs when going to the mall, searching for something, thinking, looking with your eyes, in here [in prison], there is no need for all that. […] Or things that keep the whole story alive, keep it alive,

> changes … It's just really very dull in here. And of course, people become dull much faster in here. Everyday life is very monotonous, everything is regulated. Every thought, every idea, every wish is regulated in here. The prisoner does not have to ensure that the rent is paid by the end of the month […]. You just have to sit at the table and the food is ready […] you sit at the table and then you go back to the cell, then you are locked up again, or you sit at the workplace and then you just have to pack hundreds of things somewhere in an envelope. Then go back to the cell again, then there is dinner time, the prisoner must sit again at the table, you don't need to think 'what do I want to cook today? What is seasonal now? What would I like to eat?' You simply get what is there. And then back up to the cell again, and in there again, yes, what am I doing today? Maybe I take a book, I read a book or … most of them just lie down and switch on the TV and then they stare into the TV until they fall asleep, and then it is morning again. So it's just that the everyday challenges that we have, that are also good for us, physically as well as mentally, they just fall apart in here, to a large extent. (Medical staff member E., 4.2.2014)

Certain prisoners indeed mentioned that they had experienced bodily changes since their arrival in prison, mainly weight increases, but also an unbalanced digestion. Weight increase was clearly something I could observe over time: prisoners' bellies were getting bigger and bigger. Moreover, as two of my research sites were located in the units for elderly and ill prisoners, I came across many prisoners with health issues, which was recognizable to me especially through their limited mobility and agility. Some prisoners are also well aware of the effects that monotonous prison life may have on their mental health. Based on their observations of their fellow prisoners' behaviours, some reported not only a loss of spontaneity, but also a 'loss of interest in other people and emotions' (Letter from a prisoner, 27.9.2016) and becoming 'dulled' over time (Theo,

3.5.2016).[8] In addition to this, there is the lack of any concrete perspective, which makes many prisoners become depressed, angry, or sad (see Sect. 2.3.1).

Prisoners who were at the time of my fieldwork physically capable and willing to participate in the prison's sports programme generally described sports, similarly to people in the outside world, as activities that help them to increase their physical and emotional well-being. Moreover, in the sporting context of the prison, prisoners also use their bodies as instruments of action to influence the experience of imprisonment, by re-appropriating and regaining control over their bodies (see also Milhaud 2009). Sport is often used as an 'outlet' 'to let off steam', which helps them to 'just forget the whole thing for two hours' (Leo, 23.3.206). It is also used as a means to reach 'physical tiredness', which further leads to 'mental relief' (Serge, 25.9.2013), 'calmness' (Anton, 24.3.2016) and reaching the stage of being 'free of stress and negative thoughts' (Jonathan, 2.5.2016). For certain prisoners, sport is also a means to exercise some control over time, in particular the process of ageing, and thus to prepare their bodies for the future: by doing sports, prisoners try 'to stay fit and healthy as long as possible' (Serge, 25.9.2013).

In contrast, some prisoners say that they see no reason they should care for their health. For instance, Thomas refused to follow the doctor's advice to lose weight through physical movement and a more balanced diet, mainly because, according to him, he does 'not have any future' (Thomas, 11.6.2013) (which for him is outside) and therefore does not see any meaning in remaining fit:

> As I am now [in terms of weight], I haven't been like this before imprisonment. I used to go walking with my dog every day, for several hours [...] By doing this you automatically don't get fat. And where I lived, there you had to go up the street, I lived quite high up, and mostly I

[8] Against this background, it is not surprising that studies on ageing in prison point out that prisoners tend to age faster than people outside—a phenomenon that is also called 'hyper-ageing' (Dubler, 1998, p. 150). However, this is not only the result of the institutional environment of the prison. Prisoners are generally characterized by high-risk lifestyles and exhibit a disproportionately high level of health issues. In sum, they have higher rates of morbidity and mortality compared to society as a whole (Hostettler et al., 2016, p. 29).

> went home by foot, like this you have your personal fitness, but if you cannot do this ... The medical service said I was too heavy, I replied: Listen, give me a dog, I take it for a walk every day, for two, three hours, then I will immediately lose weight [...] I don't want to go into this room and go cycling and running on the treadmill, I haven't done this on the outside and I certainly won't do that in here. [...] When the doctor comes and says: You should no longer do this and that, then I reply: Do you know what, what should I then still live for? In the beginning, he wanted me to lose at least 20 kilos, and I said: Then please explain to me why I should still live, and [he answered]: But you too have a future, I said: Yes, I would be pleased to change [places with you]. [...] I don't chasten myself in here, what for, whether I die in five years or in eight months, this is a detail. But I will most probably die in here. Maybe I still live for 20 years, who knows, but I'm not unnecessarily hoping for a vague future out there, because for me, as you've rightly said, the future is outside and not in here. (Thomas, 11.6.2013)

Moreover, some prisoners participate in sport, above all, to 'kill time', and, when it takes place during work hours, to reduce the hours they have to be at their workplace.

The sporting context in prison is also a social space, which enables interactions that are not common in other contexts. As explained by Leo, while engaging in physical activities, and especially when playing team games, 'one behaves differently' and is 'more easy-going' (Leo, 23.3.2016). This is something I realized myself, particularly when I joined the prisoners playing badminton or table tennis—games that allow great physical activity and maybe foster an ambition to win the match. This is also connected to the experience (and maybe expression) of emotions, in a way that is probably not possible in other carceral spaces (see also Crewe, 2014). As I further explore in the following, the fact that one 'behaves differently' during sports lessons also influences interpersonal interactions in a way that may complicate the institutionally established boundary between staff and prisoners and affect the relations among prisoners.

6.4.2 Experiencing Encounters Between 'Human Beings'

Sporting contexts in prison are social spaces where prisoners interact with both fellow prisoners and sports teachers, who are either from the outside or part of the regular prison staff, such as prison officers or foremen. As I show in the following, when they actively participate in sports (and not just supervise the lesson), institutionally ascribed (opposed) roles and individual status can fade into the background as prisoners and staff face each other in the roles of equal partners or opponents—or maybe apprentices and trainer. Collective sports activities thus also challenge the important but fragile relationship of both closeness and distance between staff and prisoners and may even blur the institutionally established boundary or 'basic split' (Goffman, 1961, p. 7) between them.

Some members of the prison staff who also gave sports lessons explicitly mentioned that they frame these as situations that should differ from the everyday (working) routine. One of the foremen who teaches sport once a week told me that he 'clearly deal[s] differently' with prisoners during sports lessons, during which he wants to be 'not their boss, but their opponent' (Foreman A., 27.6.2016). He makes this clear by wearing sportswear and actively participating himself, and also by shaking the prisoners' hands before and after sport—'like in the outside world'—to indicate that he 'respects' them as equal opponents (Foreman A., 27.6.2016). With this practice, which is very uncommon in prison, he also (physically) makes the beginning and the end of this particular activity tangible for the prisoners. Moreover, he wants the sports lesson to be an occasion during which prisoners are 'allowed to express emotions', for instance 'to get upset' and 'to swear'—things he would not accept in the workplace in his role as foreman (Foreman A., 27.6.2016). From his point of view, he thereby releases prisoners from playing the role of the prisoner and lets them slip into the role of the athlete, or simply of an emotional human being:

> *Foreman A.*: And you realize that they behave completely differently, it makes them feel more relaxed. Yes, because they don't have to play a role, they are allowed to swear a bit, yes, to show emotions. Which

I think is important, especially in sports you should be able to show emotions and even let off some steam.

Irene: So you actually provide them with some free space, right?

FA: Yes, I think so, it's a free space. Especially for them to sometimes break out of the whole, out of all the rules, out of the whole, which is so strictly ordered, to break out a bit, even if it's just a little bit. But for once to simply be the athlete, and not the prisoner, a human being, you know, the athlete, not the prisoner. (Foreman A., 27.6.2016)

The extract above also clearly indicates that for this foreman, sport is not only a perfect framework but also a legitimate one for the expression of emotions, as something that is commonly associated with athletes. Moreover, according to him, allowing prisoners to spend some time out of the prison routine gives them pleasure and satisfaction, which, in the end, also contributes 'to a better atmosphere' in prison as a whole, and 'makes it easier for [the foreman] to work [with them]' (Foreman A., 27.6.2016). This echoes Norman's (2017) argument that sport in prison is also used to exercise social control over prisoners. In this sense, to let prisoners simply be human beings during sports can also be interpreted as a strategic decision.

However, facing each other as 'human beings' during sports lessons is particularly challenging as it brings staff 'again a step closer' (Foreman B., 27.6.2016) to the prisoners—and vice versa. Facing each other not only in the role of prisoner and foreman but also as game partners 'sharing the same hobby' creates an 'additional connection' between prisoners and the teaching staff member (Foreman A., 27.6.2016). This is not without problems, as staff and prisoners are supposed to keep a 'social distance' (see also Goffman, 1961, p. 7). From the institution's perspective, close relations between staff and prisoners automatically increase the potential for inappropriate and illegal practices—such as doing a favour for the prisoner, for instance by smuggling something in for him—which 'could put the prison's security in danger' (Foreman A., 27.6.2016). For this reason, from the staff members' perspective, in the end, the prisoner has to remain a prisoner: 'You must always keep in mind that he is a prisoner' (Foreman A., 27.6.2016). The social boundary between staff and prisoners is thus not static but constantly redrawn and re-negotiated, by both staff and prisoners. This dynamic also becomes apparent in the following extract from my fieldnotes:

> During table tennis, I became involved in a discussion between a prisoner and a foreman who had just played a match together. [The prisoner] mentioned several times that this prison was the best because of the staff: playing table tennis together and 'to talk personally' with staff, this is unique, he told me. [The foreman] intervened by saying: 'but we [prison staff] still don't tell private things'. I joined in the conversation and wanted to know from [the foreman] whether the interactions are nevertheless a bit more collegial, as they take place in the frame of leisure time. He then agreed, saying: 'Yes, you [as staff member] certainly have to distinguish between work and leisure'. (Fieldnotes, 3.2.2016)

As this extract further clarifies, while some prisoners, such as the one quoted above, welcome the blurring of the boundary between themselves and prison staff during sports lessons, this is something which makes staff feel uncomfortable—maybe not so much while practising it, but certainly while reflecting upon it. Through discursive practices, the staff foreman quoted in the extract above tried, to some extent, to re-establish the social boundary between himself and the prisoner after they had faced each other as (equal) game partners while playing table tennis together. He nevertheless agreed that this boundary did not need to be as distinct as in the work context.

In addition to the discursive and behavioural strategies illustrated above, staff members may also create distance between themselves and prisoners through hidden and symbolic practices without the prisoners' knowledge. The following example, however, should probably also be interpreted as a performance of the foreman's positioning vis-à-vis me:

> Together with [a foreman] I went to the gym, and we set up the ping-pong tables. We expected ten prisoners. [...] He got the rackets and asked me if I brought my own (which I didn't) and if not I would just have to wash my hands afterwards. I said that I don't mind at all to use the same rackets as the prisoners. But he insisted on giving me a new one, saying that 'the inmates don't need to know that you got a new one'. 'It's always

good to keep a certain distance', he added, and smiled. The prisoners arrived […]. (Fieldnotes, 3.2.2016)

In this situation, the foreman emphasized and maintained the boundary between 'us' (the prison staff and me) and 'them' (the prisoners) by making sure that I did not get *in touch* with prisoners by using one of the rackets they usually use. In case I did, he recommended that I wash my hands afterwards. This conversation would certainly not have taken place if I had been a guest in a sports club in the outside world.

During sports lessons, prisoners also interact among themselves, which again entails redrawing and re-negotiating social boundaries. While the literature points out that sports provide prisoners with resources to perform masculinity and create a hierarchical and violent inmate culture (see, e.g. Abrams et al., 2008; Ricciardelli, 2014; Sabo, 2001; Sabo et al., 2001), these elements did not emerge during my fieldwork. I assume that this is in part because such dynamics are more common among younger prisoners. The majority of the prisoners I spoke to are part of the elderly prison population, and indeed weightlifting and bodybuilding, which are in particular considered to contribute to the issues mentioned above, were not among their preferred activities. Those who nevertheless used to go to the gym (illustrated in Fig. 6.15) typically indicated health issues like back pain as their main reason for going. Some of the prisoners who used to stay in one of the special units also participated in the gymnastics lessons for elderly people. The younger ones preferred activities such as football, badminton, table tennis or yoga.

However, certain prisoners mentioned that during sport, one is 'more easy-going, out of the daily routine' (Leo, 23.30.2016). Sport may thus also offer positive opportunities for prisoners 'to know each other better' (Leo, 23.30.2016). On the other hand, however, as explained by another prisoner, it is important 'to not express too many emotions', because otherwise 'one becomes vulnerable'. This prisoner told me that he worried that he had been 'too cheerful' during his last sport lesson, that he had 'forgotten for a moment where [he] was', which is not good, according to him (Fieldnotes, 11.2.2016). This echoes Crewe et al. (2014, p. 57), who point out that the prison environment is often described as 'low in trust', a place where prisoners feel the need to 'mask'

Fig. 6.15 The prison gym (*Source* Photo by a prisoner)

their emotional expressions and put on 'fronts' of courage and aggression (see also Sect. 4.4). Hence, regarding relations between prisoners during sports, where one tends to forget where one is, it is nevertheless important for prisoners to maintain a certain distance—maybe not a social distance, but an emotional one. Like prison staff, prisoners feel the need to keep in mind that the opponent, in the end, is a prisoner. Interestingly, being (too) cheerful and joking with prisoners was also designated as a danger by some of the staff members. As explained by one of the foremen, joking with prisoners is not a problem in itself, but it creates a mood that can lead the prison staff to 'suddenly [...] tell them [the prisoners] too much. Suddenly, you talk about your holidays' (Foreman C., 7.7.2016). Such behaviour again carries the danger of blurring the institutionally established social distance between staff and prisoners.

As I show in the following, blurring boundaries is also an issue during education and training.

6.5 Escaping Spatio-Temporal Stasis Through Education and Training

As mentioned in the introductory section, the prisoners' right to access education and training is stipulated in Art. 82 of the SCC. As showed by Richter et al. (2011), the status of education within the Swiss penal system has been improved through the reform of the Criminal Code in 2007 and the equating of education with work. This newly stipulated equivalence of work and education corresponds to a worldwide tendency to pay more attention to education, which is considered an important tool in the prisoners' rehabilitation process. Moreover, in 2007, Switzerland launched a nationwide programme that provides basic education for prisoners called '*BiSt*' (*Bildung im Strafvollzug*). According to its website, the aim of the basic education programme is (1) to improve the prisoners' capacity for coping with daily life in prison and (2) to increase their chances of reintegrating into society and the world of work (BiST Fachstelle Bildung im Strafvollzug, 2019). Basic education primarily promotes skills in mathematics, reading and writing, but it also focuses on social behaviour and basic computer skills. Lessons take place once a week for half a day, during the prisoners' work hours. The duration of the prisoners' participation is undetermined.

Richter et al. (2011) employ the metaphor of an 'island' to describe the meaning of this particular education programme, because it basically allows prisoners to retreat from the monotonous prison routine. Moreover, in the classroom, they feel like individuals, and they have the opportunity to get in touch with the outside world and to engage in something they consider meaningful. The authors also describe school lessons as 'safe spaces' ('*geschützte Räume*') characterized by relations of trust and openness both among prisoners and between prisoners and teachers. These elements clearly also emerged in the interviews I conducted with prisoners. For instance, education as a change in the monotonous prison routine was put forward by the majority of the prisoners with whom I talked:

> Very little happens in here. I'm glad when I'm in school, then I hear something new from the teacher, he always brings news, has experienced

> this and that, he experiences in a week as much as I experience in a year. It's normal, so much happens outside, whether you like it or not, it just happens. And there you always hear something new, have fun, work on some topics and … otherwise, nothing happens, what should I tell you? (Jonathan, 2.5.2016)

Yet, as the basic education programme is oriented towards prisoners who have to be rehabilitated, the curriculum is based on repetition. Additionally, none of the courses are designed for long-term prisoners, such as courses that build upon one another—not least because these prisoners are clearly outnumbered in prison. Participation in education as well as other training courses is therefore (as with prison life in general) characterized by the experience of repetition and routine. At the time I met Jonathan, he was participating in the *BiSt* programme for the second time: 'The teacher asked me if I didn't mind going through the same topics again. It doesn't bother me' (Jonathan, 24.9.2013). While the lack of any advanced training did not seem to bother Jonathan, Clément clearly complained about it:

> The computer course offered in here, I also participated once, but then I quit after the third time, that was the lowest drawer. It was supposed to be an advanced computer course, but I just had to laugh. But of course, in here, there are just so many different people, and for some it might have been a good thing. (Clément, 25.6.2013)

As I show in the following, despite the limitations, school lessons nevertheless provide prisoners held in indefinite incarceration with particular opportunities regarding the experience of time and their sense of self.

6.5.1 Tracing the Rhythms of the Outside World—And Finding One's Own

I met prisoners who participated in school lessons not only to achieve some distraction from the prison routine, but also to exercise control over the passage of time—by tracing the rhythms of the outside world and therefore remaining (to some degree) up to date. This, of course, also strongly depends on the teacher and his or her personal way of shaping the lessons:

> For example, when we talk about a topic, I understand it this way, others understand it maybe the other way round, and then we discuss that, and you get a correct answer. […] I also learned how to use the computer. I understood many topics better. For example, at school we discussed news that we saw on TV. And so I got a much better understanding than just from the TV. (Jonathan, 24.9.2013)

I argue that by staying informed, prisoners *synchronize* their lives with the lives of people from the outside world from whom they are not only spatially but temporally segregated: the rapid progress—especially technological progress—that takes place in the outside world does not to a great extent find its way inside the prison. For instance, although prisoners do have computers, they do not have access to the Internet, nor are they allowed to use mobile phones. The prisoners' lives are therefore in some ways acted out in a past era.

Moreover, despite the limited education offered, some prisoners engage in mental work within the frame of school lessons with the aim of escaping the feeling of *temporal stasis* that they experience in prison and, connected to this, the fear of mental deterioration. In learning something new, and especially pursuing personal projects (e.g. writing a cookbook, developing a computer programme, preparing and giving a school lesson), they 'use time' constructively, which enables them to maintain their sense of self and to develop further as human beings—according to their own *individual rhythm*.

Hence, although prisoners sentenced to indefinite incarceration are, from an institutional perspective, not supposed to be concretely prepared for a future in society, and despite the limited education programme, certain prisoners nevertheless use the available education and training offer to create for themselves a liveable present and future—inside prison.

> I asked Lars if he also had contact with the prisoners kept in indefinite incarceration. He said no, because most of them have completely

'resigned'; were like 'backward', because of the long detention. To see this scares him. He tries to keep 'mentally fit'; he goes to school and takes a course in programming. That's important to him. (Fieldnotes, 9.2.2016)

In sum, education and training programmes indeed constitute 'islands' and 'safe spaces' for prisoners, as argued by Richter et al. (2011). However, as I have shown in this section, prisoners serving indefinite incarceration also use these occasions to deal with temporality (to trace the rhythms of the outside world and use time constructively), which allows them to experience themselves both as part of society as a whole and as an individual and thus to build *a bridge* to 'the mainland'.

6.5.2 'Playing Through Certain Emotional States'

During my stay in the units for the ill and elderly, the number of prisoners taking part in the organized leisure activities that I presented in the previous section was very small. This is due in part to the fact that the prisoners in the *AGE* were excluded from the prison's general evening leisure programme, as mentioned above. According to staff, in the *60plus*, although the prison offered different activities, the interest on the part of the prisoners was, with the exception of the cooking class, very low. Only towards the very end of my fieldwork was there one prison officer who managed to establish two afternoon programmes per week, one for prisoners interested in engaging in handicrafts and another one offering more movement-oriented activities. During my fieldwork in the *AGE*, in addition to gymnastics lessons for the elderly, for a short period of time one of the foremen offered music lessons once a week over the lunch break. Whenever possible, I participated too:

Together with a group of three to four prisoners, we met in one of the workrooms. We sat in a circle and the foreman encouraged us, one after the other, to create a rhythm by playing one of the available rhythm instruments. Then the rest of the group joined in, picking up the proposed rhythm. While playing music together, everyone was focused on the sound we were producing. Roles, statuses, and even the context became irrelevant. One prisoner once said (clearly delighted) that playing music let him 'completely forget' that he was in prison. (Fieldnotes, 18.8.2013)

That playing music allows for moments when the prison becomes irrelevant was also described by Leo and Markus. For Leo, it is a way to 'immerse' himself in his own world. As he told me, by playing the guitar, he sometimes achieves a state similar to the one he reached when using drugs (Fieldnotes, 24.2.2016). But, as Markus explained to me, music in prison can signify much more than gaining the feeling of being free. During our walking interview, he showed me the room where a band workshop took place once a week (illustrated in Fig. 6.16). As he revealed during our conversation, playing music in prison is for him also about living through, or, as he nicely put it, 'playing through', certain 'emotional states':

> This here, it's also a bit of freedom, it's about switching off. As you play the guitar yourself, when you make music yourself, then you know that then you really have such moments like that, or when you play certain songs, that you just feel free, or even sentimental, melancholic, [...] that you can play through certain emotional states, by playing certain songs or some kind of music. (Markus, 28.9.2017)

When entering the room with me, he both verbally and non-verbally expressed the importance this place had for him:

Irene: Oh, it's already open! (We are entering the room that was not locked as expected).

Markus: It's open; the cleaning cart is standing outside. But this is a place ... nobody else is allowed to go in, nobody else uses it, there's no other group or anything [than those participating in the band workshop]. And also ... oh I quickly have to air the room a little bit (he opens a window). Eh! Strange, why has my chair gone //(laughs)//. So, this is the band room. Here we make music. Everything has to be in order (he rearranges a chair).

I: So this is your place (pointing to the chair)?

M: That's my place, yes (laughs). We come here on Friday evening, to make some sounds. I've been playing the guitar for over ten years now. (Markus, 28.9.2017)

Fig. 6.16 The prison music room (*Source* Photo by a prisoner)

As this extract illustrates, through narrative (by pointing out his *privileged access* to this room, where he has a *personal place*, objectified in a particular chair), and by using particular gestures and action patterns when presenting it to me (airing the room, rearranging it in the 'right' order), Markus ascribed new meanings and values to this place. More concretely, following Tuan (2001 [1977]), he transformed it into a familiar and intimate (personal) place. This is also strongly related to the (functional) significance of this place, used by Markus to live through his emotions.

6.6 Events Out of the Ordinary

Encountering the outside world also takes place in the frame of special and extraordinary events, for instance where prisoners meet external guests (Baechtold et al., 2016, p. 182). During my fieldwork, I witnessed several such events, including a theatre production, a film workshop and a football match with an external team. I also attended several Christmas parties where external guests, such as musicians, were invited.

During my walking interview with Leo, at some point he guided me to the building where some of these events usually take place, of which he took a 'special' picture (see Fig. 6.17):

Leo: I think this is just a nice room, that's why I have chosen it [for the walking interview]. [...]

Irene: Yes, it's really nice indeed.

L: And also in terms of what we've already done in here. Concerts, or church visits, which were very interesting, very impressive, the Christmas party took place here too (laughs), [together] with representatives of the governing council. Yes and there is the organ. [...] And of course [here] you have a projector, it's a pretty modern one. Of course music is also cool in here [...] we had already a lot, the acoustics are ideal.

I: So then this is a place that brings back nice memories?

Fig. 6.17 A 'special picture' of a 'special place' (*Source* Photo by a prisoner)

> *L*: Yes, there is always something going on in here [...] I associate this place with joy, also with awareness, for example during a worship service or lectures, also for reflection. Also with fun and letting off steam when there's a concert. Recently, an artist came here, who painted with sand and projected this onto the canvas. She worked with light, and the shadow alone looked really cool, and in the background her husband told a story and she painted accordingly. (Leo, 31.8.2017)

As his description reveals, such special events constitute time–space constellations outside of the ordinary prison routine, and they allow prisoners to gain new impressions and experiences. They can also be considered particular 'emotional zones' (Crewe et al., 2014) as they enable forms of emotional experience and expression—for example 'to let off steam'—in a way that is probably not possible elsewhere. Moreover, Leo's statement suggests that this room, which is designated for special events, is not simply a place where entertainment is consumed, but where prisoners are involved as individuals. It is thus a place where they 'do' things, where they experience not only joy but moments of awareness and reflection.

In addition to these organized events, special or extraordinary events may also be experienced on an individual level, which is often related to the prisoners' awareness and attitude. They usually happen by surprise, such as *seeing* (not only hearing) a flock of sheep:

> We [workers in the prison's construction service] had to build scaffolding, then we took a break, me, I was up there [on the roof], preparing things, masking tape, I thought, I would rather continue than take a break, told this to my boss, and then I sat up there on the gable and smoked a cigarette and then I looked out. You can hear the sheep from time to time, and as I sat there on the gable, I suddenly saw the flock of sheep. This doesn't sound special, but if you imagine, I haven't seen a sheep in seven years, it's weird, and I just sat up there, just enjoying watching these sheep. That was something ... You can see a dog [in prison] from time to time, you hear it barking now and then, but a sheep! I've never been interested in sheep, and also now I don't really care about them, but I saw animals again. I saw animals again. And I saw and heard them, I saw them out in the fields, and I saw the shepherd, or whoever that was,

> the owner. I sat up there for half an hour, smoking a cigarette one after the other, watching these sheep. Totally stupid! […] But for me it was, it was special, something different. And such moments, special, beautiful, funny, cool moments are what one is looking for in here as much as outside. Because what else is life than the search for such moments. And you have this experience very rarely in here. But when you have that, it's really cool. (Markus, 28.9.2017)

Another special event prisoners mentioned was a barbecue that may be authorized once or twice a year. In addition, having access to some 'nice food'—preferably (certain) meats they are allowed to order from the outside world—and eating it during a social gathering among prisoners was mentioned by many prisoners as a highlight, because the prison food is generally rather unpopular:

> When you sit together in a little round, of course, one does not forget that one is in prison, but that one could once again play a trick on the prison, for example when sitting in front of a good piece of meat and then maybe forget it for a moment. […] Many things can be acquired legally, we buy it. Have you heard of the possibility to order fresh meat? //yes// We just buy 500 gram filet steaks per head. (Juris, 22.3.2016)

> From time to time, they let me receive cigars, through the husband of my friend, then I smoke a fine cigar from time to time, or […] something good from outside, something you don't get in here, some special meat, and then from time to time during a cell visit, I make a nice meat platter, with *Bündnerfleisch* [air dried meat], ham, and so on, doing something good for yourself once again. (Hugo, 23.3.2016)

As these examples suggest, the experience of extraordinary moments—no matter whether they are formally organized for the whole community, planned informally among prisoners, or appear in the shape of a surprise for an individual prisoner—nourishes and intensifies a prisoner's life and leaves 'traces' on the individual.

From time to time, the prisoners also come across external visiting groups. However, many of the prisoners mentioned that whenever the prison management informs them about a visiting group, they try to avoid them. They feel like these visitors often behave as if they were walking around in a 'zoo' (Theo, 3.5.2016), or speak to prisoners in a way that makes them feel 'treated like a little dog' (Fieldnotes, 9.2.2016). Of course, there are also researchers who visit the prison from time to time. On one of the first days of my fieldwork (and hence when I was still unknown to the prisoners), I had the chance to join such a group, consisting of people who were newly employed by the cantonal prison authority. As the following extract from my fieldnotes illustrates, I developed mixed feelings during this tour:

> Guided tour through the house: We gathered early in the morning [in the middle of the prison]. Our tour guide arrived, and after a short welcome we went on our way. There were still prisoners around [waiting to go to their workplaces], and I felt uncomfortable that they could see me in this role, like a tourist. I hoped they noticed that I was the only one in the group carrying a bunch of keys [like officers] and thus not really belonging to this group. At first, I tried to (physically) distance myself a little from the group, but then I gave up. Our guide led us through the entire building. As we passed through workshops, where there were also some prisoners held in indefinite incarceration at work, he usually said: 'Now you will see some famous prisoners', and after we left the place he asked: 'Did you recognize them?'. Without naming them, he helped us with hints; sometimes he also mentioned (in detail) their offenses. There was no interaction between prisoners and the visitors. It felt like being in a zoo. (Fieldnotes, 3.2.2016)

While the visits in the visiting room generally involve encounters between friends or relatives, prisoners experience encounters with visitor groups more as a reinforcement of the social distance between the *citizens* of the free world and the *criminals* inside the prison.

As explored in detail in Sect. 4.5, the prisoners can also connect with the outside world through media, such as radio, television or newspapers, which, as I discussed, fulfils several functions while prisoners spend time in their cells (a means to 'kill time' or 'transcend' the prison context). Of course, journalists are also interested in the prisoners' stories—especially these prisoners, as they generally committed serious violent or sex offences—not as much after they have been sent to prison, but certainly while they are still outside, after they committed an offence, and during the time they stand trial. Thus, it may happen that prisoners who, among themselves, generally do not talk that openly about their crimes learn from the newspaper about their fellow prisoners' crimes. This can have negative consequences for themselves as well as for the relations between them:

> Provocations, brawls, death threats, mobbing, all that. Yes, but I was aware that this would come. I knew that I wouldn't be welcomed with open arms [by fellow prisoners]. And that I certainly would have to subordinate myself, due to the crime I committed. So, I behaved accordingly, very adapted, which I still am actually, and also very reserved, very decent, very careful. And I had to earn respect, and also fight for it. And that was actually really an issue during the first two years. And that's what I was talking about everywhere. Because I didn't feel well mentally, and also because of what I did, had feelings of guilt […] [Today], it is no longer the crime, but more the human being [that fellow prisoners see], those I have known for some time now. Sure, the new ones they know about me from the media, or just know the case. […] For me, this has become a normal thing that certain people simply, yes … detest [what I did]. Which is right, in a way. (Leo, 23.3.2016)

> In the workshop: Again, Lars started to talk about the topic of social contacts, mentioned how difficult it is, because people you start to like always leave one day. That's why he tries not to get involved too much. But he has a friend […]. When they met, his friend didn't talk about the actual crime he committed, said he was in [prison] because of robbery. When Lars learned about his offense through the newspaper, he broke off the contact for several months. But then he realized that they really get on well together, so they decided 'to leave the past behind'. (Fieldnotes, 23.2.2016)

In some cases, especially if the prisoner is staying in one of the units for ill and elderly prisoners (units that come into public focus now and again), it occasionally happens that newspapers, or more precisely particular journalists, develop an interest in the daily lives of these prisoners, or rather the lives of prisoners living in this particular unit. During the time of my fieldwork, there was a lot of media coverage of the two units for elderly and ill prisoners, including interviews with one or two prisoners carefully selected by the prison management. As I witnessed, those who have to speak for the whole prison community may afterwards be blamed by their fellow prisoners, for example for 'whitewashing the reality' in prison.

Prisoners who told me about their personal encounters with journalists who afterwards wrote about them generally expressed disappointment and frustration with the way they (or the story they told) were represented. While dissatisfaction may arise from the fact that their statements were not reproduced 'correctly', some prisoners also experience more serious consequences. One prisoner mentioned that the newspaper published his full name and former address without his knowledge. As a consequence, one of his relatives broke off contact with him, saying that she was concerned about her own reputation. Another prisoner, who has communicated a lot with the outside world, especially in his attempts to exhaust all legal means and make his situation public, felt that the way his case was (and from time to time still is) represented by one particular Swiss newspaper also negatively affects the way prison officers interact with him. According to him, they are influenced by the 'negative' and 'wrong' stories that have been written about him.

6.7 Going on Release on Temporary License

A break from the prison routine par excellence is release on temporary license. According to Art. 84 para. 6 SCC, '[t]he prison inmate shall be granted release on temporary licence to an appropriate extent in order to cultivate relations with the outside world, prepare for his release or where there are special circumstances'. However, temporary absences or furloughs are only provided when the prisoner's 'conduct in custody does not preclude this and there is no risk that he will abscond or commit further offences' (Art. 84 para. 6 SCC). Temporary absences are regulated by the cantonal enforcement authorities and can be shortened, cancelled or provided with additional conditions at any time. One reason they are granted is to maintain social relationships (*Beziehungsurlaub*). This kind of temporary absence is limited to 36 to a maximum of 56 hours, including an overnight stay. Temporary absences are also sometimes granted to take place during the day for a maximum of 16 hours, which allow prisoners to deal with urgent and non-delegable important matters of a personal, legal or existential nature (*Sachurlaub*) (Schweizerisches Kompetenzzentrum für den Justizvollzug). These rights also apply to prisoners held in indefinite incarceration, but not to those serving lifelong incarceration (Art. 84 para. 6bis SCC).

As mentioned, the cantonal decisions regarding permission for absences or furloughs are embedded in a wider socio-political context, currently characterized by increased public demands for security and a general attitude of 'zero-tolerance', especially towards prisoners sentenced to indefinite incarceration. Hence, any request for temporary prison leave by a so-called high-risk offender today has to be reviewed by an expert committee (Art. 62d para. 2 SCC), consisting of—at a minimum—representatives of the prosecution services, the enforcement authorities and psychiatrists. Moreover, any incident—such as escapes by prisoners on prison leave, even though both the prison leaves and the escapes are relatively rare and generally without serious consequences[9]—increases the pressure on political actors and authorities, and generally results in more restrictions for this particular prison population as a whole (see also Sect. 2.2.1).

For example, as the *Tagesanzeiger* reported in July 2011: 'The canton of Bern wants to learn the lessons of the four-day escape of a detained criminal. For the time being, it has cancelled all accompanied exits and vacations for the 19 prisoners held in indefinite incarceration and the other 130 prisoners, who are considered to be a public danger' (Spirig, 2011, my translation). After this incident, the right-wing party *SVP* introduced a motion (without success, however) that aimed to 'instruct the Federal Council to submit to the parliament an amendment to Art. 64 SCC to the effect that prison leaves and vacations

[9] At the end of December 2013, 144 offenders were held in indefinite incarceration. Regarding the loosening of the prison regime, between 2007 and 2013 escorted absences were the type of release most frequently granted (459), usually only for a few hours. In contrast, unaccompanied temporary absences (11) and furloughs (7) were only occasionally granted. In connection with these measures, four incidents, such as escapes and assaults against executors, therapists or other persons, were registered (Der Bundesrat, 2015).

for prisoners sentenced to indefinite incarceration are excluded' (Die Bundesversammlung – Das Schweizer Parlament, 2011, my translation).

In addition, certain informal practices are also influenced by the political context, one of which became public in 2015. According to several newspapers, since 2013, the penal system in the Canton of Berne had been keeping a so-called 'watch list' of all prisoners who made headlines in the media due to the crime they committed (usually crimes for which prisoners were sentenced according to Art. 64 SCC). At the instruction of the management of the Office of Corrections, any planned measures aiming to loosen the regime of detention (such as temporary prison leaves) had to be submitted to the management whenever the prisoner concerned appeared on the 'watch list' (Mühlemann, 2015). Protests from prisoners who were not being heard by the penal enforcement authority ended in a further and successful appeal at the cantonal High Court of Appeal: the list was declared illegal in 2017 (Müller, 2017).

While several cantons used to apply the so-called 'prison leaves for humanitarian reasons' (my translation) for prisoners held in indefinite incarceration, since 2013, the Federal Supreme Court stated that according to the SCC, there can be no temporary prison absence for *purely* humanitarian reasons (Künzli et al., 2016, p. 50). Prison leaves and furloughs thus constitute temporary authorized absences from the correctional facility, which are part of the individual enforcement plan and play an important role within the rehabilitative process of the offender. In particular, they should serve to maintain or cultivate social relationships with people outside the prison, to deal with urgent personal, existential and legal matters, to maintain a connection to the outside world and to structure a long sentence, for therapeutic purposes or preparation for release, without impairing the safety of the public (Künzli et al., 2016, p. 50).

Of all the prisoners I interviewed, four had access at that time to temporary prison absences. Three were at that time sentenced according to Art. 64 SCC, one according to Art. 59 SCC. These prison leaves took place between two and four times a year, for four to eight hours each, and the inmate was escorted by at least two staff members. According to Moran and Keinänen (2012), due to the escorted nature of prison leaves, they can be considered as a 'heterotopic, quasi-carceral space outside of the prison' (Moran & Keinänen, 2012, p. 72), and the prison guards who escort prisoners embody the disciplinary regime of the prison beyond the prison walls. Thus, 'access to the "outside" is not only strictly controlled by the enforcement authorities' selection procedures, but the "outside" is actively surveilled and prisoners on furlough are constantly reminded of their incarcerated status' (Moran & Keinänen, 2012, p. 72). I talked to two staff members who used to escort prisoners to the outside. However, they both described these situations less by referring to their task to survey and control the prisoner, but to the degree of closeness to the prisoners that may emerge during these situations, and the (potential) related role conflict:

> You're not in here [in prison] anymore, behind the walls, but you're really out there, it's also about security, they could jump out of the car anytime. And then maybe you meet his family, you are actually a stranger, but for the prisoner or the client, you are almost more a reference person than his family, which he sees much less. And yes, during the first time with the family you are reserved, the second time you know the people a bit, know the constellations, at some point you feel almost like part of it (laughs) [...] and by then they're also treating you like this. They don't say: now the troublemaker comes again, but: yes, come in, sit down, here is something to eat. So this is another level. With these people [the prisoners] it's probably important that when they're back in here [in prison] and then back at this table, that you switch to the other level, to the business level. It should also be fair to the others who are not granted any prison leave. (Social assistant B., 27.6.2016)

> This is quite difficult sometimes, I accompanied [a prisoner] during a prison leave, five hours, and all in all it really went well, and three days later, I have to control his cell and tell him: this and that is not good. (Prison officer B., 8.10.2013)

How do prisoners deal with prison leave, considered here as quasi-carceral time–spaces? They all emphasized the fact that they always complied with the prison's requirements: 'Everything always went perfectly; I came back on time, followed the rules' (Louis, 22.3.2016):

> I've always proven myself again and again [during the prison leaves]. I was accompanied by [two prison officers] and I walked maybe 500 meters in front of them, along the *Bahnhofstrasse*, while they were behind me, I only had eye contact and I also went to the toilet by myself. I could have run away any time. But I'm not interested. (Patrick, 3.5.2016)

> I once even came back by myself. It was stupid, I wanted to see the airfield again, and because I'm not so familiar with the trains, I grew up in a village, and then the prison officer was next to me and got on the train and at that moment the door was closing, that sliding door, and I was standing outside with four blacks, and I don't speak English [...] [But] then I thought, I do what I've learned. Then I went to the main station, back to Zurich, by train. You know, Zurich is still written in big letters. And I thought once I'm in Zurich, I know to which track I need to go. And indeed, I found the right platform [...] and came back [to the prison]. (Theo, 3.5.2016)

As these statements suggest, while prison staff refers to the more relaxed atmosphere that may develop during prison leaves and the fact that one is 'really out there', prisoners are highly aware that they are (still) under surveillance, and in this sense, that prison leaves indeed constitute (quasi-)carceral time–spaces. They are, to some degree, 'still in there'. Technically, these spaces simultaneously provide them with the opportunity to prove their reliability and trustworthiness, as there are always moments where they could have 'run away'. From their point of view, however, this fact is rarely acknowledged by the competent authority.

Despite their rule-following behaviour, I met five prisoners who experienced having their permission to go on prison leave suddenly restricted or even cancelled completely. The reasons they put forward were generally collective punishment by the competent authority due to an incident caused by another prisoner on prison leave (see also Sect. 2.3.1):

> For ten years I was granted unaccompanied prison leave, I worked outside the wall for two years, and today I'm even worse off than when I came to prison for the first time. And only because somebody else messed things up. (Clément, 25.6.2013)

Other reasons mentioned were changing interpretations of the prisoner's behaviour by the forensic psychiatrist in the frame of a risk assessment, which is decisive for the enforcement authority's decisions regarding, for instance, the possibility of converting Art. 64 SCC into Art. 59 SCC or granting conditional release. One example comes from Louis:

> From 2006 to 2013, I had temporary prison leaves, twice a year, which I enjoyed with my family, my wife. Then they were suddenly cancelled, even though I haven't done anything, on the contrary, everything went always perfect: I came back on time, followed the rules … I just enjoyed being outside the walls, with the family, with my wife, and that was suddenly, yes … stopped by the authority, because somehow, for whatever reason, it was suddenly assumed that there is a risk of absconding, but I've never been on the run, there was no sign, it was never a plan […]. And then I started to defend myself, by legal means, and I was classified as rebellious and they transferred me to [another prison, and again another prison] […]. (Louis, 22.3.2016)

A similar experience was faced by Theo. He was also engaged in therapy and went on several successful prison leaves, until they were suddenly cancelled:

> I was allowed to go on prison leaves between 2008 and 2012. […] One and a half years ago, an assessment of my case had to be made and we wanted to achieve the conversion of Art. 64 SCC into Art. 59 SCC, [so] that I get one step closer to the outside. Because all the prison leaves went well, I had therapy, so nothing should have been standing in the way. But, and now that's what scared me, and also a lot of the employees too, I had to take an assessment and this expert put everything I've had done in here, prison leaves, therapies, everything in a negative light. He said I was even more dangerous, that I was even more dangerous than when I came in. After 20 years of therapy and prison leaves and so on. (Theo, 3.5.2016)

As mentioned several times, prison leaves, among other elements, increase the possibility that prisoners' will ever have a future outside as it provides them with the opportunity to prove themselves. However, as the quotes by Louis and Theo illustrate, the actions required of them in order to progress within the system are often perceived as unclear or unattainable and the authorities' decisions as arbitrary and confusing. As I explored in detail in Sect. 2.3.1, this reinforces uncertainty and may have a significant impact on the prisoners' sense of self. Of course, there are also prisoners who refuse to enrol themselves in therapy (even when they have the opportunity) or do not want to work with the available psychiatrist. In these cases, the prisoners generally have no chance at all to achieve change. Finally, however, there was one prisoner who mentioned that he himself 'messed it up' during a prison leave (without going into detail), and that this was the main reason that the authority cancelled permission for further prison leaves.

Despite their (quasi-)carceral characteristics and importance for the prisoners' potential progression within the penal system, prison leaves are of course experienced in different ways by the prisoners. Louis and Theo mentioned that they always 'enjoyed' and 'appreciated' these moments, and that they visited their family members and places that have high emotional value for them: 'I visited my family, I went there with the pastor, the one we have in the house [in prison], and I visited my favourite chapel where I met my girlfriend' (Theo, 3.5.2016). For Erwin, prison leaves are moments during which he can 'go to where [*he*] want[s] to', a change from the ever-same environment, and a possibility 'to enjoy a nice meal' (Erwin, 18.10.2017).

Prison leaves are also moments that confront prisoners with various (changing) conditions and rhythms of the outside world that are in stark contrast to everyday prison life. This is a stressful experience for Patrick. He said that whenever he left the prison he was especially 'scared of all the cars'. However, he 'adores' observing people and standing in the middle of the main station, which he described as a 'pure adrenaline rush' (Fieldnotes, 3.5.2016). For Clément, being outside from time to time allows him to keep up to date with the larger changes that occur over time:

> I get along quite well [with the changes], except for the damn Internet and the mobile phone. So if I want something, then I have to ask my son or brother. Me I don't get it. [But] as I've been going out regularly since 1998, one gets used to it. You see the changes, for example, at home,

> yes, the cottage on the lake, you used to see the lake from it, today you can't see anything. Previously, we had a little cabin with a small boat, together with my brother, everything has gone, and that's all built over. The infrastructure is totally different than when we were there. And of course, if you pass certain things, you know … it really changed. And then, when you come out after let's say 20 years, for the first time, me I wouldn't get along with it. (Clément, 26.9.2017)

Clément's statement was confirmed by a prisoner who, by contrast, never had any access to prison leave. He realized that in prison, he is missing out particularly on changes in technology, such as the invention of the iPhone:

> I mean, stuff like … iPhone, or things like that. I know such things only by hearsay. And then, depending on how they [fellow prisoners] describe it to me (laughs), how that functions. But as I said, that is a detail now. Other things like buying a ticket at the ticket machine outside, for the train … this information I get from my mother, when she has difficulties with it herself (laughs). Also employees who have known me since the beginning, they sometimes also say there and there, a lot has changed, it's clear that you wouldn't recognize it again. I have a big deficit in here. If I would come out, I wouldn't have a clue. I would first of all keep away from everything. (Anton, 24.3.2016)

How does it feel to go back to prison after one has spent several hours in the 'free world'? As I was told by Clément, it was 'extremely difficult in the beginning', but in the meantime, he 'got used to it' (Clément, 26.9.2017).

Prison leaves also provide prisoners with 'highlights' to look forward to and memories to live on for some time, allowing them to stay connected to the outside world. In the *60plus* unit, there were two prisoners who always told me (weeks) before and (weeks) after they had been on a prison leave. During my fieldwork, there was one prison officer who usually took pictures when he escorted someone on prison leave and later gave them to the prisoners, who kept them as souvenirs. As Erwin explained: 'If somebody sends me a postcard, I pin it here [on the pinboard], or if I had been outside and eaten somewhere for example, I'll pin that [e.g. a brochure of the restaurant] here too' (Erwin, 18.10.2017) (see Fig. 6.18). Usually, the prisoners reported to me in detail where they had been, what they had been doing, and precisely what food they had eaten.

That prisoners may get used to returning to prison after spending some time in the 'free world' is something one of the social assistants who has been escorting one particular prisoner for a while now finds difficult to understand:

> The return is usually not … I don't have the feeling that [for him] it is harder than driving off in the morning. [The prisoner shows] the same emotional state. Me I have more trouble with it, each time I'm thinking: Now he has to go back, in there, at least for the next four months, until the next vacation. And me, I can go back [out] afterwards. So, sometimes I have more trouble imagining how it must be for him now […] Sometimes […] when we're back [in front of the prison] a little bit earlier, then [the prisoner] says: Yes, let's smoke a cigarette, then we can go in – ten

Fig. 6.18 A prisoner's personal pinboard: keeping memories alive (*Source* Photo by a prisoner)

> minutes or 15 minutes earlier. And I think: Would I do that? Would I give a single minute of mine, of that little freedom, would I give it away? (Social assistant B., 27.6.2016)

As I have mentioned, there are currently few prisoners sentenced to indefinite confinement who are allowed to spend some hours outside the prison walls. Those who are authorized to temporarily leave the prison must be aware that it can be cancelled at any moment, for any reason. Moreover, in the case of this prison population today, even when successfully accomplished, temporary prison leaves are not guaranteed to contribute positively to their progression within the system. I assume that these layers of uncertainty also influence the meaning prison leaves hold for prisoners and their emotional and personal engagement, although I have no information concerning this matter. Generally, prisoners held in indefinite incarceration have to prepare themselves for a future inside prison—until the end of their lives.

6.8 Conclusion

Leisure time in prison is usually explored in direct comparison with the outside world, often linked to the question of whether leisure or 'free' time can even exist in prison (see e.g. Matthews, 2009). What I have explored in this chapter basically corresponds to what Clemmer (1958 [1940]) designated as 'regulated leisure time'. This means that I approached leisure time first from the angle of the prison system. I also included additional time–spaces that provide prisoners in one way or another with a break from the prison (working) routine, such as the daily walk in the courtyard, encountering people from the outside world or going on temporary prison leave. I looked at the concept of leisure less in direct comparison with the outside world and did not primarily focus on its concrete function from the perspective of the prison or the prisoners. Instead, I explored in this chapter the prisoners' spatial, temporal and embodied experiences *of* and *during* this particular everyday period that is labelled and organized by the prison as 'leisure time', taking place in a wide range of contexts.

Generally, during leisure time, the prisoners are—in various ways and to different degrees—confronted with the outside world. Therefore, their lived experiences often oscillate between a sense of confinement and a sense of freedom. In other words, it is during the confrontation with 'freedom' that they often become most aware of their confinement. The prisoners' subjective and embodied experience of the outside world is intertwined with their particular (legal) status as well as their individual experience of time. Their diverse ways of making use of these time–spaces thus also reveal their individual ways of dealing with the indefinite nature of their incarceration. Some of these prisoners (still) need to feel connected to the outside world and its rhythms as it provides them with hope and a sense of the future; for others, however, it is particularly challenging to be reminded of the outside world and to realize that 'normal' life goes on. These prisoners generally try to concentrate on the present and the (prison) inside, and they usually cut off their bonds to the outside world as it is emotionally too demanding and too painful to live in two worlds at the same time.

References

Abrams, L. S., Anderson-Nathe, B., & Aguilar, J. (2008). Constructing masculinities in juvenile corrections. *Men and Masculinities, 11*, 22–41. https://doi.org/10.1177/1097184X06291893

Baechtold, A., Weber, J., & Hostettler, U. (2016). *Strafvollzug: Straf- und Massnahmenvollzug an Erwachsenen in der Schweiz* (3rd ed., Kriminalität, Justiz und Sanktionen KJS: Vol. 17). Stämpfli Verlag.

BiST Fachstelle Bildung im Strafvollzug. (2019). BiST - Bildung im Strafvollzug. https://www.bist.ch/de/. Accessed 23 December 2019.

Bundesamt für Justiz BJ. (2011). Fokus: Sexualität. *Information zum Straf- und Massnahmenvollzug – info bulletin, 2.*

Calkins, K. (1970). Time: Perspectives, marking and styles of usage. *Social Problems, 17*(4), 487–501.

Clemmer, D. (1958 [1940]). *The prison community*. Holt, Rinehart & Wilson.

Cohen, S., & Taylor, L. (1972). *Psychological survival: The experience of long-term imprisonment*. Penguin Books.

Comfort, M. L. (2002). 'Papa's house': The prison as domestic and social satellite. *Ethnography, 3*, 467–499. https://doi.org/10.1177/146613810200300 4017

Crewe, B. (2009). *The prisoner society: Power, adaptation and social life in an English prison*. Oxford University Press.

Crewe, B. (2014). Not looking hard enough: Masculinity, emotion, and prison research. *Qualitative Inquiry, 20*(4), 426–437.

Crewe, B., Warr, J., Bennett, P., & Smith, A. (2014). The emotional geography of prison life. *Theoretical Criminology, 18*, 56–74. https://doi.org/10.1177/1362480613497778

Cunha, M. I. (1997). Le temps suspendu. Rythmes et durées dans une prison portugaise. *Terrain* (29), 59–68.

Der Bundesrat. (2015). *Verwahrungspraxis in der Schweiz; Bericht in Erfüllung des Postulats 13.3978 Rickli vom 27. September 2013*. https://www.bj.admin.ch/dam/data/bj/sicherheit/gesetzgebung/archiv/verwahrung/ber-br-d.pdf. Accessed 10 December 2019.

Die Bundesversammlung – Das Schweizer Parlament. (2011). *11.3767 Motion. Keine Hafturlaube und Ausgänge für Verwahrte*. https://www.parlament.ch/de/ratsbetrieb/suche-curia-vista/geschaeft?AffairId=20113767. Accessed 10 December 2019.

Dubler, N. N. (1998). The collision of confinement and care: End-of-life care in prisons and jails. *The Journal of Law, Medicine & Ethics, 26*, 149–156. https://doi.org/10.1111/j.1748-720X.1998.tb01670.x

Flanagan, T. J. (1980). The pains of long-term imprisonment: A comparison of British and American perspectives. *The British Journal of Criminology, 20*, 148–156. https://doi.org/10.2307/23636693

Gallant, D., Sherry, E., & Nicholson, M. (2015). Recreation or rehabilitation? Managing sport for development programs with prison populations. *Sport Management Review, 18*(1), 45–56.

Goffman, E. (1959). *The presentation of self in everyday life*. Doubleday.

Goffman, E. (1961). *Asylums: Essays on the condition of the social situation of mental patients and other inmates*. Anchor Books, Doubleday & Co.

Hostettler, U., Marti, I., & Richter, M. (2016). *Lebensende im Justizvollzug. Gefangene, Anstalten, Behörden*. Stämpfli Verlag.

Jewkes, Y., & Reisdorf, B. C. (2016). A brave new world: The problems and opportunities presented by new media technologies in prisons. *Criminology & Criminal Justice, 16*, 534–551. https://doi.org/10.1177/1748895816654953

JVA Lenzburg. (2010). *Orientierung an die Gefangenen*.

JVA Lenzburg. (2011). *Hausordnung: Justizvollzugsanstalt Lenzburg* .
JVA Pöschwies. (2016a). *AGE-Info. Kanton Zürich* .
JVA Pöschwies. (2016b). *Justizvollzugsanstalt Pöschwies. Jahresbericht 2016*.
JVA Pöschwies. (2016c). *Wochenplan AGE*.
JVA Pöschwies. (2017). *Hausordnung: Justizvollzugsanstalt Pöschwies (HO PöW)*.
Künzli, J., Eugster, A., & Schultheiss, M. (2016). *Haftbedingungen in der Verwahrung: Menschenrechtliche Standards und die Situation in der Schweiz*. Bern.
Kusenbach, M. (2003). Street phenomenology: The go-along as ethnographic research tool. *Ethnography, 4*, 455–485. https://doi.org/10.1177/146613810343007
Largey, G., & Watson, R. (2006 [1972]). The sociology of odors. In J. Drobnick (Ed.), *The smell culture reader* (pp. 29–40). Oxford.
Lefebvre, H. (2014). *Rhythmanalysis: Space, time and everyday life*. Bloomsbury.
Leigey, M. E., & Ryder, M. A. (2015). The pains of permanent imprisonment: Examining perceptions of confinement among older life without parole inmates. *International Journal of Offender Therapy and Comparative Criminology, 59*, 726–742. https://doi.org/10.1177/0306624X13517868
Lussault, M., & Stock, M. (2010). 'Doing with space': Towards a pragmatics of space. *Social Geography, 5*, 11–19. https://doi.org/10.5194/sg-5-11-2010
Marti, I. (2021). Sensing freedom: Insights into long-term prisoners' perceptions of the outside world. *Incarceration, 2*, 26326663211013704. https://doi.org/10.1177/26326663211013703
Martos-García, D., Devís-Devís, J., & Sparkes, A. C. (2009). Sport and physical activity in a high security Spanish prison: An ethnographic study of multiple meanings. *Sport, Education and Society, 14*, 77–96. https://doi.org/10.1080/13573320802615189
Matthews, R. (2009). *Doing time: An introduction to the sociology of imprisonment*. Palgrave Macmillan.
Meek, R. (2014). *Sport in prison: Exploring the role of physical activity in correctional settings*. Routledge.
Milhaud, O. (2009). *Séparer et punir. Les prisons françaises: mise à distance et punition par l'espace* (PhD thesis). Université Michel de Montaigne - Bordeaux III, Bordeaux. https://tel.archives-ouvertes.fr/tel-00441473
Moran, D. (2013a). Between outside and inside? Prison visiting rooms as liminal carceral spaces. *GeoJournal, 78*(2), 339–351.

Moran, D. (2013b). Carceral geography and the spatialities of prison visiting: Visitation, recidivism and hyperincarceration. *Environment and Planning D Society and Space, 31*, 174–190. https://doi.org/10.1068/d18811
Moran, D., & Keinänen, A. (2012). The 'inside' and 'outside' of prisons: Carceral geography and home visits for prisoners in Finland. *Fennia—International Journal of Geography, 109*(2), 62–76.
Moran, D., & Turner, J. (2018). Turning over a new leaf: The health-enabling capacities of green space in prison. *Social Science & Medicine*. https://doi.org/10.1016/j.socscimed.2018.05.032
Moran, D., Turner, J., & Schliehe, A. K. (2018). Conceptualizing the carceral in carceral geography. *Progress in Human Geography, 42*, 666–686. https://doi.org/10.1177/0309132517710352
Mühlemann, S. (2015). Häftlinge wollen gegen schwarze Liste vorgehen. *20 Minuten*. https://www.20min.ch/schweiz/bern/story/Haeftlinge-wollen-gegen-schwarze-Liste-vorgehen-22432489. Accessed 10 December 2019.
Müller, P. (2017, November 20). Käsers «Watch-Liste» mit Risikostraftätern ist illegal. *Berner Zeitung BZ*. https://www.bernerzeitung.ch/region/kanton-bern/kaesers-watchliste-ist-illegal/story/24458854. Accessed 10 December 2019.
Norman, M. (2015). Prison yoga as a correctional alternative? Physical culture, rehabilitation, and social control in Canadian prisons. In J. Joseph & W. Crichlow (Eds.), *Alternative offender rehabilitation and social justice: Arts and physical engagement in criminal justice and community settings* (pp. 78–98). Palgrave Macmillan.
Norman, M. (2017). Sport in the underlife of a total institution: Social control and resistance in Canadian prisons. *International Review for the Sociology of Sport, 52*, 598–614. https://doi.org/10.1177/1012690215609968
O'Donnell, I. (2014). *Prisoners, solitude, and time*. Oxford University Press.
Oxford Dictionaries. (2018). *Leisure*. https://en.oxforddictionaries.com/definition/leisure. Accessed 29 June 2018.
Ricciardelli, R. (2014). *Surviving incarceration: Inside Canadian prisons*. Wilfrid Laurier University Press.
Richards, B. (1978). The experience of long-term imprisonment: An exploratory investigation. *The British Journal of Criminology, 18*, 162–169. https://doi.org/10.1093/oxfordjournals.bjc.a046888
Richter, M., Kirchhofer, R., Hostettler, U., & Young, C. (2011). Wie eine "Insel" im Gefängnis. Bildung im Schweizer Strafvollzug. *Tsantsa* (16), 50–60.

Ricordeau, G. (2012). Between inside and outside: Prison visiting rooms. Translated from the French by Cadenza Academic Translations. *Politix, 1*(97), 101–123.

Sabo, D. (2001). Doing time, doing masculinity: Sport and prison. In D. Sabo, T. A. Kupers, & W. J. London (Eds.), *Prison masculinities* (pp. 61–66). Temple University Press.

Sabo, D., Kupers, T. A., & London, W. J. (Eds.). (2001). *Prison masculinities*. Temple University Press.

Schweizerisches Kompetenzzentrum für den Justizvollzug. Leben im Freiheitsentzug. Ausgang und Urlaub. https://www.skjv.ch/de/fachwissen/justizvollzug-ch/leben-im-freiheitsentzug. Accessed 10 December 2019.

Schweizerisches Kompetenzzentrum für den Justizvollzug. (2019). Leben im Freiheitsentzug. Freizeit. https://www.skjv.ch/de/fachwissen/justizvollzug-ch/leben-im-freiheitsentzug. Accessed 29 June 2018.

Spirig, J. (2011, July 7). Bern stoppt Ausgang für verwahrte Straftäter. *Tages-Anzeiger*. https://www.tagesanzeiger.ch/schweiz/standard/Bern-stoppt-Ausgang-fuer-verwahrte-Straftaeter/story/13432749?track. Accessed 10 December 2019.

Sykes, G. M. (1971 [1958]). *The society of captives: A study of a maximum security prison*. Princeton, NJ: Princeton University Press.

Thibaud, J.-P. (2011). The sensory fabric of urban ambiances. *Senses and Society, 6*(2), 203–215.

Thompson, E. P. (1967). Time and work discipline in industrial capitalism. *Past and Present* (36), 56–97.

Toch, H. (1996 [1977]). *Living in prison: The ecology of survival*. Princeton University Press.

Tuan, Y. F. (2001 [1977]). *Space and place: The perspective of experience*. University of Minnesota Press.

Turner, J., Moran, D., & Jewkes, Y. (2020). Serving time with a sea view: The prison cell and healthy blue space. In J. Turner & V. Knight (Eds.), *The prison cell: Embodied and everyday spaces of incarceration* (pp. 215–238). Palgrave Macmillan.

Turner, V. (1969). *The ritual process: Structure and anti-structure*. Penguin Books.

van Gennep, A. (1960). *The rites of passage*. Chicago University Press.

Wener, R. (2012). *The environmental psychology of prisons and jails: Creating humane spaces in secure settings*. Cambridge University Press.

7

Conclusion

Based on ethnographic data generated in two secure prisons for male offenders, this book provided insights into the everyday lives of long-term prisoners in Switzerland, who are labelled 'dangerous' and categorized as posing an 'undue risk' to society and are therefore held in undetermined, most probably lifelong detention in secure prisons. They are either sentenced to a measure called 'indefinite incarceration' (Art. 64 of the Swiss Criminal Code [SCC]), or in-patient 'therapeutic treatment of mental disorders' (Art. 59 SCC). Compared to the majority of long-term prisoners, this prison population faces particular challenges: in contrast to prisoners sentenced to a finite (though long) custodial sentence, these prisoners do not have any date of release and may have to remain in prison for the rest of their lives; however, they are not in the same situation as prisoners sentenced to a 'real' life sentence (where the fixed end date is usually death) as the possibility of release is legally anchored in both Art. 64 SCC and Art. 59 SCC. Their chances for a future perspective (outside prison) depend on the decisions of the courts and the penal enforcement authorities, which regularly evaluate the prisoners' situations based on prison reports, psychiatric assessments and the recommendations of an expert committee. Due to a more hard-line

I. Marti, *Doing Indefinite Time*, Palgrave Studies in Prisons and Penology,
https://doi.org/10.1007/978-3-031-12590-4_7

approach towards crime and a zero-tolerance attitude towards these prisoners since the 1990s, the majority of them will, however, most likely remain in prison for the rest of their lives and even spend the end of their lives in a secure setting. In other words, these prisoners' lives are characterized by *indeterminacy*.

In addition, they have to deal with the particularity of everyday life in prison, which is characterized by coercion, heteronomy and a high density of rules and repetition that allows for little spontaneity and few contingencies, creating the impression of living in an *ever-same present*. In the dominant public discourse, these prisoners—violent and sex offenders who committed the most serious or 'unusual' crimes—are categorized as 'evil and sub-human', often portrayed by the media as 'monsters' or 'beasts'. Hence, they constitute today's 'absolute others' (Greer & Jewkes, 2005) as they are not only physically, but also socially and morally excluded from society. In this book, I explored the lived experiences of these prisoners, whose number is increasing, by looking more closely at the formal organization of their everyday lives, their subjective perceptions of the prison context, and their agentic ways of arranging their daily lives under these conditions.

7.1 To Apprehend 'the Prison' as It Is Lived

In contrast to many prison studies, I explored the prisoners' lived experiences ethnographically and inductively, detached from a priori ideas of what the prison *is* and what it *does*, and tried primarily to gain an understanding of the prison from within, as it appears to the prisoners. To do this, I used the lens of the everyday and ordinary as a methodological entry point. This allowed me to study their ways of *being* and *doing indefinite time* by remaining empirically grounded—that is, to capture their diverse modes of engagement in various everyday situations that are all contextually embedded. More concretely, guided by the idea of the relativity and subjectivity of the experience of the carceral, I started my analysis with the small (everyday) details of these prisoners' lives, which are formally divided into 'resting' (in the cell), 'work' and 'leisure' time. This allowed me not only to trace the everyday habits, practices, routines and rhythms that characterize their lives, but also to uncover profoundly existential issues that are all engendered and anchored in these various everyday contexts, which they in turn (re)arrange according to their individual needs, interests and possibilities.

At the analytical level, I accessed the prison and the experience of imprisonment by using space, time and embodiment as key concepts. More concretely, I comprehended 'the prison' through its *regime*—that is, its formal creation of everyday life, or in other words the *spatio-temporal order* that is imposed on the prisoners, expressed in routines and rhythms, and shaped by the prison's 'institutional logics' (Thornton et al., 2012; Thornton & Ocasio, 2008) of punishment and rehabilitation (materialized in the prison's legal basis, architecture and design, norms, rules and staff practices). As I have illustrated, everyday life in prison is, on the one hand, organized in such a way that it corresponds to 'normal life' (Art. 75 para. 1 SCC). On the other hand, however, it is strongly regulated and constrained in the name of security.

To grasp the prisoners' subjective experience, I adopted a phenomenological approach inspired by Merleau-Ponty (1962) and the pragmatist perspective developed by Lussault and Stock (2010). Drawing on their concept of 'inhabiting' allowed me to capture (1) the prisoners' subjective *emplaced* and *embodied perceptions* and the meanings they ascribe to various (material and social) prison contexts or time–spaces, and how these perceived contexts influence prisoners' sense of self and their experience of imprisonment in general; and (2) their multiple ways of dealing with the various contexts through their *everyday practices*. By tracing the prisoners' ways of *doing with* space and time, I explored how they (re)arrange the institutional spatio-temporal order according to their personal needs, interests and possibilities, whereby they attribute (new) meanings and values to the various prison contexts, create personal and intimate spaces, redefine carceral rhythms and thus shape the experience of imprisonment in general.

As I demonstrated throughout this book, my analytical perspective opens up a unique and fruitful perspective on the prison and the subjective experience of imprisonment. First, it allows us to understand the prison not as a space in the sense of a (pre-defined) container that holds people, but as a formally established *set of arrangements of space and (clock) time* that is *lived*—that is, individually perceived, used, appropriated and constantly (re)arranged. From this perspective, what is experienced by prisoners as, for example, 'the cell', is not only related to the ambiance produced by the cell's architecture, design and furnishings, but also, among other things, by the prison officers' handling of the boundary between the inside and outside of the cell, for instance when unlocking or locking the door, and respect for prisoners' privacy when entering and searching their cells, as well as the prisoners' individual ways of arranging these living spaces. Simply put, a prison is not the same to all its prisoners. Second, the concept of *inhabiting* enables the exploration of the prisoners' embodied, agentic and practical engagement with imprisonment without necessarily labelling it 'resistance', 'coping' or 'adaptation' to the prison environment as previous research has often done (Cohen & Taylor 1972; Crewe 2009; Ugelvik, 2014), as from a pragmatist perspective, space and time can not only constitute a 'problem' but also be mobilized as a 'resource'. Moreover, it also reveals the usually unnoticed, apparently insignificant and banal activities, habits and routines that prisoners develop and carry out when residing in this place, which, as I demonstrated in this book, are maybe less 'spectacular', but by no means less revealing from a phenomenological perspective.

7.2 Public and Political Pressure, Institutional Indecisiveness, Challenged and Challenging Prison Staff

While in Switzerland indefinite incarceration is nothing new in itself, the fact that sex offenders and violent offenders (some of them first-time offenders) constitute today's 'dangerous' and thus 'ungovernable' (Pratt, 1997, p. 97) members of society and are preventively locked up, combined with an increased focus on the risk they may pose, is a relatively new phenomenon. Moreover, while people sentenced to indefinite incarceration generally used to be released after some time, due to changing political and public demands regarding public security since the 1990s, the penal enforcement authorities are today more cautious regarding the loosening of the penal regime or the granting of conditional release to these so-called 'high-risk' offenders. Also, the courts today sentence a much greater number of people to in-patient therapeutic measures according to Art. 59 SCC for a duration of five years, which is also known as 'small indefinite incarceration' (*kleine Verwahrung*), because it can be extended (for additional five-year periods) or even converted into indefinite incarceration (Art. 64 SCC). As a result, by the end of 2018, of the approximately 7,000 total prison inmates, 731 people were serving a measure without a concrete (or any) date of release (Bundesamt für Statistik, 2019)—20 years earlier, their number was 173. Finally, although these prisoners are sentenced to a (preventive) measure and not a custodial sentence, due to security concerns, they are almost all held in a secure prison, where they live under the same regime and conditions as prisoners who serve ordinary (finite) sentences.

While penal enforcement authorities feel pressure from all sides when dealing with these prisoners (political and public demands for zero tolerance towards these offenders on the one hand, the law that obliges them to work with these prisoners towards rehabilitation on the other), this prison population rarely appears on the radar screen of the prison management. Long-term prisoners sentenced to indefinite incarceration constitute not only a minority within the prisons but are mostly perceived as well integrated into the prison routine. However, the fact that the vast majority of them will grow old, became frail and eventually die in prison has already started to cause trouble and will continue to challenge these authorities further as the prisons are at present not adequately equipped to provide proper long-term care, and public care institutions are usually unwilling to accommodate 'dangerous' offenders (see Hostettler et al., 2016).

Today, those most directly challenged by prisoners who may stay until the end of their lives are prison employees who work with them in face-to-face situations and encounter them on a daily basis. The long-term nature of their stay in particular challenges established roles and the fragile balance between (physical and emotional) proximity and distance between staff and prisoners. It is also on this level that institutionally established structures, rules and regulations are challenged. Most of the prison officers I interviewed mentioned that although they have no official mandate, they (informally) consider these prisoners' particular status and (within the given scope of discretion) attempt to help them find perspective within the walls, for instance by providing them with a bit more variety and autonomy at work, creating some kind of free spaces for them and implementing certain rules a bit less strictly. They also highlight the need for additional and differently trained staff (e.g. in social or occupational pedagogy, but also care staff) to ensure the appropriate handling of these prisoners, including shifting the focus from their crime towards their individual resources.

The key actors interviewed (representatives of the enforcement authorities, prison management and staff) generally agree that these inmates' status as prisoners who are preventively held in prison should be considered, mainly by granting them more freedom, individuality and autonomy, and fewer restrictions regarding social contact within the prison and with the outside world. This echoes the positions of the UN Human Rights Committee (UN Human Rights Committee, 2014) and the European Court of Human Rights Convention (European Court of Human Rights, 2010), which both call for explicit consideration of the non-punitive character of indefinite incarceration in its enforcement. However, the key actors I interviewed do not agree on what concretely could or should be improved for these prisoners and how this should be implemented—and what it may cost. However, most doubt that a spatial separation of these prisoners from the rest of the prison population (as implemented in Germany in the name of the *Abstandsgebot*) would be in the prisoners' best interest and rather plead for mixing the prisoners in the name of 'normalisation' according to Art. 75 para. 1 SCC.

7.3 Shifting Between Continued Hope and Resignation

From the perspective of those directly concerned, *doing indefinite time* is essentially about dealing with feelings of uncertainty, dependence and disorientation, and living a prescribed, monotonous daily life that leaves hardly any 'traces' on the individual. The lack of any release date and regular assessment of these prisoners' situation (with the aim of eventually changing it) by the penal enforcement authorities creates a particular condition that affects the prisoners' experience of space and time, their future and their present. Moreover, the enforcement authorities' examinations (which according to the prisoners do not take place as regularly as they should according to the law) are often perceived as arbitrary and inconsistent, because of suddenly changing or contradictory statements regarding the prisoners' personal attributes, behaviour or development, which creates confusion and additional uncertainty, causing them to lose orientation in their lives and maybe even faith in the reliability of the world beyond them.

Generally, the time-based indefiniteness of their imprisonment and lack of any concrete perspective confront prisoners with a dilemma regarding their ways of living and thinking: should they continue to hope for release and therefore remain focused on the future and the outside world, waiting for a change, or should they give up hope and rather concentrate on the here and now? Due to the lack of perspective, those who concentrate on the future may have difficulty finding meaning in their present lives; others who have decided to stop hoping may feel the need to cut their bonds to the outside world, even to their loved ones and their 'pre-prison selves', because it is too complicated and stressful to live emotionally in two different and separate worlds.

Most importantly, due to the uncertainty and unpredictability created by both the legal and penal enforcement authorities, the prisoners' decision might turn out to be 'a mistake' as their situation suddenly may change or, in contrast, never change again. Given these circumstances, many of the prisoners' attitudes shift between hope and resignation. As I showed throughout this book, their ways of *living* the prison are strongly shaped by their attitude towards indeterminacy, or, in other words, their mode of *being with time*, but also by the prison context, which, as I sum up in the following, constitutes various conditions for *being* and *doing* time.

7.4 Maintaining a Sense of Self and Personal Integrity

The prison cell—the place in prison where these men spend most of their time, alone—turned out to be the crucial context for the foundation and maintenance of the prisoners' sense of self and personal integrity. This becomes visible, for instance, in their description of the cell's ambiance, related not only to its materiality but also the way they feel treated by prison staff, for instance during the locking and unlocking of their cells, all 'filtered' through their self-perception as preventively locked-up prisoners who have (mostly) already served their sentences and, above all, human beings who deserve respect. The prisoners' experiences of the cell are further related to the prison surroundings, to which they may have (partial) access through the window by using their senses (i.e. hearing and seeing), which some enjoy and others avoid as it can intensify as well as ease the pain caused by the deprivation of liberty and removal from society. In this regard, the curtain—a banal and ordinary object—turned out to be of existential importance for those who cannot bear the view of the outside community.

As I further clarified, their personal ways of arranging the prison cell can be understood as a direct manifestation of their attitude towards indefinite incarceration or their mode of *being with time*, for example, concentrating on the (outside) future or on the (prison) present. Although it is highly constrained by the prison's accommodation regime and prison officers who constantly remind them of their status as prisoners (by means of rules, controls and complaints regarding the degree of order and tidiness in their cell as well as related sanctions), the prisoners find various techniques to (re)arrange the spatio-temporal order that defines the prison cell, thereby ascribing new meanings to this place and creating an intimate space. Through narratives, the use of objects, individual and collective activities, and by using their senses, there are prisoners who transform the cell (and the experience of it) into a 'home', while others want the cell to remain a cell, meaning a simple 'place' where they currently have to stay, but not a place for comfortable or cosy 'living'.

However, regardless of their attitudes towards the prison and their imprisonment, their cell—which they inhabit and where they store personal objects and can spend some unobserved time—constitutes for all of them a private and personal space, related to feelings of belonging and attachment, and which they try to defend by applying a wide range of techniques, including controlling access to their cell and personal objects (e.g. by installing an additional curtain or using 'inconspicuous' behaviour to influence the intensity and frequency of cell searches), or scheduling private and intimate activities according to the prison officers' rhythms and routines. They also use their time in the cell for bolstering their embodied self by developing the body's energy and skills through physical exercise or spiritual activities (e.g. yoga, meditation), to counteract feelings of vulnerability and retreat into their inner self.

The experience of the cell as a private and personal space is further shaped by staff behaviour, for instance when entering (with or without first knocking) or searching the prisoners' cells. It is to a great extent also linked to the experience of closeness and intimacy with fellow prisoners when they visit each other in their cells, although the prison context is characterized by mutual distrust and 'real' friendship is generally described to happen rarely in prison. Moreover, when socializing with fellow prisoners, for instance in the evening in one of the prisoner's cells, those held in indefinite incarceration often face a certain dilemma: on the one hand, the younger, short-term prisoners (being the vast majority) may bring in welcomed inputs from the outside world, but often have different ('bad') habits and interests (e.g. to participate in illicit activities such as drug trafficking or getting access to the Internet, which may lead to collective sanctions and withdrawal of privileges) and also will sooner or later leave the prison again. On the other hand, long-term prisoners who are in the same situation may have a similar criminal background and stay longer, but the older ones especially are often perceived by the younger prisoners as particularly marked by their long-term imprisonment (and often extensive medication use), which, from their perspective, has led to dullness, mental disruption and a loss of any ability or interest in interpersonal exchange. This not only makes it difficult for these prisoners to find a friend, but also raises fears regarding their own future. Certain prisoners also worry that spending time with the 'dangerous' inmates may create a bad impression of them and lead to negative remarks in prison reports.

After being locked up in the evening, the cell becomes the place where the prisoners pass time according to their individual rhythm, which they create again depending on their personal needs and attitudes towards imprisonment. As I showed, the time span in the cell has many different meanings for prisoners: some want it to be over as soon as possible and are mainly interested in 'killing time', while others want to 'use' the hours in the cell in a 'productive' and self-reflective way, for example by writing, studying or developing and implementing personal projects (e.g. the development of a computer programme or the preparation and later presentation of a lecture in a school lesson). Yet others use it to transcend the prison context, by means of consuming audio-visual media, playing (offline) computer games or daydreaming, and to gain experience in other time–space constellations. As I explained, the prisoners' ways of using the TV, which they may rent from the prison and watch in their cells, reflect in an exemplary way the various modes of *being* and *doing* indefinite time: it is used for distraction and entertainment, for 'killing time', but also to keep mentally fit by gaining new (scientific) knowledge, or staying up to date about developments and trends in the outside world by following the news. Interestingly, there are also prisoners, especially those who are particularly concerned about their mental health, who perceive watching television as a pure waste of time and manipulation, and therefore do not have a TV in their cells.

7.5 Searching for Normalcy, Social Belonging and Individuality

While the cell is the place that is most crucial for the maintenance of their sense of self and personal integrity, the work context is essentially linked to the prisoners' experience of 'normality' and personal identity, through which they (re)constitute themselves as both unique individuals and members of society. This is particularly crucial for prisoners who are physically, socially and morally excluded from society. Also, as I illuminated, during work, through their (more or less) moving bodies and sensory perception and depending on the particularity of the workplaces and assigned activities, they can enrich their individual geographical experience of the prison, which also shapes their general sense of (the prison) space.

The fact that work constitutes the prison context where prisoners may experience a sense of what they call 'normalcy' results from various factors. For instance, workshops are generally perceived as spaces that are less marked by the carceral—both regarding their material equipment and social interactions taking place there (among *workers*). Moreover, prisoners often have to process orders from external customers, which directly connects them with and allows them to contribute to the outside community. Yet, the opposite experience is possible as well, for instance in the units for ill and elderly prisoners, where work is to a great extent not supposed to be productive in an economic sense, but mainly serves to occupy time and structure the prisoners' day, and the products are hence mainly sold in the prison shop. Combined with the experience of not being allowed to work 'properly'—that is, in one's own professional manner learned in the outside world (which may not be permitted by the prison foreman), using 'proper' work tools (due to security reasons)—and producing something 'useful', some prisoners working there feel forced to carry out work which for them is anything but 'normal'. This gives prisoners, especially those with a high work morale, the impression of being not only a useless but also a worthless person. I also showed that the often repetitive and monotonous prison work is not necessarily a burden for everyone, because not being challenged intellectually (as well as physically) also provides certain prisoners with a distraction from personal worries and allows them to *immerse* themselves into the present, or, in contrast, let their thoughts wander and thereby *transcend* the present.

For prisoners held in indefinite incarceration, work signifies above all an important social space where they seek recognition, which can be experienced in the form of the prison foremen's appreciation and valorization of their individual (work) skills, competences and potential as well as the attribution of trustworthiness. This is crucial for the prisoners' sense of self as it allows them to construct a particular role for themselves as workers, to neutralize their stigma as 'dangerous' and 'evil' individuals, and also to be more than a 'simple' prisoner, but a specialist or expert in one particular domain. Especially through the limited number of so-called *Vertrauensjobs*—jobs that are based on trust as they provide prisoners with more responsibility, autonomy and access to staff spaces (e.g. jobs in the housekeeping and maintenance services)—which are indeed often assigned to long-term prisoners who are generally known for following the rules and knowing the system—they may (re)gain the feeling of (still) being a member of human society and at the same time experience individuality and exclusivity vis-à-vis fellow prisoners.

Generally expressed, the experience of recognition (in all its manifestations) nurtures the experience of their existence—as social beings—because it leaves *traces* on both the prisoners and others. However, the opposite experience, in the shape of contempt, misrecognition and indifference, is possible as well, which not only causes a high degree of frustration but may also reinforce their experience of physical, social and moral exclusion from society.

7.6 Balancing on the Boundary Between Freedom and Captivity

Finally, leisure time constitutes time–spaces where prisoners are most directly confronted with the outside world—physically, intellectually and emotionally—which not only provides them with a break from the (work) routine, but also evokes ambivalent feelings. Simply put, leisure activities generally intensify their lives and allow them to feel free, or less imprisoned, but at the same time alert them most intensively of their imprisonment. This takes place, for instance, in the courtyard, where prisoners can experience time outside, in the open air, and with all senses, yet very close to the prison wall and its related infrastructure. While some enjoy this time of the day and the sensory impressions they gain of the outside world, intentionally 'filtering' out everything that reminds them of the prison (the wall, the fences, the cameras), for others, it is the place where they become most painfully aware of their imprisonment and exclusion from society, and therefore they mainly avoid it. Thus, the daily hour in the courtyard signifies for some a time–spaces for recovery, while for others it is almost like a prison within the prison, perceived as particularly (emotionally) constraining.

Similar to the courtyard, although more intense, receiving visitors is again a highly ambivalent and emotionally charged part of the prisoners' everyday lives because it allows them to get most directly (intellectually, emotionally and physically) in touch with the outside world. It also serves as a time marker as receiving visitors signifies an event outside of the ordinary prison routine and provides them with a stage on which to perform and experience a non-prisoner self (e.g. a husband, a friend, a brother, etc.). As I identified, the particularity of the visiting place is crucial to this experience. While prison visits generally take place in a room where the prisoners and their guests have to meet while sitting at a table, in one prison, certain prisoners also have access to an open-air visiting area that allows them to move around more freely (like in a public park), where they are less directly supervised by staff, and maybe can even spend some intimate time with their spouse or girlfriend in the public toilet (implicitly tolerated by the prison management). Many of the prisoners who have access to this open-air visiting space described it as their favourite or the most beautiful place in prison.

However, although visitors generally help prisoners to keep motivated and not lose hope, for prisoners held in indefinite incarceration, visitors can also turn into a burden as they constantly remind them of their indefinite imprisonment, and thus not only of what they have lost but also what they will probably never have (again), such as being physically present for their family, living in an (unrestricted) partnership, having a love life or simply having something to share, which may also hinder them, as well as their loved ones, from moving on with their lives. For this reason, there are prisoners who decide to break off all social contact with the outside world. More often, however, the relationship is ended by those outside due to the prisoner's criminal history, the emotional burden of having and visiting someone in prison, the indeterminacy of their stay, or because they have become too old and weak to continue to visit them in prison.

Furthermore, I also explored the prisoners' ways of communicating with people in the outside world through letters and phone calls. I showed how these means of communication are not only used by the prisoners to maintain their bonds to the outside world, but also to construct spaces for living out emotions and fantasies. However, their use is highly restricted by the prison management, which hinders the prisoners from communicating freely and spontaneously. Prisoners also do not have access to new media, which again increases their feelings of social exclusion and being left behind.

During sports, in the role of the sportsman and through the use of their bodies, prisoners can in particular live out emotions—and temporarily, although not entirely, relax control over their self-presentation—which they cannot do in other contexts. Moreover, they can also regain control over their bodies, which are shaped by the prison's spatio-temporal regime as well as time, and thus maintain (or increase) their physical and emotional well-being.

The education and training context is mainly used by the prisoners as a window to the outside rhythms and an opportunity to synchronize their lives with those of people in society by gaining skills important in the outside world (e.g. using a computer) and learning about important events, news and trends. It also allows future-oriented prisoners to use time productively and to develop further (intellectually) as individuals and thereby to escape the feeling of *temporal stasis* created by the prison regime. However, due to the fact that the prison's basic education and training programme is anchored in the logic of rehabilitation as it aims to prepare prisoners who are serving finite sentences for their release, the curriculum is generally based on repetition; thus, the benefits of school lessons for long-term prisoners strongly depend on each teacher's motivation.

I also described how, from time to time, prisoners may experience extraordinary events, both formally organized (such as Christmas parties or a barbecue) and individually lived surprises (e.g. encountering animals), which are crucial in these prisoners' lives as they temporarily change the carceral rhythm and, most importantly, intensify their lives. In the form of memories, these events leave traces and also shape their experience of the passage of time. The prisoners' (regular) encounters with external visiting groups, in contrast, mainly lead to negative feelings as the visits make them feel like zoo animals and reinforce the social distance between the (innocent) *citizens* of the free world and the (dangerous) *offenders* inside prison.

Finally, according to the law, the rights concerning release on temporary license, which aims at preparing prisoners for release and allowing them to cultivate their relations to the outside world, technically also apply to prisoners held in indefinite incarceration. These temporary absences are crucial to the prisoners' perspective as they can increase their probability of someday having a future outside by providing them with room to prove themselves. However, due to the more restrictive approach to loosening the regime in the case of these 'high-risk' prisoners, only a few of those I met were at that time granted temporary prison absences. These moments are experienced as a change from the ever-same routine, the ever-same food and the ever-same people, and in some ways also a chance to (physically and emotionally) visit their former lives. At the same, however, they are also confronted with the changes that have occurred in the outside world (especially developments in technology), and the disappearance of former points of reference, as well as a completely different rhythm, which can also lead to stress. Despite their rule-following behaviour, I met prisoners whose permission to go on prison leave was suddenly restricted or even completely cancelled, either due to an incident caused by another prisoner on prison leave, or a changing evaluation of the prisoner's risk potential. These restrictions, which are often not self-inflicted, may create additional uncertainty and reinforce feelings of frustration.

7.7 Final Thoughts from the Other Side of the Prison Wall

Although they are banished from society, these individuals are still *alive.* In this book, I revealed the manifold implications indefinite incarceration can have for human beings. One aspect that came out most clearly is that the carceral aspects of the prisoners' experience are related to the indeterminate nature of their imprisonment, combined with institutional structures that are—despite international and European human rights requirements and, as I showed, the prison staff's desire for adaptations—established not for prisoners incarcerated for preventive reasons *and* for an undetermined duration, but for (mostly younger) prisoners serving (finite) custodial sentences. This situation affects the prisoners' whole being and ways of inhabiting the world: their possible need to settle or belong somewhere as well as to move on, to pursue and achieve goals, to develop further as individuals, to possibly affect and be affected as human beings, to use and feel their body, to create and live according to individual rhythms, and to establish and maintain meaningful social relations. Keeping these prisoners under the same regime as prisoners serving a custodial sentence, imposing the same restrictions, but framed in non-rehabilitative terms and without any formal 'compensation' in order to, as required by law, guarantee 'human dignity' (Art. 74 SCC) and 'counteract the harmful consequences of the deprivation of liberty' (Art. 75 para. 1 SCC) and, in the case of these prisoners, indeterminacy, begs the question of whether we—as a society that stands for a humane penal system and yet decided to exclude them, possibly forever—can live with this situation. As one prisoner once mentioned, people like him, sentenced to indefinite incarceration, are in some ways the 'lost ones' (Fieldnotes, 17.2.2016). I would add that within the prison system, they are in particular the 'forgotten ones'.

References

Bundesamt für Statistik. (2019). *Kriminalität und Strafrecht. Justizvollzug. Inhaftierte Erwachsene*. https://www.bfs.admin.ch/bfs/de/home/statistiken/kriminalitaet-strafrecht/justizvollzug/inhaftierte-erwachsene.html#-1879612962. Accessed 27 February 2020.

Cohen, S., & Taylor, L. (1972). *Psychological survival: The experience of long-term imprisonment*. Penguin Books.

Crewe, B. (2009). *The prisoner society: Power, adaptation and social life in an English prison*. Oxford University Press.

European Court of Human Rights. (2010). *Case M. vs Germany* (App 19359/04). https://hudoc.echr.coe.int/eng?i=001-96389. Accessed 10 December 2019.

Greer, C., & Jewkes, Y. (2005). Extremes of otherness: Media images of social exclusion. *Social Justice, 32*(1), 20–31.
Hostettler, U., Marti, I., & Richter, M. (2016). *Lebensende im Justizvollzug. Gefangene, Anstalten, Behörden.* Stämpfli Verlag.
Lussault, M., & Stock, M. (2010). 'Doing with space': Towards a pragmatics of space. *Social Geography, 5*, 11–19. https://doi.org/10.5194/sg-5-11-2010
Merleau-Ponty, M. (1962). *Phenomenology of perception.* Routledge and Kegan Paul.
Pratt, J. (1997). *Governing the dangerous: Dangerousness, law and social change.* Federation Press.
Thornton, P. H., & Ocasio, W. (2008). Institutional logics. In R. Greenwood, C. Oliver, R. Suddaby, & K. Sahlin-Andersson (Eds.), *Handbook of organizational institutionalism* (pp. 99–129). Sage.
Thornton, P. H., Ocasio, W., & Lounsbury, M. (2012). *The institutional logics perspective: A new approach to culture, structure, and process.* Oxford University Press.
Ugelvik, T. (2014). *Power and resistance in prison: Doing time, doing freedom.* Palgrave Macmillan.
UN Human Rights Committee. (2014). *International Covenant on Civil and Political Rights: General Comment No. 35.* https://tbinternet.ohchr.org/_layouts/15/treatybodyexternal/Download.aspx?symbolno=CCPR%2fC%2fGC%2f35&Lang-=en. Accessed 10 December 2019.

Correction to: Doing Indefinite Time

Correction to:
I. Marti, *Doing Indefinite Time*, Palgrave Studies in Prisons and Penology, https://doi.org/10.1007/978-3-031-12590-4

The original version of the book was previously published without OA funding acknowledgement lines in the Frontmatter, which has been now incorporated as "The open access publication of this book has been published with the support of the Swiss National Science Foundation". The book has been updated with the change.

The updated original version of the book can be found at https://doi.org/10.1007/978-3-031-12590-4

I. Marti, *Doing Indefinite Time*, Palgrave Studies in Prisons and Penology,
https://doi.org/10.1007/978-3-031-12590-4_8

Index

I. Marti, *Doing Indefinite Time*, Palgrave Studies in Prisons and Penology,
https://doi.org/10.1007/978-3-031-12590-4

The manufacturer's authorised representative in the EU is Springer Nature Customer Service Centre GmbH, Europaplatz 3, 69115 Heidelberg, Germany. If you have any concerns regarding our products, please contact ProductSafety@springernature.com

Printed and bound by CPI Group (UK) Ltd, Croydon, CR0 4YY
28/09/2026
02224064-0001